THE OFFICIAL RED BOOK®

A Guide Book of
UNITED STATES
COMMEMORATIVE COINS

History • Rarity • Values • Grading • Varieties

Q. David Bowers

Foreword by
Donn Pearlman

Valuations Editor
Lawrence Stack

Whitman
Publishing, LLC
PUBLISHING SINCE 1934

A Guide Book of
UNITED STATES COMMEMORATIVE COINS
History • Rarity • Values • Grading • Varieties

© 2008 by Whitman Publishing, LLC
3101 Clairmont Road, Suite C, Atlanta, GA 30329

The WCG™ data grid used throughout this publication is patent pending. THE OFFICIAL RED BOOK is a trademark of Whitman Publishing, LLC.

Correspondence concerning this book may be directed to the publisher, at the address above.

ISBN: 0794822568
Printed in China

Disclaimer: Expert opinion should be sought in any significant numismatic purchase. This book is presented as a guide only. No warranty or representation of any kind is made concerning the accuracy or completeness of the information presented, or its usefulness in numismatic purchases or sales. The opinions of others may vary. The author, a professional numismatist, regularly buys, sells, conducts auctions, and sometimes holds certain of the items discussed in this book.

Caveat: The price estimates given are subject to variation and differences of opinion. Before making decisions to buy or sell, consult the latest information. For certain issues that are normally found with areas of light striking, well-struck coins may command significantly higher prices. Past performance of the rare-coin market or any coin or series within that market is not necessarily an indication of future performance, as the future is unknown. Such factors as changing demand, popularity, variations (sometimes wide) in grading interpretations, strength of the overall coin market, and economic conditions will continue to be influences.

Advertisements within this book: Whitman Publishing, LLC, does not endorse, warrant, or guarantee any of the products or services of its advertisers. All warranties and guarantees are the sole responsibility of the advertiser.

Prices and population reports: Estimated market prices are given in various grades by valuations editor Lawrence Stack, with information from multiple sources. These are given simply as an opinion and guide at the time of compilation in 2007. Certain actual transactions may take place at higher or lower figures. The population reports are the combined figures from the American Numismatic Association Certification Service (ANACS), the Numismatic Guaranty Corporation of America (NGC), and the Professional Coin Grading Service (PCGS). As time goes on, many such figures are apt to increase, due to submissions of new coins and resubmissions of examples already certified. A population-report figure may or may not reflect the actual rarity of a coin and should be used very carefully as an aid to determining value. Among modern commemoratives, most are in very high grades, many at or approaching MS-70 and PF-70, but only a small percentage have ever been certified. Well-worn commemoratives of certain issues exist in large numbers (1892 and 1893 World's Columbian Exposition half dollars are examples), but few have ever been certified.

CONTENTS

ABOUT THE AUTHOR

Q. David Bowers became a professional numismatist as a teenager in 1953, later earning a B.A. in finance from Pennsylvania State University, which in 1976 bestowed its Distinguished Alumnus Award on him. The author served as president of the American Numismatic Association (1983–1985) and president of the Professional Numismatists Guild (1977–1979); is a recipient of the highest honor bestowed by the ANA (the Farran Zerbe Award); was the first ANA member to be named Numismatist of the Year (1995); in 2005 was given the Lifetime Achievement Award; and has been inducted into the ANA Numismatic Hall of Fame, currently one of just 12 living recipients with that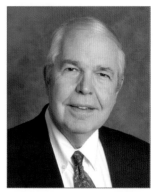
distinction. Bowers was given the highest honor awarded by the Professional Numismatists Guild (the Founder's Award), and has received more "Book of the Year Award" and "Best Columnist" honors from the Numismatic Literary Guild than any other writer. In 2000 he was the first annual recipient of the Burnett Anderson Memorial Award for writing. In July 1999, in a poll published in *COINage*, "Numismatists of the Century," by Ed Reiter, Bowers was recognized in this list of just 18 names. He is the author of more than 50 books, hundreds of auction and other catalogs, and several thousand articles, including columns in *Coin World* (now the longest-running by any author in numismatic history), *Paper Money*, and, in past years, *Numismatist*. His prime enjoyments in numismatics are knowing "coin people," from newcomers to old-timers, and studying the endless lore, technical aspects, and history of coins, tokens, medals, and paper money. As co-chairman of Stack's (New York City and Wolfeboro, New Hampshire) and numismatic director for Whitman Publishing, LLC, he is in the forefront of current events in the hobby.

Donn Pearlman: The writer of the foreword, Donn Pearlman, a former award-winning Chicago radio and television newscaster, is president of Donn Pearlman, Inc., a public relations firm in Las Vegas, Nevada. He is a member of the Numismatic Literary Guild and a former governor of the American Numismatic Association (with scars to prove it). His writing has been enjoyed by many, including readers of *Numismatist*.

CREDITS AND ACKNOWLEDGMENTS

Sources for this book include a large file maintained for many years on commemorative coins and their history; the continuing parade of commemorative news in U.S. Mint news releases and Web-site postings; and stories in *Coin World*, *COINage*, *Coins* magazine, *Numismatic News*, *Numismatist*, and other media. *The Commemorative Trail*, journal of the Society for United States Commemorative Coins (SUSCC), has been particularly useful. Other sources are given in the endnotes and the selected bibliography.

Of special help in the preparation of this book have been the following:

The **American Numismatic Association,** Colorado Springs, Colorado. The **American Numismatic Society,** New York City. **Wynn Bowers** reviewed the manuscript and made suggestions. **Roger W. Burdette** provided information from the National Archives. **Roberta French** assisted the author with the compiling of information and research. **Michael Garafalo** provided images of ephemera associated with commemoratives. **Jenna King** reviewed the manuscript and made suggestions. **Patty Moore** reviewed the manuscript and made suggestions. **Ronald E. Patten** provided information. **Donn Pearlman** wrote the foreword. **Stephen Schechter** provided images of historical items from his extensive collection. **Robert Shippee** reviewed the manuscript and provided valuable suggestions. **Michael White, U.S. Mint,** provided information about modern issues. **Frank Van Valen** reviewed the manuscript and made suggestions.

The staff of **Stack's** assisted in many ways: Most photographs are by **Douglas Plasencia** and are from the Stack's auction and other files, including the **Richard Jewell** and **Robert Prescott** collections. **Susan Novak,** assistant to the author, helped with correspondence, research, and coordination of the book. **Larry Stack** provided valuations.

The staff of **Whitman Publishing, LLC** provided photographs of commemoratives from 1982 to date from their files, including some photos taken by **Tom Mulvaney.** Additional photos were provided by Troy Thoreson.

In 1992 my book *Commemorative Coins of the United States: A Complete Encyclopedia* was published. Some text from that book has been adapted into the present volume. Below is a list of those who helped with information for that book, some of which has been included or adapted in the present text:

John W. Adams
Burnett Anderson
Roger Bear
Aubrey E. Bebee
Harry X. Boosel
Walter H. Breen
Donald L. and
   Helen L. Carmody
Lynn Chen
R.W. Colbert
Dr. Andrew Cosgarea Jr.
Hugh Courteol Jr.
William C. Cousins
Charles Davis
Beth Deisher

Frank DuVall
Bill Fivaz
John Jay Ford Jr.
David L. Ganz
Frank Gasparro
Lori Germaine
Cory Gillilland
Margaret Gray
Nancy Green
Robert Harwell
Donna Hayashi
Wayne K. Homren
Elizabeth Jones
Ron Karp
Charles Kirtley

Sue Kohler
Robert Korver
Abe Kosoff
Robert Lamb
Greg Lauderdale
Dwight Manley
Arnold Margolis
Chester Y. Martin
John H. McCloskey
Ed Metzger
Meredith H. Miller, M.D.
Eric P. Newman
Matthew Peloso
Donna Pope
William Pukall

Jon B. Rawlson
Ed Reiter
Gilroy Roberts
Gloria Rovelstad
P. Scott Rubin
Marika Somogyi
Bill Shamhart

Arlyn Sieber
Harvey G. Stack
Edgar Z. Steever
Donald J. Sterling Jr.
Anthony Swiatek
Cornelius Vermeule
Patricia Lewis Verani

Robert Weinman
Scot Willingham
Mark Van Winkle
Sherl Joseph Winter
Stewart Witham
William Woodward

In reviewing the above roster in 2007, I was impressed with the fact that many people who helped years ago are in different positions today, and some are no longer living. Still others are as active as ever, and we've crossed paths in the past year. The dynamics of the hobby are constantly changing as are the people in it. The present book relies essentially on my long-maintained historical archives, including original correspondence files of several issuers and commissions. The bibliography gives other valuable sources as do the end notes. All photographs are of actual coins (not composites by using the obverse and reverse of different specimens). Certain historical, numismatic, and archival information and illustrations are used on a nonexclusive basis by special arrangement with the author.

FOREWORD

Universally acclaimed prolific author Dave Bowers has produced yet another important reference book that takes readers through time to compellingly capture the "flavor" of numismatic events and personalities. (My pocket calculator died when I tried to compute it, but I believe *A Guide Book of United States Commemorative Coins* is Dave's 123,000th book, although my figures may be off by one or two thousand.)

I like commemoratives, you like commemoratives—we all like commemoratives. And, their stories can be even more fascinating than the coins themselves—as the following pages will reveal.

A not-so-funny thing happened on the way to the United States' most popular commemorative coinage program. It almost didn't get approved. With literally billions of commemorative state quarter dollars in circulation since 1999, it may be difficult for some people to even imagine there was a time when the U.S. Mint and members of Congress were vehemently against the concept of striking commemoratives of any kind. The anti-commem antagonists pointed to actual and perceived abuses of special coin programs in the 1930s and 1950s, and there were also tangled political considerations that created frustrating roadblocks. Despite the rich history of U.S. commemorative coinage dating back to 1892, there were decades in the 1960s and 1970s when the topic of commemoratives in Congress was about as welcome as a CBS *60 Minutes* investigative television crew camped outside the door.

Negative attitudes began changing with introduction of the dual-dated 1776–1976 quarter, half dollar, and dollar coins produced to celebrate the country's 200th anniversary. (If the Buffalo nickel design had been used for the 1976 coinage, we'd have to refer to them as "Bison-tennial," but that's a bad joke and has absolutely no place in this serious book about commemoratives.) The Bicentennial coins remain popular today. Living in Las Vegas, where half dollar coins are often used to pay a portion of a player's winning, natural blackjack hand, I've seen people get excited to receive a 1776–1976 coin in change. With more than 1.6 billion Bicentennial quarters and more than 500 million of the half dollars struck for circulation, these coins obtained as pocket change will not be considered "rare" until the first McDonald's opens for business on one of Jupiter's moons. But they started a trend—the resumption of commemoratives—although it took circulating coins to do it.

Given the overwhelming public acceptance of the circulation-strike and silver clad Proof Bicentennial coins, you'd think Congress and the Mint would quickly move to give the public more commemoratives to enjoy and collect. In Washington, a six-year lag could be considered moving quickly. The next commemorative coin wasn't issued until 1982, and was in the traditional mode—limited edition, and sold for a premium, just as commemoratives have been since way back in 1892 with the Columbian half dollar. The 1982 George Washington commemorative half dollar was the country's first noncirculating, legal-tender commemorative coin design since the demise, by expiration, of the unlamented Carver-Washington coins in 1954. Although some nitpicking critics complained about the artistic depiction of Washington's horse on the new 1982 half dollar, the solid popularity of the coin showed that commemoratives were viable. Collectors and the general public wanted them, and the federal government could actually make a profit producing and selling them. The era of modern commemoratives began.

Soon, members of Congress were introducing or happily co-sponsoring legislation to strike commemoratives to raise money for various projects requested by constituents and special interest groups. Commem after commem was approved, commem after commem struck and offered for sale. The designs of our daily pocket change remained nearly stagnant except for the brief bicentennial creative burst of excitement, but the proliferation of special-interest-group commemorative coins intended for coin collectors or simply as souvenirs accelerated faster than paparazzi chasing Brad Pitt. Illinois Congressman Frank Annunzio, then chairman of the U.S. House Committee on Administration, repeatedly blocked legislation in the House for new designs on circulating coins. (On one occasion, just before the House was to vote on coinage redesign, someone on Capitol Hill started an absolutely false rumor that under the proposed legislation the motto "In God We Trust" would be removed from circulating coins. The erroneous rumors killed the bill.) But Rep. Annunzio supported measures that led to the striking of fund-raising commemoratives for the 1984 Olympic Games in Los Angeles and 1986 Statue of Liberty coins that helped pay for that landmark's restoration.

The Olympic Games and the Statue of Liberty are popular themes with the public. But consider two of unusual themes that actually won Congressional approval and were made into commemoratives. There's the 38th anniversary of the end of the Korean War in 1991 (not the 30th, not the 40th, but the 38th anniversary); then there's the 1995 Special Olympics Games dollar that depicted a living person, Eunice Shriver, the mother of television newscaster Maria Shriver and mother-in-law of California governor Arnold Schwarzenegger. When it appeared that not all the Shriver coins would be purchased by collectors and the general public by the Mint's cutoff deadline, a buyer came out of the woodwork and placed an order for most of the production, apparently to avoid any non-sellout embarrassment to the family and those who supported creation of those fund-raising coins for a worthy cause.

Collectors often refer to coins as "history you can hold in your hands." The next time you look at any commemorative coin, remember, it's more than just a piece of metal produced with artistic and technical skill. There's undoubtedly a fair amount of unrecorded political manipulation that went into its creation, along with weird anniversaries, the commemoration of obscure things, and designs that would flunk Art 101. In the mix are coins of importance and beauty. No third-party certification service can assign a grade to these extra features that go with the commemorative you are looking at right now.

Donn Pearlman
Las Vegas, Nevada

INTRODUCTION

Commemorative coins have been favorites of mine for a long time. I am in good company, since the passion is shared by other numismatists everywhere. This succinct comment from the *Guide Book of United States Coins* tells why:

> The unique position occupied by commemoratives in United States coinage is largely due to the fact that, with few exceptions, all commemorative coins have real historical significance. The progress and advance of people in the New World are presented in an interesting and instructive manner on the commemorative issues. Such a record of facts artistically presented on gold and silver memorial issues appeals strongly to the collector who favors the historical side of numismatics.

Actually, while *many* commemoratives have "real historical significance," there are others that do not—enough others that much intrigue, illogic, and other interesting aspects are part of the series. To me, these byways are often more interesting than the stories behind the standard coin issues. While few would argue that the sesquicentennial (a recurring word that means 150th anniversary) of American Independence celebrated in 1926 was worthy of both a commemorative silver half dollar and gold quarter eagle, it is likely that you will find more fascinating the coins with meaningless or trumped-up reasons for being coined.

Among these illogical varieties, consider the 1936 Norfolk (Virginia) half dollar issued to observe the 200th anniversary of this town changing its status from a township to a royal borough in 1736. Or what about Thomas G. Melish, who in 1936 persuaded Congress to grant him the personal right to distribute commemorative half dollars? He came up with the notion that 1936 was the 50th anniversary of "Cincinnati as a musical center of America." Intrigued as to what happened musically in Cincinnati in 1886 to merit the U.S. government's memorializing it 50 years later by issuing a set of three coins (one each from the Philadelphia, Denver, and San Francisco mints), I spent several days looking through news accounts of the city as well as through city and state histories and, for good measure, texts dealing with music. I discovered not a single unusual thing, founding, or event of particular musical importance in Cincinnati for 1886!

Then there is the curious case of C. Frank Dunn, who was in charge of ordering half dollars for the Boone bicentennial in 1934. Bear-trapper Daniel was commemorated that year with a half dollar struck at the Philadelphia Mint. One might think if the bicentennial was in 1934, then on December 31 of that year it would be over. Not so. The "bicentennial" celebration went into high gear with *six* different date, mintmark, and die varieties of Boone halves in 1935! It was not until 1938 that coining presses at the Philadelphia, Denver, and San Francisco mints stopped stamping out the things.

As if this were not enough, commemoratives offer a lot of other weird celebrations, beginning with the 1893 Columbian half dollar (the *401st* anniversary of Columbus's "discovery" of America, not that it was lost in the first place, this being the successor to the logical 1892 half dollar), the 1919 centennial of the state of Alabama commemorated on a 1921-dated half dollar, and for good measure, the oddest-dated anniversary of all, the 1991 dollar observing the 38th anniversary of the end of the Korean War (mentioned by Donn Pearlman in the foreword).

Beauty is in the eye of the beholder, it is said. Commemoratives give a wide opportunity for you to pick favorites as well as critique the selections of others. In 1937, dealer

B. Max Mehl published a monograph which included this commentary on the 1925-S California Diamond Jubilee half dollar:

> This is my favorite coin because San Francisco is my favorite city (not that you give a damn). This beautiful coin was struck to commemorate the 75th anniversary of California being admitted into the Union (this coin should have been struck in gold). Obverse is a very fine piece of art work showing a miner washing gold. The reverse is a polar bear [*sic*], the emblem of California (why, I don't know). I have traveled and toured California from one end to the other and have never yet seen a bear.

In contrast to such praise, in *Numismatic Art in America*, 1971, Cornelius C. Vermeule opined that the art on the 1935 Old Spanish Trail half dollar was "wretched." Poor designs, or at least those that have been viewed as such, are aplenty among the classic commemoratives of the 1892 to 1954 period, but strong competition is mounted by a number of modern issues.

That said, there are many designs, old and new, that just about everyone considers attractive. The Oregon Trail Memorial motif was voted as the top favorite by Society for United States Commemorative Coins (SUSCC) members in a 1985 poll. Among modern issues, both the 1986 Statue of Liberty Centennial and the 1988 Olympic Games $5 gold coins created by Elizabeth Jones have earned high praise from the numismatic community. In the pages that follow you can view the different designs and draw your own conclusions.

In addition to art, significance (or lack thereof) of things to be commemorated, unusual and sometimes irregular situations in distributing the coins, and other aspects, a collection of commemorative types is very distinctive—each one with its own story to tell. It is no wonder that these coins have been favorites for a long time.

In creating this book I drew on numerous resources, including an extensive historical and research file I have been keeping for many years. The present Whitman book is concise, but it includes facts not available in any other current source. I believe you'll find it to be a one-stop depot for most information you might desire on the subject. I have added a measure of numismatic history to the narrative, telling how various issues were distributed and the cast of characters involved—ranging from the wily Farran Zerbe to the honest and conscientious Walter P. Nichols. Most of these characters—saints and scoundrels—are from the classic era of commemoratives, from 1892 to 1954. Since that time distribution has been by the U.S. Mint, and curious capers and irregularities have disappeared, but not the issuance of some commemorative coins for unremarkable occasions, or as sops to special interests with connections to Congress.

"Time, like an ever-rolling stream, bears all its sons away," hymnist Isaac Watts wrote two centuries ago. Apart from commemorative enthusiasts, who today would recognize the names C. Frank Dunn, L.W. Hoffecker, Thomas G. Melish, and A.W. Parke—to mention just four of many individuals of the 1930s who considered collectors to be ripe for plucking? Or bit players who suggested designs or even created art, such as Frederick Lewis, Constance Ortmayer, Harry H. Cochrane, or David Goode Parsons? Not even a *Jeopardy!* winner would likely recognize even one. When you read this book, however, you will learn that David Goode Parsons was an art student at the University of Wisconsin in 1936 and was tapped to prepare the designs for the Wisconsin commemorative of that year. You'll also read about the live beaver in artist Constance Ortmayer's studio.

Walt Disney once said, "We have always tried to be guided by the basic idea that in the discovery of knowledge there is great entertainment." To me there is entertainment indeed in some of the byways of commemoratives, and I hope you will delight in learning some of those little-known facts given in this book.

The story of commemoratives is ongoing. No doubt by the time a new edition of this book is prepared there will be new issues to contemplate—their designs, logic (or lack thereof) for issuing them, and more.

In a word, commemoratives are *interesting*.

Enjoy!

Q. David Bowers
Wolfeboro, New Hampshire

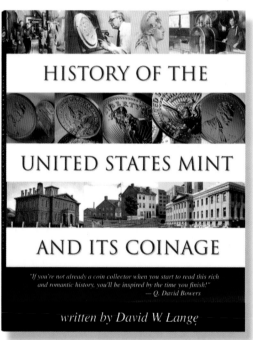

CHAPTER ONE
CHRONICLE OF COMMEMORATIVES

Defining a *Commemorative* Coin

What is a commemorative coin? There is no hard and fast rule that covers all issues. In general, a commemorative coin is one that was produced with the primary intention of creating a special souvenir to be sold (at a premium above face value) to observe or memorialize an anniversary, special occasion, or other event. Although they are legal tender, such pieces differ in design from regular circulating coinage of the time. A case in point is the modern statehood quarter program inaugurated in 1999. While each quarter dollar commemorates one or several aspects of a state's history and traditions, it is a circulating coin issued at face value and thus is not grouped with commemorative coins. Had it been available only at a premium, it would be known as a commemorative.

There is a distinction between a commemorative *coin* and a commemorative *medal*. United States commemorative coins are those that have a designated face value and are legal tender, although they were primarily issued as commemoratives. Accordingly, anyone desiring to spend a 1903 Louisiana Purchase gold dollar or a 1928 Hawaiian Sesquicentennial half dollar can certainly do so—although such a scenario is unlikely. In contrast, commemorative medals, such as made for the 1825 opening of the Erie Canal, the 1876 Centennial Exhibition, or the 1925 Norse-American Centennial, have no legal tender status at all.

The classic era of commemoratives ended with the final Carver/Washington half dollars in 1954. At the time, silver was the standard metal for circulating denominations of the dime, quarter, and half dollar. After a long span of inactivity, the new era of commemoratives commenced with the Washington half dollar in 1982, commemorating the 250th anniversary of the birth of the Father of Our Country. These were made of silver alloy, but at the time of issue each coin contained much more than fifty cents' worth of silver. Accordingly, the inscription HALF DOLLAR on each did not mean much.

Similarly, beginning with the 1983 and 1984 commemoratives struck in silver for the Los Angeles Olympic Games, coins were made with the ONE DOLLAR denomination lettered on them, but with much more than a dollar's worth of silver used in their production. Following suit, $5 and $10 commemorative gold coins inaugurated in the 1980s were marked with these denominations, although their metal value was higher. Such commemoratives were and continue to be sold at prices reflecting their metallic value plus a profit to the Mint. The inscribed face value has absolutely no relevance. The same situation pertains to various silver and gold "eagles" sold by the Mint from 1986 to date. These bear irrelevant denominations inscribed on them.

In summary, a commemorative U.S. coin is one that is legal tender and inscribed with a denomination and is intended to memorialize a person, place, thing, or event, but not intended for circulation. Commemoratives are produced, in limited quantities and for a limited time, per the enabling legislation for each.

Early Commemorative Coins

The first American coins that can be called commemoratives took the form of tokens and medals from the colonial era, most of which could be spent in commerce. We have, for example, the silver three pence issued by Standish Barry, Baltimore silversmith and entrepreneur, inscribed BALTIMORE TOWN JULY 4.90. Featuring a portrait of the issuer on the obverse, these must have been distributed on Independence Day, possibly as part of some special participation by Barry in the national holiday. Today, examples are highly prized numismatic rarities.

George Washington was featured, perhaps commemorated in a way, on a number of tokens of the 1790s, such as the 1792 WASHINGTON PRESIDENT and WASHINGTON BORN VIRGINIA issues, the reverses of which give important dates in his biography.

While the first official *federal* commemorative, called at first a *souvenir coin*, is generally considered to be the 1892 half dollar for the World's Columbian Exposition, there are at least two antecedents worthy of note—not to overlook several unadopted ideas, including this:

A proposal made by Elias Boudinot and described in the *Annals of Congress*, January 1, 1793, would have, in a sense, made all subsequent U.S. coins commemoratives:

> Mr. Boudinot, after remarking that the artists who had exhibited specimens of the figure of Liberty on the several samples of coins which he had seen all differed in their conceptions on this occasion, for the sake, therefore, of uniformity, he moved to add a clause to the present bill, providing that, in lieu of the figure of Liberty, the head of Columbus should be substituted. Mr. Boudinot supported his motion by some pertinent remarks on the character of Columbus and the obligations the citizens of the United States were under to honor his memory. . . . On the question being put, the motion was negatived.[1]

WASHINGTON BORN VIRGINIA copper "cent" or medalet of 1792. The reverse gives highlights of his life in public service. The February 11, 1732, birth date on the obverse is from the Julian calendar in effect at the time; today we use the Gregorian calendar date of February 22.

Thus Columbus commemorative coins were not to be—at least not for the time being. Generations later the famous navigator would be depicted on commemorative half dollars of 1892 and 1893 and a set of coins in 1992.

When the Marquis de Lafayette, French hero of the American Revolution, revisited the United States in 1824 and 1825, Congress declared him to be "the Nation's Guest." Joseph Lewis, a New York City engraver, cut dies for small (9 mm) medalets with Washington's portrait on one side and Lafayette's on the other. These were ready by September 2, 1824, to honor Lafayette, who arrived in New York on August 15.[2] A grand soiree was staged for Lafayette at the Castle Garden, and the committee for the ball selected the Lewis medalet as the official remembrance. These proved to be immensely popular, and an

Half dollar of 1824 counterstamped on the obverse and reverse with the portraits of Washington and Lafayette. The James B. Longacre estate, auctioned on January 21, 1870, included a similar coin, which earned this comment in a review of the sale by E.B. Mason Jr.: "1824 silver half dollar; medallions of Washington and Lafayette; a beautiful and very rare piece; sold for the small sum of $11; lucky [Edward] Cogan was the buyer."

advertisement placed by Lewis in the Philadelphia *National Gazette* stated that he had sold more than 2,000 of them.

Important to the present narrative, Lewis used his dies to counterstamp hundreds if not thousands of current federal coins, particularly copper cents and silver half dollars. Whether such pieces were sold at a premium, or simply created as souvenirs on coins quickly put back into circulation, is not known today. They must have been very popular in their time.

Large copper cent of 1822 with Washington/Lafayette counterstamps.

Without question a certain variety of the 1848 $2.50 gold quarter eagle was intended as a commemorative and specifically authorized as such. On December 8, 1848, Secretary of War W.L. Marcy wrote to Mint Director Robert Patterson concerning a shipment of 228 ounces of gold nuggets and dust that had been sent from California, to be deposited at the Philadelphia Mint on behalf of the federal government:

The 1848 quarter eagle with CAL. counterstamped on the reverse is perhaps the first federal commemorative coin. Mintage was 1,389 pieces.

> If the metal is found to be pure gold, as I doubt not that it will be, I request you to reserve enough of it for two medals ordered by Congress and not yet completed, and the remainder, with the exception of one or two small bars, I wish to have coined and sent with the bars to this department.
>
> As many may wish to procure specimens made with California gold, by exchanging other coin for it, I would suggest that it be made into quarter eagles with a distinguishing mark on each, if any variation from the ordinary issues from the Mint would be proper and could be conveniently made.

Not having received any information, Marcy inquired concerning the progress of the coinage. On January 5, 1849, Director Patterson replied:

> The amount of your deposit of gold, made on the 15th ult., is now ready for delivery in California gold. It is our practice to pay for deposits as soon as their value is ascertained; but this could not be done in the present case because payment was required in coins made of the bullion deposited.
>
> Before the Cal. gold could be used it had to undergo the process of *parting* in order to separate it from the excess of silver which it contains. This was one source of delay. Another occurred by the time required for stamping the letters CAL. on the quarter-eagles as you desired. Your payment of $3,910.10 will be made up of $3,474.64 in coins and $435.46 in two bars of gold as melted from the grains.

At the time of Marcy's letter the smallest U.S. gold coin was the quarter eagle. (The gold dollar was not introduced until the following year, 1849.) The estimated 1,389 quarter eagles from the first government deposit bore the notation CAL. on the reverse.

Apparently, 1848 CAL. quarter eagles were available for face value to anyone desiring them. Probably, fewer than two or three dozen numismatists—if, indeed, even that many—learned of them at or near the time of issue and added the coins to their cabinets. Among those acquiring such pieces was Chief Engraver James B. Longacre, who preserved at least three specimens in his personal collection.

In the ensuing years many different commemorative *medals* were struck in America, but no coins. The Crystal Palace opened in New York City on July 14, 1853, with the Exhibition of the Industry of all Nations, an occasion for several varieties of medals to be issued. Today, the building's inaugural event is considered by some to be the first of the international expositions to be held in our country. This was a private endeavor that failed to make money, despite P.T. Barnum's lending his talents to the venture. On October 5, 1858, the steel and glass structure, with

Copper medalet, 31 mm, from dies by George H. Lovett, issued in 1858 to observe the burning of the famous Crystal Palace. During the 19th century many medals were issued to commemorate people, places, and events. Unlike later commemorative *coins*, these usually had limited circulation and were soon forgotten.

about 750,000 square feet of wooden flooring, burned to the ground. This furnished the occasion for teenaged numismatist Augustus B. Sage to issue a medal depicting it in flames, with ALL IS VANITY on the reverse, a mournful line taken from Ecclesiastes.

Although many industrial expositions and fairs were held during the next several decades, the 1876 Centennial Exhibition, held in Philadelphia, was the only official event of importance to be sponsored by the American government. Hundreds of different tokens and medals were issued in connection with it, including some struck on an antique (1836) Mint press, but no commemorative *coins*.

Classic Era Launched in 1892

What numismatists today often refer to as the classic era of commemoratives began in 1892 with the issuance of a souvenir (as it was called) half dollar minted to commemorate the World's Columbian Exposition, scheduled to be opened in Chicago that year, but delayed until 1893. These pieces were produced at the Philadelphia Mint in 1892, and shipped to exposition officials, who paid face value plus transport for them, and offered them for $1 each (retail). The occasion was to celebrate the 400th anniversary of the "discovery" of America by Christopher Columbus.

An undeveloped 686-acre site on the shore of Lake Michigan was selected for the exposition grounds. In January 1891 a group of architects met in Chicago to plan the buildings, which were subsequently constructed mainly in the classical style reflecting Greek and Roman influences, and with exteriors made of an artificial composition resembling marble, called "staff," giving rise to the name "White City" for the structures. The brightness was further emphasized at night, when the grounds were illuminated by electric lights—then a relatively new innovation.

Work proceeded apace, and the exposition was dedicated on October 21, 1892, but since all exhibits were not yet in place, it was not possible to open the fair to the general public in the 400th anniversary year. Finally, at noon on May 1, 1893, the 401st anniversary, President Grover Cleveland officiated at a ceremony that opened the exposition grounds to the public. An estimated 300,000 individuals attended opening-day festivities.

The exposition showcased American progress in art, architecture, technology, science, agriculture, and other endeavors. No expense was spared to create a new city, complete with 160 buildings (many of which were connected by canals plied by gondolas and small steam-powered craft) and 65,000 exhibits devoted to commercial, national, artistic, and other subjects. Separate structures showcased the attractions and products of different states and foreign countries. Sculptures and other works of art decorated many of the open spaces as well as building interiors. The prime attraction at the Columbian Exposition was the gigantic Ferris Wheel, which consisted of cars the size of railroad coaches, mounted to a gigantic steel framework. A 20-minute ride (one rotation) cost fifty cents.

As a publicity stunt Wyckoff, Seamans & Benedict, makers of the Remington typewriter, gave this $10,000 check to buy the first 1892 Columbian half dollar made available for sale.

There were many numismatic features. The U.S. Mint exhibit in the Government Building featured a coining press that struck thousands of brass souvenir medals, which were offered for sale at 25¢ each. Coins from the Mint collection, taken to Chicago from their home in Philadelphia, were on view and were highlighted by the rare 1804 silver dollar and the unique 1849 $20 gold piece—in company with coins from all eras of civilized history. Most popular with the general public was a widow's mite of biblical fame. In addition, there were many private exhibits and vendors. For souvenir hunters, hundreds of different inexpensive tokens, badges, and medals were available, struck in brass, aluminum, white metal, and bronze.

Ultimately the event cost an estimated $30 million to stage and attracted 28 million visitors.

The exhibit of the U.S. Mint and the Treasury Department at the Columbian Exposition. Many rarities were on view, including an 1804 silver dollar and the unique 1849 double eagle.

More Commemoratives

The next exposition of note in America was the 1898 Trans-Mississippi Exposition held in Omaha, which saw the production of medals, but no coins. The 1901 Pan-American Exposition in Buffalo, New York, a world's fair that attracted many exhibitors, followed, but again, no coins. The organizers of events after 1893 contemplated the Columbian Exposition commemoratives, and did not see the potential for either great public enthusiasm or profit. In the meantime, in 1900 the Lafayette commemorative silver dollar was distributed. The intent was to help finance a statue by an American sculptor, Paul Bartlett, to be erected in Paris for the International Exposition of that year (remembered today for showcasing the Art Nouveau Movement, with the work of printmaker Alphonse Mucha at the forefront, among other displays). As stipulated in the legislation, the coins themselves were actually prestruck, all in one day on December 14, 1899, the 100th anniversary of Washington's death. The date on the coin is that of the exposition, not of the coin itself. In a way it can be said that the coin is dateless—one of many little interesting facts that are scattered through the history of American commemorative issues.

The St. Louis World's Fair

Enter Farran Zerbe, an avid collector, writer, and entrepreneur who came up with the idea of creating commemorative gold dollars to be sold at the 1904 Louisiana Purchase Exposition, popularly called the St. Louis World's Fair. Exuding optimism, Zerbe persuaded the exposition organizers and influential members of Congress that there would be an overwhelming demand for new gold dollars.

Congress authorized 125,000 commemorative gold dollars to be made with the portrait of Thomas Jefferson, who had been president when the Louisiana Purchase was consummated, and another 125,000 depicting William McKinley, who had been assassinated in September 1901 at the Pan-American Exposition in Buffalo. Jefferson would appeal to historians and traditionalists, while McKinley would surely encourage sentimentalists to acquire a coin. Congress did little or no research as to the practicality of a commemorative and imposed no restriction as to the retail price charged. Moreover, there was no *ex post facto* review for unexpectedly low sales. Instead, it was onward to the next commemorative proposal. Despite much ballyhoo and the addition of innovative products (such as gold dollars mounted in spoons, brooches, and pendants) by Zerbe, the effort to sell them for $3 each was a failure. Including thousands that Zerbe held back for his own account, just 35,000 were distributed.

By 1905, the aftermarket for the Louisiana Purchase Exposition gold dollars was poor, and examples were readily available for less than the $3 issue price. To make matters worse, examples of the 1900 Lafayette commemorative dollar, issued at $2, were available for not much more than face value. To any outside observer, buying commemoratives or investing in them would seem to be a fool's errand—except, perhaps, to obtain one each for a collection and that could likely be done at a discount later.

In 1905 in Portland, Oregon, the regional Lewis and Clark Exposition was held, but not at all on the scale of the 1893 Columbian Exposition or the 1904 St. Louis World's Fair. Commemorative gold dollars illustrating explorer Meriwether Lewis on one side and William Clark on the other,

Spoon with a 1903 McKinley gold dollar as part of the bowl. Commemoratives were fashioned into several types of souvenir articles.

were produced. These were offered at $2 each. As might be expected previous issues, collector interest was at a very low ebb. Probably not more than a thousand were sold to individual collectors, though dealers bought some as well. Most went to the general public.

How rare is it? How much is it worth? These are the questions most often asked by anyone who owns an old coin—commemorative or otherwise. With commemoratives, the method of distribution has a strong correlation to both of these basic questions. The rarity of pieces in higher grades is often more dependent on the method of distribution than on the quantity struck. Prime examples are these Lewis and Clark commemorative gold dollars. Today, in gem grade of MS-65 or better, the 1905 Lewis and Clark gold dollar is far and away the rarest commemorative of that denomination. Compare this commentary to my remarks about the 1922 Grant gold dollars.

In 1907 the Jamestown (Virginia) Tercentenary Exhibition was held, and Farran Zerbe's proposal to strike $2 commemorative gold coins died, as did his proposal for coins for the 1909 Alaska-Yukon-Pacific Exposition.

All Eyes on San Francisco

In 1915 the Panama-Pacific Exposition was held in San Francisco. Every effort was made to create what would truly be the greatest world's fair to be held in America.

By this time Farran Zerbe's reputation had been severely tarnished and he was in even deeper trouble. In the 1909 American Numismatic Association (ANA) election, when he was president of the association, he contrived to rig the election for his chosen successor, Dr. J.M. Henderson, by signing up new, short-term ANA "members" at a discount, so they could vote. He had also gone to visit with Lucy Heath, widow of the late George F. Heath, founder and owner of *The Numismatist*, who had died in 1908. Everyone thought that the magazine, the official publication of the ANA, would be bought on behalf of the ANA. Wrong! Zerbe bought it for himself. As it turned out, although the magazine was improved greatly in appearance and in editorial content, it proved unprofitable, and in 1910 W.W.C. Wilson bought the magazine and presented it as a gift to the ANA.

Now, with the Panama-Pacific Exposition in the offing, Zerbe persuaded the organizers and also Congress that this would be an ideal occasion to reap great profits from an extensive issue of commemoratives. The program, unprecedented and unrepeated, consisted of an panorama including a silver half dollar, gold dollar, quarter eagle, and two varieties of $50 gold pieces, to be sold individually or as a complete set at $200.

The exposition opened in San Francisco on February 20, 1915. The exhibits were extensive, and the event was a great success for its founders, who sought to commemorate both the opening of the Panama Canal (in 1914) and the rebirth of San Francisco since the disastrous earthquake and fire of April 1906. Elegant structures in the classical style were erected of temporary materials, many in the form of Greek temples or derivations thereof, with fountains, sculpture, and other ornaments. A memorable time was had by anyone who visited.

The ANA held its annual convention in San Francisco that year. It seems that Zerbe's reputation was at such a low ebb, few people endeavored to attend. Fewer than 20 members were there, the lowest head count of any annual convention in ANA history. In the meantime, Zerbe mounted his Money of the World Exhibit at the exposition, and offered for sale the commemorative coins as well as various tokens and medals, pieces of obsolete bank notes, and other souvenirs, probably doing a good business overall.

Sales of the commemorative coins fell far short of expectations, and of the 1,500 minted of each of the impressive $50 gold coins—one of octagonal shape and the other

Farran Zerbe's "Money of the World" exhibit and concession at the Panama-Pacific International Exposition in San Francisco in 1915.

round—only 645 and 483, respectively, escaped the melting pot. The numismatic market eventually took note of their rarity, and soon the gold issues of the exposition became highly prized. Today they are classics.

McKinley Issues and Onward

Next in the chronicle appeared commemorative gold dollars dated 1916 and 1917 issued on behalf of the McKinley Memorial in Niles, Ohio, the president's birthplace. With no associated fair or exposition, public interest was very low. The net distribution amounted to 15,000 of the 1916-dated dollars and just 5,000 of those dated 1917. Quantities were wholesaled to dealers. Today, McKinley Memorial gold dollars are nearly all seen in Mint State.

In 1918, Illinois commemorated its centennial of statehood with a half dollar, depicting on the obverse the portrait of Lincoln, and on the reverse the state seal. Distribution was largely in the state of Illinois during the anniversary year, as well as to the numismatic community. For the first time, a commemorative issue sold out completely, with 100,000 distributed.

Into the 1920s

In 1920, Maine celebrated its centennial as a state. A commemorative half dollar was devised, featuring the state arms on the obverse and an inscription on the reverse. The planning of this half dollar was strictly a regional event, mainly involving citizens of Maine, and not with any hype by Farran Zerbe or anyone else. Of the 50,000 that were made available for distribution, all were eventually sold, and everyone was satisfied. Both the 1918 Illinois and 1920 Maine half dollars are poster examples of what a commemorative coin should be—observing an important centennial involving an entire state, with a reasonable number coined, and all of them distributed.

In 1920 the 300th anniversary of the landing of the Pilgrims at Plymouth, Massachusetts was commemorated. The coin's obverse featured Governor Bradford holding a Bible (presumably), while the reverse showed the *Mayflower*. More examples (200,112) than the market could bear were struck, with the result that by the end of the year, tens of thousands remained unsold. Undaunted, the anniversary commission ordered 100,053 more to be struck, to exploit the numismatic and souvenir market—the new issue distinguished by having the 1921 date added to the obverse field. Of those, 20,053 pieces were sold, representing a profit.

The State of Alabama celebrated 100 years of statehood in 1919, but the commemorative half dollar did not appear until 1921. The obverse featured the portraits of William Wyatt Bibb, governor in 1819, and the 1919 governor, T.E. Kilby, the latter being alive when the coin was produced, thus making this the first instance in which a federal legal tender coin bore a living person's portrait. Although a law had been in place since 1866 prohibiting the use of the portraits of living persons on paper money, there was no such rule in effect for coins—nor is there today.

In the same year, Missouri legitimately celebrated its 100th anniversary of statehood, and issued a commemorative half dollar. The obverse featured a portrait of Daniel Boone, while the reverse showed Boone (presumably) with an Indian. This was the second instance in American coinage in which the portrait of the same person appeared on two sides of the same coin (the first was the 1900 Lafayette dollar).

In 1922 the 100th anniversary of the birth of Ulysses S. Grant was celebrated by two commemorative coins, a half dollar and a gold dollar, both of the same design. The Grant coins were mainly sold in Ohio by local and regional advertising, and into numismatic circles. Sales fell short of expectations, and thousands of coins went back to the melting pot. Very few reached the general public, with the result that today most of the Grant half dollars and nearly all of the Grant commemorative gold dollars are found in Uncirculated grade—the last usually in gem preservation.

The 1921 Alabama Centennial half dollar observed an anniversary that took place in 1919. To exploit collectors, two varieties were made—one with "2x2" on the obverse, recognizing Alabama as the 22nd state, and the other "plain" without this feature.

Hollywood

In 1923 the motion picture industry in Hollywood issued a commemorative half dollar, the ostensible occasion being the centennial of the Monroe Doctrine of 1823. It seems that most of the 274,077 minted were simply dumped into circulation at face value. Fred Woodson, a California banker who was also an active coin collector during the 1930s (and the grandfather of the author's wife), recalled that such pieces were common in pocket change and were frequently received at tellers' windows. He amassed a small hoard of pieces in this manner. Graded in the late 1970s, the coins were found to be mostly in the AU-55 to MS-60 range.

As no mention of motion pictures appears on the coin, only historians are aware of the connection. As to any significant nationwide celebration in 1923 for the anniversary of the Monroe Doctrine, there was none. Today, nearly all of these half dollars, even those certified as MS-64 and MS-65, are rather unprepossessing in appearance and often are poorly struck—this in addition to the low relief to begin with.

Next in the chronicle was the 1924 commemorative observing the 300th anniversary of the settling of Huguenots and Walloons in North America, and the founding of New Netherland (today's New York City) in 1624. Its obverse depicts Admiral Coligny and William the Silent, who had nothing to do at all with the celebration in question. Most were sold or distributed as souvenirs, not placed into circulation.

Diverse Issues

In 1925 a suite of commemorative half dollars appeared, including the Lexington-Concord Sesquicentennial, the Stone Mountain Memorial, the California Diamond Jubilee, and the Fort Vancouver Centennial. The designs of these were widely appreciated at the time, and each became popular with collectors. More than a million were distributed of the Stone Mountain issue, which achieved wide popularity throughout the South. The Lexington-Concord Sesquicentennial coin, of which more than 160,000 were distributed, was also widely popular, but it seems that many coins were either placed into circulation as unsold, or were quickly spent by those who acquired them as souvenirs, for such pieces were often seen in pocket change for a decade afterward. In contrast, the California Diamond Jubilee half dollar went to buyers who saved the coins. The Fort Vancouver Centennial, strictly a local event, is perhaps the most curious issue of 1925, because it was produced in San Francisco, but the S mintmark was inadvertently left off one of the dies. Just 14,994 reached circulation, a tiny fraction of the other issues of the year.

Small wooden boxes were used to distribute many 1925 Lexington-Concord half dollars. An image of the Old Belfry was rubber stamped on the sliding lid.

In 1926 in Philadelphia, the Sesquicentennial Exposition was held to commemorate the 150th anniversary of American independence. A grand world's fair was planned, but attendance lagged, and the event was not a commercial success. Two commemorative coins were issued in conjunction with it: a half dollar struck in low relief, and a gold quarter eagle. In terms of poor aesthetics, the Sesquicentennial half dollar gives the 1923-S Monroe a run for the money.

In the same year, the first of the great continuing series of half dollars was launched, the Oregon Trail Memorial—intended to commemorate the tradition of those who traveled through the Midwest and West in the 1840s, to settle in Oregon. Coins were struck at the Philadelphia and San Francisco Mints, the first time that multiple facilities were used for a single issue. The pieces were stored at each mint until needed. Despite low sales and large quantities in storage, at the Philadelphia Mint in 1928 thousands more were minted. These, however, could not be released until the 1926 coins were claimed! Shortly

Many different packages and promotions were used to sell 1925 Stone Mountain half dollars, including this certificate from the United Daughters of the Confederacy, stating the coin was among those purchased by Bernard Baruch, famous American financier, a later distribution.

after Herbert Hoover moved into the White House in March 1929, he declared there would be no more commemorative coins, and not even Oregon Trail half dollars were made during his administration. A businessman, Hoover thought that the past practice of coining vast quantities of commemorative coins and then melting most of them was extremely wasteful and that further abuses of this nature would not be tolerated. Just about anyone could have come to the same conclusion: of the 1,000,528 half dollars struck for the Sesquicentennial, 859,408 were shipped back to the Mint to be melted. It was for this reason that the creation of new varieties had to await the presidency of Franklin Delano Roosevelt in March 1933.

In the meantime, and continuing to the 1930s, the Oregon Trail Memorial Commission switched distributors, eventually including coin dealer Wayte Raymond as one. Issues continued to be produced, including a 1933-D variety (the first Denver Mint commemorative striking) struck for sale at the Century of Progress Exposition in Chicago—a world's fair which was modestly successful, despite its being held in the middle of the nationwide Depression. Then followed scattered issues such as the 1936-S, 1937-D, and the last two years, 1938 and 1939, with Philadelphia, Denver, and San Francisco pieces. Promotions included many misleading statements, including phony "sold out" notices and the like. Finally, in 1939, Congress put an end to commemorative half dollars. When all was said and done, 14 different varieties had been issued from 1926 to 1939. Although this was widely viewed as the worst example of exploiting numismatists, today the Oregon Trail half dollars are widely appreciated for their design. Returning to the 1920s, in 1927 the State of Vermont observed the 150th anniversary of the Battle of Bennington, a famous incident in which Ira Allen and the Green Mountain Boys vanquished all comers. At the time, the coin issued was widely known as the Bennington half dollar, though today it is known as the Vermont Sesquicentennial commemorative. Pieces seen today are well struck. Distribution of the Vermont half dollar amounted to slightly more than 28,000 pieces.

Next in line is the 1928 Hawaii Sesquicentennial half dollar, observing the 150th anniversary of the arrival of Captain James Cook at the Sandwich Islands, today known as the Hawaiian Islands, in 1778. Just 10,000 were ordered, a modest expectation. These were offered to residents of the Hawaiian Islands, who snapped up more than half of the issue, and also to numismatists. The issue was quickly sold out, and soon rose to a premium, this being the first time that a quick profit was shown for any buyers of a commemorative issue.

During this era, other commemoratives were proposed, but did not see reality. The most famous of these was for the 1925 Norse-American Exposition. Proponents of that event had to settle for a commemorative medal, struck at the Philadelphia Mint, from designs by James Earle Fraser. In 1929 various proposals were made to issue commemorative coins to celebrate the 125th anniversary of the Lewis and Clark expedition, the 300th anniversary of the founding of the Massachusetts Bay Colony, and the 250th anniversary of the founding of Trenton, New Jersey—all of which legislative efforts were unsuccessful. In 1930 the idea of a $1.50 gold coin arose again, in a proposal to observe the discovery of anesthesia, whereas another proposal suggested that $3 gold pieces be made for the Washington Bicentennial. Much effort was expended by L.W. Hoffecker and others to

Organizers of the 1925 Norse-American Exposition sought to have a commemorative half dollar issued, but had to settle for a medal. Designed James Earle Fraser, these were struck at the Philadelphia Mint.

authorize a half dollar observing the 100th anniversary of the Gadsden Purchase, and in April 1930 an appropriate bill was passed, but was vetoed by President Hoover. By that time there were five bills for commemoratives pending in Congress.

The Early 1930s

The next new commemorative design was the 1934 Maryland Tercentenary issue, celebrating the 300th anniversary of the establishment of that colony by Cecil Calvert. The issue, of which 25,000 were distributed, was a success, and was widely appreciated both by the collecting community and by citizens of that state. In the same year, the backers of the 1936 Texas Centennial celebration launched a half dollar dated 1934, meaningless in terms of the anniversary of independence, but still of interest to collectors. (Because it existed, it was necessary to add to a collection.) Texas Centennial half dollars of 1934 were produced at the Philadelphia Mint, after which exploitation went into high gear, with P-D-S sets made from 1935 through 1938, including the proper centennial year of 1936.

The bicentennial of Daniel Boone's birth was celebrated in 1934 with the issuance of a handsome commemorative half dollar featuring Boone on both sides. Distribution was placed in the hands of C. Frank Dunn, of Lexington, Kentucky, who sold 10,000 coins of the first year release. These were popular, and with greed as the guiding light, Dunn launched a continuing series, which grew to include P-D-S sets from 1935 through 1938. In November 1935, Dunn pulled off a great caper. He offered special-issue Boone coins for sale, then returned most requests as "sold out." With only a limited number minted, the price jumped. At first, scandal erupted, lawsuits were threatened, and distributor Dunn transferred his assets into his wife's name. Mysteriously, he just happened to have some sets available for sale later, saying that he had reacquired them from some original purchasers. Boone sets, thoroughly tarnished in reputation, continued to be made through 1938.

New Designs of 1935

In the meantime, in 1935 Connecticut celebrated its 300th anniversary of the founding of the colony, with issuance and successful distribution of 25,000 commemorative coins. The design was and is attractive, and remains popular to this day. In the same year, Arkansas began celebrating its 1936 centennial ahead of time by issuing 1935 P-D-S commemorative sets, an exploitation that continued through 1939—again with many false statements and phony "sold out" notices.

In 1935 the city of Hudson, New York, celebrated its 150th anniversary with the issuance of a commemorative half dollar. Just 10,000 were struck, and shipped to the First National Bank in that town, which hoped to sell them for $1 each as souvenirs. Some local publicity was initiated, but apparently little interest resulted, this being a Depression year, and Hudson being anything but a wealthy community. What to do with all of these coins? A white knight appeared on the scene in the form of Julius Guttag, a New York dealer, who offered 95 cents each for all that the issuers wished to sell, thereby relieving them of having an unsold glut on hand. An estimated 7,500 pieces were acquired by Guttag. Those in charge breathed easier, little realizing that the state had been set for a rush on their commemorative.

With this background, the issue of the 1935 Old Spanish Trail half dollar was a scenario made in heaven. This was the personal brainchild of L.W. Hoffecker, an El Paso, Texas, entrepreneur who had been trying to launch a commemorative since the late 1920s, but without success so far. With appropriate connections, including with President

Franklin D. Roosevelt, he persuaded Congress to authorize a half dollar which he alone was in charge of distributing, although a local museum was named as the nominal issuer. Buying the coins at face value, and adding the costs of die preparation and shipping, he offered them at $2 each, quickly selling out. Because the 10,000 mintage was the same as for the red-hot Hudson issue, who could resist? Actually, the wily Hoffecker hadn't quite sold out, but kept a nice reserve on hand to sell later, even into the 1940s. By the latter time he had served as president of the ANA.

L.W. Hoffecker had his own personal commemorative half dollars, so to speak. The ostensible purpose was to memorialize the Old Spanish Trail (shown here on a detail from the coin).

Also in 1935, the California Pacific International Exposition launched commemorative half dollars with the 1935-S issue, followed by the 1936-D coin of irrelevant date (but needed to fill numismatic collections). Since enough strikes were made of each to meet demand, little attention was paid to them in the marketplace.

The Commemorative Explosion of 1936

At the beginning of 1936, the commemorative market was as hot as a firecracker. Hudson Sesquicentennial half dollars continued in strong demand, the Old Spanish Trail pieces continued to rise in price, and despite continuingly higher posted prices, the 1935-D and S Boone with Small "1934" seemed nowhere to be found. All earlier commemoratives now sold at a premium over issue price, with the 1928 Hawaiian Sesquicentennial and the 1922 Grant With Star being the highest ranked among earlier half dollars, and the gold issues dating back to 1903 being in good demand as well.

Sniffing windfall profits, thousands of citizens decided to investigate what was going on, and decided to become coin collectors. A few of them even learned to pronounce *numismatist*. All bets were off—more than a dozen individuals, municipalities, and other entities advertised forthcoming types of commemorative half dollars, these in addition to long-running series such as the Boone, Arkansas, Oregon Trail Memorial, Panama-Pacific International Exposition, and Texas issues.

New subjects of the year included, in alphabetical order, the Albany (New York) Charter Anniversary, Battle of Gettysburg Anniversary, Bridgeport (Connecticut) Centennial, Cincinnati Musical Center, Cleveland Centennial, Columbia (South Carolina) Sesquicentennial, Delaware Tercentenary, Elgin (Illinois) Centennial, Long Island Tercentenary, Lynchburg (Virginia) Sesquicentennial, Norfolk (Virginia) Bicentennial, Providence or Rhode Island Tercentenary, Senator Joseph Robinson of Arkansas, San Francisco-Oakland Bay Bridge, Wisconsin Territorial Centennial, and York County (Maine) Tercentenary. Wow! Actually, not all were new in 1936, because some were still in gestation. Although dated 1936, several were not struck until 1937.

The 1936 Cincinnati issue was created by Thomas G. Melish, an Ohio industrialist who came up with the notion that 1936 would celebrate the 50th anniversary of Cincinnati as a "Musical Center of America," never mind that nothing happened 50 years earlier that was memorable. The 1936 Gettysburg Anniversary bore this date, but actually was issued for the 75th anniversary of the Battle of Gettysburg, which did not take place until 1938. The 1936 Delaware half dollar bore this date on the obverse, and 1938 on the reverse. You figure it out! Each of the 1936 issues has its own story to tell, as related later in the present text.

By late summer of 1936 the bloom was off the investment rose, and certain issuers had large quantities of unsold pieces, sometimes amounting to thousands. Gloom descended, and commemoratives went into a quiet mode.

The End of the Trail

With apathy the order of the day, the next new issues in the commemorative series, the 1937 Roanoke Island (North Carolina) 350th anniversary issue and the 1937 Battle of Antietam anniversary half dollars, both met indifferent receptions.

Then came the 1938 New Rochelle half dollar, a most interesting production conceived by the Westchester (New York) Coin Club, but minted and issued *in 1937*. The issue was well publicized in numismatic circles, and great care was given to fill all orders, and to make all public statements factual.

By 1938, commemoratives were passé. In 1939, the time-worn Arkansas and Oregon Trail sets continued to be issued, amid testimony in Congress about the abuses of recent years. Among those at the hearing was L.W. Hoffecker, one of the scoundrels, who cast himself as a model of ethical behavior! The Act of August 5, 1939, prohibited the further issuance of any commemoratives authorized prior to March 1, 1939. For all anyone knew, the United States would never issue any more such coins.

What Might Have Been

Congress had been inundated by bills proposing new half dollars during the period 1935 to 1939. While many of them became realities, most did not. Had some of the proponents pushed harder, then today we would be collecting such items as half dollars commemorating the 50th anniversary of the founding of Wilkinsburg, Pennsylvania; the centennial of Montgomery, Alabama; the 100th anniversary of the University of Louisville; and the 350th anniversary of the introduction of American-grown tobacco in England.

The list also includes proposals for commemoratives relating to the 100th anniversary of the arrival of Marcus and Narcissa Whitman in the Walla Walla Valley in Washington and the founding of the Waiilatpu Mission; the 160th anniversary of the arrival of General Washington and the Continental Army in Morristown, New Jersey; the 1939 World's Fair; the 300th anniversary of the founding of Hartford, Connecticut; the centennial of the founding of the city of Shreveport, Louisiana; the 20th anniversary of the 42nd (Rainbow) Division of the U.S. Army; the memory of humorist Will Rogers; and the 180th anniversary of the death of John Beckley (the founder of Beckley, West Virginia). And this is only a partial list!

After autumn 1936, prices of already-issued commemoratives trended downward. News that huge unsold quantities remained of certain varieties dampened interest further. Down prices went, finally touching bottom, on average, in 1941. Then came World War II. Inflation prevailed as cash became common on the home front, but consumer goods were difficult to find. The idea of issuing new commemoratives was forgotten. Almost.

A New Era

In 1946, Iowa celebrated its centennial of statehood, and Congress allowed a commemorative half dollar to be produced, to the extent of 100,000 pieces for distribution. Interestingly, 500 were set aside for distribution on the 150th anniversary of statehood in

1996, which was accomplished in due course, and another 500 for the 200th anniversary in 2046 (which a future generation of numismatists awaits).

In the same year, an arrangement was made to produce the Booker T. Washington Memorial half dollars, a tribute to this famous black educator and leader. P-D-S sets were made from 1947 through 1951 as well, in erratic (but usually low) quantities, with many melted. Few records were kept as to the quantities destroyed or sold.

This series wound down in 1951, when the same issuers tried to revive the enthusiasm but with a new design, the Carver/Washington motif, now featuring Booker T. Washington's portrait in combination with George Washington Carver. P-D-S sets were minted from 1951 through 1954. The coins were viewed as dull and uninteresting. The series was exploitative, again no account was kept of profits made, and the series was closed down in 1954.

It was 1939 all over again. The Treasury Department, which advised Congress on certain matters, unofficially declared that commemoratives were dead forever.

As the years went by, the numismatic community missed legitimate commemoratives, and many pleas were made by letters to congressmen and others, often reprinted in pages of *The Numismatist*, the *Numismatic Scrapbook Magazine*, *Numismatic News*, and *Coin World*. Certainly, enough events arose that were worthy of commemoration.

Surprise!

In 1982, the Treasury Department backed the issuance of the first commemorative since 1954—a half dollar celebrating the 250th anniversary of the birth of George Washington. This time around distribution was placed in the hands of the Bureau of the Mint (today called the United States Mint) rather than with commissions or private individuals. The profits accrued to the Treasury Department and the United States government.

The issue was well received in the numismatic community, although toward the end sales were sluggish. Then came the 1983 and 1984 Los Angeles Olympiad coins, minted in the subject years for the Los Angeles Olympiad held in 1984. This was a diverse and somewhat experimental series, with dollars of two different designs (the 1984 coin with headless torsos was condemned in its era) and, for the first time, a commemorative $10 coin. Sales were satisfactory, with all comers able to acquire whatever they needed.

The concept of a surcharge, or built in fee, was introduced, with a certain amount per coin going to a designated beneficiary—in this instance the Los Angeles Olympic Organizing Committee. These and related surcharges became controversial with collectors, many of whom resented making involuntary donations when they bought coins. Today, the practice continues and remains controversial. It is, however, the linchpin that has ignited most commemorative programs—as potential recipients of the surcharges launch intense lobbying campaigns in Congress.

In 1986, the 100th anniversary of the completion of the Statue of Liberty was commemorated by the issuance of a copper-nickel clad half dollar (first of its kind in the commemorative series), a silver dollar, and a $5 gold coin, with varied motifs, but each depicting on the obverse the Statue of Liberty, or an element therefrom. Unprecedented quantities were sold, although not as many as had been authorized.

The Dismal Era

Then followed the dark ages of modern commemorative issuance, including the 1987 Constitutional Bicentennial issue, the 1988 Olympiad issue, and more. Most designs were viewed by numismatists as being unattractive, boring, repetitive, or all of the above. A notable exception was Elizabeth Jones's 1988-W $5 Olympiad coin. Sales generally fell short of expectations.

In 1990 the Eisenhower Centennial dollar featured two portraits of the same person on the obverse, a first for a legal tender coin, and quite curious in its aspect. Whether such a coin was needed aroused comment, especially in view of the unpopularity of the recent (1971 to 1978) Eisenhower clad dollar intended for general circulation, but mostly used on gaming tables in Nevada.

In 1991 the 50th anniversary of the Mount Rushmore National Memorial was celebrated with a clad half dollar, silver dollar, and gold $5. All three depicted the Mount Rushmore carvings on the obverse, but numismatists took no great interest in them. Many thought if three coins had to be made for a given celebration, at least the designs could be different in each instance. In the same year came the oddest anniversary observation of all, a commemorative dollar for the 38th anniversary of the end of the Korean War. The United Service Organizations also turned out a commemorative this year, of a rather bland design that might have befitted a cheaply made arcade token, some suggested. Pressured to turn out an unceasing stream of motifs, the Mint, even with occasional help from outside artists, was not able to rise above mediocrity in many instances—in the view of many coin buyers as expressed in the columns of *Coin World, Numismatic News,* and other publications.

Coins minted in 1992 for the XXV Olympiad, the 200th anniversary of the White House, and the 500th anniversary of Columbus's discovery of America were marketed, followed by other issues in succeeding years. Some were well received, but sales of most fell far short of projections. Sometimes the low sales quantities had benefits for those wise enough to place orders, such as the 1995 $5 issue honoring baseball star Jackie Robinson, of which just 5,174 Uncirculated pieces were made, creating a rarity, the extent of which was not known until sales ended and figures were published.

Commemoratives saturated the market. Numismatic and other complaints were heard, and in recent years, issues have been limited to no more than two celebrations annually. While the future is unknown, since 1994 these have taken the form of silver dollars observing Thomas Alva Edison and the Lewis and Clark Bicentennial (2004); Chief Justice John Marshall and the Marine Corps 230th anniversary (2005); Benjamin Franklin and the San Francisco Old Mint (2006); and Jamestown's 400th Anniversary and Little Rock Central High School's Desegregation Anniversary in 2007.

Most ugly modern commemorative? Many collectors found the 1984 Olympic Games silver dollar, with headless torsos, to be unattractive.

Most beautiful modern commemorative? Many numismatists and design award committees thought so. This $5 gold coin depicting the goddess Nike, by Chief Engraver Elizabeth Jones, was made for the 1988 Olympics.

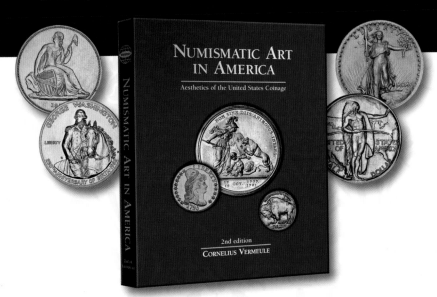

CHAPTER TWO
MINTS AND THE MINTING PROCESS

From Concepts to Coinage Dies

Creating and Reviewing Designs

For commemorative coins, the sponsoring commission or other entity usually suggested motifs. If the coins were intended to honor a specific person or event, this was usually the first choice—to depict Columbus on the obverse and one of his ships on the reverse of the 1892 Columbian half dollar was a logical approach. State arms or seals of Illinois (1918), Maine (1920), Maryland (1934), and other issues represented anniversaries of colonies and various states. Historical ships were depicted on many issues, while buildings (Monticello, old and new Iowa Capitols, White House, U.S. Capitol, and more) were seen on others. The yucca tree (Old Spanish Trail, 1935), oak (Connecticut Tercentenary, 1935), palmetto (South Carolina Sesquicentennial, 1936), rose (Botanic Garden, 1999), and other plants form still further motifs.

From the 1915 Panama-Pacific coins onward, the Commission of Fine Arts has reviewed the designs. Sometimes the commission was given a wide selection of artists' sketches. Other times the members were shown a design that the Treasury Department had already approved, rendering further commentary redundant—although sometimes suggestions were made as to lettering and style.

Hubs and Dies

Once a design was finalized, a talented sculptor, often an engraver at the Mint, translated the motifs onto a plaster, clay, or composition model of large size, often eight to 12 inches in diameter. From the model a hard copy was made by electrotyping, to create a *galvano* or metal impression, with the features being in mirror image. This galvano was then placed into a transfer lathe, a pantograph-style device with a tracer point slowly moving over the slowly turning original, while at the other end of the arm a reduced image was made by a tiny rotating cutting drill translating the design into a soft steel blank, the face of which is the size of the finished coin. At the Mint, a reducing or transfer lathe was used to make hubs, as part of the sequence needed to create dies. The Medallic Art Company, a private contractor, was sometimes enlisted to use its Janvier lathe to make transfers.

The transfer lathe can be used to copy just the main motifs of a coin, such as designs. At a later stage the lettering and numerals can be punched in by hand. In recent generations, the entire design, with all lettering and other features, has been mechanically transferred. The newly created soft steel hub, as it is called, is then examined under magnification, and an engraver sharpens certain features and otherwise finishes the surface. (The hub bears a raised image, similar to a coin in relief.)

Next, the hub is hardened by heating it to a high temperature, then quickly quenching it in oil or water. It is then cleaned, examined, and made ready to create copies by impressing it into soft steel blanks. On these blanks, relief portions of the hub design become incuse or intaglio. These are then hardened and pressed into other soft steel blanks, which are then hardened to become working dies for use in coining presses. Mintmarks, if any, were added by punching the appropriate letter into the working die.

In the 1980s the die-making process was modernized. Modern commemorative master hubs, used to create working dies, are made complete with date, mintmark, and all other features. Since 1927, most working dies have been chrome plated to extend their lives.

The Coining Process

Preparing Planchets

Commemoratives as well as other coins are struck on planchets—circular discs the approximate diameter of the finished coin.[3] For the typical half dollar blank, discs were cut out of long strips of silver alloy, much as a cookie cutter would punch out pieces of dough. At the Mint this was accomplished by using ingots to create narrow strips by means of a rolling mill, and punching out one disc at a time. Later, gang punches were made, creating a loud racket as they stamped out multiple blanks in one blow. Each blank had to conform to the statutory weight and specifications applicable to the same denomination's regular coinage.

For silver half dollars of the 1892 to 1954 classic era this meant a weight of 192 grains (in alloy of 90 percent silver, 10 percent copper) with a tolerance of plus or minus 1.5 grains, a standard adopted on February 21, 1853, and used ever since. For modern commemoratives in clad metal, such as the 1989-D Congress Bicentennial half dollar, this meant an outer layer of 25 percent nickel and 75 percent copper (with a silvery appearance) bonded to a solid copper core, with an overall weight of 175 grains, with a tolerance of plus or minus seven grains. In recent years, commemoratives have been made either of silver (90 percent silver and 10 percent copper) or gold (90 percent gold and 10 percent copper). In each instance, copper is added to give strength to the alloy.

Silver and gold discs not meeting specifications were melted down and recycled into the ingot-strip-disc process.

After the circular blank is ready it is put into a milling or upsetting machine and run at high speed between a roller and an edge, in an area in which the diameter decreases slightly, forcing the metal up on ridges on both sides of the coin. This process creates what is called a *planchet*. This is blank on both sides but has a raised rim.

Although processes have varied over time, it is customary to anneal the planchets by heating followed by cooling, to soften the metal. If this is not done correctly, a planchet will be too hard, and coins made from it will not strike up completely in the deeper recesses of the die. After annealing, they are cleaned in a soapy or acidic mixture, rinsed, and then dried by tumbling in sawdust or by exposure to currents of air. The dry planchets are ready for coining. Tumbling around in a cleaning machine imparts countless nicks and marks to both sides. It was hoped, at least by numismatists during the 1892 to 1954 classic era, that during the squeezing and compression of the planchet in the coining press, these would be obliterated. This proved to be the case for most (but not all) commemoratives. In contrast, coins made for everyday circulation, such as Lincoln cents and Jefferson nickels, often had incompletely struck features. For modern commemoratives 1982 to date, striking is nearly always complete, with no weak areas on the finished coins.

Striking the Coins

Commemorative coins are struck by a pair of dies fitted to a coining press. The top or hammer die moves up and down, and the lower or anvil die remains fixed in position.

On top of the anvil die is a plate with a circular opening, the collar, which defines the diameter of the coin. A planchet is inserted into the collar and rests on top of the anvil die. For all commemoratives of the 1892 to 1954 classic era, and most since then, the collar has had vertical indentations or *reeding*. As the top die descends and impresses the planchet, it imparts designs from both dies as well as the reeded edge from the collar. Although high-speed presses with different mechanisms, some with multiple pairs of dies, have been used for cents, nickels, and other circulating coins over the years, the machines used to make commemoratives—known as *knuckle-action presses*—retain the traditional style.

For a half dollar minted in the early 20th century, the pressure required for properly stamping the coin was 98 tons, as compared to 160 tons for a silver dollar (such as the 1900 Lafayette commemorative) and 35 tons for a quarter eagle (such as the 1915 Panama-Pacific). Presses striking half dollars and silver dollars were driven by a 7.5 horsepower electric motor running at 950 rpm, and producing 90 coins per minute. In time, knuckle-action presses were replaced by new designs by Bliss, Schuler, and others, for more efficient coinage of circulating issues in large quantities—sometimes billions. Commemoratives, however, continued to be struck on the old-style presses.

It seems that for most commemoratives minted during the classic era, little or no attention was paid to handling the coins carefully. After coining, they were dumped into a box behind the press, transferred to a larger bin, then run through a mechanical counter, and put into cloth bags. Afterward, the typical half dollar might be in what we might call MS-63 or MS-64 grade today.

Although I have seen no records to substantiate this, inspection of the coins themselves suggests that for a few classic-era coins, care was indeed taken in their handling—examples are the 1935 Old Spanish Trail, 1936 York County (Maine) Tercentenary, and 1938 New Rochelle half dollars, with typical examples grading MS-65 or finer. Significantly, each of these issues was distributed by a *numismatist* (or group of numismatists), who must have furnished the Mint with requirements as to care in minting, packing, and shipping.

Full Details on Commemoratives

For circulating denominations of coins it was and still is the intention of the mints to produce the largest number of pieces in the shortest time and with the least amount of effort. There was no consideration whatsoever to pleasing numismatists who might later collect such coins. In happy contrast, commemoratives were struck on slow-speed presses and, for the most part, more carefully.

For a commemorative or other coin to strike up with *Full Details*—with every design feature sharp—this process has to occur:

First, the planchet must be annealed properly, to the appropriate softness to bring up the design features. A planchet that has bypassed the annealing process or that has been cooled too quickly is apt to be too hard, and thus more difficult to strike.

Second, the dies have to be spaced closely in the coining press, so that when they are closest together in the minting cycle, they will force the planchet metal into the deepest recesses.

Commemoratives for which the above process was *not* followed include the 1921 Missouri Centennial, 1921 Alabama Centennial, 1946 to 1951 Booker T. Washington, and 1951 to 1954 Carver/Washington half dollars. Even on many if not most coins certified as gem Mint State—that is, MS-65 or above—the highest parts are apt to lack detail and show tiny nicks and marks from the original planchet. On Booker T. Washington coins this appears as a grainy effect on the highest part of the obverse portrait. For *you*, the collector seeking top-quality examples, the advantage is that few numismatists are aware of this, and by carefully searching, you can find coins with Full Details.

Proof Coins

Beginning with the Washington 250th Anniversary half dollars in 1982, Proofs have been made in addition to regular coins with "Uncirculated" finish. The Proofs have often been made at a different mint, as were, for example, the 1982-D Uncirculated Washington half dollars and their corresponding 1982-S Proofs.

Proofs are struck from dies having the fields polished to a high mirror finish. The designs and lettering are typically in a matte or frosty finish, giving a nice contrast sometimes called *cameo*. The planchets are specially prepared as well. Striking is typically done with two, or sometimes three, blows of a slowly operated knuckle-action press.

Assay Coins

Prior to 1980, additional specimens of commemoratives and regular issues were produced at the various mints to be set aside for viewing by the Assay Commission. This was a panel of citizens and government officials who selected at random a small number of coins from those reserved, and tested them for weight and correctness of alloy. In studying the mintage figures given for each coin in the classic era from 1892 to 1953, we can see additional numbers of assay coins. As an example, the mintage of 1920 Maine Centennial half dollars totaled 50,028, equivalent to 50,000 intended for distribution and 28 for assay; and the mintage of 1928 Hawaiian Sesquicentennial half dollar reached 10,008, with the odd eight being assay coins.

As to the disposition of the assay coins that were not tested, the intent was to melt these for conversion into other coins. In practice, from time to time Assay Commission members and Mint employees obtained specimens by exchanging other current coins for them, a legitimate procedure. Because of this it is reasonable to assume that some commemorative coins intended for assay were in fact distributed. (At the time they were novelties.) Net distribution figures given in the present text reflect that assay pieces were *not* destroyed unless Mint records specifically state otherwise (as, for example, with the 1903-dated Louisiana Purchase Exposition gold dollars, of which 258 assay pieces were made with 250 later melted, and the 1915 Panama-Pacific half dollars, of which 30 assay pieces were struck and then listed in government records as having been melted).

Mints that Have Made Commemoratives

The Philadelphia Mint

When the first Columbian half dollars were struck in 1892, the Philadelphia Mint was located in the second structure to bear that name, a Greek Revival building that succeeded the first Mint erected in 1792. The cornerstone for the Second Mint, as historians designate it, was laid on July 4, 1829, in a ceremony in which silver half dimes were given out as souvenirs. The structure was occupied in January 1833, and commenced the production of coins. Steam power replaced horsepower in 1836, after which knuckle-action presses of the Thonnelier type were employed for most coinage. Beginning in the early 1890s, slow-speed electric motors were installed to run the coining presses.

Within the Philadelphia Mint were complete facilities for refining silver and gold, producing ingots and planchet strips, making planchets, and striking coins. The Engraving Department was also located there, as was a shop for making dies.

The Second Philadelphia Mint, which began operation in 1833 and continued into 1902, is where the first commemorative coins were made.

In October 1901 the Third Philadelphia Mint became operational, in a new building situated on a full city block defined by Sixteenth, Seventeenth, Buttonwood, and Spring Garden streets, with the main entrance on Spring Garden Street. The Mint Cabinet, or Mint Collection, was stored and displayed at the Mint until spring 1923, when it was removed to the Smithsonian Institution—where today it is known as the National Numismatic Collection in the Museum of American History.

The facility on Spring Garden Street remained in use until the late 1960s, when the present or Fourth Philadelphia Mint was opened on Independence Square.

All models for commemorative coins were either prepared or finished at the Philadelphia Mint, beginning in 1892, and continuing to the present day. Various reduction processes, hubs, and dies have been made there as well, including working dies for branch mints.

The chief engravers at the Mint from 1892 onward have each been involved in the production of at least some commemorative coins. These have been Charles E. Barber (1880–1917), George T. Morgan (1917–1925), John R. Sinnock (1925–1947), Gilroy Roberts (1948–1965), Frank Gasparro (1965–1981), and Elizabeth Jones (1981–1990). No chief engraver has been appointed since that time, although as of this writing in 2007, the talented sculptor-engraver John Mercanti seems to have this position *de facto*.

Gilroy Roberts joined the Mint in 1936 as an understudy to Chief Engraver Sinnock. In a letter to the author he recalled the era:

> The commemorative half dollars of our country were in full swing at the time, and artists' models were arriving for processing to coining dies on a regular basis. This happened at a time when I was striving to improve my skill as a low-relief sculptor and engraver. It was a wonderful opportunity to study the creations of some of our country's leading medallic artists, both good and not so good. It was a great influence on furthering my career.[4]

Chief Engraver Gasparro saw no new commemoratives during his tenure. His successor, Elizabeth Jones, was in the right place at the right time, and was central to the success of many of the commemoratives of the 1980s.

The Denver Mint

The present Denver Mint was constructed beginning in 1904 and struck its first coins, in silver and gold, in 1906. The ice was broken for commemoratives with the 1933-D Oregon Trail Memorial half dollar. The mint was enlarged in 1937. Today, the same structure is in use, although with many improvements in technology. In recent years limited die-making operations have been set up there, but not involving the design process.

The San Francisco Mint

The San Francisco Mint struck its first commemorative coins, a suite of five different coins including two formats of $50 gold pieces, in 1915, for the nearby Panama-Pacific International Exposition. From that time onward the mint has been important in the commemorative series. The 1915 building, as the second structure to bear that name, had been in service since its opening in 1874. It was the only building in its district to survive the April 1906 earthquake and fire. In 1937 the mint moved to a new building on Duboce Street in the same city, a modern fortress-like facility.

In 1955 the Treasury Department announced that the San Francisco Mint would close its coining operations forever. Its last commemorative coin had been the 1954-S Carver/Washington half dollar. The government determined that it was more economical to strike circulating coins in Denver and haul them to the West Coast, than to continue a coining facility in California. During a coin shortage in the 1960s the facility was reactivated, and it has remained in use ever since.

When commemorative production, in suspension since 1954, was resumed with the Washington 250th Anniversary half dollar in 1982, pieces with Proof finish were struck in San Francisco, while those with "Uncirculated" or "circulation strike" finish were made in Denver.

The West Point "Mint"

In 1974, during a shortage of cents in circulation—fueled by hoarding due to the rising price of copper on world markets—Mint Director Mary Brooks proposed that the Bureau of the Mint install coin presses at the West Point Bullion Depository. Located on the grounds of the United States Military Academy, the structure was well fortified, and in a secure area. The facility had been constructed in the late 1930s for the storage of silver, a counterpart to the gold storage facility at Fort Knox in Kentucky.

Soon, the necessary equipment was installed. Using planchets obtained on contract, the West Point Mint, as it became known in numismatics, commenced striking millions of Lincoln cents. No mintmark was used, giving the coins the appearance of Philadelphia Mint products. In time, other coins were struck there, including American Eagle silver and gold bullion coins, and certain commemoratives, some of which bore a W mintmark.

The first of these was the 1984-W $10 for the Los Angeles Olympiad. In 1986, West Point was the only mint where the highly acclaimed Statue of Liberty $5 gold coin was struck, inaugurating a list of different $5 issues made only at that location.

It is likely that the West Point Bullion Depository will continue to produce commemoratives for many years to come.

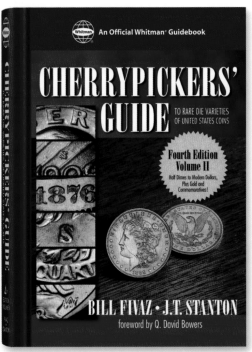

CHAPTER THREE
GRADING COMMEMORATIVE COINS

Grade as a Determinant of Value

Descriptions of Condition

As is true in most other numismatic series, the grade assigned to a commemorative coin is a key component in determining its market value. Stated simply, the grade of a coin is a designation reflecting how much wear or contact it has received. A pristine or "like new" commemorative half dollar is referred to as being in *Mint State*, the term most often used, although *Uncirculated* means the same thing. Commemoratives made with special mirror finish to the fields and sold as Proofs are called that today.

While today in the early 21st century we have 11 different Mint State grades to deal with from MS-60 to MS-70 (see ANA Grading Standards below), and even more at lower levels, it was not always so. Prior to 1960—the year that coin collecting underwent a great boom and expansion catalyzed by the launching of *Coin World* and excitement about the 1960 Small Date Lincoln cent—the typical advertisement for commemorative coins simply listed them as "Brilliant Uncirculated," or "BU." There were no gradations. Sometimes, modifiers such as "choice" or "gem" would be used in auction listings. Commemoratives with wear might be called Extremely Fine or About Uncirculated.

In a way it seems like only yesterday, but it was about 1957 or so that I went with my friend Ken Rendell on a multiple-day trip to examine the inventories of all the dealers in the Boston area. Arthur Conn, who conducted business from an office in his home in nearby Melrose, had a particularly generous stock. At the time he was one of the most important advertisers in the *Numismatic Scrapbook Magazine*, the most popular rare coin periodical of the time. Each month he owned the center spread of two pages, and usually featured Uncirculated and Proof coins. At the time I had been a rare coin dealer for a few years, since 1953, and had built a nice mail-order clientele by looking for especially nice coins and selling them to collectors who appreciated quality. Then as now, buyers either had the chance of obtaining the best quality or the lowest price, but not both in the same coin! Among my customers were Emery May Holden Norweb, John Jay Pittman, and most other connoisseurs of the era. My operation was small scale, for at the same time I was attending the Pennsylvania State University.

I asked Mr. Conn if I could look through his extensive inventory of commemorative coins. Then as now, certain issues were known as being rather "scruffy" or unappealing, and were hard to find in truly gem preservation, while others were usually found as gems. As examples, the 1923-S Monroe Doctrine half dollar is usually unprepossessing or downright ugly, while just about every 1938 New Rochelle I've ever seen is a beautiful gem. Accordingly, I didn't waste my time with the "gemmy" issues, but sought to find petunias among the onion patch of coins that were usually unattractive.

I was very impressed that Conn had the best part of a long cardboard box filled with 1900 Lafayette silver dollars, nearly 200 of them, each in a paper envelope marked "Brilliant Uncirculated," or similarly. Some were nicked up and unattractive, while a few were flashy gems. I bought all of the latter, perhaps a half dozen or so. I then went through the other difficult commemorative varieties and cherrypicked for quality. Mr. Conn didn't mind at all, for his typical mail order customers would keep just about anything he sent them, so long as it was reasonably "brilliant."

While I learned the hard way—by doing—and became well acquainted with grading, most collectors and some dealers did not bother to invest time in such study. Market emphasis was mostly on price. In 1957 the typical market price for a brilliant Uncirculated Lafayette dollar was perhaps $45. An unattractive example with many nicks and marks would sell instantly at the bargain price of $40, but a hand-picked superb gem at $55 would find only a handful of buyers.

In 1957, or at any other time in that long-ago era, you could have formed a choice collection of commemoratives by cherrypicking for quality—one coin at a time. Today, Uncirculated coins—usually called Mint State, although the term is hardly new—are typically graded by numbers, such as MS-61 or MS-63, not simply as "Uncirculated" or "Mint State." Within these assigned grades there can be wide differences. Grading is not scientific. Because of this, cherrypicking can still pay.

The ANA Grading Standards

In 1977 the ANA sponsored *The Official ANA Grading Standard for United States Coins*, largely supervised by dealer Abe Kosoff, and compiled by Kenneth E. Bressett, of Whitman Publishing Company, editor of the *Guide Book of United States Coin* (the successor to Richard S. Yeoman). I wrote the general introductory material.

The system is one of numbers, building upon a scheme devised by Dr. William H. Sheldon in 1949 and published in his *Early American Cents* book. The number 1 denoted a coin worn nearly smooth and barely identifiable. Sheldon called this Basal State-1. Today, we would say Poor-1. The number 70 represented absolute perfection. Sheldon conceived the Basal State number as a multiplication factor to calculate market price, using Basal Value for each variety. A coin in VF-30 grade with a Basal Value of $2 would be worth 2 times 30, or $60, by his system, while the same variety in MS-60 grade would be worth 60 times $2, or $120.

Today, there is a huge difference between VF-30 and MS-60, and the system is even more absurd, or perhaps beyond absurd. In any event, in the commemorative series, most grades below Mint State are irrelevant to most buyers, and for some issues, such as modern commemoratives 1982 to date, may not even exist. The concept of using numbers lives on, however, although the Basal Value idea has been dropped. No longer are numbers the base for any price calculation.

At first, the ANA Grading Standards of 1977 mirrored the Sheldon system of 1949, more or less, but in successive editions intermediate grades were added by the ANA board of governors, as MS-63 and MS-67, then the full range of Mint State possibilities, giving 11 grades from MS-60, 61, 62, and, so on, all the way to MS-70. On the other hand, the grade of Very Fine runs from VF-20 until we find EF-40, or a range of 20 numbers, but they are not all used. Perhaps some day we will have VF-21, VF-22, etc. I hope not. The ANA book became well accepted and has gone through multiple editions, now at the sixth.

Below are given the guidelines as outlined in *The Official ANA Grading Standards for U.S. Coins*, sixth edition, narrative by Q. David Bowers, grading guidelines by Kenneth Bressett. These criteria represent an adaptation and distillation of information and opinions gathered from many leading experts in the field.

While they and any other standards are subject to interpretation, those propounded by the ANA are the most widely used in the marketplace, including by all of the leading grading services. Understanding them is the *first step* to being able to evaluate the grade of a coin. It is not the be-all and end-all, and by no means the final answer to smart buyers. It is, however, the final answer for perhaps 90 percent or more of the buyers of coins today.

Official ANA Grading Standards Adapted for Commemorative Coins

MS-70 A flawless coin exactly as it was minted, with no trace of wear or injury. Must have full mint luster and brilliance or light toning. Any unusual striking traits must be described.

MS-67 Virtually flawless, but with very minor imperfections.

MS-65 A coin possessing full mint luster with no major detracting features such as slide marks on the high points, deep contact marks, visible or excessive hairlines, or evidence of cleaning.

MS-63 A coin with half or more of its original luster, but with noticeable detracting marks or minor blemishes.

MS-60 A Mint State coin with no trace of wear, but numerous contact marks or blemishes may be present. Surface may be fully lustrous or exhibit little or no luster (caused naturally or from chemical cleaning).

Reading the above carefully, you might notice some problems or potential things to watch for. In an effort to make five definitions cover dozens of different commemorative issues and designs, the guidelines are necessarily fuzzy.

Under MS-70 I am not quite sure what "unusual striking traits" are. If this is to mean weak details on high points, such as on the reverse of many 1921 Alabama half dollars, I would not want to pay an "MS-70 price" for such a coin.

If I were buying an MS-60 coin I might not want one that has no luster because of "chemical cleaning." On the other hand, I don't quite know what lack of luster "caused naturally" means.

Not Complicated

If you have read certain of my other studies in the Whitman "Official Red Book" series you will know that for such series as Lincoln cents and Indian Head / Buffalo nickels, grading can be exceedingly complex. With commemorative coins it is much simpler. While adhering to the ANA guidelines quoted above can raise questions, in the marketplace most commemorative coins have few, if any, complications.

Making things still easier is the availability of coins certified by such leading services (alphabetically) as ANACS (ANA Certification Service), ICG (Independent Coin Grading), NGC (Numismatic Guaranty Corporation), and PCGS (Professional Coin Grading Service). While these services and the ANA standard are far from infallible, they are very useful.

Higher Grade = Higher Price

Today, the use of the ANA standards as well as certification makes everything more understandable to buyers. That unattractive coin might be graded MS-60 (PCGS) today, while the superb gem might be MS-66 (PCGS). The catch is that today the MS-66 coin costs a heck of a lot more than the MS-60. Cherrypicking for hidden values in dealers' stocks, while not impossible, does not have the possibilities it did 50 years ago. Higher grade coins sell for higher prices, sometimes much higher.

Here are retail price estimates for the 1900 Lafayette dollar in the July 2007 issue of the *Rare Coin Market Report*, giving values for PCGS-certified coins:

Prices of the 1900 Lafayette Dollar (PCGS)

EF-40: $475	**MS-62:** $1,350	**MS-65:** $12,000
AU-55: $750	**MS-63:** $2,300	**MS-66:** $20,000
MS-60: $1,000	**MS-64:** $4,000	**MS-67:** $82,500

The above price schedule also showcases some points for future discussion. Namely, if you win the lottery and have $82,500 to spend for an MS-67 Lafayette dollar, is this a good value for the money? Or, would it be better to buy an MS-66 for $20,000—less than 25 percent of that price? After all, it takes an expert to tell the difference. Further, are all coins in the same grade apt to be

The market value of a 1900 Lafayette commemorative silver dollar can vary greatly depending upon the grade assigned to it.

of the same overall quality? What is *quality?* Is it the same as *grade?* If you could visit a latter-day equivalent of Arthur Conn and sort through 10 coins now certified as MS-66, would some be better than others?

With that food for thought, here are additional comments about the ANA standards.

Scientific or Not?

For a grading system or any other system to be truly scientific, it should be able to be used at a distance by a qualified person having the guidelines in hand. If I were to send a box of 100 ungraded 1900-dated Lafayette dollars, along with the book giving the ANA grading standards, to an intelligent person in Juneau, Alaska, the recipient could not possibly sort them into such grades as MS-60, 61, 62, and onward to 70. In fact, I dare say that he or she would have problems defining MS-63 as compared to MS-65. If the system were sci-entific, the coins, after being returned to me, could be sent to another person, say in Havre de Grace, Maryland, who would assign exactly the same numbers to them.

In the real commemorative marketplace, a coin graded by NGC as MS-66 in Janu-ary, if removed from its holder and sent back in September, might be returned as MS-65, or MS-67, or perhaps in a "body bag" marked "environmental damage," or some similar situation. Likely, in most instances it would come back as MS-66, but differences do occur, and very often. The possibility that an MS-66 coin might be returned as MS-67 is very real, and is exactly why thousands of collectors and hundreds of dealers play the "resubmission game"—sending back coins to see if they can be upgraded.

Continuing with my example of a 1900 Lafayette dollar, if you owned a beautiful gem MS-66 at $20,000, and you sent it back to the grading service 100 times, paying $100 each time for expedited service, and *finally* received an $82,500 coin, you would be $52,500 richer, after paying $10,000 in grading fees. It is easy to see that this system is win-win for both players: the coin owner as well as the grading service.

The downside, of course, is that in the marketplace the average quality of an expen-sive commemorative you may be offered, graded, say, MS-65 or 66, becomes less and less. Any "high end" or conservatively graded MS-65 is likely to be moved to an MS-66 holder, while a "low end" or optimistically graded MS-65 will stay in its MS-65 holder forever!

If there is a point to this it may be: don't worship numbers. When you are contemplating paying a huge differential in price for just a single higher grading point, be very careful.

Advantages of the ANA Grading Standards

That said, there are multiple distinct *advantages* the ANA Grading Standards have to offer. Here are some that come to mind:

1. **Grades are easy to compare.** It is instantly obvious that a 1915-S Panama-Pacific gold dollar in MS-65 grade is a nicer coin than an MS-60, but not as nice as one certified MS-67. There may be differences within grades, but usually not with large jumps. If you are building a collection of classic 1892–1954 commemorative silver coins in MS-65 grade, you can hone in on listings at that level, and not concern yourself with offerings of higher or lower examples.

2. **No information is given about quality.** Yes, this is an *advantage* for you. It means that if you become a connoisseur and seek, for example, an MS-64 1923-S Monroe Doctrine half dollar, you may be able to find a really nice one. For this particular variety, most, but not all, are rather unattractive. Indeed, they are downright ugly. While others will be satisfied by simply seeing the "MS-64" label on a certified holder, you will be wiser, and will carefully study the coin itself. Perhaps after reviewing 20 coins you will find one that has significantly finer eye appeal. This is called cherrypicking.

3. **Undesirable coins sell to most buyers.** Yes, this is yet another advantage for you, and it is a godsend for dealers. A really crummy-appearing 1923-S Monroe Doctrine half dollar certified as MS-64 will sell instantly if it is priced at an attractive discount from market price. Ditto for a certified MS-65, never mind that it is as ugly as a toad. This is wonderful for people who have coins for sale. This keeps overall market values strong.

Certified Coins

Different Services

In the 1970s the ANA Certification Service (ANACS) set up in the business of grading coins for a fee. A submitted coin would be assigned a grade, photographed for identification, and sent back with a certificate showing the coin and its evaluation. In time, the ANA sold ANACS to Amos Press, parent company of *Coin World*, which later sold it to Anderson Press, parent company of Whitman Publishing, LLC (publisher of this book).

In 1986 PCGS popularized the encapsulation of coins in a plastic holder, soon popularly called a "slab." NGC followed suit in 1987, and, soon, ANACS developed its own holder. Later, more than 100 services were born, but most died. Today, NGC and PCGS have the lion's share of the business, with ANACS and IGC joining them in terms of acceptance and reputation. There are, no doubt, other fine services as well. There are also a lot of exploitative and fly-by-night services, some of them with "official" or high-sounding names. My advice: on your own, approach several different dealers and collectors and ask about the grading services. Just say something like: "If you were buying a 1928 Hawaiian Sesquicentennial half dollar for your own collection, and desired the MS-63 grade, which certification service would you prefer?" The services are continually discussed, and you'll soon become well informed as to which labels are worthwhile and which should be ignored.

The certification services use the same ANA Official Grading Standards that you have just read. Because the standards are not scientific, a commemorative half dollar or other coin can be assigned a different grade if resubmitted to the same service, or the grade can remain the same.

That said, some services have "tighter" interpretations than do others. If a certain MS-65 commemorative half dollar from Certification Service A is listed at $1,000 in the *Certified Coin Dealer Newsletter*, and the same coin from Certification Service B is posted at $900, it means that the dealer community values A's coins slightly higher than B's, meaning that they are perceived as being of slightly higher quality. It is important to remember that even with such differences, there are likely some coins graded by B that are of higher quality than some of those certified by A. Stated another way, each leading service has some coins that are apt to be finer than those of a competing service, and some that are to be lesser in quality.

Registry Sets

Some years ago David Hall, prime founder of PCGS, came up with the idea of the PCGS Registry Set. This developed into a very popular program whereby collectors and investors can form a set or collection in just about any series, and register it with PCGS. The total of the numbers (ANA grading numbers) in each set is added up, with more weight being assigned to rarer issues, and a score is assigned.

For participants, this is like owning a stable of race horses. When one of your coins is improved, your score rises, and perhaps with the improvement of a half dozen coins, you will move from fourth best set to third. As an auctioneer I know that when PCGS coins that are the highest graded are offered, there is a lot of excitement. Such coins do not need to be at all rare at lower levels. A Registry Set leader at MS-69 might be one of just three graded at that level and may be very expensive, while a very nice MS-65 may be valued at a very nominal and affordable sum.

My advice is that Registry Set participation can be exciting—just like betting in Las Vegas or on the Kentucky Derby, or buying options in the stock market—but there are losers as well as winners. Keep your eye on the series in which you are involved, and watch out for the real possibility that a coin, which today may have just three graded at MS-69, might have 10 at that level a few years hence, or even some at MS-70.

Population Reports

In a word, *beware!* From the inception of PCGS in 1986 and NGC in 1987, the values of certain certified coins have been driven by the numbers appearing in their periodic population reports. As more and more coins are sent into the services, the populations expand. This is particularly true for the "ultra" grades such as MS-68 to 70 and PF-68 to 70. *Populations never get smaller. They usually get larger, often much larger.* Take heed of this when buying, and you'll pay for the price of this book many times over!

A lot of "investors" and viewers of television shopping programs have overpaid by huge sums when buying modern commemoratives implied as being *rare* in such numerical grades as 68, 69, and 70, whereas in actuality, *most* modern coins are in those grades. Make money as the dealers do: buy directly from the United States Mint.

If you are a Registry Set participant, or if you have a lot of money and want the best, then ultra grades are for you. For the rest of us, gem 65 and 66 coins will be just fine, if selected with care.

Common Sense When Analyzing Reports

Further, the population reports for commemoratives are heavily biased toward ultra-grade coins. One of the most common of all commemoratives is the 1893 Columbian half dollar, of which 4,052,105 were struck and 2,501,700 melted, leaving a distribution of 1,550,405 coins. While many have disappeared, still today there are at least 100,000 or more still around, perhaps even two or three times that.

Recent population report totals (ANACS, NGC, and PCGS combined) are as follows:

1893 Columbian Half Dollar Population Report Totals

VG-8: 7	**AU-53:** 85	**MS-63:** 2,833
F-12: 18	**AU-55:** 487	**MS-64:** 3,025
VF-20: 43	**AU-58:** 1036	**MS-65:** 1,037
EF-40: 103	**MS-60:** 287	**MS-66:** 280
EF-45: 118	**MS-61:** 643	**MS-67:** 31
AU-50: 192	**MS-62:** 1,992	**MS-68:** 2

What do these numbers mean? What do they not mean?

A newcomer to the hobby might read these numbers and think, "The most common grade of an 1893 Columbian half dollar is MS-64, since more than 3,000 have been certified. Really rare is a VG-8, with only seven certified. In fact, a VG coin is far rarer than an MS-67."

Then he or she would think: "How can this be, if more than a million were distributed? Why are worn coins so *rare*?" A eureka moment would then suggest that since it typically costs at least $10 to certify such a coin, there would not be much point in submitting a potential VG-8 coin, which is worth very little. In actuality, there are 100,000 worn Columbian halves in existence, although only slightly more than 2,000 have been certified in grades from VG through AU.

What *is* useful from this report? In comparing these numbers for *high-grade* coins, MS-65 and upward, with other commemoratives, you can gain an idea of the relative availability of the 1893 Columbian half dollar. If you are working on a Registry Set, the knowledge that just two have been certified means that such a coin will be difficult to locate and expensive, especially if certified by PCGS (the focal point of Registry Sets).

Because of the above, it would be a waste of time and space to give population reports for commemorative coins except in Mint State for classic era coins and higher level Mint State and Proof grades for commemoratives from 1982 to date. This is what I have done in this book. For more details, refer to the population reports themselves.

Chapter Four
How to Be a Smart Buyer

Introduction

The following paragraphs tell you what I would do if I were building a high-quality collection of commemorative coins, a reiteration of some of the things already mentioned, the addition of some ideas not yet discussed, and a summary. If you've read some of my other books you know that buying coins in some series can be very complex. Commemoratives are fairly straightforward.

Step 1: The Numerical Grade

Look at market listings and determine what grades you would like to buy for each of the coins you need. This will be a combination of your budget plus the desire to obtain a good value for your money. You might like to consider what I call the Optimal Collecting Grade. Generally, this means that if the next higher grade of a coin is multiples of the price, it may not be a good value. Refer to the analysis of prices in the next chapter.

As an illustration, I return to the price structure of the 1900 Lafayette dollar mentioned in the last chapter.

Prices of the 1900 Lafayette Dollar (PCGS)

EF-40: $475	**MS-62:** $1,350	**MS-65:** $12,000
AU-55: $750	**MS-63:** $2,300	**MS-66:** $20,000
MS-60: $1,000	**MS-64:** $4,000	**MS-67:** $82,500

For my money, for a Lafayette dollar or just about any other commemorative of the 1892 to 1954 classic era, I would probably pick MS-64 as a goal, and then cherrypick for quality, knowing full well that sooner or later I will find a "high end" MS-64 that will be every bit as nice as an MS-65 (as many do when they resubmit coins to the services). Or, I might pick MS-65 and cherrypick to find one that is as nice as an MS-66. I would see no point in making MS-67 a goal, even if I could afford it—in reality there is hardly any difference between a 67 and a 66.

For modern commemoratives 1982 to date, "as issued" is a good goal—coins in Mint holders. These are usually MS-67 to MS-70 or PF-67 to PF-70. The typical coin approaches perfection.

Let's say you pick MS-64 as a goal for 1892 to 1954 coins and MS-67 and PF-67 as a goal for modern commemoratives.

Now it is time to go coin hunting.

If your budget calls for an MS-64 1900 Lafayette dollar and if you are at a coin show, ask to see pieces in the MS-64 category. I'd stick with coins certified by one of the leading services. There is no particular point in asking for an MS-60 or an MS-66.

Now, that certified MS-64 Lafayette dollar (or 1892 Columbian half dollar, or 1946-S Booker T. Washington half dollar, etc.) in your hand is a candidate for your further consideration.

Step 2: Eye Appeal at First Glance

At this point, take a quick glance at the coin. Is it "pretty"? Is the toning (if present) attractive, or is it dark or blotchy? Is the coin stained? If it is brilliant, is it attractively lustrous, or is it dull and lifeless?

For all the commemoratives you will be considering for your collection, there are many opportunities in the marketplace. It is not at all necessary in any instance to compromise on eye appeal! I would buy brilliant coins, or pieces that are delicately and beautifully toned. I would not buy deeply toned coins, or ones with intense "rainbow" colors. This is a matter of preference. In my opinion, deep or vivid toning often hides a multitude of grading sins.

If it is not attractive, then reject it and go on to look at another. The price is not important. An ugly coin graded as MS-67 is still ugly, and if it were my decision I would not buy it for half of the current market price! And, there are a lot of ugly MS-65, 66, and 67 coins out there.

If the coin is attractive to your eye, then in some distant future year when the time comes to sell it, the piece will be attractive to other buyers, an important consideration. Among commemoratives of the early era, most brilliant or delicately toned coins have good eye appeal. Exceptions for which many or most have problems (necessitating special care on your part) include the 1900 Lafayette dollar, and the following half dollars: 1915-S Panama-Pacific, 1921 Alabama, 1921 Missouri, 1922 Grant With Star, 1923-S Monroe Doctrine (the worst), 1925 Fort Vancouver, 1926 Sesquicentennial of American Independence, and all of the Booker T. Washington and Carver/Washington issues. In contrast, high quality examples of nearly all issues of the 1930s are easy to find. Modern commemoratives from 1982 to date are nearly always found as high-grade gems. You can almost (but not quite) buy with your eyes closed—the quality is that nice! Now, with an attractive commemorative in your hand, it is a candidate for your further consideration.

Step 3: Evaluating Sharpness and Related Features

At this point you have a coin which you believe to be more or less in the numerical grade assigned, and one with excellent eye appeal. The next step is to take out a magnifying glass and evaluate its sharpness. When weakness is found, it is usually on the higher parts of the design, often at the center. While all should be checked, in particular the 1892 and 1893 Columbian half dollars, the 1900 Lafayette dollar, and the following half dollars can have problems: 1921 Alabama, 1921 Missouri, 1923-S Monroe Doctrine, 1926 Sesquicentennial, and all Booker T. Washington and Carver/Washington issues. Early commemorative gold coins are usually well struck, but on gold dollars of 1903 to 1905, check the highest areas of the portraits. For modern commemoratives 1982 to date, virtually all are very sharp.

Examine your prospective coin carefully, and reject it if there are any problems with the surface or planchet. No compromise of any kind need be made. If the commemorative you are considering buying has passed the preceding tests, it is a candidate for your further consideration.

 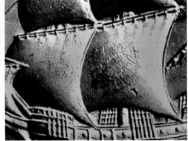

The eagle's neck and shoulder on a 1921 Alabama. The image at left shows feathers and other details. The image on the right is from a lightly struck example (as usual) and displays few details in this area.

The largest sail on the ship on the reverse of the 1936 Delaware Tercentenary is usually not struck up fully, and thus displays nicks and marks from the original planchet. On such a coin the fields can be almost perfect, if *after* *striking* the coin was handled with care.

Step 4: Establishing a Fair Market Price

Now, you have a very nice coin at hand! Next comes the evaluation of its price.

For starters, use one or several handy market guides for a ballpark estimate. This book is a handy guide, but should be verified with one of the weekly or monthly listings, such as in *Coin Values* (published by *Coin World*), the "Coin Market" feature of *Numismatic News*, or the *Coin Dealer Newsletter*. The *Rare Coin Market Report*, published by PCGS, gives prices for coins of that service. Nearly all early commemoratives in grades up to MS-65 have standard values and trade within certain ranges, as do later issues up to, say, MS-67 and Proof-67. For commemoratives in ultra high grades and for which just a few have been certified, prices can differ widely. Be careful.

If the commemorative is easy enough to find in a given grade, with sharp strike, with fine planchet quality, and with good eye appeal, then be sure the coin is offered for about the going market price. If the going price is $500, and you are at a convention or coin shop and are offered a nice one for, say, $525, buy it anyway—as your time and the opportunity have value. On the other hand, if it is priced at $650, you can wait. If it is offered for $425, better look at it more carefully!

The modern commemoratives are so plentiful that they are almost a commodity. Probably a good way to get all or most is to pick a dealer you like, with reasonable prices, and buy as many as you can from this single source—then fill in any open spaces later. For the early ones, take your time, and pick and choose wisely.

Enjoyment

The commemorative coins in your collection are meant to be enjoyed. Use a 4x or 8x hand magnifier and study their characteristics. You will see many interesting things. If motivated, study their history as well. The Internet is a fine place to learn more about the people, places, or events commemorated.

Ways to Collect Commemorative Coins

Possibilities

With hundreds of varieties minted from 1892 to the present day, relatively few numismatists opt to collect one of everything. This is possible to do, however, given an adequate budget, but obstacles are presented by such items as the two 1915 Panama-Pacific International Exposition $50 gold coins, octagonal and round, which run into the tens of thousands of dollars apiece. An alternative is to form a collection within a collection—perhaps designs or locations that you find interesting, or particular themes, or from a particular time in history.

As commemoratives are divided into the classic era from 1892 to 1954 and the modern series from 1982 to date, quite a few people pick one or the other to concentrate on. Within those two areas there are many other possibilities. The following are some ways that have been popular over the years.

Complete Collection of Silver Commemoratives, 1892–1954

In the classic era of commemorative issuance for the period indicated, there were 142 varieties of half dollars made, these including added features (such as 2x2 on the 1921 Alabama half dollar and 2★4 on the 1921 Missouri) or extended dates, such as the superfluous issuance of a 1921 half dollar to help commemorate the tercentenary of the landing of the Pilgrims, which was celebrated in 1920 with a half dollar. Dates and mintmarks proliferated among later issues, with dozens of varieties in the 1930s alone.

To form a complete set, start with the earliest issue, the 1892 Columbian, and proceed until the last, the 1954-S Carver/Washington. Along the way there will be quite a few scarcities and rarities, among which are the 1922 Grant With Star, 1928 Hawaiian, 1935 Hudson, 1935 Old Spanish Trail, and the low mintage coins in the Arkansas and Boone series. All are available, however, and some inexpensively, because the present market levels in most instances are a fraction of what they were in 1989 and 1990 when investors bid up commemoratives to unprecedented levels.

Two other silver coins also belong to this set, the 1893 Isabella quarter and the 1900 Lafayette dollar. With 142 half dollars plus these two coins, the total number of pieces is 144.

Arranged in date order, such a collection is a veritable museum of commemorative history, reflecting dozens of different designs, engravers, and issuing practices. By revisiting the present book as well as other commemorative texts, such a collection can be enjoyed for a long time. For maximum appreciation, read about each issue, and they will come to life. A 1935 Hudson Sesquicentennial half dollar can be *exciting* if you know its history! Otherwise, it is just a coin with a specific grade and value.

Type Set of Silver Commemoratives, 1892–1954

One of the most popular methods to collect classic commemoratives is to form a type set of every issue from 1892 to 1954. By this method, you will acquire one of each design. There are two Columbian half dollars, the 1892 and 1893 dates, but you will pick just one—your choice. For the 1922 Grant half dollar there is the With Star variety which is rare and expensive, and the readily available Without Star. Again, you will select your favorite. For the Oregon Trail series which began in 1926 and wound down in 1939, by which time 14 different varieties had been made, you will select one.

The most expensive issues in a type set are the 1928 Hawaiian, 1935 Hudson, and 1935 Old Spanish Trail, each with a distribution of just 10,000 pieces. To the 48 different basic design types you will add the 1893 Isabella quarter and 1900 Lafayette dollar, bringing the total to 50 coins.

As each piece is of a completely different design, such a type set gives a capsule view of the panorama of early commemoratives, without having to acquire dates, mintmarks, and other varieties.

The 1928 Hawaiian Sesquicentennial half dollar is the rarest single issue in an 1892–1954 type set of commemorative silver coins.

A Collection Within a Collection

Many commemorative enthusiasts have picked a particular series issued in multiple varieties, and have concentrated on getting one of each. A favorite is the 1926 to 1939 Oregon Trail Memorial, a particularly beautiful design. Although some issues are scarce, and the 1939 set of three pieces has the remarkably low distribution of just 3,000 pieces per coin, all are quite affordable. A specialist in Oregon Trail halves might not have any Boone or Texas half dollars, for example. Collections of Texas Independence Centennial half dollars made from 1934 to 1938 are very popular, particularly with citizens of the Lone Star State.

Glancing through this book or any other listing of classic era commemoratives might suggest other opportunities—such as issues of New England, or with motifs related to the Civil War, or connected with fairs and expositions. Relatively few people have pursued these avenues, but they do exist. A pleasing thing about this is that if you begin your interest by getting one of each piece produced in connection with an exposition, these will continue to be important if you decide expand your collection into a full type set of 50 silver coins or a full collection of 144 varieties.

Classic Era Gold Commemoratives

From the 1903 Louisiana Purchase commemorative gold dollars (Jefferson and McKinley varieties) to the 1926 Sesquicentennial quarter eagle, nine varieties of gold dollars were issued, two quarter eagles (1915-S Panama-Pacific International Exposition and 1926 Sesquicentennial), and two $50 issues for the 1915 event just mentioned.

While a complete collection can be gathered by those who can afford the $50 pieces, a more popular route is to acquire one of each of the gold dollars and quarter eagles, or just 11 pieces. The rarity and value of these depends on the grade. At the MS-65 level, the key issue is the 1905 Lewis and Clark gold dollar.

Modern Commemoratives

From the 1982 half dollar commemorating the 250th anniversary of George Washington's birth, down to the latest issues you might read about in *Coin World* and *Numismatic News*, a virtual panorama of coins is in the offing. These are of different denominations, most popularly dollars in silver (not a regular coinage metal due to its premium value) and $5 gold coins, but also including a wide selection of half dollars in earlier years, and one type comprising four varieties of $10 gold coins for the 1984 Olympic Games.

These pieces can be collected by one of each basic design, or by variety, the last sometimes including different mintmarks as well as different finishes (frosty or regular Mint State finish, as well as Proof finish). A full collection of every date and mintmark will run into many thousands of dollars.

A popular way to collect is to buy one of each type, since this is considerably more affordable. In time, more subspecialties will arise, but denominations offer an opportunity—such as one of each half dollar, inexpensive enough. One of each dollar will include some clad varieties as well as some in silver—later issues being silver, as well as having mintmark variations. Enough $5 gold coins can be collected to make these a little series in themselves. And then there are several varieties of $10 gold pieces.

Packaging of commemoratives has varied over the years, with different cases, boxes, and assemblies of coins within the packages, some including non-commemoratives such as Proof sets. Collecting commemoratives in such holders and boxes offers another opportunity, but this activity is tempered by the appeal to many collectors of having their coins put in certified holders. The original boxes and cases can still be kept, however, but they usually have a way of being separated from the coins when they are later sold.

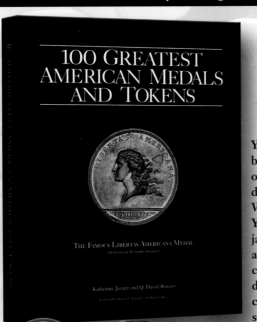

A GUIDE BOOK OF

40 A GUIDE BOOK OF

on a fanciful portrai
an authentic porte
George T. Mo
recent mod
World a
Min

CHAPTER FIVE
COMMEMORATIVES, 1892
HISTORY AND MARKET ANALYSIS

A Note on Presentation

Commemorative coins are presented in chronological ord
instances in which a series was started in one year and c
listing is given after the first year. Accordingly, the Oregon Trail Memorial half dollars,
which commenced in 1926 and ran through 1939, are listed under 1926. Otherwise, the
continuity would have been lost if the series had been broken up by individual years.

(1892–1893) COLUMBIAN EXPOSITION HALF DOLLARS

Distribution
1892: 950,000
1893: 1,550,405

Whitman Coin Guide (WCG™)—1892 Columbian Exposition 50¢

MS-60	MS-63	MS-64	MS-65	MS-66	MS-67	MS-68
$30	$90	$205	$750	$1,725	$9,270	

CERTIFIED POPULATIONS

MS-60	MS-61	MS-62	MS-63	MS-64	MS-65	MS-66	MS-67	MS-68
222	477	1,635	2,832	3,300	1,364	344	41	1
PF-60	PF-61	PF-62	PF-63	PF-64	PF-65	PF-66	PF-67	PF-68
2	3	3	19	26	13	6	1	2

1893 Columbian Exposition 50¢

MS-60	MS-63	MS-64	MS-65	MS-66	MS-67	MS-68
$45	$85	$220	$842	$1,815	$10,450	

CERTIFIED POPULATIONS

MS-60	MS-61	MS-62	MS-63	MS-64	MS-65	MS-66	MS-67	MS-68
268	631	1,982	2,799	2,930	967	243	27	2
PF-60	PF-61	PF-62	PF-63	PF-64	PF-65	PF-66	PF-67	PF-68
0	0	0	1	1	0	0	0	0

Points of Interest: Officially designated as a *souvenir* coin, not a commemorative. The
first such souvenir/commemorative in American coinage. The first legal tender coin to
depict a foreigner. The 1893 issue is the first illogical date on a commemorative, because
it honors the odd 401st anniversary of the 1492 "discovery" of America by Columbus.

Subject of Commemoration: 400th anniversary of Columbus's landing in the New
World and the 1893 World's Columbian Exposition. Authorized August 5, 1892, to the
extent of 5,000,000 coins.

Designs: *Obverse*—Portrait of Columbus designed by Charles E. Barber from a plaster
model by Olin Levi Warner, taken from Columbus's portrait on an 1892 medal issued
in Spain, derived from a statue in Madrid by Jeronimo Suñel, which in turn was based

by Charles Legrand. There is considerable debate as to whether ...ait of the explorer exists. *Reverse*—Ship and two globes, designed by ...rgan from a plaster model by Olin Levi Warner, taken in turn from a ...l made in Spain of the flagship *Santa Maria*. The globes represent the Old ...d the New and are reminiscent of Spanish pillar dollars.

...age and Melting Data: **1892:** *Maximum authorized*—5,000,000 (also includes ...ins dated 1893). *Number minted* (including an unknown number of assay coins)— 950,000. *Net distribution*—950,000. **1893:** *Number minted* (including 2,105 assay coins)—4,052,105. *Number melted*—2,501,700. *Net distribution*—1,550,405.

Original Cost and Issuer: Sale price $1. Issued by the Exposition.

Commemorative Coins of the Exposition

To raise funds and promote the World's Columbian Exposition in Chicago, 5,000,000 souvenir (as they were called) half dollars were authorized by Congress. These were to be sold to the exposition for face value, after which it was planned to offer them to the public for $1 each.

The first Columbian coin was struck at the Philadelphia Mint on November 19, 1892, too late for the opening ceremony of the fair on October 21. Wyckoff, Seamans & Benedict, makers of the Remington typewriter, offered $10,000 for the very first coin, soon donating it to the Columbian Museum (later known as the Field Museum of Natural History). More than 2,000 were struck on the first day, with the first, 400th, 1,492nd, and 1,892nd coins being given to Col. James W. Ellsworth of the exposition commission.

The first coins were distributed soon afterward. Nationwide interest was strong, and many were sold. In anticipation of great sales, additional pieces were struck dated 1893, this being the actual date that the exposition was open to the public.

Displays of Columbian half dollars helped promote sales and were set up in many places. In the rotunda of the Administration Building was a model, constructed of Columbian half dollars, of the Treasury Building in Washington. It measured 20 feet long, 11 feet wide, and four feet high. In the Liberal Arts building, an obelisk 20 feet high was made of the half dollars, billed as the only "official" souvenirs of the exposition.

Almost as an afterthought, the Board of Lady Managers sponsored a commemorative 25¢ piece, the Isabella (discussed separately below). Sales of the coins did not come up to expectations, and many were melted. Quantities of unsold half dollars were placed into circulation for face value, to the consternation of those who had paid $1 each for similar pieces.

Key to Collecting

Both dates of the Columbian half dollars are common in all grades through MS-65, and are often available beyond that. The design is attractive, and the typical high-grade coin is lustrous and frosty—a great start to a commemorative coin collection! Some with *original* light blue or iridescent toning can be particularly attractive. If you want just a single coin for type, the 1892 is the logical choice, since it is the first one.

Worn coins are very common today, from quantities placed into circulation by the Treasury Department and from pieces spent by purchasers after their novelty had passed.

Striking is usually good, although some can be weak at the center, such as on the higher areas of the portrait and, on the reverse, in the details of the ship's sails. As a rule of thumb, high-grade 1892 coins are better struck than are those struck in 1893. The typical coin has more than just a few bagmarks from handling and being rolled around in kegs.

For many years, experts said that no Proofs had been struck, ⬚ of some coins that had completely mirrored fields. Today, the certifica⬚ ognize Proofs. In this category quality and eye appeal can vary widely, s⬚ ship is advised while spending the large sums required to obtain such coins.⬚

(1893) COLUMBIAN EXPOSITION "ISABELLA" QUARTER DOLLAR

Distribution
24,214

Whitman Coin Guide (WCG™)—1893 Columbian Exposition, Isabella 25c

MS-60	MS-63	MS-64	MS-65	MS-66	MS-67	MS-68
$800	$970	$1,400	$3,950	$6,235	$12,925	$55,000

CERTIFIED POPULATIONS

MS-60	MS-61	MS-62	MS-63	MS-64	MS-65	MS-66	MS-67	MS-68
250	442	1,338	1,794	1,922	726	263	69	111
PF-60	PF-61	PF-62	PF-63	PF-64	PF-65	PF-66	PF-67	PF-68
2	0	6	5	12	8	2	0	0

Points of Interest: Depicts a foreign monarch, unique in American coinage. The first and still the only commemorative quarter dollar.

Subject of Commemoration: The industry of women.

Designs: *Obverse*—Portrait of Queen Isabella of Spain, sponsor of Columbus's voyages to the New World. *Reverse*—Kneeling woman with distaff. Charles E. Barber is credited with the designs, but is believed to have followed ideas supplied by contemporary artist Kenyon Cox (most familiar for his Brownies cartoon characters, which were a sensation in their time).

Mintage and Melting Data: Authorized on March 3, 1893. *Maximum authorized—40,000. Number minted (including 23 assay coins)—40,023. Number melted—15,809. Net distribution—24,214.*

Original Cost and Issuer: $1. Sold by the Board of Lady Managers, World's Columbian Exposition.

Story of the Isabella Quarter

In January 1893, well after the Columbian half dollar was a reality, Mrs. Potter Palmer, well-known Chicago socialite, patron of the arts, and *grande dame* of the exposition, suggested to the Appropriations Committee of the House of Representatives that $10,000 of the money earmarked for the Board of Lady Managers of the World's Columbian Exposition be given in the form of a special issue of souvenir (as they were called) quarter dollars. This was translated into a law approved March 3, 1893, which stated that the production of these quarters would not exceed 40,000 and that the pieces would be of standard weight and fineness.

The Board of Lady Managers had been formed at the insistence of Susan B. Anthony, who was determined that women should be adequately represented in the administration of the exposition. Interestingly, there was also a Board of Gentlemen Managers, but this did not get much publicity because it was taken for granted. The Board of Lady Managers took complete charge of the quarter-dollar project and stated

male motifs. Kenyon Cox, a well-known illustrator, was
...tches, apparently furnishing motifs that were eventually
... at the Mint.

Philadelphia Mint on June 13, 1893. The first, 400th,
...s were reserved with certificates, and the same were sent
...ers in Chicago. Unlike the Columbian half dollars, the
... been handled with a degree of care at the Mint, for con-
... minimal on specimens delivered to the distributor.

...re offered for sale for $1 each. Relatively few were sold,
probably because they represented less of a "good buy" at the dollar price demanded,
for someone could buy a Columbian half dollar—a coin of twice the face value—for the
same amount. While Columbian half dollars were sold through exhibits at several places
at the fair, the only notable exhibit of Isabella quarters was in the Woman's Building.

Possibly as many as 15,000 were sold at the exposition and by mail to collectors and
dealers in 1893. The biggest buyer is believed to have been the Scott Stamp & Coin
Company, which purchased several thousand.

After the fair ended and a quantity had been disposed of to Scott, the Board of Lady
Managers still had about 25,000 unsold pieces on hand, of which 10,000 were bought
for face value by Mrs. Potter Palmer and several of her friends and were parceled out
through coin dealers and others through the mid-1920s. Returned to the Mint for
remelting were 15,809 unwanted coins.

Key to Collecting

The 1893 Isabella quarter is an anomaly among early commemoratives, in that most in
the marketplace are Mint State, and in that category choice and gem coins abound.

The typical Isabella quarter is well struck and shows full details. The fields are richly
lustrous. Enough choice and gem examples exist, even at MS-65 and higher, that finding one with good eye appeal will present no problem. Connoisseurship is still worthwhile—there are some coins out there that should not be bought. Avoid darkly toned,
stained, or recolored coins. Lower-grade Mint State coins often have marks on Queen
Isabella's cheek and on the higher parts of the reverse design. The left obverse field
often has bagmarks.

Some with mirrored fields have been classified as Proofs, although years ago ANACS
and others did not recognize Proofs. A related situation occurred with the Columbian
half dollars (see above). No official records exist for the production of such Proofs.

As the only commemorative quarter dollar, the Isabella has been a "must have"
numismatic favorite for a long time.

(1900) LAFAYETTE MEMORIAL SILVER DOLLAR

Distribution
36,026

Whitman Coin Guide (WCG™)—1900 Lafayette Memorial, $1

MS-60	MS-63	MS-64	MS-65	MS-66	MS-67	MS-68
$1,100	$2,350	$4,205	$11,500	$19,635	$90,750	

CERTIFIED POPULATIONS

MS-60	MS-61	MS-62	MS-63	MS-64	MS-65	MS-66	MS-67	MS-68
276	412	897	1,098	1,340	390	146	13	0

Points of Interest: First commemorative silver dollar. First legal tender coin to depict an American president (Washington). First legal tender coin to depict the same person on both sides (Lafayette portrait on the obverse, Lafayette statue on the reverse). Only commemoratives struck from hand-made dies. The denomination is expressed as LAFAYETTE DOLLAR. These coins were *pre-struck* in 1899.

Subject of Commemoration: Erection of a statue of Lafayette in Paris in connection with the 1900 Paris Exposition (Exposition Universelle).

Designs: *Obverse*—Portraits of Lafayette and Washington. *Reverse*—Statue of Lafayette on horseback. The statue motif, by Paul Wayland Bartlett, was taken from an early model that differed in certain ways with that later erected in Paris. Designer Charles E. Barber claimed inspiration from the 1824 "Defender of American and French Liberty" medal made in Paris by François Augustin Caunois. Numismatic scholar Arlie Slabaugh has pointed out, however, that Barber swiped the jugate portraits of Washington and Lafayette from the obverse of the Yorktown Centennial medal of 1881, made from dies engraved by Peter L. Krider—but Barber's die work was much shallower and less pleasing than that done by Krider. The Bartlett statue was to have been unveiled in Paris on July 4, 1900, but progress was so slow that a large plaster model was shown instead. Finally, in 1908, the bronze statue was finished and was set up in the Place du Carrousel in the court of the Tuileries adjacent to the Louvre.

Die Varieties: This is the only commemorative issue for which die varieties can be collected, although interest in them is limited to specialists. There can be quite a bit of action, however, when an attributed rare die combination crosses the auction block. These characteristics are adapted from David M. Bullowa's 1938 study: Obverse varieties: (1) With a small point on the bust of Washington. The tip of Lafayette's bust is over the top of the L in DOLLAR. The AT in STATES is cut high. (2) With left foot of the final A in AMERICA recut, and with the A in STATES high. Second S in STATES repunched (this is diagnostic). (3) With the AT in STATES recut and the final S low. The letters F in OF and LAFAYETTE are broken from the lower tip of the crossbar and to the right base extension, and AMERICA is spaced A ME RI C A. The period after OF is close to the A of AMERICA. The tip of Lafayette's vest falls to the right of the top of the first L in DOL-LAR. (4) With C in AMERICA repunched at the inside top (this is diagnostic). With CA in AMERICA differently spaced from the obverses just described. Reverse varieties: (A) With 14 long leaves and long stem. Tip of lowest leaf over 1 of 1900. (B) With 14 shorter leaves and short stem. Tip of lowest leaf over space between 1 and 9 in 1900. (C) With 14 medium leaves and short, bent stem. Tip of lowest leaf over 9 in 1900. (D) With 15 long leaves and short, bent stem. Tip of lowest leaf over 9 in 1900. (E) Tip of lowest leaf over space left of 1 in 1900. Rarity estimates: 1-A: Scarce. 1-B: Most often seen variety. 1-C: Very rare.[5] 2-C: Rare. 3-D: Very rare. 4-E: Very rare.[6]

Mintage and Melting Data: Authorized March 3, 1899. *Maximum authorized*—50,000. *Number minted* (including 26 assay coins)—50,026. *Number melted*—14,000. *Net distribution*—36,026.

Original Cost and Issuer: $2. Lafayette Memorial Commission through the American Trust & Savings Bank of Chicago.

The Lafayette Memorial Commission

In 1899, the Lafayette Memorial Commission sought to raise funds to erect in Paris a statue of General Lafayette on horseback, to be sculpted by Paul Wayland Bartlett. This was to be a gift of the American people on occasion of the 1900 International Exposition in Paris, to honor the Frenchman who in 1777, when he was not quite 20 years old, risked life and fortune to bring French troops to America to aid the Revolutionary War patriots. In 1824 he returned to the United States as "the Nation's Guest" and was honored on coins counterstamped with his portrait.

The Commission petitioned Congress for an appropriation to coin 100,000 souvenir *half* dollars. When the legislation was approved on March 3, 1899, the authorization was for 50,000 silver one-dollar pieces, to be known as Lafayette dollars. It was intended that the coins be sold for $2 each to the public.

A nationwide campaign was mounted, with schoolchildren selling the coins for $2— with the hope that the $50,000 profit would pay for the statue. Work on the statue lagged, and it was not ready for the exposition. Instead, a large plaster model was shown there.

Striking the Coins

The Commission desired that the coins be struck as soon as possible in 1899, so they could be sold on a timely basis. They were to be dated 1900, however, in keeping with the year of the Paris International Exposition. The denomination was expressed as "Lafayette Dollar."

Striking of all 50,026 Lafayette dollars was accomplished in one day, on December 14, 1899, at the Philadelphia Mint, utilizing an old press which spewed out the pieces at the rate of 80 per minute, equal to 4,800 coins per hour. An account from the Philadelphia *Public Ledger* described the event:

> There was very little ceremony Friday, only a small group of Mint officials, members of the Memorial Association and representatives of the press being present. The coin press used was an old one in the Mint, and has been exhibited all over the country at international and state expositions. It was made years ago at Merrick's. It was operated by Miss Gleary.
>
> As the first coin, heated by tons of pressure put upon it, was taken from the dies, she handed it to Superintendent Boyer, of the Mint, and it was then inspected by the engraver [Charles E. Barber] and pronounced perfect. After showing it to Robert J. Thompson, secretary of the Lafayette Memorial Commission, it was given to Mr. Roberts, Director of the Mint, who had come on from Washington to be present on this occasion. After placing it in a suitable case it will be given to president McKinley, who will send it to the president of the French Republic.

Most remarkably, the die pairs used to produce the coins were made by hand, with the letters and numbers individually punched. Accordingly, die varieties can be identified—a situation unique in the commemorative coin field.

The first coin was sent to President William McKinley, who had it encased in an expensive ($1,000) presentation casket, and forwarded it by sea on the S.S. *Champagne* to France. Robert J. Thompson, secretary of the Lafayette Memorial Commission, delivered the coin to President Loubet in a special ceremony intended to be held on Washington's birthday, February 22, but which actually took place in the Elysée Palace on March 3, 1900.

Perhaps because Columbian half dollars originally sold at $1 v lation for face value, there was little public interest in paying $2 for lar. It is not known how many were actually sold, but 14,000 unwa Treasury Building in Washington, where, unknown to collectors, in cloth bags of 1,000 each in a vault used to store large bundles $5,000 and $10,000 notes). Others reached the wholesale market a little as $1.10 each, if not even less.[7] In 1945 the Treasury melted the remaining 14,000 coins, unaware that by that time they had significant numismatic value!

Key to Collecting

Lafayette silver dollars of 1900 are at once interesting, impressive, and well worth owning. Most examples in the marketplace show evidence of circulation, with AU being typical, due to original owners handling or spending the coins. In the Mint State categories, the vast majority are MS-60 to 63. Many of these are dull or unattractive, the result of multiple dippings or cleanings over time. Many, if not most, have marks and dings, usually most prominent on the cheek of Washington. Properly graded MS-64 coins are very scarce, and MS-65 or higher gems are very rare, especially if with good eye appeal.

(1903) LOUISIANA PURCHASE EXPOSITION GOLD DOLLARS

Distribution

Jefferson: 17,500 Uncirculated (estimated)
and 100 Proof
McKinley: 17,500 Uncirculated (estimated)
and 100 Proof

Whitman Coin Guide (WCG™)—1903 La Purchase Exposition Gold $1-Jefferson

MS-60	MS-63	MS-64	MS-65	MS-66	MS-67	MS-68
$850	$1,200	$2,255	$3,245	$4,310	$10,038	

CERTIFIED POPULATIONS

MS-60	MS-61	MS-62	MS-63	MS-64	MS-65	MS-66	MS-67	MS-68
45	95	370	803	1,362	1,029	772	124	0
PF-60	PF-61	PF-62	PF-63	PF-64	PF-65	PF-66	PF-67	PF-68
3	2	5	12	10	10	11	4	0

1903 Louisiana Purchase Exposition Gold $1-McKinley

MS-60	MS-63	MS-64	MS-65	MS-66	MS-67	MS-68
$850	$1,100	$2,250	$3,300	$4,345	$8,525	

CERTIFIED POPULATIONS

MS-60	MS-61	MS-62	MS-63	MS-64	MS-65	MS-66	MS-67	MS-68
74	147	515	777	1,153	807	702	139	2
PF-60	PF-61	PF-62	PF-63	PF-64	PF-65	PF-66	PF-67	PF-68
3	1	2	8	20	16	7	2	0

Points of Interest: Some of the coins were *pre-struck* in 1902. These are the first legal tender coins to portray Jefferson and McKinley. Of the immense quantity of 125,000 coins minted of each variety, only about 17,500 were sold of each.

Subject of Commemoration: 100th anniversary of the Louisiana Purchase.

Designs: Jefferson: *Obverse*—Portrait of Thomas Jefferson. Designed by Chief Engraver Charles E. Barber (obverse portrait copied from an early 19th-century medal by John in turn used a Houdon bust as a model) assisted by George T. Morgan. Inscription and branch. Designed by Barber. **McKinley:** *Obverse*—McKinley's ιt borrowed from Barber's own presidential medal, an image which Augustus Saint- ιdens, no fan of either Barber or the Mint engraving staff, characterized as "deadly." Reverse—As preceding.

Mintage and Melting Data: Authorized June 28, 1902. *Maximum authorized*—250,000 (total for Jefferson and McKinley varieties). *Number minted* (including 258 assay coins comprising both varieties)—250,258 (125,000 of each variety). *Number melted*—215,250 (total for both varieties; no account was kept of the portraits; 250 assay coins were melted). *Net distribution*—35,000; estimated to be divided into about equal quantities of each variety.

Original Cost and Issuer: $3. Louisiana Purchase Exposition Company, St. Louis, Missouri (sales through Farran Zerbe). Some were sold as mounted in spoons, brooches, and stick pins; 100 certified Proofs of each design were made, mounted in an opening in a rectangular piece of imprinted cardboard.

The Louisiana Purchase Exposition

The Louisiana Purchase Exposition, popularly known as the St. Louis World's Fair, was intended to commemorate the 100th anniversary of the purchase of a vast tract of interior land from France in 1803, which took place during the administration of President Thomas Jefferson. This purchase paved the way for the Lewis and Clark expedition, which left St. Louis in 1804 to explore the upper reaches of the Missouri River, and beyond to the Columbia River and the Pacific Ocean, and included districts later known as the states of Louisiana, Arkansas, Iowa, Kansas, Oklahoma, Missouri, Nebraska, North Dakota, South Dakota, and Montana, and parts of Colorado, Wyoming, and Minnesota.

Delays postponed the opening of the event until April 30, 1904. The fair continued until closing day on December 1 of the same year, by which time about 20 million people had attended, many of whom enjoyed humming or singing the popular song, "Meet Me in St. Louis." The exposition was situated on a 1,272-acre tract in Forest Park, one of the largest expanses of land ever allotted to an event of this type in a U.S. city. Fifteen major buildings, including four art palaces (one of which exists today), formed the focus of the fairgrounds with numerous smaller buildings, exhibit areas, fountains, gardens, and other attractions providing interest.

Among the exhibits were many automobiles, dirigibles, and other vehicles, demonstrations of wireless telegraphy, and displays of the uses of electricity. Works of hundreds of different artists, mainly painters, were on display. Among the sculptors represented at the exposition were John Flanagan, Adolph A. Weinman, Evelyn Beatrice Longman, James Earle Fraser, Hermon A. MacNeil, and Daniel Chester French, all of whom would subsequently have connections with coin designs, commemorative or otherwise.

Commemorative Gold Dollars

On June 28, 1902, legislation was approved that provided for the coinage "at the mints of the United States 250,000 gold dollars of legal weight and fineness, to be known as the Louisiana Exposition gold dollar, struck in commemoration of said exposition." These were the brainchild of numismatist and entrepreneur Farran Zerbe, from Tyrone, Pennsylvania, who was to have exclusive charge of their distribution. He suggested that sales would be expanded if two styles of gold dollars were created. The subjects chosen were Thomas Jefferson, who engineered the Louisiana Purchase in 1803, and President William McKinley, who had been assassinated in September 1901, and whose memory was still fresh in the minds of citizens.

Chief Engraver Charles E. Barber set about designing the coins, each and with a common reverse. In December 1902, 75,080 gold dollars were st January 1903 an additional 175,178 were made, completing the authorization. In 250,258 pieces were struck, including 258 for assay purposes. Later 250 of the a coins were melted. One hundred specimens of each of the two designs were struck with Proof finish and were distributed to favored insiders as well as exposition and government officials, though not to the collecting fraternity. Proofs were affixed to imprinted cards, with the coins held under a waxed paper window secured with cords and a red wax seal. Each card included this notation, this for a Jefferson dollar:

> This is to certify that the accompanying Louisiana Purchase Exposition gold dollar struck at the Mint of the United States, Philadelphia, in accordance with an Act of Congress approved June 28, 1902, is one of the first one hundred impressions from the Jefferson dies.

Promotion

Zerbe promoted the gold dollars to the numismatic fraternity, offering them at $3 each, a nominal price to a later generation of readers but at the time a figure considered to be excessive, for it represented three times face value. Zerbe reasoned that regular-issue gold dollars, which had not been minted since 1889 and which were selling at a premium, even for worn pieces, would set the pace for the sale of the freshly minted Uncirculated coins. The commemorative gold dollars did not catch on, however, and interest lagged—despite the siren song of such lofty prose as the following (by Zerbe):

> The Louisiana Purchase gold dollar is the fourth child in the numismatic family of United States commemorative issues; it is the diminutive member of that family but the most artistic and powerful, as it is the finest example of designing, engraving, and stamping and is of gold. The older members of the family are less fine and all in the baser metal, silver.

Articles submitted by Zerbe to *The Numismatist* paint an enthusiastic view of the fair and the various numismatic souvenirs sold in connection with it, promoting them as a wonderful investment. Seeking to attract even more attention, Zerbe issued news releases outlining his proposal that the government produce a *billion-dollar* gold piece to exhibit at the fair. This mammoth "coin" was to be 40 feet in diameter, 30 inches thick, and would weigh 4,480,000 pounds.

All of this hoopla did not sit well with many collectors and dealers. In particular, Thomas L. Elder, a dealer whose business was just beginning to become important on the national scene, later wrote a virulent condemnation, stating that Zerbe, contrary to all standards of numismatic professionalism, was simply a huckster who engaged in misleading advertising and promotions.

Writing in *The Numismatist*, January 1903, George C. Arnold, a well-known dealer, suggested that the $3 market price could not be sustained, and would fall in the resale market to "$1.85 to $2 each, or even lower figures."

Despite Zerbe's heroic efforts, the promotion was an unmitigated disaster. Of the 250,000 minted for distribution, back to the Mint went the staggering quantity of 215,000, leaving 35,000 as the number actually distributed.

Within a year or so after the fair closed, the gold dollars were readily available for $2 or even less, bringing much discredit upon Farran Zerbe—for it was taken for granted that he intended to maintain or even increase the market price later, protecting

...ased coins for $3 each. Much ill will was engendered. So wide-
...tion for the Louisiana Purchase Exposition gold dollars, that sales
...rized by the government, the Lewis and Clark gold dollars, were
...negative way.

...ng

...umismatics there are many Cinderellas—coins that are despised or overlooked in
one market, but which become highly appreciated and desired later. So it is with the Jefferson and McKinley gold dollars of 1903. Today, the demand for them is strong, not
only from collectors, but also with investors, for most coins remain in choice or gem
Mint State. Proofs come on the market only at widely separated intervals, and usually
only in major auctions or other important sale events.

When buying these coins look for friction or contact marks on the cheek (which are
usually more evident on the McKinley variety than on the Jefferson). Most specimens
are very lustrous and frosty, but occasionally a prooflike coin will be encountered. Avoid
coins with copper stains (from improper mixing of the alloy). The eye appeal is usually
quite good. Finding pieces that are just right will be no problem.

(1904–1905) LEWIS AND CLARK EXPOSITION GOLD DOLLARS

Distribution
1904: 10,025
1905: 10,041

Whitman Coin Guide (WCG™)—1904 Lewis & Clark Exposition Gold $1

MS-60	MS-63	MS-64	MS-65	MS-66	MS-67	MS-68
$1,500	$3,075	$6,015	$12,034	$17,600	$35,145	

CERTIFIED POPULATIONS

MS-60	MS-61	MS-62	MS-63	MS-64	MS-65	MS-66	MS-67	MS-68
41	109	370	531	936	390	175	30	1

PF-60	PF-61	PF-62	PF-63	PF-64	PF-65	PF-66	PF-67	PF-68
0	0	0	2	2	0	0	0	0

1905 Lewis & Clark Exposition Gold $1

MS-60	MS-63	MS-64	MS-65	MS-66	MS-67	MS-68
$2,000	$3,400	$7,090	$19,930	$35,440	$62,425	

CERTIFIED POPULATIONS

MS-60	MS-61	MS-62	MS-63	MS-64	MS-65	MS-66	MS-67	MS-68
57	177	446	626	985	301	89	4	0

Points of Interest: This is the first commemorative gold coin issue to be struck in
more than one year; it is a two-headed coin with a portrait on each side.

Subject of Commemoration: The Lewis and Clark expedition of 1804 to 1806.

Designs: 1904 and 1905: *Obverse*—Portrait of Meriwether Lewis. *Reverse*—Portrait of
William Clark. Designed by Charles E. Barber using portraits by Charles Willson Peale.

Mintage and Melting Data: 1904: Authorized on April 13, 1904. *Maximum authorized*—250,000 (total for 1904- and 1905-dated coins). *Number minted* (including 28 assay
coins)—25,028. *Number melted*—15,003. *Net distribution*—10,025. **1905:** *Number minted*
(including 41 assay coins)—35,041. *Number melted*—25,000. *Net distribution*—10,041.

Original Cost and Issuer: $2 (some at $2.50), many probably discounted further. Lewis and Clark Centennial and American Pacific Exposition and Oriental Fair Company, Portland, Oregon (sales through Farran Zerbe and others).

The Exposition

Held in 1905 in Portland, Oregon, the Lewis and Clark Exposition attracted an estimated 2,500,000 visitors from opening day on June 1, 1905, until closing on October 14. The 406-acre site accommodated seven large buildings, many smaller ones, and the usual concessions and midway attractions. Exposition exhibits emphasized natural resources including fishing, mining, and forestry, but arts and manufacture were not neglected. The Forestry Building, measuring more than 200 feet in length and constructed of native Oregon fir (including some logs of six or more feet in diameter) was a focal point of interest. After the exposition closed, the structure was maintained as a museum of the lumber industry.

Unlike the St. Louis fair of the preceding year, the Lewis and Clark Exposition was not designated by Congress as an international event, and no official government invitations were extended to foreign nations to exhibit. Notwithstanding this, 16 countries accepted offers from the exposition itself. In the annals of fairs in the United States, the Lewis and Clark Exposition is not one of the more memorable. No doubt the Louisiana Purchase Exposition of the preceding year, having essentially the same theme, stole much of its thunder. Numismatically, however, it is very important.

Two More Gold Dollars

On April 13, 1904, a congressional act provided the following:

> The secretary of the Treasury shall, upon the request of the Lewis and Clark Centennial and American Pacific Exposition and Oriental Fair Company, cause to be coined at the mints of the United States not to exceed 250,000 gold dollars, of legal weight and fineness, to be known as the Lewis and Clark Exposition gold dollar, struck in commemoration of said exposition.

Farran Zerbe, the entrepreneur who facilitated the issuance of the 1903 Louisiana Purchase Exposition gold dollars, was the moving force behind this legislation as well, although his name did not officially appear in connection with it. The authorized quantity of a quarter million pieces was identical to that approved earlier for the Louisiana Purchase Exposition, and reflected Zerbe's aspirations for widespread sales. By this time, Zerbe had not acknowledged the market failure of the 1903 coins and was still promoting them heavily as investments.

Chief Engraver Charles E. Barber designed the gold dollars, using portraits by Charles Willson Peale. Meriwether Lewis was depicted on the obverse, which bore the date 1904 or 1905, and William Clark was shown on the other side. Concerned that sales would not reach even close to the authorization of 250,000 coins, the Philadelphia Mint was careful. David M. Bullowa in *The Commemorative Coinage of the United States*, 1938, told the story of production:

> Although the Mint records state that 60,069 pieces were struck, 25,028 dated 1904 and 35,041 dated 1905, these figures do not tell the true story. Of the 25,028 struck in September 1904 at the Philadelphia Mint, 10,025 were sold, and 15,003 were melted down at the San Francisco

Mint. The fair management ordered from the Philadelphia Mint 10,000 pieces dated 1905. This mint, prior to its summer closing, struck an additional 25,000 during March and June, to meet possible orders; and as none of these were needed subsequently, the entire 25,000 were melted. In other words, about 10,000 of each date were distributed, and 40,000 of the 60,000 pieces struck were returned to the melting pot.

As the preceding commentary indicates, the Lewis and Clark coins were not popular. In the numismatic community commemorative gold dollars were an anathema, and collectors who had recently paid $3 each for 1903-dated Louisiana Purchase Exposition gold dollars and who now found they were worth $2 each or less (and virtually unsalable even at that low price), were not interested in buying more coins of the same denomination, even though the issue was of a different design.

Very little information concerning the 1904 and 1905 Lewis and Clark gold dollars appeared in the numismatic press, and it can be supposed that the editor of *The Numismatist*, Dr. George F. Heath, who had condemned the folly of the earlier 1903-dated Louisiana Purchase Exposition gold dollars, simply elected not to print any publicity notices that Zerbe may have sent in. The July 1905 issue of the *American Journal of Numismatics* noted that the first 25,000 of the new souvenir dollars had been received by the First National Bank of Portland, Oregon from the Philadelphia Mint. "They will be sold for $2 each, and to the purchaser of five an additional one will be presented," the account related.

The firm of D.M. Averill & Company, 331 Morrison Street, Portland, was involved in the distribution, possibly in connection with Zerbe, although details are not known. In early 1905, Averill offered 1904-dated dollars by mail at $2.50 each and 1905 pieces at $2 each—falsely noting, concerning the 1904 coins, "These are nearly exhausted." Sales were made by Zerbe at the fair, and through local banks. Likely, the vast majority of the 10,000 coins sold of each date went to the general public, not to numismatists. Most were mishandled, and this had profound implications on the survival rate of high-quality pieces.

Key to Collecting

Most extant examples of 1904 and 1905 Lewis and Clark Exposition gold dollars show evidence of handling. Typical grades range from AU-50 to AU-58 with an occasional coin grading in the MS-60 to MS-63 range. MS-64 coins are difficult to find, and MS-65 pieces are rare. It is usual for Mint State coins to have areas of prooflike finish.

The 1905-dated issue is at least 20 percent scarcer than the 1904. It may have been the case that quantities of 1905 coins in the possession of Zerbe were never officially returned for melting but were simply cashed in at face value or melted in 1933. In any event, among all commemorative gold coins of this denomination, the Lewis and Clark issues of 1904 and 1905 are singularly distinctive for their rarity in higher grades. They are far rarer than any other commemorative gold dollar varieties.

When contemplating a purchase, check the portraits on both sides for evidence of friction, which is usually there. Use medium magnification and a strong light. Some exhibit die problems, seen as a rough raised area of irregularity at the dentils. While some specimens are deeply lustrous and frosty, most are partially prooflike. Pristine coins are very rare.

(1915) PANAMA-PACIFIC INTERNATIONAL EXPOSITION COMMEMORATIVES

Distribution
1915 silver half dollar: 27,134
1915 gold $1: 15,000
1915 gold $2.50: 6,749
1915 round gold $50: 483
1915 octagonal gold $50: 645

Whitman Coin Guide (WCG™)—1915 Panama-Pacific Int'l Exposition 50¢

MS-60	MS-63	MS-64	MS-65	MS-66	MS-67	MS-68
$600	$900	$1,700	$2,780	$4,210	$7,015	$60,500

CERTIFIED POPULATIONS

MS-60	MS-61	MS-62	MS-63	MS-64	MS-65	MS-66	MS-67	MS-68
103	148	598	1,055	1,598	861	413	129	2

1915 Panama-Pacific International Exposition Gold $1

MS-60	MS-63	MS-64	MS-65	MS-66	MS-67	MS-68
$1,000	$1,100	$1,550	$2,700	$4,500	$12,375	

CERTIFIED POPULATIONS

MS-60	MS-61	MS-62	MS-63	MS-64	MS-65	MS-66	MS-67	MS-68
78	171	703	1,374	2,304	1,617	1,030	85	0

na-Pacific International Exposition Gold $2.50

	MS-63	MS-64	MS-65	MS-66	MS-67	MS-68
00	$4,648	$6,650	$8,270	$10,430	$20,779	

RTIFIED POPULATIONS

MS-60	MS-61	MS-62	MS-63	MS-64	MS-65	MS-66	MS-67	MS-68
17	43	231	450	991	933	779	102	0

1915 Panama-Pacific International Exposition Gold $50 Round

MS-60	MS-63	MS-64	MS-65	MS-66	MS-67	MS-68
$60,000	$86,500	$105,050	$153,040	$192,500	$214,500	

CERTIFIED POPULATIONS

MS-60	MS-61	MS-62	MS-63	MS-64	MS-65	MS-66	MS-67	MS-68
12	46	113	211	221	46	17	2	0

1915 Panama-Pacific International Exposition Gold $50 Octagonal

MS-60	MS-63	MS-64	MS-65	MS-66	MS-67	MS-68
$55,000	$81,950	$99,275	$144,800	$233,750	$302,500	

CERTIFIED POPULATIONS

MS-60	MS-61	MS-62	MS-63	MS-64	MS-65	MS-66	MS-67	MS-68
17	62	148	247	256	55	5	3	0

Points of Interest: The octagonal $50 is the only U.S. commemorative coin ever to be struck in other than round shape. With just 483 pieces, the round $50 has the lowest distribution quantity of any U.S. commemorative coin.

Subject of Commemoration: The Panama-Pacific International Exposition held in San Francisco in 1915, to celebrate the opening of the Panama Canal.

Designs: Silver half dollar: *Obverse*—Columbia standing with her arms outstretched, cherub near her, rising sun in distance. Designed by Chief Engraver Charles E. Barber. *Reverse*—Eagle perched on a shield with branches to each side. Designed by George T. Morgan. **Gold dollar:** *Obverse*—Head of Panama Canal laborer. *Reverse*—Two dolphins encircle ONE DOLLAR. Designed by Charles Keck. **$2.50 gold:** *Obverse*—Columbia with a caduceus in her left hand, seated on a hippocampus, signifying the use of the Panama Canal. Designed by Charles E. Barber. *Reverse*—Perched eagle facing left. Designed by George T. Morgan (adapted from one of his pattern half dollar reverses of 1877). **$50 gold, round:** *Obverse*—Helmeted head of Minerva. *Reverse*—Owl, symbol of wisdom, on a pine branch. Designed by Robert I. Aitken. **$50 gold, octagonal:** *Obverse* and *Reverse*—Same as the $50 round, except there are eight dolphins in the angles on both sides.

Mintage and Melting Data: Silver half dollar: Authorized by the Act of January 16, 1915. *Maximum authorized*—200,000. *Number minted* (including 30 assay coins)—60,030. *Number melted*—32,896, including 30 assay coins (29,876 were melted on September 7, 1916 and the balance on October 30, 1916). *Distribution*—27,134. **Gold dollar:** Authorized by the Act of January 16, 1915. *Maximum authorized*—25,000. *Number minted* (including 34 assay coins)—25,034. *Number melted*—10,034, including 34 assay coins (melted at the San Francisco Mint on October 30, 1916). *Net distribution*—15,000. **$2.50 gold:** Authorized by the Act of January 16, 1915. *Maximum authorized*—10,000. *Number minted* (including 17 assay coins)—10,017. *Number melted*—3,268, including 17 assay coins (melted at the San Francisco Mint on October 30, 1916). *Distribution*—6,749. **$50 gold, round:** Authorized by the Act of January 16, 1915. *Maximum authorized*—1,500. *Number minted* (including 10 assay coins)—1,510. *Number* *melted*—1,027. *Distribution*—483. **$50 gold, octagonal:** Authorized by the Act of January 16, 1915. *Maximum authorized*—1,500. *Number minted* (including 9 assay coins)—1,509. *Number melted*—864. *Distribution*—645.

Original Cost and Issuer: Half dollar: $1. **$1 gold:** $2 (a few at $2.25). **$2.50:** $4. **$50 gold, round and octagonal:** each $100. Combination offers included a set of four coins (buyer's choice of one $50) in a leather case for $100, and a set of five coins in a copper frame for $200, this issued after the exposition closed. Coin and Medal Department (Farran Zerbe), Panama-Pacific International Exposition, San Francisco, California.

The Panama-Pacific International Exposition

The 1915 Panama-Pacific International Exposition, a name chosen to reflect the Panama Canal and Pacific Ocean commerce, was planned to be the ultimate world's fair. The rebuilding of San Francisco since the April 1906 earthquake and fire and the 1914 opening of the Panama Canal furnished the occasions for the celebration. Foreign countries, domestic manufacturers, artists, concessionaires, and others were invited to become part of what eventually constituted a miniature city, whose sculptures and impressive architecture were intended to remind one of Rome or some other distant and romantic place, but which at night was more apt to resemble Coney Island. The object was to attract attention, draw visitors, make money, and enhance the glory of the new and dynamic San Francisco.

The buildings of the exposition were arranged in three areas. Festival Hall and several large exhibition "palaces" furnished the center of activity, flanked to the west by buildings containing the exhibits of 44 states, several U.S. territories, and 36 foreign nations, a racetrack, and a livestock building. To the east were the amusement midway and seemingly innumerable concessions.

Situated on 635 acres in Golden Gate Park in San Francisco, the exposition cost about $50 million, opening on February 20, 1915, and closing on December 4. In the intervening 10 months, it drew an estimated 19 million visitors. The event was a smashing success by nearly all standards.

Five Commemorative Coins

Coin dealer and entrepreneur Farran Zerbe conceived an unprecedented program of five different commemorative coins and was given the right to distribute them. It was not until the relatively late date of January 16, 1915, that a congressional act providing for commemorative coins was signed into law. This provided that no more than 3,000 gold coins of the denomination of $50, 10,000 gold coins of $2.50 value, and 25,000 gold dollars were to be coined and that no more than 200,000 silver half dollars were to be made. The $50 coins were to capture the tradition of the famous $50 "slugs" made in San Francisco in the early 1850s during the Gold Rush. Production of the gold coins was to begin as soon as possible, but not later than the day of the opening of the exposition. The Treasury was to sell the pieces at face value, and the fair (via Zerbe) could charge the public whatever it pleased.

The silver half dollar pieces had a slightly different arrangement of production and timing under the legislation, which stated: "Said fifty-cent coins herein authorized shall be issued only upon the request of the Panama-Pacific International Exposition Company and shall be delivered to it by the secretary of the Treasury, at par, during the period when said Panama-Pacific International Exposition shall be officially opened."

It was further authorized that, at the discretion of the secretary of the Treasury, the half dollars should be "coined or finished and issued from the machinery to be installed as a part of the exhibit at the United States Mint at said Exposition, and for the purpose of maintaining the exhibit as an educative working exhibit at all times the coins so minted may be remelted and reminted."

The provision for melting coins was intended to keep the exhibit in full operation. If the coining press was to be operated continuously during the fair, far more than 200,000 half dollars might have to be produced, but since no more than that were authorized, this production would be accomplished by destroying earlier minted pieces to preserve the intended net amount. It developed that medals were struck on the exposition grounds, but coins were not.

Due to the lateness of the act's passage, it was impossible to have any of the coins produced until about three months after the opening of the exposition. In order to have them even at that time, hubs for the gold dollar were made on contract in New York City by the privately owned Medallic Art Company, at the exposition's expense. That firm had a Janvier portrait lathe in operation, offering modern technology in the reduction of models to hubs in the process of making dies. Later the Medallic Art Company was to produce many models and some dies for other commemorative issues.

Designs of the Coins

The Treasury Department assumed that Chief Engraver Charles E. Barber, who had designed the Louisiana Purchase Exposition and Lewis and Clark Exposition gold dollars, would create motifs for the different Panama-Pacific coins. The Commission of Fine Arts, however, in its first cooperation with the Treasury Department in the matter of coin designs, felt differently and submitted the names of Robert I. Aitken, Miss Evelyn Beatrice Longman, Paul H. Manship, and Charles Keck, all of New York City, as its first choices. The Commission suggested, as alternates, in the event that satisfactory arrangements could not be made for those first named, John Flanagan, Augustus Lukeman, Sherry Fry, and Miss Janet Scudder, all of New York City, plus Leonard Grunelle of Chicago and Bela Lyon Pratt of Boston.

The 1915 Panama-Pacific half dollar, the only silver coin of the exposition, incorporated an obverse design by Barber and a reverse motif by Barber and George T. Morgan, his principal assistant (who was to succeed Barber in the chief engravership following the former's death in 1917). On the right of the obverse was an allegorical representation of Columbia scattering flowers, and behind her, a naked child, holding a large cornucopia to represent the abundant resources of the American West. In the background was seen the Golden Gate and the setting sun with resplendent rays. The radiant sun motif was a popular one in American coinage and had been used on regular-issue $20 pieces since 1907. It would be used beginning in 1916 on regular issue Liberty Walking half dollars. The Barber-Morgan reverse was dominated by an eagle perched on a shield, with oak and olive branches to the left and right, representing stability and peace.

Charles Keck was eventually selected to design the gold dollar and created several sketches as proposals. These were revised to just four: one featuring explorer Balboa, another with Poseidon holding a trident, and two others consisting of different versions of a Panama Canal worker wearing a cap. Secretary of the Treasury William G. McAdoo preferred the worker—and shown on the finished coin was the head and neck of a typical laborer at the Panama Canal, wearing a cloth cap, facing to the viewer's left, with UNITED STATES OF AMERICA in two lines in front of the worker's face. The public then and numismatists today thought the depiction was of a baseball player! The reverse illustrated two dolphins, symbolizing the meeting of two oceans, the Atlantic and Pacific.

Evelyn Beatrice Longman, a New York City sculptress, was selected to prepare the design of the $2.50 gold coin following the recommendation of the Commission of Fine Arts. After preparing some sketches she became ill and was unable to complete the work. Secretary of the Treasury McAdoo reviewed Longman's ideas and rejected them. The project was given to Chief Engraver Charles E. Barber and his assistant, George T. Morgan, at the Philadelphia Mint, which suited William Malburn, assistant secretary of the Treasury, who felt that *all* the Panama-Pacific coin designs should be prepared by in-house artists at the Mint. Barber designed an obverse showing an allegorical figure of the goddess Columbia holding in her left hand a caduceus (representing the medical triumph over yellow fever in Panama during the canal construction), and seated astride a hippocampus, a Greek mythological seahorse with the head and forefront of a horse and the tail of a dragon. For the reverse, Morgan created an eagle standing on a plaque inscribed E PLURIBUS UNUM, a motif borrowed from that used in 1877 on pattern half dollars and in 1879 for his "Schoolgirl" pattern silver dollar. The quarter eagle version looked much less elegant.

Robert I. Aitken, a New York artist, designed the octagonal and round 1915 Panama-Pacific International Exposition $50 pieces, both of which have the same design, except that unlike the round issue, the octagonal coins display dolphins in the angles on the obverse and reverse between the inscription and the points of the border.

The obverse depicts Minerva, according to the official description "The Goddess of Wisdom, Skill, Contemplation, Spinning, Weaving and of Agriculture and Horticulture"—obviously, an all-around mythological person (who is also seen on the arms of the State of California). The reverse, according to the original publicity, depicts an "owl, sacred to Minerva, the accepted symbol of wisdom, perched upon a branch of western pine." The dolphins in the angles of the octagonal piece were placed there, "suggesting as they encircle the central field, the uninterrupted water route made possible by the Panama Canal." Both varieties of coins bore the date as MCMXV—perhaps following the Roman numeral dating precedent set by Saint-Gaudens's beautiful $20 MCMVII of 1907.

Selling the Coins

Distribution of the various commemorative coins was placed in the hands of Farran Zerbe, who set up his Money of the World exhibit as part of the Coin and Medal Department under his management. The sales depot consisted of a large booth within the Palace of Fine Arts (which today is the only building from the exposition still standing); a white latticework structure appearing somewhat similar to a fancy grape arbor, with open top and sides, enclosing a spacious area in which numismatic specimens in frames and cases were displayed.

Advance orders for the Panama-Pacific commemorative coins amounted to $40,000. Half dollars were offered at $1 each or six for $5. Gold dollars were pegged at $2 (or $2.25 each; offering prices varied) or six for $10, whereas $2.50 pieces were offered at $4 each or six for $20, and $50 pieces in both octagonal and round shapes cost $100 each.

Most of these coins were sold singly in paper envelopes or as part of a group in velvet-lined black leatherette cases. Later in the sales program Zerbe commissioned Shreve & Co., a local jewelry firm, to create glass-fronted copper frames suitable for displaying sets of the five different coins. Double sets containing two of each could be ordered in the same frames. Sales were continued after the exhibition closed, which seemed to be at variance with the original enabling legislation, but no one complained.

Five pieces in a copper frame under glass cost $200, while a double set, mounted to show the obverse and reverse of each, was listed for $400. The number of sets sold was about 300, mostly to banks, of which about 60 were accompanied by "certification papers" issued by Zerbe. I estimate that perhaps fewer than a half dozen double sets were sold. A set containing a half dollar, gold dollar, $2.50, and buyer's choice of either a round or octagonal $50 was available in a leather case for $100. Smaller sets in leather presentation cases, including a half dollar, gold dollar, and quarter eagle, were available for $7.50. As a clearance Zerbe offered, in late 1915, quantities of six each of half dollars and quarter eagles, $25 the lot, or six half dollars, gold dollars, and quarter eagles for $37.

Zerbe's reputation in the numismatic community was so poor that when the ANA decided to hold its annual convention in San Francisco in 1915, only a handful of members showed up, fewer than 20 in all—setting a record for poor attendance unequalled before or since. The coins themselves, as beautiful as they are to contemplate and own today, followed the usual Zerbe pattern of hype and overblown expectations. Vast quantities remained unsold and were melted, including the majority of the two largest coins, the octagonal and round $50 gold pieces.

Key to Collecting

Each of the five Panama-Pacific International Exposition coins is in strong demand today. Most activity is necessarily centered around the varieties with the largest distribution—the half dollar in particular, but also the gold dollar. Quarter eagles are scarce. The $50 issues play to a wide market as "trophy coins," often sought by well-financed buyers who otherwise are not particularly interested in commemoratives. There was a time when cased sets, particularly those in copper frames, were the *crème de la crème* of the commemorative specialty. In recent years most such sets have been disassembled, since most owners prefer to have the five coins in individual certified holders marked with their grades.

Half Dollars: The finish of the half dollar does not have the typical deep mint frost associated with earlier silver issues, but is apt to be satinlike in appearance with the high parts in particular having a microscopically grainy finish. On many pieces there is an inner "circle" or "line" near the rim of the obverse due to die characteristics. On the reverse, the eagle's breast feathers are indistinct on all specimens, an attribute which sometimes gives Mint State coins the appearance of having light wear.

Most 1915 Panama-Pacific International Exposition half dollars seen today are in grades from AU-50 to MS-63. The grainy finish of the pieces makes them difficult to grade. In particular, it is not easy to determine whether a coin has been lightly cleaned or subtly polished, because the surface of a typical piece was never deeply frosty or lustrous to begin with. It is recommended that the grade of any coin offered be checked carefully prior to purchase. This includes coins certified at high grades.

Gold Dollars: Most dollars known today are in varying levels of Mint State. The issue remains one of the most available and most popular gold dollars of the early era. Examine the laborer's cap and check it at several angles to the light to look for friction. Also check the high spots of the dolphins on the reverse. Friction is the rule (especially on the obverse), not the exception. Even the experts are apt to grade Panama-Pacific gold dollars with differences of a point or two.

Quarter Eagles: The typical specimen is apt to be graded from AU-55 to MS-63 or slightly better. MS-64 coins are elusive, and true MS-65 pieces are rare. Most Mint

State pieces show a satiny, some-times grainy luster quite unlike the deep mint frost seen on the Panama-Pacific gold dollar. Check for friction on the high points of Columbia on the obverse and, on the reverse, on the body and upper wings of the eagle. Buy a lustrous specimen and avoid dull examples.

$50 Gold Coins: In keeping with the small quantities originally issued, 1915 Panama-Pacific $50 gold coins are rare in all grades today, with the round pieces being slightly more elusive than the octagonal versions. The typical grade encountered is apt to be about MS-63 or MS-64 if the coin has been kept in an original box or frame, or AU-58 to MS-63 if it has not. The cheek of Minerva and her helmet are the checkpoints for friction and/or handling marks (usually just friction). The upper part of the owl is also a point to check. Avoid coins which have been cleaned or lightly polished (as evidenced by a myriad of microscopic hairlines).

(1916–1917) McKinley Memorial Gold Dollars

Distribution
1916: 15,000 (estimated)
1917: 5,000 (estimated)

Whitman Coin Guide (WCG™)—1916 McKinley Memorial Gold $1

MS-60	MS-63	MS-64	MS-65	MS-66	MS-67	MS-68
$725	$875	$1,500	$2,620	$4,035	$12,392	

CERTIFIED POPULATIONS

MS-60	MS-61	MS-62	MS-63	MS-64	MS-65	MS-66	MS-67	MS-68
80	221	632	1,027	1,857	1,171	748	95	0
PF-60	PF-61	PF-62	PF-63	PF-64	PF-65	PF-66	PF-67	PF-68
0	0	0	1	1	0	0	0	0

1917 McKinley Memorial Gold $1

MS-60	MS-63	MS-64	MS-65	MS-66	MS-67	MS-68
$900	$1,525	$2,510	$4,005	$5,885	$14,300	

CERTIFIED POPULATIONS

MS-60	MS-61	MS-62	MS-63	MS-64	MS-65	MS-66	MS-67	MS-68
27	104	374	687	1,102	742	440	79	0

Points of Interest: This gold dollar was created on behalf of regional interests in Ohio and had no national importance.

Subject of Commemoration: The sale of these helped to pay for a memorial building at Niles, Ohio, the president's birthplace.

Designs: *Obverse*—Portrait of William McKinley. Designed by Charles E. Barber. *Reverse*—Proposed McKinley Birthplace Memorial to be erected in Niles, Ohio. Designed by George T. Morgan.

Mintage and Melting Data: Authorized February 23, 1916. *Maximum authorized*— 100,000 (total for both years). **1916:** *Number minted* (including 26 assay coins)—20,026 *Number melted*—5,000 (estimated). *Distribution*—15,000 (estimated). **1917:** *Number minted* (including 14 assay coins)—10,014. *Number melted*—5,000 (estimated). *Distribution*—5,000 (estimated).

Original Cost and Issuer: $3. National McKinley Birthplace Memorial Association, Youngstown, Ohio.

McKinley Again

On February 23, 1916, congressional legislation was passed that provided for the production of not more than 100,000 gold dollars, to be known as McKinley souvenir dollars, "for the purpose of aiding in defraying the cost of completing in a suitable manner the work of erecting a memorial in the city of Niles, Ohio to William McKinley, late president of the United States." The National McKinley Birthplace Memorial Association, located in Youngstown, Ohio, was to be the recipient of the coins and anticipated profits.

Possibly licking its wounds from the Panama-Pacific commemorative coins, for which the Mint Engraving Department designed only the half dollar and quarter eagle (and those by default), the Treasury did not call for outside help with the McKinley gold dollar motifs. The project was assigned to Chief Engraver Charles E. Barber and his associates. On March 31, 1916, Mint Director Robert W. Woolley submitted the Mint's own designs to the Commission of Fine Arts, which made suggestions for revision, but the Commission's ideas were ignored.

Barber created the obverse design, which consisted of a portrait of McKinley quite unlike that used on his 1903-dated coins of the same denomination. The reverse design by George T. Morgan represents the planned McKinley Birthplace Memorial in Niles, Ohio. In August and October 1916, the quantity of 20,026 McKinley gold dollars was struck at the Philadelphia Mint. In February 1917 a further 10,014 McKinley gold dollars of the same design, these dated 1917, were struck at the same facility.

Distribution

Of the 30,000 1916- and 1917-dated McKinley gold dollars produced for distribution, about 20,000 were sold. About 10,000, probably mostly dated 1917, were returned to the Mint for melting.

B. Max Mehl in his 1937 monograph, *The Commemorative Coins of the United States*, related:

> This issue of these gold dollars was prompted by some personal friends of the president. The original plan was to strike 100,000 of the gold dollars to sell them at $3 each and use the proceeds to erect a memorial building at the birthplace of McKinley at Niles, Ohio. However, like all similar plans promulgated by those who are inexperienced in numismatics, the sale of the coins met with meager success. In 1916, 20,026 of the coins were struck, of which approximately 15,000 were sold.
>
> In 1917 another issue of 10,000 were minted of which only about 5,000 were sold. By that time the Committee in charge apparently realized that the number of collectors in the country could not and would not absorb an issue of 100,000 coins at $3 each. The Committee had 20,000 coins left on hand. About 10,000 of these were disposed of at a greatly reduced price to the "Texas dealer" [Mehl himself], who in turn distributed them extensively among collectors of the country at a reduced price from the original issue price of $3 each.

I estimate that original sales were approximately as follows: 1916: Sold by the Commission to the public and numismatists at the time of original distribution, 8,000 or so coins. Later sold to B. Max Mehl, 7,000 or so coins; 1917: Sold by the Commission to the public and numismatists at the time of original distribution, 2,000 or so coins. Later sold to B. Max Mehl, 3,000 or so coins. The Mint did not keep track of the specific dates melted.

Key to Collecting

The McKinley dollars are popular today as a necessary part of a commemorative gold collection. The obverse of the 1916 issue often displays friction, while the reverse of the same coin can appear as choice Mint State. Prooflike fields are common, and some are highly prooflike on both sides. Those dated 1917 are much harder to find and usually are in higher grades, with rich luster on both sides, and often of a pale yellow color.

(1918) ILLINOIS CENTENNIAL HALF DOLLARS

Distribution
100,058

Whitman Coin Guide (WCG™)—1918 Illinois Centennial 50¢

MS-60	MS-63	MS-64	MS-65	MS-66	MS-67	MS-68
$200	$225	$275	$615	$900	$2,010	$41,250

CERTIFIED POPULATIONS

MS-60	MS-61	MS-62	MS-63	MS-64	MS-65	MS-66	MS-67	MS-68
91	91	562	1,917	3,483	2,059	709	144	3
PF-60	PF-61	PF-62	PF-63	PF-64	PF-65	PF-66	PF-67	PF-68
0	0	0	0	2	0	0	0	0

Points of Interest: All were distributed, the first time any authorized mintage of commemoratives was fully used, with none returned for melting.

Subject of Commemoration: The 100th anniversary of Illinois statehood.

Designs: *Obverse*—Portrait of Abraham Lincoln facing right. Designed by George T. Morgan. *Reverse*—Illinois State Seal. Designed by John R. Sinnock.

Mintage Data: Authorized on June 1, 1918. *Maximum authorized*—100,000. *Number minted*—100,000 plus 58 for assay.

Original Cost and Issuer: $1. The Illinois Centennial Commission through various outlets.

Illinois Celebrates Its Centennial

Commemoratives were struck in 1918 to celebrate the centennial of the admission of the state of Illinois into the Union, setting the precedent for numerous other state and local anniversaries to be observed on commemorative coinage during the next several decades. Legislation provided for the striking of 100,000 half dollars.

The obverse design was created by George T. Morgan, now chief engraver at the Mint, following the death of Charles E. Barber in 1917. Morgan, whose talents far eclipsed those of Barber, had worked as an engraver at the Mint since 1876. Portrayed was a youthful head of Lincoln, beardless, taken from the head of Andrew O'Connor's statue created for the Centennial and subsequently unveiled in Springfield in August 1918.

The reverse, by assistant engraver John R. Sinnock, was adapted from the Illinois State seal. The border of the obverse and reverse consists of beads and pellets, an attractive substitute for denticles. The models for both sides were reduced by Sinnock on the Mint's Janvier portrait lathe, which had been on hand more than a decade.

Offered for sale at $1 each through the Springfield Chamber of Commerce and other outlets, the Illinois half dollars met with a popular reception, and most were sold, including several thousand remaindered to B. Max Mehl at a price of just slightly more than face value. A Springfield bank bought 30,000 pieces and kept them in its vault until the Bank Holiday of March 1933, after which the cache was sold to dealers for a small premium over face value. By early 1936 all were widely distributed.

Key to Collecting

The design of this coin has made it a collectors' favorite. Examples were struck with deep, frosty finishes, giving Mint State pieces an unusually attractive appearance today. On the obverse the typical coin shows contact marks or friction on Lincoln's cheek and on other high parts of his portrait. The field typically shows contact marks. The reverse is usually from one to three points higher due to the protective nature of its complicated design. Most examples are lustrous and frosty, although a few are seen with partially prooflike fields.

(1920) MAINE CENTENNIAL HALF DOLLARS

Distribution
50,028

Whitman Coin Guide (WCG™)—1920 Maine Centennial 50¢

MS-60	MS-63	MS-64	MS-65	MS-66	MS-67	MS-68
$200	$250	$330	$616	$1,120	$5,225	

CERTIFIED POPULATIONS

MS-60	MS-61	MS-62	MS-63	MS-64	MS-65	MS-66	MS-67	MS-68
39	61	258	980	2,164	1,615	562	33	0

Points of Interest: Originally envisioned to circulate at face value to promote Maine.

Subject of Commemoration: The 100th anniversary of the admission of the state of Maine to the Union in 1820.

Designs: *Obverse*—Arms of the state of Maine: the Latin word DIRIGO means "I direct." *Reverse*—Heavy wreath enclosing inscription. Anthony de Francisci modeled the coin from a design by Harry H. Cochrane.

Mintage Data: Authorized on May 10, 1920. *Maximum authorized*—100,000. *Number minted*—50,028, including 28 for the Assay Commission.

Original Cost and Issuer: $1. Maine Centennial Commission.

A Half Dollar for Maine's Centennial

In colonial times and in the early federal era the district of Maine, east of New Hampshire, was part of the state of Massachusetts. Numismatists today are familiar with many varieties of bank notes issued by towns such as Portland, with the Massachusetts address of the early

days. Following a referendum, citizens of the district formed the sta
There was no controversy involved, and the transition was made smoot

To celebrate the state's 100th anniversary the governor and Council
Maine requested that the Treasury issue an appropriate commemorative half
April 21, 1920, John A. Peters, a delegate to the House of Representatives from
sought to promote his bill for a centennial half dollar by noting that the pieces
intended to "simply go into circulation with the special design upon them." It was fel
that if the pieces passed from hand to hand in pocket change they would help publicize
the centennial observation. At this time Columbian souvenir half dollars were common
in everyday circulation.

Congress approved the coinage on May 10, 1920, well into the centennial year. The
authorization provided for up to 100,000 coins. By this time it had been decided to sell
the coins at a premium to the public for $1 each. On May 14, Secretary of the Treasury
David F. Houston sent a sketch of the proposed design to Charles Moore, chairman of
the Commission of Fine Arts. The motifs were drawn by Harry H. Cochrane, a Maine
artist and legislator, and featured the state arms on the obverse and an inscription within
a wreath of pine on the reverse.[8]

Moore sent the sketch to Commission member James Earle Fraser, a talented sculptor who had designed the 1913 Indian Head / Buffalo nickel among other things, who
condemned the motifs as "very ordinary" and suggested they "should not be used." To
this, Moore added his own comments in a letter to the secretary of the Treasury, stating that if accepted the design "would result in a coin far below the standard set by the
new fifty-cent piece" (a reference to the highly acclaimed 1916 Walking Liberty design
by Adolph A. Weinman), continuing:

> The design proposed is positively bad, and would bring humiliation to
> the people of Maine if it should be executed. . . . The Treasury Depart-
> ment and the Mint also would be made to suffer criticisms from the
> people who have now been aroused to a feeling and demand for an
> artistic coinage.

Further allusions were made by Moore to other coin designs of earlier times, probably Charles E. Barber's dime, quarter, and half-dollar motifs of 1892 through 1916,
which had been widely criticized from nearly the first day they were produced:

> We should not return to the low standards that have formerly pre-
> vailed. This is especially true in the present instance, where the coin
> goes ultimately to collectors and becomes a permanent memorial of
> the state of Maine.

The Maine Centennial Commission did not buy Moore's argument and insisted
that Cochrane's sketches be used. The Commission of Fine Arts enlisted sculptor
Anthony de Francisci to create models.

Dies were made, and 50,000 coins were struck, plus 28 for the Assay Commission.
These were not available until the end of the summer, by which time the centennial festivities in Portland had already concluded. Sales of the half dollars were fairly brisk, and
30,000 or more were disbursed soon after receipt. The others were kept by the office of
the state treasurer and were parceled out through much of the year 1921, although
quantities remained on hand for years afterward.

The demand by the numismatic community was lukewarm at best, and likely no
more than 5,000 coins went to dedicated collectors. The over-promotion by Farran

till had its effect in lowered market prices, and enthusi-
was minimal.

lars were sold to the numismatic fraternity, with the result
00 pieces distributed saw careless handling by the public.
n or handling marks on the center of the shield on the
completely finished in the dies and always show tiny *raised*
ks, which at quick glance may appear to be hairlines or
scratches, this ... fect on the grading.

Today examples in higher Mint State levels are much more elusive than the fairly
generous mintage would indicate. Strictly graded MS-65 coins of excellent surface quality and aesthetic appeal are rare, much more so than generally recognized.

(1920–1921) PILGRIM TERCENTENARY HALF DOLLARS

Distribution
1920: 152,112
1921: 20,053

Whitman Coin Guide (WCG™)—1920 Pilgrim Tercentenary 50¢

MS-60	MS-63	MS-64	MS-65	MS-66	MS-67	MS-68
$150	$200	$250	$515	$1,210	$3,815	

CERTIFIED POPULATIONS

MS-60	MS-61	MS-62	MS-63	MS-64	MS-65	MS-66	MS-67	MS-68
101	111	717	2,121	3,603	1,714	408	40	0

1921 Pilgrim Tercentenary 50¢

MS-60	MS-63	MS-64	MS-65	MS-66	MS-67	MS-68
$250	$275	$320	$635	$1,540	$6,050	

CERTIFIED POPULATIONS

MS-60	MS-61	MS-62	MS-63	MS-64	MS-65	MS-66	MS-67	MS-68
25	38	225	695	1,707	1,208	381	37	0

Points of Interest: Dallin's initial D is incuse or recessed under Bradford's elbow on
the coin—an unexplained departure from all other motifs, indicating it was probably
added by the use of what seems to have been a D mintmark punch, possibly as an afterthought in the hub. On the original plaster model his initials C.E.D. appeared in relief.

Subject of Commemoration: The 300th anniversary of the landing of the Pilgrims at
Plymouth.

Designs: *Obverse*—Waist-up portrait (artist's concept, since no likeness exists) of Governor Bradford holding a book. *Reverse*—The *Mayflower*. Cyrus E. Dallin executed the
designs furnished to him by the Pilgrim Tercentenary Commission.

Mintage and Melting Data: Authorized May 12, 1920. *Maximum authorized—*
300,000. **1920:** *Number minted* (including 112 assay coins)—200,112. *Number melted—*

48,000. *Net distribution*—152,112. **1921:** *Number minted* (including 53 assay coins)—100,053. *Number melted*—80,000. *Net distribution*—20,053.

Original Cost and Issuer: $1. Pilgrim Tercentenary Commission.

300th Anniversary of the Pilgrims' Landing

In 1920 the 300th anniversary of the landing of the Pilgrims at Plymouth furnished the opportunity for numerous celebrations throughout New England. On May 12 of that year, Congress authorized the production of 300,000 (the bill originally stated 500,000 but was amended, apparently inadvertently) silver Pilgrim Tercentenary 50-cent pieces to commemorate the event. No provision was made for issuing the coins for more than one year, but doing so was not in violation of the legislation, for neither was it prohibited.

The Pilgrim Tercentenary Commission suggested a design, which was modeled by Cyrus E. Dallin, a Boston sculptor who was known for Indian subjects. The obverse bore a stylized portrait of Governor William Bradford (1590–1657), who was said to represent a typical Pilgrim of the time. On the coin Bradford's left arm supported a Bible, representative of the Separatist religious group, of which the governor was a member, which endeavored to lead their lives in strict accordance with that book's teachings. (Alternatively, *Old Colony Memorial*, published in 1920, states that the book supported by Bradford is his *History of Plimoth Plantation*.)

The reverse showed a view of the *Mayflower* but with an error in the ship's rigging, for it showed a flying jib type of sail that had not been used at that early date; a square water-sail under the bowsprit should have been depicted. The reverse displayed the date expressed as 1620–1920.

As the legislation authorizing this issue was not approved until May 12, and since, during the summer of 1920, many celebrations were planned, artist Dallin was urged to work quickly. His motifs were shown to members of the Commission of Fine Arts. James Earle Fraser found the devices to be well done but the inscriptions to be crudely lettered. The hour was late—there was no time to modify Dallin's work, and it was used as he created it.

Minting and Distribution

In October 1920, by which time many celebrations were history, 200,112 Pilgrim Tercentenary half dollars were struck at the Philadelphia Mint. Except for the odd 112 pieces reserved for the Assay Commission, the production was shipped to the National Shawmut Bank in Boston, which put them on sale for $1 each beginning in November, with the profits going to the Pilgrim Tercentenary Commission.

Although more than 100,000 coins found ready buyers, tens of thousands of coins remained unsold by year's end. Defying all logic, the Commission sought to have the remaining 100,000 authorized coins struck. This was done in July 1921, with a small "1921" date added to the left obverse field. Though commemorating the 301st anniversary made no sense, the Commission felt that the public as well as numismatists would have to buy the 1921 coins in order to have a complete set. The new idea laid a big fat egg, and fewer than 20,000 were sold. Eventually, the glut of unwanted pieces was shipped back to the Mint to be melted, amounting to 48,000 pieces dated 1920 and 80,000 (80 percent of the mintage!) dated 1921.

Writing in 1937 in *The Commemorative Coins of the United States*, B. Max Mehl commented on the 1921 Pilgrim half dollar and its effect upon collectors:

> This was the beginning of the hot idea of trying to "get" the collector at least twice. And the way collectors have responded to the various subsequent issues is indicative that collectors, whether they like it or not, are going in for minor varieties of commemoratives.

Indeed, the genie could not be put back in the bottle, and it was onward and upward for future commemorative commissions to devise all sorts of odd and illogical varieties to tap the numismatic market.

Key to Collecting

The 1920 issues are common today. The 1921 is slightly scarce. MS-64 and higher coins usually have excellent eye appeal, but there are many exceptions. For grading, on the obverse check the high areas of Governor Bradford's portrait and hat for friction. On the reverse check the ship's rigging and the stern of the vessel. Most coins have scattered contact marks, particularly on the obverse. Nearly all 1921 coins are this way. Many coins (particularly coins which are early impressions from the dies) show tiny *raised* lines in the obverse field, representing die finish marks; these are not to be confused with hairlines or other evidences of friction (which are recessed).

(1921) Alabama Centennial Half Dollars

Distribution

2x2: 30,000 (estimated)
Plain: 35,000 (estimated)

Whitman Coin Guide (WCG™)—1921 Alabama 2x2 Centennial 50¢

MS-60	MS-63	MS-64	MS-65	MS-66	MS-67	MS-68
$375	$700	$1,150	$2,520	$5,500	$33,000	

CERTIFIED POPULATIONS

MS-60	MS-61	MS-62	MS-63	MS-64	MS-65	MS-66	MS-67	MS-68
55	134	517	1,126	1,345	710	105	6	0

1921 Alabama Centennial 50¢

MS-60	MS-63	MS-64	MS-65	MS-66	MS-67	MS-68
$300	$575	$810	$2,050	$5,545	$29,634	

CERTIFIED POPULATIONS

MS-60	MS-61	MS-62	MS-63	MS-64	MS-65	MS-66	MS-67	MS-68
48	85	342	774	1,491	674	119	5	0

Points of Interest: The first instance of the use of a living person's portrait on a U.S. coin (T.E. Kilby).

Subject of Commemoration: These half dollars were authorized in 1920 for the centennial, which was celebrated in 1919, but they were not struck until 1921.

Designs: *Obverse*—Portraits of William Wyatt Bibb, the first governor of Alabama, and T.E. Kilby, governor at the time of the centennial. *Reverse*—Alabama State Seal with eagle perched on a shield. Designed by Laura Gardin Fraser.

Mintage and Melting Data: Authorized on May 10, 1920. *Maximum authorized*—100,000. *Number minted*—70,044 (including 44 for assay). *Number melted*—5,000. *Net distribution*—**2x2:** estimated as 30,000. **Plain:** estimated as 35,000.

Original Cost and Issuer: $1. Alabama Centennial Commission.

A Confusing Array of Dates

Adventurers from Spain may have traversed the area known as Alabama by 1528, more than a decade before Hernando DeSoto's 1540 visit. Settled by the French in 1702, the region later came under the dominion of Great Britain, which retained possession until the American Revolution. In 1798 the land became part of the Territory of Mississippi, of which it remained a part until Alabama became its own territory in 1817, and a state on December 14, 1819.

The 1820 government census tallied 127,900 white residents of Alabama. Tuscaloosa served as capital of the state from 1826 to 1846; in the latter year it was relocated to Montgomery, a city which later served as capital of the Confederate States of America.

It seems reasonable to suggest that, if a 100th anniversary of statehood commemorative half dollar were to be created, 1919 would have been the logical year to do it. Indeed in 1919 many centennial celebrations were held throughout the state.

Now enters the element of greed. Early in the year 1920, the Alabama Centennial Commission devised the idea and promoted a piece of legislation in Congress to provide for a commemorative quarter dollar, which was amended on April 21, 1920, to be a half dollar. On May 10, 1920, a bill was passed providing for 100,000 silver 50-cent pieces to be produced "in commemoration of the 100th anniversary of the admission of the State of Alabama into the Union," completely overlooking the fact that the centennial had already passed, and it was now the 101st anniversary!

The situation dragged on, designs were proposed and discussed, and finally on June 28, 1921, *two years after the centennial*, committee chairman Owen suggested a new design showing William Wyatt Bibb and Thomas E. Kilby, representing the governors in 1819 and 1919. This was the motif used, with the models being made by Laura Gardin Fraser.

The Alabama Centennial coins, authorized in 1920 to celebrate a 1919 anniversary, were not struck until 1921, and to reflect this the auxiliary date of 1921 was placed on the obverse in addition to the 1819–1919 dating on the reverse, a bewildering confusion of dates to the casual observer.

Two Varieties Created

The first examples were struck on October 21, 1921, and bore on the obverse a special notation, 2x2, representing the fact that Alabama was the 22nd state to enter the Union, the two digits being divided by a St. Andrew's cross taken from the Alabama state flag (the design of which inspired the Confederate flag). Some 6,006  pieces with 2x2 were struck in October 1921, it was reported, and likely many more later (revisionist comment), after which the 2x2 inscription was removed from the master die; and a second variety, later known as the "plain" issue, was produced.

On the morning of October 26, the first pieces with 2x2 were put on sale in Birmingham during President Warren G. Harding's visit to the city. Later examples were distributed through banks for $1 each. Per conventional wisdom and Mint records, likely incorrect, in December 1921 a further 10,008 pieces with 2x2 were produced plus 54,030 of the "plain" type, giving a total mintage of 16,014 with 2x2 and 54,030 without that distinguishing feature.

Although various mintage, melting, and net distribution figures have been published, usually showing the 2x2 to be by far the rarer, in the real world both are nearly of equal rarity, with the plain only slightly more plentiful. We do know that 70,044 were minted totally, and that 5,000 were melted. This leaves a distribution of 65,044, perhaps divided into about 30,000 of the 2x2 and 35,000 of the plain.

The special 2x2 notation was made at the recommendation of sculptor and Commission of Fine Arts member James Earle Fraser, husband of the coin's designer, who recognized that when Missouri tried a similar trick a few months earlier, additional sales resulted.

Key to Collecting

Most Alabama half dollars were sold to citizens of that state, and relatively few were acquired by numismatists. As might be expected, the majority of pieces in existence today are MS-63 or less, with circulated pieces being abundant. In fact, the typical coin encountered is apt to be in Extremely Fine or About Uncirculated grade. Mint State examples are scarce, and coins MS-65 or finer are rare. Nearly all show friction or contact marks on Governor Kilby's cheek on the obverse, and many are flatly struck on the eagle's left leg and talons on the reverse.

The Mint did not produce the pieces with care, and even specimens carefully preserved since the day of issue are apt to appear unsatisfactory from the standpoint of sharpness and luster (although the 2x2 versions are usually better defined than the plain pieces). Nicks and marks from the original planchet are apt to be seen on the areas of light striking. Sharply struck, high-grade Mint State coins are very rare—in fact, among the very rarest in the series.

The eagle's upper leg is often seen lightly struck, particularly on the plain variety; in instances of light striking, marks from the original planchet can be seen in this area. Coins were handled carelessly, and most show contact marks in various areas. For both varieties, patience and cherrypicking will pay rewards.

(1921) Missouri Centennial Half Dollars

Distribution
2★4: 9,000 (estimated)
Plain: 11,400 (estimated)

Whitman Coin Guide (WCG™)—1921 Missouri 2★4 Centennial 50¢

MS-60	MS-63	MS-64	MS-65	MS-66	MS-67	MS-68
$850	$1,250	$1,900	$5,005	$14,300	$20,900	

CERTIFIED POPULATIONS

MS-60	MS-61	MS-62	MS-63	MS-64	MS-65	MS-66	MS-67	MS-68
22	44	298	696	1,470	436	16	6	0

1921 Missouri Centennial 50¢

MS-60	MS-63	MS-64	MS-65	MS-66	MS-67
$750	$1,075	$1,770	$5,100	$10,690	$17,600

CERTIFIED POPULATIONS

MS-60	MS-61	MS-62	MS-63	MS-64	MS-65	MS-66	MS-67
74	92	387	832	1,619	413	49	0

Points of Interest: The first instance of two varieties in the same year, to exploit the numismatic market. This was soon copied on the Alabama half dollar, to which a 2x2 was added.

Subject of Commemoration: Missouri's admission to the Union in 1821.

Designs: *Obverse*—Portrait of Daniel Boone. *Reverse*—Standing figures of Boone and an Indian, set against a starry background, with SEDALIA incused below, representing the location of the exposition for which the pieces were created. Designed by Robert Aitken.

Mintage and Melting Data: Authorized on March 4, 1921. *Maximum authorized*— 250,000 (combined for both types). *Number minted*—50,028 in all. *Number melted*— 29,600. *Net distribution*—20,428 (estimated), with 9,000 for 1921 2★4 and 11,400 for 1921 Plain. The 28 remaining were for the Assay Commission.

Original Cost and Issuer: $1. Missouri Centennial Committee through the Sedalia Trust Company.

Celebrating a Centennial

Although Spanish explorers had visited Missouri in the 1540s, it remained for the French to settle the area. St. Louis, founded by the French in 1764, became a center for fur trading and commerce on the Mississippi River. The Territory of Missouri was established in 1812. Following the Missouri Compromise of 1820, a piece of legislation developed by Henry Clay, Missouri was admitted into the Union as a slave-holding state in exchange for the 1820 admission of Maine as a free state.

Missouri was admitted to the Union on August 10, 1821. A century later, on March 4, 1921, Congress authorized 250,000 silver 50-cent pieces to be struck in commemoration of the event. Pieces were intended for distribution at the Missouri Centennial Exposition and State Fair held in Sedalia, the first capital of Missouri, from August 8 to 20, 1921.

The Design

Robert Aitken, a recognized medalist and sculptor best remembered in numismatic circles for the $50 Panama-Pacific gold coins, was named by the Commission of Fine Arts to prepare models, following ideas forwarded by a committee of the Missouri Centennial Exposition. The idea of adding a special "2★4" notation in the field apparent-  ently was the brainchild of James Montgomery, chairman of the exposition, who wrote the following in a letter to Charles Moore, chairman of the Commission of Fine Arts:

> I desire also to make the following suggestion, that the star with the figures "24" be shown on five thousand of the coins. To do this, the star and figures would have to be raised on the die and after five thousand coins were struck, the star and figures could be cut off and the balance of the coins would be without the star and figures. This would

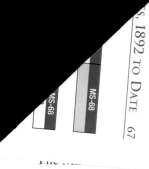

5,000 for a sufficient profit to pay the expense of ch you price at $1,750.

a design featuring on the obverse the portrait of Daniel e shown standing figures of Boone and an Indian, set against SEDALIA incused below, representing the location of the ieces were created. Much of the die work was accomplished any in New York City, in order to expedite manufacture.

ial Committee branch of the Sedalia Chamber of Commerce was made custodian of the entire issue and appointed the Sedalia Trust Company as distributor. The first coins offered, the Plain pieces without the 2★4 notation in the field, were marketed during the first week of August in 1921 at the Missouri Centennial Exposition and State Fair. The specimens with 2★4, although produced first, were offered later.

Uncertain Mintage Figures

In his 1938 monograph David M. Bullowa stated that 50,028 half dollars were struck at the Philadelphia Mint in July 1921, of which the first 10,000 bore on the obverse the designation 2★4, signifying Missouri's status as the 24th state of the Union, with the balance of 40,028 being without the star, a variety collectors would later designate as Plain.

Among others, Anthony Swiatek and Walter Breen have suggested that only 5,000 pieces were coined with the 2★4 notation on the obverse and that 45,028 half dollars were made without this feature. Contemporary advertisements specifically listed the 2★4 variety as having a mintage of 5,000. It is thought that 29,600 of the Plain style were melted, resulting in a net mintage of 15,400 (using the Swiatek-Breen figures) or 10,400 (if the Bullowa figures are used). To suggest that only 5,000 were made of the 2★4 and that 15,428 of the Plain were made strains credulity, for in practice both varieties are nearly equal in rarity today (the 2★4 being slightly scarcer), a situation borne out by catalogue values and also by statistics kept by commercial grading services.

What we do know is that 50,028 were minted totally, and 29,600 were melted, leaving a net distribution of 20,428, of which 28 were for the Assay Commission. A reasonable estimate of the original distribution might be 9,000 of the 2★4 and 11,400 of the Plain.

Key to Collecting

The typical Missouri half dollar encountered is apt to be in a grade from AU-55 to MS-63, usually with friction and contact marks on the higher areas of the design. Most are lightly struck at the center of the portrait of Boone on the obverse, and at the torsos of the two figures on the reverse. Apparently, little care was taken at the Mint during the striking of the pieces. MS-65 and higher coins, *if sharply struck at the centers*, are rarities—a situation not widely known. Patience and cherrypicking will reward you.

(1922) GRANT MEMORIAL COMMEMORATIVES

Distribution

Half dollar, No Star: 67,405
Half dollar, With Star: 4,256
Gold dollar, No Star: 5,015
Gold dollar, With Star: 5,000

Whitman Coin Guide (WCG™)—1922 Grant 50¢, No Star

MS-60	MS-63	MS-64	MS-65	MS-66	MS-67	MS-68
$140	$200	$330	$900	$1,855	$5,375	

CERTIFIED POPULATIONS

MS-60	MS-61	MS-62	MS-63	MS-64	MS-65	MS-66	MS-67	MS-68
89	155	556	1,689	2,542	1,268	373	58	1

1922 Grant 50¢, With Star

MS-60	MS-63	MS-64	MS-65	MS-66	MS-67	MS-68
$1,500	$2,200	$3,050	$7,730	$18,335	$42,765	

CERTIFIED POPULATIONS

MS-60	MS-61	MS-62	MS-63	MS-64	MS-65	MS-66	MS-67	MS-68
61	69	257	566	920	235	68	8	0
PF-60	PF-61	PF-62	PF-63	PF-64	PF-65	PF-66	PF-67	PF-68
0	0	0	0	1	1	0	1	0

1922 Grant Gold $1, No Star

MS-60	MS-63	MS-64	MS-65	MS-66	MS-67	MS-68
$2,000	$2,400	$3,600	$4,650	$5,170	$9,765	

CERTIFIED POPULATIONS

MS-60	MS-61	MS-62	MS-63	MS-64	MS-65	MS-66	MS-67	MS-68
18	45	198	423	761	601	570	162	1

1922 Grant Gold $1, With Star

MS-60	MS-63	MS-64	MS-65	MS-66	MS-67	MS-68
$2,000	$2,575	$3,800	$4,650	$5,410	$5,775	

CERTIFIED POPULATIONS

MS-60	MS-61	MS-62	MS-63	MS-64	MS-65	MS-66	MS-67	MS-68
19	19	104	312	832	741	766	286	4

Points of Interest: The With Star half dollars apparently were coined in error, for the Commission had not ordered them. This is the only classic era commemorative issue in which two different denominations have the same designs.

Subject of Commemoration: The 100th anniversary of Ulysses S. Grant's birth.

Designs: Half dollar: *Obverse*—Head of Grant in profile, depicting him in the later years of his life, with closely cropped beard, wearing a military coat. *Reverse*—Grant's log cabin birthplace amid huge trees. Designed by Laura Gardin Fraser. **Gold dollar:** Same as preceding, except for different denomination inscriptions. Designed by Laura Gardin Fraser.

Mintage and Melting Data: Authorized on February 2, 1922. *Maximum authorized*— 250,000. **Half dollar, No Star:** *Number minted* (including 55 assay coins)—95,055. *Number melted*—27,650. *Net distribution*—67,405. **Half dollar, With Star:** *Number minted* (including 6 assay coins)—5,006. *Number melted*—750. *Net distribution*—4,256. **Gold dollar, No Star:** *Number minted and distributed*—5,000. **Gold dollar, With Star:** *Number minted and distributed*—5,016. Assay coins: 16.

Original Cost and Issuer: Half dollar, No Star: $1.50, later reduced to 75¢. **Half dollar, With Star:** $1, later raised to $1.50. **Gold dollar:** $3 for either variety. U.S. Grant Centenary Memorial Commission (mail orders were serviced by Hugh L. Nichols, chairman, Batavia, Ohio).

Ulysses S. Grant

The race was on to create unusual varieties for collectors, and the next entry in the field consisted of the 1922 Grant Memorial half dollars and gold dollars, each of the same design and each made in two varieties. The occasion was the 100th anniversary of the birth of President Ulysses S. Grant.

Grant was born in Point Pleasant, Ohio on April 27, 1822. In his second year he moved with his family to Georgetown in the same state, where he spent his boyhood. In 1839 he entered West Point, from which institution he graduated in 1843, going on to serve in the army under generals Zachary Taylor and Winfield Scott during the Mexican War, 1845–1848. Grant resigned from the army in 1854 and worked as a farmer and real estate agent in St. Louis, moving to Galena, Illinois in 1860. When the Civil War erupted, he offered his services and was appointed colonel of the 21st Illinois Volunteers, later advancing to the rank of brigadier general. He captured Fort Henry and Fort Donelson (after which he was elevated to major general), saw action at Shiloh, and took charge of the decisive capture of Vicksburg. Following Grant's victory at Chattanooga, President Lincoln named him General of the American Armies. It was Grant who accepted Lee's surrender at Appomattox in April 1865.

Grant was elected president of the United States on the Republican ticket in 1868 and was re-elected in 1872. He did not serve with distinction, and his terms are remembered as corrupt and graft-ridden. Following his presidency he took a trip around the world. In 1884 he lost much of his fortune when a New York City bank failed. Devoting his time to writing his memoirs, Grant finished them four days before his death. The book earned about $450,000—a precursor of what many later presidents would earn, because telling about the administration was more lucrative than the office itself. Grant died on July 23, 1885, at Mt. McGregor, New York, and was buried—dare I say it?—in Grant's Tomb in New York City.

Special Coinage

To commemorate all of this, the Ulysses S. Grant Centenary Memorial Association was incorporated in 1921 and soon announced ambitious plans, including anniversary celebrations in Clermont County, Ohio, the erection of memorial "community buildings" in Georgetown (of his boyhood) and Bethel, Ohio (where he lived for a short time after his graduation from West Point). The laying of a highway five miles in length from New Richmond to Point Pleasant was also specified in the congressional bill. The buildings and highway were never constructed. Seemingly, the whole arrangement was phony.

With good connections in Congress the Association requested that 200,000 gold dollars be authorized. The enabling act provided that 10,000 gold dollars and 250,000 half dollars were to be coined to official Mint standards, and that the profits were to go to the construction of memorial sites in Ohio.

Laura Gardin Fraser prepared the designs and models. Depicted on the obverse was the bust of Ulysses S. Grant in military uniform, facing right, adapted from a photograph by Mathew Brady. Shown on the reverse was the fenced clapboard house in Georgetown. The Centenary Memorial Association was aware of the extra profit reaped by the distributors of Alabama and Missouri half dollars, so they too desired to have a special mark on their coins, but, not being able to devise anything significant in the way of an emblem, they came up with the idea of putting an otherwise meaningless star on the obverse of about half the issue of gold dollars.

Apparently, by error or inadvertence, a star was added to the obverse of a number of half dollars as well. Historian Don Taxay relates the arrival of 5,000 halves with stars was "a bonus which greatly surprised the committee."

Mintage and Distribution

Once again, Mint records of quantities struck are inconclusi-
state that 117,685 half dollars were made, while the *Annual R*
Mint gave the number as 100,061. Today it is generally accep
halves and 5,006 With Star pieces were minted. The With Sta

The pieces were available for sale in April 1922. The initi
or without star, a figure changed in December 1922 to 75¢ for the No St
purchased in lots of 10 or more) and $1.50 for the With Star issue. Orders were taken
until January 1, 1923, when the books were closed. The public accounted for many if not
most of the sales. Collectors bought others. In the end, many were melted. Nearly all of
the gold coins were wholesaled to dealers. Sales were satisfactory, although not up to
expectations, and 750 With Star and 27,650 No Star half dollars were melted, leaving net
distributions of 4,250 With Star and 67,350 No Star pieces, if records are correct.

In March 1922 the Philadelphia Mint struck 5,000 gold dollars with a small incuse
star in the right field, and 5,016 without this feature. The gold dollars With Star were
sold for $3.50 each and the No Star coins for $3 each beginning in April 1922. All were
eventually distributed, but mostly in bulk to dealers.

Key to Collecting

Half Dollars: The finish on the surface of Grant half dollars, even on well preserved
Uncirculated pieces, is quite "rustic" and shows numerous raised die finish lines and
other Mint preparation marks. Further, most specimens are lightly struck on the center
of the obverse. These factors combine to make it extremely difficult to differentiate
minute gradations among Mint State coins, and even grading experts are apt to differ
measurably from each other when it comes to rendering opinions. A few are prooflike.

The No Star half dollar is common, with typical grades ranging from MS-60 to 63
or so. MS-65 and higher coins are seen with some frequency, but are much scarcer.

The 1922 Grant With Star half dollar in Mint State is one
of the very rarest pieces of the series simply because the mintage
was low and most pieces did not sell to collectors. The issue has
been unappreciated in recent times, perhaps the greatest *sleeper*
among early commemorative half dollars.

Gold Dollars: Today nearly all known Grant gold dollars are in
varying degrees of choice and gem Mint State, with MS-66 and 67
coins being easy to find. Some lower-grade coins show friction on the
cheek and hair of General Grant. To locate this evidence of friction,
turn the coin carefully at several angles under strong light and medium
magnification. Some specimens have dull surfaces; avoid these.

(1923) MONROE DOCTRINE CENTENNIAL HALF DOLLARS

Distribution
274,077

ɔin Guide (WCG™)—1923 Monroe Doctrine Centennial 50¢

MS-63	MS-64	MS-65	MS-66	MS-67	MS-68
$200	$550	$3,180	$6,970	$21,590	

ΓIED POPULATIONS

S-60	MS-61	MS-62	MS-63	MS-64	MS-65	MS-66	MS-67	MS-68
83	173	868	1,995	2,551	576	99	10	0

Points of Interest: One of the most poorly struck of all commemoratives. Issued by the California film industry, which is not mentioned on the coins. Large quantities were put into circulation for face value.

Subject of Commemoration: The 100th anniversary of the Monroe Doctrine, the declaration by President James Monroe that European countries that interfered with countries in the western hemisphere or established new colonies in it would meet with disapproval or worse from the American government.

Designs: *Obverse*—Conjoined portraits of presidents James Monroe and John Quincy Adams, both of whom were instrumental in formulating the Monroe Doctrine. *Reverse*— Plagiarized copy of a medal created by Ralph Beck in 1899 (and copyrighted that year) for the seal of the 1901 Pan-American Exposition in Buffalo, showing the continents of North and South America as female figures in the outlines of the two land masses, a motif suggested by James Earle Fraser, who acted as an advisor. Perhaps Fraser did not know of the Beck precedent. Chester Beach prepared the models for this coin.

Mintage and Melting Data: Authorized on January 24, 1923. *Maximum authorized*— 300,000. *Number minted* (including 77 assay coins)—274,077. *Net distribution*—274,077.

Original Cost and Issuer: $1. Los Angeles Clearing House representing backers of the First Annual American Historical Revue and Motion Picture Industry Exposition.

Harlotry in Coinage

In 1923 the motion picture industry, by that time well settled into Hollywood and adjacent areas (the center of the industry having moved there from Fort Lee, New Jersey, and other Eastern locations the decade before), was having more than its share of problems. The slaying of film director William Desmond Taylor under mysterious circumstances, the death of Virginia Rappé after an orgy held in a San Francisco hotel with Roscoe "Fatty" Arbuckle, and a general lapse of morals in the film community brought much unfavorable publicity. Several steps were taken to correct the situation. Among the suggestions brought forward was the creation of a public film exposition with a special issue of commemorative half dollars to be sold at a premium. An inscription on the letterhead used by the promoters of the issue read: "Monroe Doctrine Centennial. First Annual American Historical Revue and Motion Picture Industry Exposition, Commemorating the One Hundredth Anniversary of the Monroe Doctrine, June 1, 1923. Under the Direction and Supervision of the Motion Picture Industry."

The group thought to legitimize the coin by giving it an older historical context. By coincidence, 1923 coincided with the 100th anniversary of the Monroe Doctrine, the declaration by President James Monroe that European countries that interfered with countries in the western hemisphere or established new colonies in it would meet with disapproval or worse from the American government. Conversely, the United States would not become involved in European politics.

On December 18, 1922, Walter Franklin Lineberger, a California representative in Congress, introduced legislation for the Monroe Doctrine Centennial commemorative half dollar, stating that the 1823 declaration had prevented France, England, and Russia from attempting to obtain California from Mexico, which controlled the territory at the time. Addressing the coinage proposal, Senator Frank Greene of Vermont (a state which was to have its own commemorative coinage in a few years) commented sarcastically: "It seems to me that the question is not one of selling a coin at a particular value or a particular place. The question is whether the United States government is going to go on from year to year submitting its coinage to this—well—harlotry."

This and other objections notwithstanding, on January 24, 1923, Congress authorized the coinage of not more than 300,000 silver 50-cent pieces.

The Design
Chester Beach, a well-known artist and medalist, was selected to prepare the models for the half dollar. The obverse depicted the conjoined portraits of presidents James Monroe and John Quincy Adams, both of whom were instrumental in formulating the Monroe Doctrine.

The reverse was a copy of a medal created by Ralph Beck in 1899 (and copyrighted that year) for the seal of the 1901 Pan-American Exposition in Buffalo. It showed the continents of North and South America as symbolic female figures having the outlines of the two land masses, a motif suggested by James Earle Fraser, who acted as an advisor. Beck protested what seemed to be obvious plagiarism of his 1901 medal, but Fraser brushed off the accusation by stating that he had not seen Mr. Beck's design earlier. A comparison of the 1901 and 1923 designs, however, shows that this was highly unlikely.

The reverse inscription bore the prominent notation MONROE DOCTRINE CENTENNIAL and LOS ANGELES around the border. Any historian familiar with the Monroe Doctrine must have scratched his head in puzzlement at the contrived connection with this particular city! The design was executed in shallow relief, with the result that newly minted coins had an insipid appearance. Few if any observers called them attractive.

Production and Distribution
In May and June 1923, 274,077 Monroe Doctrine half dollars were struck and subsequently sent to the Los Angeles Clearing House. The coins were offered for $1 each and were distributed through banks, by mail, and other means, but not significantly through the so-called First Annual American Historical Revue and Motion Picture Industry Exposition, an event which history seems to have forgotten.

While it is certain that thousands of pieces were sold at a premium for $1 each, by and large the sales effort was a failure, and soon nearly all went into circulation at face value, a situation which certainly gained no friends among those who had paid $1 each for specimens.

Key to Collecting
Today the majority of 1923 Monroe Doctrine Centennial half dollars show evidence of friction or wear. Mint State examples are not particularly difficult to find, although most of them have technical grades in the MS-60 to MS-63 range. Evaluating the numerical grade of such pieces is difficult, for even the finest preserved coins are weakly defined because of the design and have a generally unsatisfactory appearance. Inspection under low magnification usually shows nicks and graininess at the highest point of the obverse of the center, from the original planchet.

Like the 1926 Sesquicentennial half dollar, the 1923 Monroe half is an aesthetic disaster. Just pick out an acceptable one (you will never find a beautiful one) and then go on to seek the next coin needed in your collection. Many have been doctored and artificially toned, after which they have been certified at high grades and sold for high prices. Avoid these like the plague. Find one that is brilliant or very lightly toned. For my money, an MS-63 or 64 coin, cherrypicked for quality (such as it is), would do nicely.

(1924) HUGUENOT-WALLOON TERCENTENARY HALF DOLLARS

Distribution
142,080

Whitman Coin Guide (WCG™)—1924 Huguenot-Walloon Tercentenary 50¢

MS-60	MS-63	MS-64	MS-65	MS-66	MS-67	MS-68
$175	$200	$280	$575	$1,185	$4,048	

CERTIFIED POPULATIONS

MS-60	MS-61	MS-62	MS-63	MS-64	MS-65	MS-66	MS-67	MS-68
54	54	327	1,191	2,623	1,714	567	65	0

Points of Interest: The obverse portraits were irrelevant to the event commemorated.

Subject of Commemoration: The 300th anniversary of the settling of New Netherland, the Middle States, in 1624, by Walloons, French and Belgian Huguenots, under the Dutch West India Company.

Designs: *Obverse*—Portraits representing Admiral Gaspard de Coligny (1519–1572; who died 52 years before the settlement in question!) and William the Silent (1533–1584; first stadtholder of the Netherlands, who had also been dead for a long while by the time of the 1624 settlement). *Reverse*—The ship *Nieuw Nederland*. George T. Morgan prepared the models for both sides, modifications by James Earle Fraser.

Mintage and Melting Data: Authorized February 26, 1923. *Maximum authorized—300,000. Number minted* (including 80 assay coins)—142,080. *Net distribution*—142,080.

Original Cost and Issuer: $1. Huguenot-Walloon New Netherland Commission, Inc., and designated outlets.

Illogical Portraits

In the year 1624 a group of Walloons (Lowlands Calvinists) sailed from Holland aboard the *Nieuw Nederland* to make a settlement in New York. Two years later the Dutch West India Company installed Peter Minuit as director of the American colony.

Sensing an opportunity three centuries later, an outfit known as the Huguenot-Walloon New Netherland Commission, chaired by Rev. Dr. John Baer Stoudt, associated with the Federal Council of Churches of Christ in America, secured congressional approval to issue 300,000 commemorative coins as a fund-raising venture in connection with the 300th anniversary of the early settlement. Planning well in advance, the group assisted in the formulation of legislation that became a reality on February 26, 1923. Almost immediately, opponents pointed out that for the government to issue coins to raise funds for a church group was a violation of the First Amendmer tion, which mandates the separation of church and state, and was the tional. Such protests, however, went unheeded in Washington.

To help sales, the proponents of the issue enlisted the person the the most prominent in numismatics at the time: Moritz Wormser, pre: Of the 142,080 Huguenot-Walloon half dollars struck at the Philadelphia Mint in February and April 1924, it is believed the best part of 87,000 were sold for $1 each to the public, although quantities remained on hand for several years afterward. Numismatic interest was low at the time, and despite the Wormser cachet, not much notice was taken of them. A report that 55,000 pieces went back to the Treasury Department and were placed into circulation must be discounted, because very few worn pieces are known.

Key to Collecting

Examples are readily available. The typical specimen is apt to be graded in the MS-60 to 63 range with MS-64 and 65 pieces being readily obtainable as well. MS-66 coins are scarcer. Relatively few worn pieces exist. Friction and contact marks are sometimes seen on the cheek of Admiral Coligny on the obverse, and on the masts and ship's rigging on the reverse. Many coins have been cleaned or repeatedly dipped. Beware deeply toned or stained coins, many of which are in slabs with high numerical grades. Uncirculated coins usually have satiny (rather than deeply lustrous or frosty) surfaces and may have a gray appearance. High in the reverse field of most coins is a "bright" spot interrupting the luster, from a touch of polish in the die.

(1925) CALIFORNIA DIAMOND JUBILEE HALF DOLLARS

Distribution
86,594

Whitman Coin Guide (WCG™)—1925 California Diamond Jubilee 50¢

MS-60	MS-63	MS-64	MS-65	MS-66	MS-67	MS-68
$250	$350	$530	$1,265	$1,860	$3,245	$19,250

CERTIFIED POPULATIONS

MS-60	MS-61	MS-62	MS-63	MS-64	MS-65	MS-66	MS-67	MS-68
124	160	748	1,734	2,543	1,430	641	211	16

Points of Interest: The grizzly bear shown on the reverse is the state emblem of California.

Subject of Commemoration: The 75th anniversary of California statehood.

Designs: *Obverse*—Kneeling miner washing placer gold with a pan. *Reverse*—Grizzly bear, as taken from the Bear Flag. Designed by Jo Mora.

Mintage and Melting Data: Authorized February 24, 1925, part of the act also providing for the 1925 Fort Vancouver and 1927 Vermont half dollar. *Maximum authorized*— 300,000. *Number minted* (including 200 assay coins)—150,200. *Number melted*—63,606. *Net distribution*—86,594.

Cost and Issuer: $1. Sold by the San Francisco Citizens' Committee through an Francisco Clearing House Association and the Los Angeles Clearing House.

California Celebrates an Anniversary

The year 1925 represented the 75th anniversary of the admission of the State of California to the Union. Prior to statehood, California had been explored and settled by the Spanish and had been a part of Mexico. Following the termination of hostilities in the Mexican War, Mexico ceded California to the United States for $15 million under terms of the Treaty of Guadalupe Hidalgo. The January 1848 discovery of gold by James W. Marshall at Sutter's Mill on the American River set the stage for the famous Gold Rush.

By the end of 1849 the white population of California had increased by tens of thousands of inhabitants, many of whom had come from the East by ship or overland by wagon. Following organizational activities in early autumn of that year, the state government began operation on December 20, 1849. The so-called Bear Flag, depicting a grizzly bear, was adopted (taken from a design devised in 1846, when in the Bear Flag Revolt a group of Americans seized the Presidio at Sonoma and forced the surrender of General Vallejo). Following an application filed on March 12, 1850, the Republic of California, as it was called, joined the Union on September 9.

An Attractive Commemorative

The Act of February 24, 1925, provided for up to 300,000 half dollars to be minted to observe the anniversary. Joseph (Jo) Mora, an artist who lived in the seaside town of Carmel, was tapped to create the designs. Evocative of the Gold Rush, the obverse depicted a Forty Niner panning for gold, while the reverse displayed a grizzly bear.

James Earle Fraser, representing the Commission of Fine Arts, took exception to the design, calling the whole thing "inexperienced and amateurish," and recommended that a better-known sculptor Chester Beach or Robert Aitken redo the work, possibly incorporating as the design "something which would be far more interesting and with a bigger sense of what California really is."

The San Francisco Citizens' Committee, which had the final say, wisely ignored Fraser's criticism, and the design became a reality. In the 1930s David M. Bullowa, who studied the commemorative series on behalf of the American Numismatic Society, paid Jo Mora's design this tribute: "A very virile and well executed half dollar, in which obverse and reverse are definitely related to each other." Elsewhere in the numismatic community it was widely praised.

In his 1971 study, *Numismatic Art in America*, Cornelius Vermeule called the design "One of America's greatest works of numismatic art."

Between August 1 and 26, 1925, a quantity of 150,200 California Diamond Jubilee half dollars was struck at the San Francisco Mint. Offered for $1 each through the San Francisco Clearing House Association and the Los Angeles Clearing House (the latter having had some experience in the field through the earlier disbursement of the 1923 Monroe half dollars), the coins were also marketed at a pageant held in San Francisco from September 6 to 12. Quantities remained unsold, and when all was said and done, 63,606 California Diamond Jubilee half dollars were returned to the Mint to be melted.

Key to Collecting

The California Diamond Jubilee half dollar remains a great favorite with collectors today. The design is such that even a small amount of handling produces friction on the shoulder and high parts of the bear, in particular, with the result that examples today are rare in higher numerical levels of Mint State. Most seen are apt to grade AU-55 to MS-62. This issue exists in two finishes—frosty or lustrous finish like or prooflike," the second being rarer. The frosty finish pieces display some definition of the details. On the other hand, the prooflike pieces have heavily br highly polished dies.[9] The issue has always been popular with the collecting comm

Many slabbed specimens in high technical grades are toned, sometimes deeply that evidence of friction (if it exists) is masked. On the obverse, check the miner's slee (and sometimes other shirt areas), and in particular on the reverse, check the shoulder and other body parts of the grizzly bear. No matter what high grade may be assigned, coins without any traces of friction are rarities today.

(1925) FORT VANCOUVER CENTENNIAL HALF DOLLARS

Distribution
14,994

Whitman Coin Guide (WCG™)—1925 Fort Vancouver Centennial 50¢

MS-60	MS-63	MS-64	MS-65	MS-66	MS-67	MS-68
$450	$550	$660	$1,630	$2,500	$5,694	$22,000

CERTIFIED POPULATIONS

MS-60	MS-61	MS-62	MS-63	MS-64	MS-65	MS-66	MS-67	MS-68
52	61	365	1,083	1,974	1,257	385	62	1

PF-60	PF-61	PF-62	PF-63	PF-64	PF-65	PF-66	PF-67	PF-68
0	0	0	0	0	0	1	0	0

Points of Interest: Struck at the San Francisco Mint, but the S mintmark was omitted in error.

Subject of Commemoration: Centennial of the founding of Fort Vancouver, Washington.

Designs: *Obverse*—Portrait of Dr. John McLoughlin. *Reverse*—Diorama of Fort Vancouver. Laura Gardin Fraser developed designs by Sidney Bell (who adapted a portrait of McLoughlin by John T. Urquhart).

Mintage and Melting Data: Authorized February 24, 1925. *Maximum authorized*— 300,000. *Number minted* (including 28 assay coins)—50,028. *Number melted*—35,034. *Net distribution*—14,994.

Original Cost and Issuer: $1. The Fort Vancouver Centennial Corporation, Vancouver, Washington.

Frontier Fort Commemorated

The 1925 Fort Vancouver Centennial half dollar was authorized on February 24, 1925, as part of the same legislation which made possible the California Diamond Jubilee and Vermont-Bennington halves. The coin observed the 100th anniversary of the founding of Fort Vancouver, Washington by Dr. John McLoughlin in 1825, an event of regional interest at best.

an by training, became associated with the North West
oup that was active throughout the Pacific Northwest. In
n arranging a merger between the North West Company
mpany. In 1825, acting on behalf of the Hudson's Bay
blished Fort Vancouver, a fortified outpost that served as
rotection for about 1,000 white settlers who traded with
ns in the territory. McLoughlin set all of the rules for the
iron hand. Later, in 1842, McLoughlin founded Oregon
...y in the same area. This settlement soon became the main destination for travelers
over the Oregon Trail.

Sidney Bell, a Portland, Oregon artist, was selected to prepare designs for the half
dollar, which he did by adapting art from other sources. The models were made by the
talented Laura Gardin Fraser. Although up to 300,000 pieces were authorized, by
August 1, 1925, only 50,028 had been struck at the San Francisco Mint. By error, the
S mintmark was omitted. As part of the publicity, the entire shipment of half dollars,
weighing 1,462 pounds (including packing material), was delivered by air on August 1.
Pilot Oakley G. Kelly, starting in Vancouver at 5:15 am, headed to San Francisco,
picked up the coins, and was back in Vancouver at 6:15 pm. In a 12-cylinder DeHavil-
land he made the round trip of 1,100 miles in 10 hours and 55 minutes of flying time,
punctuated by two stops for gas and extra time for a diversion to Portland to circle
around the *Journal* building.

Sales at $1 per coin in August and September, and also during the week-long Fort
Vancouver Centennial celebration which began on August 17, 1925, included limited
shipments by mail to collectors. Interest was lukewarm at best, and 35,034 coins were
returned to the San Francisco Mint to be melted.

Key to Collecting

The design of the Fort Vancouver Centennial half dollar was such that even a small
amount of handling produced friction on the higher spots, with the result today that
higher Mint State level coins are rare. In 1980 Anthony Swiatek estimated that fewer
than 300 choice Mint State coins survived, "the remaining thousands being barely Mint
State or sliders or worse, many poorly cleaned."[10] In 1982 a small hoard of about 500
pieces created excitement and greatly added to the supply of Mint State pieces in collectors' hands. Still, true Mint State coins are rare.

When contemplating a coin for purchase, check the obverse portrait, for it nearly
always shows evidence of friction and handling, often on coins certified in high grades.

(1925) Lexington-Concord
Sesquicentennial Half Dollars

Distribution
162,013

Whitman Coin Guide (WCG™)—1925 Lexington-Concord Sesquicentennial 50¢

MS-60	MS-63	MS-64	MS-65	MS-66	MS-67	MS-68
$125	$150	$200	$600	$1,760	$19,470	$66,000

CERTIFIED POPULATIONS

MS-60	MS-61	MS-62	MS-63	MS-64	MS-65	MS-66	MS-67	MS-68
74	108	547	1,800	3,224	1,489	351	16	1

Points of Interest: This was one of the few events of truly national significance to be commemorated on a coin in the 1920s up to this date. Sculptor James Earle Fraser of the Commission of Fine Arts approved Chester Beach's designs for the coins, but protested that the local committees had made a poor choice of subject matter.

Subject of Commemoration: The sesquicentennial (150th anniversary) of the Battle of Lexington and Concord, which took place in Massachusetts between American patriots and British soldiers on April 19, 1775, one day after Paul Revere's famous ride.

Designs: *Obverse—Minute Man* statue by Daniel Chester French, erected in Concord. *Reverse*—the Old Belfry in Lexington, which alerted the Minute Men to action in 1775. Models made by Chester Beach.

Mintage and Melting Data: Authorized January 14, 1925. *Maximum authorized—* 300,000. *Number minted* (including 99 assay coins)—162,099. *Number melted*—86. *Net distribution*—162,013.

Original Cost and Issuer: $1. U.S. Lexington-Concord Sesquicentennial Commission, through local banks.

A Popular Coin for an Important Anniversary

Few would question the appropriateness of issuing a commemorative half dollar to mark the sesquicentennial (150th anniversary) of the Battle of Lexington and Concord, which took place in Massachusetts between American patriots and British soldiers on April 19, 1775—the day after Paul Revere's famous ride. Resentment against the British culminated in "the shot heard around the world," igniting the spark for American independence.

As the time for the 150th anniversary of the battle drew near, separate committees from Lexington and Concord endeavored in 1923 to have a commemorative coin made. Unknown to each other, both contacted Chester Beach to do the work. Beach agreed, and suggested that each town pay half of his $1,250 fee. The Concord group had charge of the obverse design and selected the famous *Minute Man* statue by Daniel Chester French; the reverse motif was the purview of the Lexington committee, which chose a Lexington landmark, the Old Belfry (which had been destroyed in 1909).

During April and May 1925, at the Philadelphia Mint, 162,099 dollars were struck. The coins were shipped to Massachusetts where they were encased in small wooden boxes with slide covers and distributed for $1 per coin by the Concord National Bank and the Lexington Trust Company.

The Sesquicentennial festivities were held from April 18 to 20, 1925, during which time approximately 60,000 half dollars were sold as souvenirs, with 39,000 finding buyers in Lexington and 21,000 in Concord. In addition, the coins were sold throughout New England and, to a lesser extent, in other areas of the United States. Most went to the general public rather than to numismatists. When all was said and done, virtually the entire coinage was sold. A paltry 86 coins were returned to the Mint for melting, and one suspects that these may have been defective pieces rather than unsold surplus, or they may have been Assay Commission coins. The public spent thousands of the coins after their novelty had passed, accounting for the availability of worn examples today. These half dollars were well received by numismatists, and no controversy ever arose concerning them.

Key to Collecting

Today examples are readily obtained in all grades with the majority of pieces being in high AU or low Mint State categories. MS-65 coins are scarce in comparison to those in MS-60 through MS-64 levels. When buying, look for friction on the legs of the Minute Man on the obverse and, in particular, on the corner of the Old Belfry on the reverse. Some specimens are deeply frosty and lustrous, whereas others have partially prooflike fields. Eye appeal can vary widely.

(1925) STONE MOUNTAIN MEMORIAL HALF DOLLARS

Distribution
1,314,709

Whitman Coin Guide (WCG™)—1925 Stone Mountain Memorial 50¢

MS-60	MS-63	MS-64	MS-65	MS-66	MS-67	MS-68
$80	$100	$120	$300	$540	$1,624	$26,400

CERTIFIED POPULATIONS

MS-60	MS-61	MS-62	MS-63	MS-64	MS-65	MS-66	MS-67	MS-68
113	280	1,254	4,377	5,317	3,553	1,146	270	15

Points of Interest: The memory of President Warren G. Harding, mentioned in the original legislation, was not reflected on the coin. The vast quantity of 5,000,000 authorized was the largest since the Columbian Exposition coins of 1892–1893.

Subject of Commemoration: The carved memorial to the soldiers of the South on Stone Mountain, and the memory of Warren G. Harding.

Designs: *Obverse*—Generals Lee and Jackson on horseback. *Reverse*—An eagle perched on a cliff. The models were prepared by Gutzon Borglum, sculptor of the Stone Mountain Memorial, and later Mount Rushmore.

Mintage and Melting Data: *Maximum authorized*—5,000,000. *Number minted* (including 4,709 assay coins)—2,314,709. *Number melted*—1,000,000. *Net distribution*—1,314,709.

Original Cost and Issuer: $1. Sold by the Stone Mountain Confederate Monumental Association through many outlets, including promotions involving pieces counter-stamped with abbreviations for Southern sates.

A Monument in Stone

Located about 15 miles northeast of Atlanta, Georgia, Stone Mountain is one of the largest known visible deposits of solid granite. Measuring 867 feet high and nearly a mile wide, the site is eminently suited for a sculpture. Although the idea had been considered earlier, it was not until 1915 that a number of Southerners took action to create a monument to the leaders of the fallen but not forgotten Confederate States of America. They invited sculptor Gutzon Borglum to visit the site to give his opinion about carving a tablet, bust of Robert E. Lee, or some other modest monument measuring perhaps 20 feet square. Borglum is said to have stated that such a small carving would be like putting a postage stamp on the side of a barn. Ideas of grandeur swept through the sculptor's mind, and within a matter of days he envisioned a grandiose pageant of multiple Southern leaders sculpted in stone. Despite the absence of a formal contract, the artist drew plans in his Stamford, Connecticut studio during the following winter, proposing an ambitious carving 200 feet high and 1,300 feet wide. A formal dedication of the project took place in May 1916. Under a donor agreement with Samuel H. Venable and members of his family, owners of Stone Mountain, the project was to be completed in 12 years, or the title would revert to them.

In 1917 preliminary work began by cutting access steps into the rock, but the efforts were cut short with the entry of America into the World War and were not resumed until June 18, 1923, when Borglum began carving General Lee's figure, as part of a group that would also include Stonewall Jackson, Jefferson Davis, and other heroes of the South. Outlines from the artist's plans were projected from glass slides onto the rock face at night, and an assistant in a sling seat painted white guidelines for the workmen to follow. Borglum's original plan envisioned a three-part project, including sculptures of Confederate heroes cut into the mountainside, the Memorial Hall cut from rock at the base of the mountain, and an Amphitheatre. After an estimate of $3.5 million was presented, the project was scaled down considerably.

Commemorative Half Dollars

Work continued, and on January 19, 1924, the dedication of the upper part of General Lee took place with about 10,000 onlookers. By that time it was envisioned that the project would be completed by profits from the sale of commemorative half dollars. On March 17 of the same year, Congress passed an act authorizing up to five million such coins. The authorization was to honor Southern heroes (specific mention of the Civil War was omitted), and, to gain votes from Northern legislators, to honor the memory of the President Warren G. Harding, who had died in 1923. Soon, scandals relating to the Harding administration dominated national news, and afterward he was forgotten, as were sketches showing his portrait to be placed on the reverse of the coin. Borglum reveled in the publicity the monument and the proposed coins brought to him. He went to Washington to meet with congressmen, promoting his ideas—including raising the issue price of the coins from $1 to $5 to permit 10,000 acres of land to be obtained for an even grander project.

The first coins were struck on January 21, 1925, on the 101st anniversary of General "Stonewall" Jackson's birth. One thousand pieces were struck on a medal press. These went to dignitaries and others involved with the project.

In the meantime the Stone Mountain Confederate Monumental Association was short of money, due to funds being secretly spent by president Hollins N. Randolph on personal expenses not related to carving the monument. Borglum's bills went unpaid. A standoff ensued, with the Association complaining about Borglum, and vice-versa. Almost everyone took the side of the Association. Borglum was fired. The artist destroyed all his models and drawings, precipitating indictments, arrest warrants, and lawsuits.

In the meantime, the marketing of the commemorative half dollars took many forms. Several corporations including the Baltimore & Ohio Railroad, Southern Fireman's Fund Insurance Company, and the Coca-Cola Company purchased quantities. Bernard Baruch (a well-known investor and later advisor to American presidents) was named honorary chairman of a committee in New York City assigned to sell 250,000 Stone Mountain half dollars, and showed his spirit by personally signing up for 1,000 coins. Additional quantities were made available to banks across the nation through the Federal Reserve system.

An early brochure noted:

> The money to finance the monument is being raised by the sale of Confederate Memorial half dollars, by Founders Roll contributions of $1,000 each, by Children's Founders Roll contributions of $1, and by other ways and means. . . . The governors of Virginia, South Carolina, Georgia, Florida, Alabama, Mississippi, Louisiana, Texas, Oklahoma, Arkansas, Kentucky, and Tennessee have each assumed a quota calculated on the basis of white [sic] population and bank deposits, and each governor has pledged his state to take his quota.

Despite intense marketing efforts—the widest in the history of any coin in the 1892–1954 Classic Era of commemoratives—sales fell far short of expectations. Of the five million anticipated, only 1,314,709 were ever distributed.

Later History

The association hired Augustus H. Lukeman, a well-known sculptor, to take on the work (in 1934 Lukeman would design the Boone Bicentennial half dollar). The work by Lukeman gathered mixed reviews as to its quality, but was abandoned in 1928 when funds ran out. By this time the peculations of association president Randolph had been revealed. An October 1, 1928, article in the New York *Herald Tribune* reported that the association's financial predicament had deteriorated so far that there was no money left and that Lukeman's bust of General Lee, which cost the association $1,421,665, was unrecognizable.

Over the next several years, calls were made for Borglum to return to the project, but by that time he was busy carving the Mount Rushmore (South Dakota) Memorial. Title to Stone Mountain reverted to the Venable family. In 1958 the Georgia Legislature funded the purchase of Stone Mountain and 3,200 acres of adjacent land from the Venable family. Walker Kirkland Hancock, a Gloucester, Massachusetts sculptor, was hired to develop plans for continuing the carving project as a scaled-down version of Lukeman's concept.

The finished carving, consisting of Lee, Davis, and Jackson, measures 90 feet high by 190 feet wide, is in relief extending more than 11 feet from the matrix, and is approximately 400 feet above the base of the mountain. Formal dedication took place on May 9, 1970.

Key to Collecting

This is the most plentiful commemorative from the 1920s. Examples are readily obtainable from lightly worn grades through gem Mint State. Many have outstanding eye appeal.

When buying, check the high points of the figures of the generals on the obverse and the eagle's breast on the reverse for friction and/or evidence of contact marks. The typical coin has very lustrous and frosty surfaces, although the somewhat satiny.

(1926) SESQUICENTENNIAL OF AMERICAN INDEPENDENCE COMMEMORATIVES

Distribution
Half dollar:
141,120
Gold $2.50:
46,019

MS64

Whitman Coin Guide (WCG™)—1926 Sesquicentennial of American Indep 50¢

MS-60	MS-63	MS-64	MS-65	MS-66	MS-67	MS-68
$115	$200	$635	$4,600	$28,105	$29,700	

CERTIFIED POPULATIONS

MS-60	MS-61	MS-62	MS-63	MS-64	MS-65	MS-66	MS-67	MS-68
144	134	803	1,972	3,299	403	20	0	0

1926 Sesquicentennial of American Independence Gold $2.50

MS-60	MS-63	MS-64	MS-65	MS-66	MS-67	MS-68
$600	$950	$1,755	$4,815	$20,720	$58,300	

CERTIFIED POPULATIONS

MS-60	MS-61	MS-62	MS-63	MS-64	MS-65	MS-66	MS-67	MS-68
208	608	2,225	3,322	5,584	1,828	150	3	0
PF-60	PF-61	PF-62	PF-63	PF-64	PF-65	PF-66	PF-67	PF-68
0	0	0	0	0	1	0	0	0

Points of Interest: Both denominations were struck in low relief. The half dollar in particular is usually unattractive when seen today. Neither was popular at the time of issue. President Coolidge, shown on the half dollar, was living at the time. Other than his being in office when the coin was made, he had no connection with the history or significance of the issue.

Subject of Commemoration: The 150th anniversary of the signing of the Declaration of Independence.

Designs: Half dollar: *Obverse*—Conjoined portraits of Washington and current President Calvin Coolidge. *Reverse*—The Liberty Bell. Designed by John Frederick Lewis and modeled by Chief Engraver John R. Sinnock. **$2.50 gold:** *Obverse*—Miss Liberty standing, holding in one hand a scroll representing the Declaration of Independence (incorrectly scaled) and in the other, the Torch of Freedom. *Reverse*—Front view of Independence Hall in Philadelphia. Designed by John R. Sinnock.

Mintage and Melting Data: Authorized on March 23, 1925. **Half dollar:** *Maximum authorized*—1,000,000. *Number minted* (including 528 assay coins)—1,000,528. *Number melted*—859,408. *Net distribution*—141,120. **Gold $2.50:** *Maximum authorized*—200,000. *Number minted* (including 226 assay coins)—200,226. *Number melted*—154,207. *Net distribution*—46,019.

Cost and Issuer: Half dollar: $1. Gold $2.50: $4. National Sesquicentennial
on Association.

Coins for an Exposition

There is no doubt that the 150th anniversary of American independence was an event
worthy of commemoration on coins. To observe the occasion, Congress authorized the
coinage of not more than one million silver half dollars and not more than 200,000 gold
$2.50 pieces for the National Sesquicentennial Exhibition Association. The term *exhi-
bition*, used in the original Congressional legislation, was taken from the 1876 Centennial Exhibition held in Philadelphia 50 years earlier. When the 1926 event took place,
it was primarily designated as the Sesquicentennial *Exposition*, although the *exhibition*
word crept into some publicity.

The original bill for the coins, before emendation, provided for the production of a
unique denomination, the $1.50 gold piece, which was later deleted from the request.
The Association had also hoped to have an expanded series of coins utilizing designs
representing different periods in the growth of the United States—for example, the
original colonies, the Louisiana Purchase, California and Texas accessions, etc. Unfortunately for numismatic posterity, this illustrious series never came to pass.

The exposition opened in Philadelphia on June 1, 1926, although many exhibits
were not yet in place and much work remained unfinished—and continued until closing
day on November 30th. On view were many artistic, cultural, scientific, and commercial displays, partially financed by $5 million worth of bonds floated by the City of
Philadelphia. The Palace of Agriculture and Food Products and the Palace of Liberal
Arts were two of the larger structures.

As it did not attract national attention or support, the fair was a commercial failure,
and most firms reported that the sales and publicity generated did not repay the expenses
involved—although nearly six million people passed through the entrance gates.

Design and Distribution

John Sinnock, chief engraver at the Mint, was named to create the designs for the two
approved commemorative coin denominations, but his proposal for the half dollar was
unsatisfactory to the National Sesquicentennial Exhibition Association. Design ideas in
the form of sketches submitted by attorney John Frederick Lewis, a prominent local
patron of the arts, were accepted and sent to Sinnock for translation to models. At the
insistence of the association, the designs were executed in very shallow relief, with the
result that the pieces struck up poorly.

Anticipating an enthusiastic reception, the Association caused the Mint to strike
1,000,528 half dollars during the months of May and June, 1926, beginning with an
inaugural striking ceremony on May 19, at which Philadelphia Mayor Kendrick produced the first coin. Relatively few people cared to part with the required $1 to pur-
chase a commemorative half dollar (or $4 for a quarter eagle). When all was said and
done, the staggering quantity of 859,408 half dollars went back to the Mint to be
melted! Collectors condemned the coin for its shallow features and perceived the
design as uninteresting.

The quarter eagle was created by Sinnock from his own sketches. The obverse motif
depicted Miss Liberty standing, wearing a gown, with a large torch in her right hand and
with drapery over her left shoulder and right forearm. A close-fitting cloth cap is on her
head. In her left hand is a scroll said to represent the Declaration of Independence (but
not of the correct proportions to depict this famous document). The reverse shows

Independence Hall in Philadelphia, of a design quite similar to that on the 1776–1976 Bicentennial half dollar. The dies for the Sesq eagle were executed in unsatisfactory low relief with the result that often indistinct in areas. On the reverse there is a feature in the field what like a fingerprint but which represents rays of the sun.

In May and June 1926, 200,226 Sesquicentennial quarter eagle Philadelphia Mint, the odd 226 being for assay purposes. These failed to stir buyer interest. Later, 154,207 quarter eagles (more than three quarters of the entire mintage) went to the melting pot, thus drawing the curtain on the last of the early United States commemorative gold coins. No new commemorative gold coins were to be produced until more than a half century later in 1984.

Key to Collecting

For certain, most present buyers of the 1926 Sesquicentennial half dollar acquire an example simply because it is needed for completion of a collection. On its own it seems to share the booby prize for ugliness with the 1923 Monroe Centennial half dollar, this being an opinion voiced by numismatists over a long period of time. B. Max Mehl commented, "Personally, I think it is one of the poorest designed and struck coins of the entire series. . . ."

That said, when you are confronted with the opportunity to buy one, accurate grading can be a problem. Many examples certified at high grades have mottled or deeply toned surfaces—precluding examination—and others have been recolored. Most have graininess on the highest part of the portrait, reflecting marks from the original planchet. It may be the case that buying a coin certified any higher than MS-64 or 65 is a waste of money. One in either of those grades, if cherrypicked for strike and eye appeal, is often more attractive than a pricey MS-67 or higher coin with toning.

The quarter eagle has its own problems. Nearly all show evidence of handling and contact from careless production at the Mint, and from later indifference by the public who bought them. Most coins range from higher AU grades to lower Mint State classifications, AU-55 to MS-62, and have scattered marks in the fields. MS-65 examples are rare. Well-struck coins in higher Mint State levels are seldom seen, although in other grades the issue remains as the most plentiful survivor of the various gold commemoratives minted during the 1903–1926 span. Take out your magnifying glass and use it when buying. Also, avoid pieces with copper stains.

(1926–1939) OREGON TRAIL MEMORIAL HALF DOLLARS

MS 66

Distribution

1926: 47,955; 1926-S: 83,055
1928: 6,028
1933-D: 5,008
1934-D: 7,006
1936: 10,006; 1936-S: 5,006
1937-D: 12,008
1938: 6,006; 1938-D: 6,005;
        1938-S: 6,006
1939: 3,004; 1939-D, 3,004;
        1939-S: 3,005

Coin Guide (WCG™)—1926 Oregon Trail Memorial 50¢

	MS-63	MS-64	MS-65	MS-66	MS-67	MS-68
$200	$220	$230	$350	$590	$2,235	$11,000

CERTIFIED POPULATIONS

MS-60	MS-61	MS-62	MS-63	MS-64	MS-65	MS-66	MS-67	MS-68
16	14	129	596	1,662	1,241	524	89	7
PF-60	PF-61	PF-62	PF-63	PF-64	PF-65	PF-66	PF-67	PF-68
0	0	0	0	0	1	0	0	0

1926-S Oregon Trail Memorial 50¢

MS-60	MS-63	MS-64	MS-65	MS-66	MS-67	MS-68
$200	$215	$235	$350	$590	$1,555	$9,350

CERTIFIED POPULATIONS

MS-60	MS-61	MS-62	MS-63	MS-64	MS-65	MS-66	MS-67	MS-68
47	60	216	815	1,945	1,629	788	198	10

1928 Oregon Trail Memorial 50¢

MS-60	MS-63	MS-64	MS-65	MS-66	MS-67	MS-68
$240	$286	$320	$410	$570	$1,969	

CERTIFIED POPULATIONS

MS-60	MS-61	MS-62	MS-63	MS-64	MS-65	MS-66	MS-67	MS-68
7	4	30	182	711	946	700	121	3

1933-D Oregon Trail Memorial 50¢

MS-60	MS-63	MS-64	MS-65	MS-66	MS-67	MS-68
$400	$420	$450	$600	$965	$2,110	

CERTIFIED POPULATIONS

MS-60	MS-61	MS-62	MS-63	MS-64	MS-65	MS-66	MS-67	MS-68
1	0	12	160	792	1,064	490	77	2

1934-D Oregon Trail Memorial 50¢

MS-60	MS-63	MS-64	MS-65	MS-66	MS-67	MS-68
$220	$255	$265	$400	$840	$2,575	

CERTIFIED POPULATIONS

MS-60	MS-61	MS-62	MS-63	MS-64	MS-65	MS-66	MS-67	MS-68
6	2	25	302	1,265	1,228	409	50	0

1936 Oregon Trail Memorial 50¢

MS-60	MS-63	MS-64	MS-65	MS-66	MS-67	MS-68
$200	$225	$250	$350	$415	$800	$13,750

CERTIFIED POPULATIONS

MS-60	MS-61	MS-62	MS-63	MS-64	MS-65	MS-66	MS-67	MS-68
5	5	29	232	891	1,266	855	230	4

1936-S Oregon Trail Memorial 50¢

MS-60	MS-63	MS-64	MS-65	MS-66	MS-67	MS-68
$200	$230	$270	$380	$585	$1,155	$13,200

CERTIFIED POPULATIONS

MS-60	MS-61	MS-62	MS-63	MS-64	MS-65	MS-66	MS-67	MS-68
6	4	32	193	473	772	716	225	13

1937-D Oregon Trail Memorial 50¢

MS-60	MS-63	MS-64	MS-65	MS-66	MS-67	MS-68
$215	$230	$250	$330	$415	$750	$3,080

CERTIFIED POPULATIONS

MS-60	MS-61	MS-62	MS-63	MS-64	MS-65	MS-66	MS-67	MS-68
6	0	36	183	621	1,372	1,822	895	80

1938 Oregon Trail Memorial 50¢

MS-60	MS-63	MS-64	MS-65	MS-66	MS-67	MS-68
$200	$225	$245	$370	$484	$1,130	$16,500

CERTIFIED POPULATIONS

MS-60	MS-61	MS-62	MS-63	MS-64	MS-65	MS-66	MS-67	MS-68
9	2	23	190	655	1,024	710	140	5

1938-D Oregon Trail Memorial 50¢

MS-60	MS-63	MS-64	MS-65	MS-66	MS-67	MS-68
$200	$225	$255	$370	$484	$782	$5,225

CERTIFIED POPULATIONS

MS-60	MS-61	MS-62	MS-63	MS-64	MS-65	MS-66	MS-67	MS-68
6	0	14	152	461	953	1,060	265	55

1938-S Oregon Trail Memorial 50¢

MS-60	MS-63	MS-64	MS-65	MS-66	MS-67	MS-68
$200	$225	$250	$370	$484	$935	$8,250

CERTIFIED POPULATIONS

MS-60	MS-61	MS-62	MS-63	MS-64	MS-65	MS-66	MS-67	MS-68
7	2	36	180	596	970	839	220	27

1939 Oregon Trail Memorial 50¢

MS-60	MS-63	MS-64	MS-65	MS-66	MS-67	MS-68
$580	$600	$620	$735	$855	$1,680	$13,200

CERTIFIED POPULATIONS

MS-60	MS-61	MS-62	MS-63	MS-64	MS-65	MS-66	MS-67	MS-68
2	4	15	117	346	573	500	140	8

1939-D Oregon Trail Memorial 50¢

MS-60	MS-63	MS-64	MS-65	MS-66	MS-67	MS-68
$600	$625	$650	$735	$840	$1,100	$4,675

CERTIFIED POPULATIONS

MS-60	MS-61	MS-62	MS-63	MS-64	MS-65	MS-66	MS-67	MS-68
4	3	31	98	304	510	554	268	20

1939-S Oregon Trail Memorial 50¢

MS-60	MS-63	MS-64	MS-65	MS-66	MS-67	MS-68
$600	$625	$650	$735	$870	$1,400	$5,500

CERTIFIED POPULATIONS

MS-60	MS-61	MS-62	MS-63	MS-64	MS-65	MS-66	MS-67	MS-68
4	1	23	130	338	571	484	144	14-

Points of Interest: This is the longest-running series of commemorative coins.

Subject of Commemoration: The Oregon Trail and the pioneers who traversed it during the early 19th century.

Designs: *Obverse:* Standing Indian with U.S. map in background. *Reverse:* Conestoga wagon heading west. *Designers:* James Earle Fraser and Laura Gardin Fraser.

Mintage and Melting Data: *Maximum authorized*—6,000,000 (for the entire series). **1926:** *Number minted* (including 30 assay coins)—48,030. *Number melted*—75 (defective coins). *Net distribution*—47,955. **1926-S:** *Number minted* (including 55 assay coins)—100,055. *Number melted*—17,000. *Net distribution*—83,055. **1928:** *Number minted* (including 28 assay coins)—50,028. *Number melted*—44,000. *Net distribution*—6,028. **1933-D:** *Number minted* (including unrecorded number of assay coins)—5,250. *Number* *melted*—242 (probably defective coins). *Net distribution*—5,008. **1934-D:** *Number minted* (including 6 assay coins)—7,006. *Net distribution*—7,006. **1936:** *Number minted* (including 6 assay coins)—10,006. *Net distribution*—10,006. **1936-S:** *Number minted* (including 6 assay coins)—5,006. *Net distribution*—5,006. **1937-D:** *Number minted* (including 8 assay coins)—12,008. *Net distribution*—12,008. **1938 P-D-S:** *Number minted* (including 6, 5, and 6 assay coins)—6,006, 6,005, 6,006. *Net distribution*—6,006, 6,005, 6,006. **1939 P-D-S:** *Number minted* (including 4, 4, and 5 assay coins)—3,004, 3,004, 3,005. *Net distribution*—3,004, 3,004, 3,005.

Original Cost and Issuer: $1. (See below for increases.) Oregon Trail Memorial Association, Inc., sold through Scott Stamp & Coin Co., Inc., some sold through Whitman Centennial, Inc., Walla Walla, Washington. 1937 onward distributed by the Oregon Trail Memorial Association, Inc.

A Long, Long Trail

The Oregon Trail Memorial Association, Inc., a New York corporation, secured the approval on May 17, 1926, of a Congressional resolution authorizing:

> The coinage of 50-cent pieces in commemoration of the heroism of the fathers and mothers who traversed the Oregon Trail to the far West with great hardship, daring, and loss of life, which not only resulted in adding new states to the Union but earned a well-deserved and imperishable fame for the pioneers; to honor the twenty thousand dead that lie buried in unknown graves along two thousand miles of that great highway of history; to rescue the various important points along the old trail from oblivion; and to commemorate by suitable monuments, memorial or otherwise, the tragic events associated with that emigration—erecting them either along the trail itself or elsewhere, in localities appropriate for the purpose, including the city of Washington.

Congress further authorized the unprecedented quantity of "not more than six million" coins, with no statement of when or where they should be minted.

On the surface the motivation seemed to be good enough, for by 1926 the Oregon Trail was well known in history and legend, and doubtless many American citizens had family ties to the famous migration along that route.

Laura Gardin Fraser, by then the grand lady of commemorative half dollar art, designed the obverse, and her sculptor husband James Earle Fraser designed the reverse. Mrs. Fraser did the models for both sides. The die hubs were the work of the Medallic Art Company of New York, which by this time had been an important player on the commemorative scene for years.

The obverse depicted a relief map of the United States behind the figure of an Indian facing to the viewer's right, a bow (spanning the continent) in his right hand and his left hand outstretched. The reverse depicted a Conestoga wagon drawn by two oxen, heading to the left toward a setting sun of monumental proportions, with resplendent rays.

Which side is the obverse of the Oregon Trail half dollar and which is the reverse has been a matter of debate among numismatists. The Frasers considered the Indian side the obverse and the wagon side the reverse, but Mint reports named the wagon side as the obverse, for it bears the date, and the Indian side the reverse, for it bears the mintmark (in instances of branch-mint issues).

Greed and Exploitation

Proponents of the issue were quick to realize that if varieties were created, the market could be expanded. In 1926 the Philadelphia Mint struck 48,030 pieces, followed soon thereafter by San Francisco Mint production of 100,055 coins, the first time that a single commemorative issue had been struck at more than one mint—setting a precedent which would be expanded and abused in the years to come.

The Oregon Trail Memorial Association offered the Philadelphia coins for $1 each, and sales got off to a good start. Aiding the promotional efforts was Ezra Meeker, a long-lived gentleman who had traveled the Oregon Trail in 1851, written several books and numerous articles about it, made numerous public appearances, and achieved renown as a living pioneer—after nearly all of his contemporaries had passed on. Nearly all of the coins were sold. The association requested an additional 100,000 pieces be struck at the San Francisco Mint, and this was done. Buyers, however, were satisfied by that time, and few new orders appeared. The coins remained in storage at the Mint, awaiting receipt of payment for them.

In the meantime, more greed had set in, and the association requested that more coins be struck, now with the date 1927. This was denied—yet somehow, the association wrangled the Philadelphia Mint into striking 50,028 coins dated 1928. Since thousands of 1926-S coins had not yet been paid for, the Treasury did not permit the 1928 pieces to be released. *Years* passed.

In 1933 the problem was solved, after a fashion, by melting 17,000 unsold specimens of the 1926-S coinage, enabling the 1928 coins to be released. The association found itself with some 1926, thousands of 1926-S, and tens of thousands of 1928 coins to sell. Coming to the rescue was the Scott Stamp & Coin Company of New York City, which agreed to market the issues under what it stated was an exclusive contract. Well-known numismatist Wayte Raymond, representing the Scott interests, suggested that the 1928 half dollars be made "rare" by melting all but 6,000 of them.

Raymond figured that if additional half dollars could be minted with the date 1933, these could be sold effectively at the Century of Progress Exposition to be held that year in Chicago. Scott, billing itself as "sole distributor of Oregon Trail half dollars," advertised in *The Numismatist*, September 1933:

> The Oregon Trail Memorial Association issues a new half dollar dated 1933 to commemorate the Century of Progress. 5,000 1933 half dollars were struck at the Denver Mint; 2,000 have been reserved for patriotic societies; 3,000 are offered to the public. 1928 Oregon Trail half dollars. None ever sold until this year. All of these coins, except 6,000 pieces, have been remelted by the U.S. Mint. We offer the 1928 and 1933 half dollars at $2.00 each. Postage and registration extra.

This represented the first time the Denver Mint produced commemoratives. Scott then planned other issues—in small quantities, so as to make them salable. In 1934 at the Denver Mint, 7,006 Oregon Trail half dollars were minted, followed by a Philadelphia coinage of 10,006 in 1936, and a San Francisco issue in the amount of 5,006 (also in 1936). In 1937, Oregon Trail halves were struck only at Denver, to the extent of 12,008. Up to this point, issue prices had been quite erratic. The 1926 and 1926-S pieces had been offered for $1 each. When Scott got into the act, the price was doubled; and the 1928 issue, released in 1933, went on the market at $2 per coin. Seeking to increase sales, and in view of the tremendous unsold quantity of 1928 issues, the 1933-D was pegged at a slightly lower $1.50. That didn't stimulate activity to the extent desired—so for the 1934-D the price was raised back to the $2 level. In due course, the issues of 1936 and 1937 were listed at $1.60 each.

Scott promoted and sold the Oregon Trail issues dated from 1928 through 1936, save for some quantities set aside by the original association for direct sale in bulk to historical societies. Apparently 1936 coins were sold by both the Scott Stamp & Coin Co. and the Oregon Trail Memorial Association—the latter doing business from a mail drop at 1775 Broadway, New York City.

1937, 1938, and 1939 Coins

Oregon Trail issues of 1937, 1938, and 1939 were marketed by the association, by which time the arrangement with Scott had been discontinued. In 1937, Oregon Trail half dollars were minted only at Denver, to the extent of 12,008 coins. These 1937-D pieces were offered for sale at $1.60 each.

In 1938, for the first time, Oregon half dollars were issued as a set from all three mints, with a coinage of 6,006 for Philadelphia, 6,005 for Denver, and 6,006 for San Francisco—the odd specimens being reserved for the Assay Commission. Sets of three were advertised for $6.25 each. The final and lowest mintage in the series consisted of 1939 sets of three pieces made to the extent of 3,004, 3,004, and 3,005, respectively, at the various mints. The price was raised to $7.50 per set.

By the end of 1939, more than a decade after the original coinage of 1926, only 264,419 Oregon Trail half dollars had been minted, and, deducting 61,317 returned for melting, just 202,928 had achieved distribution or were still on hand in the stocks of the Scott Stamp & Coin Company and the Oregon Trail Memorial Association. As late as 1943, an outfit named the American Pioneer Trails Association was attempting to sell quantities of 1936 and 1937-D halves.

Congress held hearings in 1939, and front row center in testimony were the abuses of the Oregon Trail coin issuers. Several observers later suggested that, if Congress on August 5, 1939, had not forbidden further issues of commemorative coins authorized prior to March 1939, Oregon Trail coins would probably still be minted today!

Key to Collecting

Despite their checkered background. Oregon Trail Memorial half dollars are eagerly sought by numismatists today. Some years ago, members of the Society for U.S. Commemorative Coins (SUSCC) voted this as their favorite design in the series. Most demand is for a single coin as a type, but a full collection of date and mintmark varieties can be acquired for relatively low expense. Although most of the later issues have low mintages, they are not rare in the marketplace, because most were originally sold to coin collectors and dealers. Likely, the general public bought very few.

Accordingly, most surviving coins are in varying degrees of Mint State. The quality of the surface finish on the various Oregon Trail issues varies, with earlier examples tending to be frosty and lustrous and later issues, particularly those dated 1938 and 1939, having somewhat grainy or satiny fields.

Grading this issue is tricky. Look for friction or contact marks on the high points of the Indian and the Conestoga wagon, but, more importantly, check both surfaces carefully for scattered cuts and marks. All three mints had difficulty in striking up the rims properly, causing many rejections. Those that passed muster and were shipped out usually had full rims, but it is best to check when buying.

(1927) VERMONT SESQUICENTENNIAL HALF DOLLARS

Distribution
28,142

Whitman Coin Guide (WCG™)—1927 Vermont Sesquicentennial 50¢

MS-60	MS-63	MS-64	MS-65	MS-66	MS-67	MS-68
$300	$330	$375	$1,005	$1,810	$4,445	

CERTIFIED POPULATIONS

MS-60	MS-61	MS-62	MS-63	MS-64	MS-65	MS-66	MS-67	MS-68
40	67	434	1,397	2,433	1,444	395	38	2

Points of Interest: The highest-relief design of any commemorative half dollar. The catamount pictured on the reverse is a reference to the Catamount Tavern, where the Green Mountain Boys quaffed ale.

Subject of Commemoration: The 150th anniversary of the Battle of Bennington and the independence of Vermont.

Designs: *Obverse*—Portrait of Ira Allen. *Reverse*—Catamount. Designed by Charles Keck, who also prepared the models.

Mintage and Melting Data: Authorized by the Act of February 24, 1925. *Maximum authorized*—40,000. *Number minted* (including 34 assay coins)—40,034. *Number melted*—11,892. *Net distribution*—28,142.

Original Cost and Issuer: $1. Vermont Sesquicentennial Commission (Bennington Battle Monument and Historical Association).

The Battle of Bennington Commemorated

The 150th anniversary of the independence of Vermont and the Battle of Bennington were commemorated by half dollars authorized by Congress two years in advance of the celebration on February 24, 1925, not to exceed 40,000 in quantity. This had been part of the enabling legislation that provided for the California Diamond Jubilee and Fort Vancouver half dollars. In its original form, the congressional bill (submitted on January 9, 1925) called for commemorative gold dollars and silver half dollars, but the provision for gold dollars was later dropped. It is perhaps a reflection of the conservative nature of Vermonters that the two senators from that state, Dale and Greene, requested that just 40,000 half dollars be struck—a very small authorization in this era. Undoubtedly, had they asked for 100,000 half dollars, this request would have been granted. The Vermont Sesquicentennial Commission intended that funds derived would benefit the study of history.

Although Vermont had been explored by French and British trappers and others in the 1600s, it was not until 1724 that the first permanent fort was erected in the area, a settlement by the British. Fifteen years later, Governor Benning Wentworth of New Hampshire asserted that the limits of his state extended to about 20 miles east of the general line described by the northward course of the Hudson River, including Vermont.

Governor George Clinton of New York took immediate exception to what he considered to be a brazen claim, and insisted that Vermont belonged to his state. Later British authorities resolved the dispute by awarding the land to New York.

Settlers in Vermont, most of whom felt greater allegiance to New Hampshire or believed that Vermont should be an independent area, resisted New York's claim. Ethan Allen (1739–1789) and Ira, his younger brother (1751–1814), formed a group of insurgents known as the Green Mountain Boys—"Vermont" being the French language equivalent of "green mountain." Soon thereafter the Revolutionary War erupted, and the Green Mountain Boys captured Fort Ticonderoga from the British. The boundary dispute with New York was set aside.

On January 15, 1777, at a meeting held in Windsor, a town in the eastern section of Vermont just across the Connecticut River from New Hampshire, Vermont declared its independence. On August 16, the Green Mountain Boys, by that time led by Captain John Stark and Colonel Seth Warner (a cousin of the Allens), together with New Hampshire militia and local citizens, overwhelmed and defeated a contingent of British forces (augmented by hired Hessian soldiers) at the Battle of Bennington. Vermont sought to become a state of the Union, but Congress did not approve. At one time negotiations were held with the British, and the possibility that Vermont might become a part of Canada was explored. Vermont did remain, however, an independent state until it finally joined the Union in 1791. In the meantime, it issued its own copper coinage dated from 1785 to 1788.

Ira Allen, who later was active in government, was influential in drafting Vermont's declaration as an independent state in 1777. Allen served in the General Assembly and was state treasurer 1778–1786. His gift of $4,000 established the University of Vermont.

Despite his recognition as the founder of Vermont, his life ended ignominiously. Following a purchase of arms from France for the State of Vermont in 1795, he sought to return with them to America. On the way back he was captured by the British, who accused him of supplying munitions to Ireland. Finally, in 1801, he returned to Vermont, where he found himself penniless and in danger of being thrown into debtors' prison because of tax deficiencies. Leaving the state which he founded, Ira fled to Philadelphia. His death occurred in January 1814, by which time his estate was valued at only $70.

Design, Minting, and Distribution

Sherry Fry, a New York sculptor whose work included a statue of Ira Allen on the campus of the University of Vermont and who had exhibited at the 1915 Panama-Pacific International Exposition (among many other places), was selected by the Vermont Sesquicentennial Commission to prepare designs for the new half dollar. Fry submitted a portrait of Ira Allen for the obverse and a representation of the Bennington Monument obelisk for the reverse. Her efforts were rejected. Subsequently, Charles Keck, who earlier designed the gold dollar for the Panama-Pacific International Exposition, was named as Fry's replacement. Keck suggested a different portrait of Ira Allen for the obverse and a depiction of the Catamount Tavern, a 1777 gathering spot for the Green Mountain boys, on the reverse. Operated by Stephen Fay and his sons Joseph and Jonas, the Catamount Tavern was a wooden building located on the crest of a small hill north of Bennington. A stuffed catamount (the Canada lynx, a large cat related to the puma and mountain lion) displayed on top of a 20-foot pole in front gave the tavern its name.

The Commission of Fine Arts felt that a building would not be appropriate for the reverse design, nor would the Bennington obelisk. The suggestion was made to John Spargo, chairman of the Vermont Sesquicentennial Commission, that an actual catamount or a motif depicting the trophies of battle (flags, arms, and regalia) would be more appropriate. Keck drew two sketches with catamounts and one with the implements of war. One of the catamount motifs was accepted.

Following the acceptance of his sketches, Keck created for the obverse an idealized portrait of Ira Allen in high relief, a visage different from that on Fry's statue. The reverse showed a large catlike animal of uncertain species, which had nothing to do with the history of Vermont being commemorated but was a rebus for the Catamount Tavern, a subtlety lost on just about everyone who saw it.

In January and February 1927, some 40,034 Vermont Sesquicentennial half dollars (called Battle of Bennington or Bennington half dollars in contemporary government correspondence) were struck at the Philadelphia Mint. The distribution was handled by a group titled the Bennington Battle Monument and Historical Association, which sold the pieces by mail, through banks, and elsewhere for $1 each. Sales were satisfactory but not up to expectations, and eventually 11,892 coins were returned for melting.

Key to Collecting

Vermont half dollars have always been popular with numismatists and are an integral part of many collections. The Vermont half dollar was struck in the highest relief of any commemorative issue. Despite the depth of the work in the dies, nearly all specimens were struck up properly and showed excellent detail. The prominence of the obverse portrait militated against the survival of pristine coins, and most show some evidence of contact at the central points.

Most of these are in MS-62 to MS-64 grades. Nearly all coins show some friction and evidence of handling on Ira Allen's cheek. Most coins are deeply lustrous and frosty. Avoid cleaned coins, which are often seen.

(1928) HAWAIIAN SESQUICENTENNIAL HALF DOLLARS

Distribution
9,958 Uncirculated and
50 Sand Blast Proof

Whitman Coin Guide (WCG™)—1928 Hawaiian Sesquicentennial 50¢

MS-60	MS-63	MS-64	MS-65	MS-66	MS-67	MS-68
$2,650	$3,550	$4,420	$7,300	$11,470	$42,053	

CERTIFIED POPULATIONS

MS-60	MS-61	MS-62	MS-63	MS-64	MS-65	MS-66	MS-67	MS-68
92	88	438	823	1,496	711	110	3	0
PF-60	PF-61	PF-62	PF-63	PF-64	PF-65	PF-66	PF-67	PF-68
0	1	4	4	14	4	2	0	0

Points of Interest: $2 was the highest issue price for any commemorative half dollar up to this time. Most were distributed in the Hawaiian Islands.

Subject of Commemoration: The 150th anniversary of Captain James Cook's landing in Hawaii.

Designs: *Obverse*—Portrait of Captain Cook. *Reverse*—Standing Hawaiian chieftain. Designed by Juliette May Fraser and modeled by Chester Beach.

Mintage and Melting Data: Authorized March 7, 1928. *Maximum authorized*—10,000. *Number minted* (including 8 assay coins)—10,008. *Net distribution*—10,008.

Original Cost and Issuer: $2. Captain Cook Sesquicentennial Commission, through the Bank of Hawaii, Ltd.

Hawaiian History

The year 1928 marked the 150th anniversary of the January 18, 1778 arrival of British explorer and navigator Captain James Cook at the Hawaiian Islands (at first and for a long time thereafter, called the Sandwich Islands in honor of the earl of Sandwich, a patron of Cook's voyage).

Captain James Cook, born in England on October 28, 1728, joined the Royal Navy in 1755 and eventually became one of the 18th century's most famous navigators. Following his exploration and charting of Newfoundland and the upper reaches of the St. Lawrence River, Cook took a group of scientists to the Pacific Ocean to study the predicted transit of Venus across the sun. During this and several other Pacific voyages, Cook carefully plotted the locations of many islands and laid to rest theories about an undiscovered large continent. On his fourth trip to the Pacific in January 1778, Cook "discovered" the Hawaiian Islands, possibly becoming the first white man to land there—although some historians have suggested that Spanish explorer Juan Gaetano had arrived there more than two centuries earlier, in 1555. Cook returned to Hawaii, where he was considered by the natives to be the white god Lona. He became involved in an altercation, the details of which are unknown, and was killed by natives on February 14, 1779.

The Half Dollar

In 1928 an effort was made to create a coin issue that would commemorate the 150th anniversary of Cook's landing—without the abuses that had characterized certain other issues of the decade. The enabling legislation, approved by Congress on March 7, 1928, provided for the modest coinage of 10,000 silver 50-cent pieces. A distribution commission was founded with Bruce Cartwright Jr., a well-known numismatist (and whose late father was also a collector of great prominence), at its head.

In a commentary to the editor of *The Numismatist*, published in the May 1928 issue, Cartwright explained the controlled distribution policy being considered. The commission set a price of $2 apiece and placed the Bank of Hawaii in charge of public sales. A small number of the 10,000-coin mintage would be set aside for those outside Hawaii who were interested, with approved dealers able to purchase up to 100 coins each. All profits would help form a collection of Captain Cook memorabilia for Hawaii. Well-known Honolulu artist Juliette May Fraser designed the coin with a profile bust of Captain Cook, flanked by the eight largest Hawaiian islands, on the obverse, and a Hawaiian warrior chief raising his hand in welcome on the reverse.

Sketches made by Fraser were sent to Chester Beach, who prepared the models, utilizing Miss Fraser's art and some suggestions for modifications made by the Mint and Congressman Victor S.K. Houston, after which dies were made. In keeping with practice at the time, the Medallic Art Company of New York City made the dies.

A Quick Sellout

In June 1928, 10,008 Hawaiian Sesquicentennial half dollars were struck at Philadelphia, the extra eight being reserved for assay. Of the production figure, 50 were Sandblast Proofs, made by a special process which imparted a dull, grainy finish to the pieces, similar to that used on certain Mint medals of the era as well as on gold Proof coins circa 1908–1915. Collectors considered the surface style to be quite unsatisfactory, but those at the Mint believed it to be artistic.

Distribution began through the Bank of Hawaii, Ltd. in Honolulu on October 8, 1928. Sales were brisk, and soon the supply was gone, just as Bruce Cartwright Jr. had predicted. It was intended that about half the pieces be reserved for residents of the Hawaiian Islands and the other half be distributed on the mainland, but in practice it is believed that most were distributed on the islands. Almost immediately pieces traded at a premium over the $2 issue price, despite the fact that the original price charged was the highest of any commemorative half dollar up to that time.

No controversy was associated with the authorization, the reason for creation, or the distribution of the 1928 Hawaiian Sesquicentennial half dollars, and the entire affair was a model of excellence. Many collectors wished that more had been struck, a radical departure from the oversupply of other issues of the decade, but perhaps this was balanced by the satisfaction of those who had the good fortune to obtain them at the $2 issue price and saw them rise steadily in value.

Key to Collecting
By all standards the 1928 Hawaiian Sesquicentennial half dollar is the most important single silver commemorative *type* or basic design from the standpoint of scarcity of available specimens. Examples are elusive in all grades and are highly prized. Today the majority of examples are in the range of AU-55 to MS-62 or slightly finer. Pieces in MS-65 or above are especially difficult to find.

Most examples show contact or friction on the higher areas of Captain Cook's portrait on the obverse and on the legs of the Hawaiian chieftain on the reverse. Some coins have a somewhat satiny surface, whereas others are lustrous and frosty. Many undipped pieces have a yellowish tint. Beware of coins which have been repeatedly dipped or cleaned. Problem-free examples are even rarer than the low mintage indicates.

Fake "Sandblast Proofs" exist; these are coins dipped in acid. Certification by a leading service is strongly recommended.

(1934) MARYLAND TERCENTENARY HALF DOLLARS
Distribution
25,015

Whitman Coin Guide (WCG™)—1934 Maryland Tercentenary 50¢

MS-60	MS-63	MS-64	MS-65	MS-66	MS-67	MS-68
$185	$210	$235	$405	$900	$3,179	

CERTIFIED POPULATIONS

MS-60	MS-61	MS-62	MS-63	MS-64	MS-65	MS-66	MS-67	MS-68
16	23	152	990	2,777	2,240	632	94	0
PF-60	PF-61	PF-62	PF-63	PF-64	PF-65	PF-66	PF-67	PF-68
0	0	1	0	0	0	0	0	0

Points of Interest: John Work Garrett, one of America's most prominent numismatists, helped the authorizing legislation gain passage.

Subject of Commemoration: The 300th anniversary of the founding of Maryland.

Designs: *Obverse*—Portrait of Cecil Calvert. *Reverse*—Maryland state seal including the motto FATTI MASCHII PAROLE FEMINE, which, translated from the Italian, means "deeds are manly, words womanly." Designed by Hans Schuler.

Mintage Data: Authorized May 9, 1934. *Maximum authorized*—25,000. *Number minted* (including 15 assay coins)—25,015. *Net distribution*—25,015.

Original Cost and Issuer: $1. Maryland Tercentenary Commission, various outlets.

The Founding of Maryland Commemorated

The 300th anniversary of the arrival in Maryland, in 1634, of colonist followers of Cecil Calvert, second Lord Baltimore, furnished the occasion for legislation (approved on May 9, 1934) making possible the coinage of 25,000 silver half dollars of appropriate design. Calvert sponsored the emigration of about 200 English colonists (who would form the first settlement in Maryland at St. Mary's) aboard the *Ark* and the *Dove* in 1633. Calvert himself never came to America.

John Work Garrett, distinguished American diplomat and well-known numismatist, was among the citizens of Maryland who endorsed the commemorative half dollar proposal on behalf of the Maryland Tercentenary Commission of Baltimore.

Design and Distribution

Hans Schuler, director of the Maryland Institute, designed the coins. Die work was done by the Medallic Art Company. The obverse features the portrait of Cecil Calvert. The reverse displays a representation of the arms of the State of Maryland.

In July 1934, the Philadelphia Mint struck the entire authorized issue, amounting to 25,000 pieces for distribution and 15 for assay. Details were given in a letter from the Commission to dealer (and commemorative coin distributor) L.W. Hoffecker, June 6, 1935:

> As you probably know we were granted an issue of 25,000 Maryland Tercentenary commemorative half dollars. They were all dated 1934 and all minted at the Mint in Philadelphia. The first 15,000 we sold at $1 plus postage straight, regardless of the amount ordered, but as sales slowed up somewhat and we were anxious to close the office, we made a special price of 85 cents each plus postage in lots of 200 or more up to 1,000, and 75 cents each plus postage in lots of 1,000 or more. Our first coins were received on July 10, 1934, and we disposed of the last one about the latter part of April 1935. Probably 15,000 of the issue were sold in small quantities—one to say 100, and they were scattered all over the United States.
>
> In the beginning 5,000 were purchased for Maryland banks, and just how the banks disposed of them we cannot say, but the 20,000 sold through the office went mostly to individual collectors, except the probable 8,000 sold at a discount to dealers.

The Maryland issuers were conservative for their time, created no special varieties for extra profit, and did their best to distribute the coinage in a proper manner. Relatively little commentary concerning Maryland half dollars appeared in the numismatic press.

Key to Collecting

The field of the Maryland half dollar has an unusual "rippled" appearance making it similar to a sculptured plaque. Thus nicks and other marks that would be visible on a coin with flat fields are not as readily noticed on this issue. Today most examples in collections are in the grade range of MS-62 to MS-64. MS-65 pieces, strictly graded, are quite elusive. Specimens exist struck from a reverse die broken from the right side of the shield to a point opposite the upper right of the 4 in the historical date 1634.

Nearly all specimens show flat striking and/or friction on the nose of Cecil Calvert. Friction is often seen on other areas of the portrait as well, and on the reverse, on the high parts of the central motif. This issue was not handled with care at the time of mintage and distribution, and nearly all show scattered contact marks.

(1934–1938) TEXAS CENTENNIAL OF INDEPENDENCE HALF DOLLARS

Distribution

1934: 61,463
1935: 9,996; 1935-D: 10,007;
        1935-S: 10,008
1936: 8,911; 1936-D: 9,039;
        1936-S: 9,055
1937: 6,571; 1937-D: 6,605;
        1937-S: 6,637
1938: 3,780; 1938-D: 3,775;
        1938-S: 3,814

Whitman Coin Guide (WCG™)—1934 Texas Centennial of Independence 50¢

MS-60	MS-63	MS-64	MS-65	MS-66	MS-67	MS-68
$150	$165	$200	$305	$385	$1,540	$16,500

CERTIFIED POPULATIONS

MS-60	MS-61	MS-62	MS-63	MS-64	MS-65	MS-66	MS-67	MS-68
4	24	132	589	1,935	1,761	599	70	1

1935 Texas Centennial of Independence 50¢

MS-60	MS-63	MS-64	MS-65	MS-66	MS-67	MS-68
$160	$190	$200	$325	$462	$690	$6,600

CERTIFIED POPULATIONS

MS-60	MS-61	MS-62	MS-63	MS-64	MS-65	MS-66	MS-67	MS-68
3	6	21	154	557	1,140	1,184	316	15

1935-D Texas Centennial of Independence 50¢

MS-60	MS-63	MS-64	MS-65	MS-66	MS-67	MS-68
$160	$190	$200	$325	$462	$690	$15,400

CERTIFIED POPULATIONS

MS-60	MS-61	MS-62	MS-63	MS-64	MS-65	MS-66	MS-67	MS-68
3	2	32	137	567	1,275	1,124	264	8

1935-S Texas Centennial of Independence 50¢

MS-60	MS-63	MS-64	MS-65	MS-66	MS-67	MS-68
$160	$190	$200	$325	$462	$965	$16,500

CERTIFIED POPULATIONS

MS-60	MS-61	MS-62	MS-63	MS-64	MS-65	MS-66	MS-67	MS-68
10	4	42	200	687	1,196	628	92	4

1936 Texas Centennial of Independence 50¢

MS-60	MS-63	MS-64	MS-65	MS-66	MS-67	MS-68
$160	$190	$200	$325	$462	$690	$7,150

CERTIFIED POPULATIONS

MS-60	MS-61	MS-62	MS-63	MS-64	MS-65	MS-66	MS-67	MS-68
7	3	21	141	657	1,262	925	175	11

1936-D Texas Centennial of Independence 50¢

MS-60	MS-63	MS-64	MS-65	MS-66	MS-67	MS-68
$160	$190	$200	$325	$462	$690	$5,500

CERTIFIED POPULATIONS

MS-60	MS-61	MS-62	MS-63	MS-64	MS-65	MS-66	MS-67	MS-68
7	3	23	127	499	1,089	1,378	452	17

1936-S Texas Centennial of Independence 50¢

MS-60	MS-63	MS-64	MS-65	MS-66	MS-67	MS-68
$160	$190	$200	$325	$462	$935	$16,500

CERTIFIED POPULATIONS

MS-60	MS-61	MS-62	MS-63	MS-64	MS-65	MS-66	MS-67	MS-68
10	5	27	131	638	1,245	769	98	3

1937 Texas Centennial of Independence 50¢

MS-60	MS-63	MS-64	MS-65	MS-66	MS-67	MS-68
$170	$200	$210	$355	$505	$715	$11,000

CERTIFIED POPULATIONS

MS-60	MS-61	MS-62	MS-63	MS-64	MS-65	MS-66	MS-67	MS-68
9	4	33	160	612	973	555	135	9

1937-D Texas Centennial of Independence 50¢

MS-60	MS-63	MS-64	MS-65	MS-66	MS-67	MS-68
$170	$200	$210	$355	$505	$690	$13,200

CERTIFIED POPULATIONS

MS-60	MS-61	MS-62	MS-63	MS-64	MS-65	MS-66	MS-67	MS-68
9	10	28	123	500	1,065	779	160	5

1937-S Texas Centennial of Independence 50¢

MS-60	MS-63	MS-64	MS-65	MS-66	MS-67	MS-68
$170	$200	$210	$360	$505	$990	

CERTIFIED POPULATIONS

MS-60	MS-61	MS-62	MS-63	MS-64	MS-65	MS-66	MS-67	MS-68
12	2	24	133	489	966	723	129	5

1938 Texas Centennial of Independence 50¢

MS-60	MS-63	MS-64	MS-65	MS-66	MS-67	MS-68
$275	$280	$310	$495	$710	$1,650	

CERTIFIED POPULATIONS

MS-60	MS-61	MS-62	MS-63	MS-64	MS-65	MS-66	MS-67	MS-68
4	2	32	187	483	620	329	60	1

1938-D Texas Centennial of Independence 50¢

MS-60	MS-63	MS-64	MS-65	MS-66	MS-67	MS-68
$250	$275	$305	$490	$705	$990	

CERTIFIED POPULATIONS

MS-60	MS-61	MS-62	MS-63	MS-64	MS-65	MS-66	MS-67	MS-68
4	1	29	140	364	674	486	125	4

1938-S Texas Centennial of Independence 50¢

MS-60	MS-63	MS-64	MS-65	MS-66	MS-67	MS-68
$250	$275	$305	$490	$705	$1,240	$16,500

CERTIFIED POPULATIONS

MS-60	MS-61	MS-62	MS-63	MS-64	MS-65	MS-66	MS-67	MS-68
5	4	24	130	394	664	491	105	9

Points of Interest: This is one of the most ornate designs in the entire commemorative series.

Subject of Commemoration: The 1936 centennial of Texas's admission into the Union.

Designs: *Obverse*—A perched eagle with star in background. *Reverse*—Kneeling goddess Victory and other elements representative of the history and tradition of Texas. Designed by Pompeo Coppini.

Mintage and Melting Data: Authorized June 15, 1933. *Maximum authorized—* 1,500,000 (maximum total for all coins in the series 1934 onward). **1934:** *Number minted* (including 113 assay coins)—205,113. *Number melted*—143,650. *Net distribution—* 61,463. **1935-P-D-S:** *Number minted* (including 8, 7, and 8 assay coins)—10,008, 10,007, 10,008. *Number melted*—12 Philadelphia (probably defective coins). *Net distribution*—9,996, 10,007, 10,008. **1936-P-D-S:** *Number minted* (including 8, 7, and 8 assay coins)—10,008, 10,007, 10,008. *Number melted*—12 Philadelphia (probably defective coins). *Net distribution*—9,996, 10,007, 10,008. **1937-P-D-S:** *Number minted* (including 5, 6, and 7 assay coins)—8,005, 8,006, 8,007. *Number melted*—1,434, 1,401, 1,370. *Net distribution*—6,571, 6,605, 6,637. **1938-P-D-S:** *Number minted* (including 5, 5, and 6 assay coins)—5,005, 5,005, 5,006. *Number melted*—1,225, 1,230, 1,192. *Net distribution*—3,780, 3,775, 3,814.

Original Cost and Issuer: 1934: $1. American Legion Texas Centennial Committee, Austin, Texas. **1935:** $1.50 each; $4.50 per set of three. Issuer as preceding. **1936:** $1.50 each; $4.50 per set of three. Texas Memorial Museum Centennial Coin Campaign. **1937:** $1.50 each; $4.50 per set of three. Issuer as preceding. **1938:** $2 per coin; $6 per set of three. Issuer as preceding.

Texas History Commemorated

Early in the administration of President Franklin Delano Roosevelt, on June 15, 1933, Congress passed an act to authorize the coinage of silver half dollars "in commemoration of the one hundredth anniversary in 1936 of the independence of Texas, and of the noble and heroic sacrifices of her pioneers, whose revered memory has been an inspiration to her sons and daughters during the past century." The legislation provided that no more than one and a half million pieces be created on behalf of the American Legion Texas Centennial Committee, located in Austin in that state.

The history of the State of Texas is rich and colorful. The year 1836 was especially important, because the siege of the Alamo in San Antonio took place in that year, followed by General Sam Houston's trapping of the hostile forces of Santa Anna at the Battle of San Jacinto on April 21, 1836. A few months later Texas became an independent republic.

Pompeo Coppini, a Texas sculptor who had maintained a studio in New York City since 1922, was selected to prepare designs for the new coins. Coppini's obverse depicted a large eagle perched on a branch, displayed against a five-pointed star in the background, with inscriptions surrounding—a departure from standard practice, for the eagle motif was traditionally reserved for the reverse of American coinage.

The reverse of the Texas Centennial half dollar was one of the most ornate created for a commemorative coin of this period. Within the confined space available, several highly detailed elements were presented including the winged, draped goddess Victory, kneeling slightly to the observer's right with an olive branch in her right hand, and with her left hand resting on a representation of the Alamo—the most famous shrine in Texas history. Above is the word LIBERTY on a scroll, behind which are six flags. Beneath the wingtips of Victory are two medallions depicting Texas heroes General Sam Houston and Stephen Austin.

Correspondence between Charles Moore of the Commission of Fine Arts and L.W. Robert of the Treasury Department indicates that in 1933, Moore disapproved of commemoratives in general and the proposed design of the Texas half dollar in particular. Addressing Robert, Moore protested that the design was a hodgepodge and that elements would "disappear." He urged an end to commemorative coins, calling participation in the money-making schemes undignified for the U.S. government.

Writing in *Numismatic Art in America* in 1971, Cornelius Vermeule gave a contrasting view of the Texas motif, calling it a "classic triumph of how much can be successfully crowded on a coin."

Celebrating the Centennial Early

The Centennial Committee intended to use the profits to help finance the 1936 Centennial Exposition, which eventually was held in Dallas on a 186-acre site at a cost of $25 million, attracting about seven million visitors. The idea of profits to be made from multiple issues was not lost on the Texas entrepreneurs. They began celebrating the centennial two years early, with the first issues produced in Philadelphia during October and November 1934, to the extent of 205,113 pieces. Examples were offered for sale for $1 each through the Centennial Committee. Distribution, which according to advance announcements was to commence in November, began in December 1934, primarily through Texas banks. At the outset sales were much lower than anticipated, and before additional varieties could be struck the Treasury Department insisted that the 1934 issue be paid for. This was not possible, so 143,650 coins were sent to the melting pot, perhaps indicating that the world did not need any more Texas Centennial half dollars.

The Centennial Committee felt differently, however, and in November 1935, 10,000 coins were struck at each of the Philadelphia, Denver, and San Francisco mints, plus a few additional specimens for assay purposes. The greed factor entered into play with the latest version of tapping collectors' bank accounts. In 1936, A. Garland Adair, chairman of the American Legion Texas Centennial Committee, influenced Senator John Connally to introduce a law to introduce five new designs for the coins (S. 3721). Testimony revealed that this would involve 15 Texas coins *each year*, if they were struck at each of the three mints.

By 1936, the half dollars were offered by 314 different banks in the state. Sales went on and on, with P-D-S sets minted each year through 1938. Interest declined steadily, and in the last year fewer than 4,000 sets were sold.

Although 304,000 pieces were coined for distribution during the 1938 series, plus a few additional coins for assay purposes, eventu... returned to the Treasury for melting. The net sale of the issue amou... seemingly an inefficient distribution—but one which raised little unfa... at the time among collectors.

Key to Collecting

Ever since the time of issue the Texas Centennial half dollars have remained popular with numismatists. Although there have been naysayers, the Texas design was and is considered to be attractive by many collectors, and a ready demand has always existed for nicely preserved specimens. Most coins in existence are in Mint State with the typical grade being MS-64 to 65.

For evidence of friction and/or contact marks, check the eagle's breast on the obverse, and on the reverse, the head and knee of Victory. Early issues are very lustrous and frosty, whereas those produced toward the end of the Texas series are more satiny than frosty.

(1934–1938) BOONE BICENTENNIAL HALF DOLLARS

Distribution

1934: 10,007
1935: 10,010; 1935-D: 5,005; 1935-S: 5,005
1935 "small 1934" P: 10,008; D: 2,003; S: 2,004
1936: 12,012; 1936-D: 5,005; 1936-S: 5,006
1937: 9,810; 1937-D: 2,506; 1937-S: 2,508
1938: 2,100; 1938-D: 2,100; 1938-S: 2,100

Whitman Coin Guide (WCG™)—1934 Boone Bicentennial 50¢

MS-60	MS-63	MS-64	MS-65	MS-66	MS-67	MS-68
$140	$150	$170	$305	$440	$1,628	

CERTIFIED POPULATIONS

MS-60	MS-61	MS-62	MS-63	MS-64	MS-65	MS-66	MS-67	MS-68
11	8	60	223	688	897	328	40	2

1935 Boone Bicentennial 50¢

MS-60	MS-63	MS-64	MS-65	MS-66	MS-67	MS-68
$130	$170	$200	$290	$425	$1,150	

CERTIFIED POPULATIONS

MS-60	MS-61	MS-62	MS-63	MS-64	MS-65	MS-66	MS-67	MS-68
13	3	66	325	828	887	331	50	0

1935-D Boone Bicentennial 50¢

MS-60	MS-63	MS-64	MS-65	MS-66	MS-67	MS-68
$180	$215	$250	$320	$755	$1,150	

CERTIFIED POPULATIONS

MS-60	MS-61	MS-62	MS-63	MS-64	MS-65	MS-66	MS-67	MS-68
4	0	19	105	260	355	241	98	11

Boone Bicentennial 50¢

MS-60	MS-63	MS-64	MS-65	MS-66	MS-67	MS-68
$180	$215	$250	$320	$755	$1,150	

CERTIFIED POPULATIONS

MS-60	MS-61	MS-62	MS-63	MS-64	MS-65	MS-66	MS-67	MS-68
5	9	32	200	599	468	163	12	0

1935 Small 1934 Boone Bicentennial 50¢

MS-60	MS-63	MS-64	MS-65	MS-66	MS-67	MS-68
$135	$170	$200	$290	$425	$1,150	

CERTIFIED POPULATIONS

MS-60	MS-61	MS-62	MS-63	MS-64	MS-65	MS-66	MS-67	MS-68
6	11	47	293	938	1,040	428	69	2

1935-D Small 1934 Boone Bicentennial 50¢

MS-60	MS-63	MS-64	MS-65	MS-66	MS-67	MS-68
$300	$375	$390	$580	$975	$2,580	

CERTIFIED POPULATIONS

MS-60	MS-61	MS-62	MS-63	MS-64	MS-65	MS-66	MS-67	MS-68
7	7	44	187	470	701	328	43	1

1935-S Small 1934 Boone Bicentennial 50¢

MS-60	MS-63	MS-64	MS-65	MS-66	MS-67	MS-68
$260	$300	$340	$580	$1,020	$2,855	$27,500

CERTIFIED POPULATIONS

MS-60	MS-61	MS-62	MS-63	MS-64	MS-65	MS-66	MS-67	MS-68
0	0	22	94	326	336	163	31	7

1936 Boone Bicentennial 50¢

MS-60	MS-63	MS-64	MS-65	MS-66	MS-67	MS-68
$130	$170	$200	$300	$425	$985	$19,250

CERTIFIED POPULATIONS

MS-60	MS-61	MS-62	MS-63	MS-64	MS-65	MS-66	MS-67	MS-68
14	4	83	338	1,095	1,131	476	88	3

1936-D Boone Bicentennial 50¢

MS-60	MS-63	MS-64	MS-65	MS-66	MS-67	MS-68
$170	$210	$250	$320	$540	$1,205	

CERTIFIED POPULATIONS

MS-60	MS-61	MS-62	MS-63	MS-64	MS-65	MS-66	MS-67	MS-68
5	1	19	162	588	787	362	27	0

1936-S Boone Bicentennial 50¢

MS-60	MS-63	MS-64	MS-65	MS-66	MS-67	MS-68
$170	$210	$250	$320	$495	$985	

CERTIFIED POPULATIONS

MS-60	MS-61	MS-62	MS-63	MS-64	MS-65	MS-66	MS-67	MS-68
1	4	22	164	484	753	381	64	1

1937 Boone Bicentennial 50¢

MS-60	MS-63	MS-64	MS-65	MS-66	MS-67	MS-68
$135	$200	$400	$410	$425	$985	$13,750

CERTIFIED POPULATIONS

MS-60	MS-61	MS-62	MS-63	MS-64	MS-65	MS-66	MS-67	MS-68
6	6	53	270	948	1,173	529	101	3

1937-D Boone Bicentennial 50¢

MS-60	MS-63	MS-64	MS-65	MS-66	MS-67	MS-68
$350	$360	$375	$505	$645	$1,260	$16,500

CERTIFIED POPULATIONS

MS-60	MS-61	MS-62	MS-63	MS-64	MS-65	MS-66	MS-67	MS-68
4	2	19	102	345	445	243	61	2

1937-S Boone Bicentennial 50¢

MS-60	MS-63	MS-64	MS-65	MS-66	MS-67	MS-68
$350	$360	$405	$550	$704	$1,620	$22,000

CERTIFIED POPULATIONS

MS-60	MS-61	MS-62	MS-63	MS-64	MS-65	MS-66	MS-67	MS-68
8	20	102	338	444	268	51	5	0

1938 Boone Bicentennial 50¢

MS-60	MS-63	MS-64	MS-65	MS-66	MS-67	MS-68
$370	$400	$410	$520	$865	$2,310	$27,500

CERTIFIED POPULATIONS

MS-60	MS-61	MS-62	MS-63	MS-64	MS-65	MS-66	MS-67	MS-68
3	4	17	85	310	416	181	17	1

1938-D Boone Bicentennial 50¢

MS-60	MS-63	MS-64	MS-65	MS-66	MS-67	MS-68
$370	$400	$415	$520	$842	$1,425	$15,950

CERTIFIED POPULATIONS

MS-60	MS-61	MS-62	MS-63	MS-64	MS-65	MS-66	MS-67	MS-68
4	2	15	76	273	384	253	66	2

1938-S Boone Bicentennial 50¢

MS-60	MS-63	MS-64	MS-65	MS-66	MS-67	MS-68
$370	$400	$410	$520	$900	$1,865	$33,000

CERTIFIED POPULATIONS

MS-60	MS-61	MS-62	MS-63	MS-64	MS-65	MS-66	MS-67	MS-68
3	3	21	114	335	320	195	49	2

Points of Interest: Of the many varieties of Boone Bicentennial half dollars made from 1934 to 1938, the 1934 is the only one with true bicentennial status.

Subject of Commemoration: The 200th anniversary of the birth of Daniel Boone, famous frontiersman, trapper, and explorer.

Designs: *Obverse*—Portrait of Daniel Boone, an artist's conception. *Reverse*—Standing figures of Boone and an Indian. Designed and modeled by Augustus Lukeman.

Mintage Data: Authorized May 26, 1934 and, with "1934" added to modify the design, on August 26, 1935. *Maximum authorized*—600,000 (for total of all issues 1934 and onward). **1934:** *Number minted* (including 7 assay coins)—10,007. *Net distribution*—10,007. **1935-P-D-S:** *Number minted* (including 10, 5, and 5 assay coins): 10,010, 5,005, 5,005. Net distribution: 10,010, 5,005, 5,005. **1935 "small 1934" P-D-S:** *Number minted* (including 8 assay coins)—10,008, 2,003, 2,004. *Net distribution*—10,008. **1936-P-D-S:** *Number minted* (including 12, 5, and 6 assay coins)—12,012 5,005, 5,006. *Net distribution*—12,012, 5,005, 5,006. **1937-P-D-S:** *Number minted* (including 10, 6, and 6 assay coins)—15,010, 7,506, 5,006. Number melted: 5,200, 5,000, 2,500. *Net distribution*—9,810, 2,506, 2,506. **1938-P-D-S:** *Number minted* (including 5, 5, and 6 assay coins)—5,005, 5,005, 5,006. Number melted: 2,905, 2,905, 2,906. *Net distribution*—2,100, 2,100, 2,100.

Original Cost and Issuer: 1934: $1.60. **1935:** $1.10 for the Philadelphia issue; $1.60 each for the Denver and San Francisco coins. **1935 "small 1934":** $1.10 (raised to $1.60 on December 21, 1935); Denver and San Francisco $3.70 per pair. **1936:** $1.10 Philadelphia; $1.60 each Denver and San Francisco. **1937:** Philadelphia $1.60 singly; later as a pair with a Denver coin for $7.25 (Denver coins were not offered singly); P-D-S sets $12.40; San Francisco coins singly $5.15. **1938 P-D-S:** $6.50 per set of three. Daniel Boone Bicentennial Commission (and its division, the Pioneer National Monument Association), Phoenix Hotel, Lexington, Kentucky (C. Frank Dunn, "sole distributor").

Origin of the Boone Half Dollars

The 200th anniversary of the birth of Daniel Boone, famous frontiersman, trapper, and explorer, furnished the occasion for the most flagrant abuse of commemorative coins seen in the series. The Daniel Boone Bicentennial Commission, located in Lexington, Kentucky, ostensibly desired to raise money in coordination with a group known as the American Order of Pioneers, Inc., with the approval of Boone's descendants, to restore several historical sites pertaining to the famous frontiersman. Legislation passed on May 26, 1934 provided for the coinage of 600,000 silver half dollars.

The subject being commemorated, Daniel Boone, was born in 1734 near Reading, Pennsylvania and by 1752 had moved to North Carolina. He became an explorer and hunter on the frontier. In the late 1760s Boone explored Kentucky, and in March 1775 he and 30 others cut the Wilderness Road from the eastern region of Tennessee to the Kentucky River, at which point the settlement of Boonesborough was established. During the Revolutionary War Boone was captured by Indians and turned over to the British authorities in Detroit. Released back into the custody of the Indians, he was adopted as a son of Shawnee Chief Black Fish and was given the name of Big Turtle. While thus engaged, Boone learned of a strategy between the British and Indians, who intended to seize Boonesborough. Boone escaped in time to travel 160 miles by foot and warn the Boonesborough settlers, thus allowing them to prepare for the attack. After a series of incidents, Chief Black Fish came to believe that Boone had supernatural powers and opted for peace. In later years, Boone moved several times and served in several sessions of the Virginia legislature. Boone's skirmishes with Indians and his activities in the Revolution, discussed only briefly here, made him an American folk hero.

The Design

Augustus Lukeman, the New York sculptor who had taken the place of Gutzon Borglum in the carving of the epic memorial on Stone Mountain in Georgia in 1925, was selected to prepare the models for the Boone half dollar. Depicted on the obverse is the bust of a young man said to represent Boone—an artist's conception, for no original portrait is known to exist of the pioneer. (Another depiction of Boone is found on the 1921 Missouri half dollar, and an 1834 artist's conception by Chester Harding is in the National Portrait Gallery.) The reverse shows Shawnee Chief Black Fish standing with Daniel Boone, who holds in one hand a peace treaty and in the other a musket.

Correspondence preserved in the National Archives reveals that Lukeman's designs sparked a bitter debate between the artist and C. Frank Dunn, secretary of the Boone Bicentennial Commission, who had examined the models and stated them to be "historically impossible." Supporting Dunn was the Boone Family Association, which requested that the Commission of Fine Arts fire Lukeman and select another artist. This the Commission refused to do, and over a period of time the Boone faction and Lukeman worked out a few compromises—not to the complete satisfaction of anyone. The controversies surrounding the design were soon forgotten and indeed were never prominent in the numismatic press.

Distribution Begins

Although the legislation provided that 600,000 Boone Bicentennial half dollars be struck, it was somewhat curious that in October 1934 the entire first issue amounted to just 10,007 pieces, obviously a portent of the future. The pieces were shipped to Kentucky, where C. Frank Dunn, operating from an office on the second floor of the Phoenix Hotel in Lexington, dutifully set about selling as many as he could for the issue price of $1.60 each. Those not sold were simply kept on hand. There was no particular stir about them made in the numismatic community.

In 1935 the exploitation of collectors began, seemingly in an innocent way, when 10,010 pieces were struck in Philadelphia in March and 5,005 each at the Denver and San Francisco mints in May. These were dated 1935 on the reverse of the coin, representing the issue date. Philadelphia coins were offered for $1.10 each, and $1.50 was charged for each Denver and San Francisco coin. A 1935 Boone set of three coins cost a total of $4.10. So far the only problem was that it was no longer the bicentennial of Boone's birthday, and there was no reason to continue celebrating a 1934 anniversary in 1935. (Of course, in some people's minds this was reason enough to mount the charge of exploitation.) More was to come, however.

Strange Happenings

Dunn was well connected in Congress. Legislation approved on August 26, 1935, read as follows:

> That, inasmuch as the annual change in coinage date required by law has caused the removal of the commemorative date of 1934 from the design originally approved and in use for the coinage of the 50-cent pieces commemorating the two hundredth anniversary of the birth of Daniel Boone . . . it is hereby authorized to supplement said design so that the reverse of said 50-cent piece will show the figures "1934" immediately above the words "PIONEER YEAR."

Although 1935 Boone sets of three coins had already been produced during the year, in October 1935 at the Philadelphia Mint 10,008 more 1935-dated Boone half dollars were made but with the addition of the date 1934 in small numerals on the right side of the reverse. In November the Denver and San Francisco mints produced the very small quantity of just 2,003 and 2,004, respectively, of this new variety. News releases calling attention to the rare issues were sent out by Dunn. New York City newspapers, among others, carried the information that a pair of low-mintage Boone half dollars had been created at the Denver and San Francisco mints and could be ordered for $3.70 by sending remittances to Dunn.

Detail of the 1935-S Boone with small "1934" added in the field to the right.

In a quarter-page advertisement on page 905 of the December 1935 issue of *The Numismatist,* Dunn offered the new issues for sale at $1.10 for the Philadelphia coin ("will advance December 21 to $1.60 . . . if any are left") and a new high price of $3.70 for the rare Denver and San Francisco pair, for a total of $4.80 (although they were never sold as a set of three). The 1935-D and S coins with "small 1934" were sold only as a separate pair. Collectors who thought that their collections were complete were greeted with the news that they weren't.

Dunn stated that so many orders had been received as a result of advance newspaper notices that by the time collectors were generally aware of the coins through advertisements in *The Numismatist* and elsewhere, the entire limited issue had been sold out. So far as is known, not a single person who responded to the advertisement in *The Numismatist* was able to secure a set at the issue price of $3.70!

Indeed only a few collectors obtained the coins from *any* source. Writing in the *Numismatic Scrapbook*, May 1936, editor and owner Lee F. Hewitt commented:

> Many collectors do not believe that all the "famous 2,000 issue Boones" were distributed. Most of the correspondents on the subject have placed the number mailed between 500 and 1,000 sets. New York and Chicago represent approximately 20% of the nation's collectors. Twenty-eight sets have been located in New York and 11 sets here in Chicago.

On the market the low-mintage Boone pair immediately jumped to $25, then to the $50 level! In the $50 range some sets just happened to be available through dealers, and C. Frank Dunn just happened to be able to "buy some sets from earlier purchasers who wanted a profit," so the story went. Less charitable was the allegation that Dunn had secretly reserved many 1935 with "small 1934" pairs, quite possibly the majority of them, which he later sold privately under the guise that he had purchased them on the aftermarket.

Veteran dealer Abe Kosoff stated in later years that Dunn's scheme consisted of having two offices on the second floor of the Phoenix Hotel, one being the official Boone sales office and the other being his private office down the hall, the latter place being the location for many special deals.

Collectors who had endeavored to order the 1935 "small 1934" pair for $3.70 to complete their sets—but who had their remittances returned—were angered when they found that their only alternative was to pay dealers $50 or even up to $100.

The Numismatist, January 1936, printed a two-page letter from Dunn, dated December 16, 1935, in which he endeavored to explain away the situation by stating that he simply had received more orders than he could handle. He referred to the coins as "Frankensteins" (monsters of one's own making).

A poignant commentary concerning the Boone sets was submitted by Charles M. Prager to *The Numismatist*, October 1936:

> A centennial celebration is, after all, a birthday party. And isn't it queer when a birthday party lasts three years? It would seem to indicate the host is doggone hungry. . . . If Daniel Boone were alive today, he could learn plenty about trapping. . . . There is not much danger of commemorative half dollars being counterfeited these days. It's so much simpler to apply to Congress and get out an issue of your own.

Details of the Boone controversy appeared in letters and articles in *The Numismatist* throughout the year 1936. In brief, wounded would-be buyers justifiably complained about the inequities of the situation, whereas C. Frank Dunn issued pious pronouncements about how fair he was, and continued to be, and that he was simply caught in the middle of the distribution of an issue of commemorative coins that had become more popular than he or anyone else had anticipated. In view of threatened lawsuits, Dunn secretly transferred many assets to his wife's name.

After-Effects

The 1935 "small 1934" Boone situation had a dramatic and immediate impact on the coin collecting fraternity. Numismatics would never be the same.

First, a number of other enterprising individuals and commissions considering the issuance of new commemorative half dollars immediately contemplated the profits to be made if the appearance could be given that an issue was sold out, thereby causing the price to rise on the collectors' market. Quantities held back could then be parceled out for profits far beyond the amounts originally thought possible.

Second, collectors, dealers, and speculators (the term *investors* was not as popular then) immediately determined that, if they missed out on the 1935 "small 1934" Boone issues at the original price, this was certainly not going to happen with other issues, so not only would they order one piece for a collection, they would also order many extras for investment purposes.

More Boone Varieties

Undaunted by the wave of overwhelmingly unfavorable publicity, C. Frank Dunn proceeded full speed ahead, after 1935, to order more varieties from the Treasury Department. The year 1936 saw the creation of 12,012 Philadelphia Mint coins, offered for $1.10 each, and 5,005 Denver and 5,006 San Francisco pieces offered for $1.60 each. Because of left-over demand from earlier issues, and the enthusiastic nature of the commemorative market in general during the first part of 1936, all of the 1936 pieces found buyers.

The story was different in 1937, when the mintage of Philadelphia coins was 15,010 pieces, Denver 7,506 coins, and San Francisco 5,006 examples. Eventually quantities of 5,200, 5,000, and 2,500, respectively, were melted of the three issues. In an effort to stimulate demand, several marketing strategies were tried.

Dunn publicly stated that 1937 would see the last of the Boone issues, implying that collectors would do well to complete their sets by ordering those currently offered. But he did not keep his promise. In 1938 the Daniel Boone Bicentennial Commission ordered more coins from the Treasury, and 5,005, 5,005, and 5,006, respectively, were struck at the Philadelphia, Denver, and San Francisco mints. Seeking to do something to stimulate flagging sales, and probably with the expectation that Boone sets would be issued for many years thereafter if only the market could be counted upon, Dunn resorted to an age-old stratagem: discounting. The price of a set of three coins was nearly halved from the year before, and the 1938 sets were offered for $6.50 each.

The effort to sell 1938-dated sets proved largely a failure, for the commemorative market was moribund, there were far more dissatisfied collectors than there were enthusiastic buyers, and, in any event, Dunn's reputation had sunk to the level of despicability. Only 2,100 1938 sets were eventually distributed, and it seems that a number of these were wholesaled through dealers. Many thousands of unsold 1938-dated Boone half dollars were melted.

Of the total of 600,000 Boone half dollars authorized by Congress early in the game, only 86,600 saw distribution—another sorry tale. Relatively few Boone half dollars were ever sold to the general public. From beginning to end, the Boone half dollars were made for the exploitation of the collectors' market.

Key to Collecting

Today Boone coins are highly prized in view of the restricted distribution of certain issues, particularly the famous 1935 Denver and San Francisco coins with "small 1934" and the 1938 set of three pieces. While most collectors desire but a single Boone to illustrate the type, there are enough specialists who want one of each date and mintmark to ensure a ready market whenever the scarcer sets come up for sale.

Most surviving Boone coins are in varying degrees of Mint State with MS-64 to 66 pieces readily available for most issues. Early issues in the series are characterized by deep frosty mint luster, whereas issues toward the end of the run, particularly 1937 and 1938, often are seen with a satin finish and relatively little luster (because of the methods of die preparation and striking). The 1937-S is very often seen with prooflike surfaces. Until recent years these did not attract much attention, but now certain of them have been certified in holders as "PL," and the situation has changed. The 1938-S is occasionally encountered with a prooflike surface.

In general, these were carefully handled at the time of minting and distribution, but scattered marks are often seen, particularly on the portrait of Boone on the obverse. On the reverse, the left shoulder of the Indian is a point where friction is sometimes seen.

(1935) CONNECTICUT TERCENTENARY HALF DOLLARS

Distribution
25,018

Whitman Coin Guide (WCG™)—1935 Connecticut Tercentenary 50¢

MS-60	MS-63	MS-64	MS-65	MS-66	MS-67	MS-68
$290	$325	$405	$615	$1,265	$3,311	$27,500

CERTIFIED POPULATIONS

MS-60	MS-61	MS-62	MS-63	MS-64	MS-65	MS-66	MS-67	MS-68
33	54	280	1,102	2,533	2,161	767	89	2
PF-60	PF-61	PF-62	PF-63	PF-64	PF-65	PF-66	PF-67	PF-68
0	0	0	0	0	1	0	0	0

Points of Interest: On the obverse the leaves were engraved at various angles, giving a "windblown" effect when the coin is turned. The modernistic eagle design on the reverse was later adopted by Henry G. Kreis for use on the 1936 Bridgeport half dollar.

Subject of Commemoration: 300th anniversary of the founding of Connecticut.

Designs: *Obverse*—Modernistic eagle. *Reverse*—Charter Oak. Designed by Henry Kreis.

Mintage Data: Authorized June 21, 1934. *Maximum authorized*—25,000. *Number minted* (including 18 assay coins)—25,018. *Net distribution*—25,018.

Original Cost and Issuer: $1. Connecticut Tercentenary Commission.

A Commemorative for Connecticut

The year 1935 marked the 300th anniversary of the founding of the colony of Connecticut. On June 21, 1934, President Franklin D. Roosevelt approved an act of Congress

providing for 25,000 silver half dollars of appropriate design. S
was selected to prepare the models under the supervision of Pau
medalist of the era.

The obverse design was adapted from an 1855 painting
Brownell owned by the Connecticut Historical Society that depi
the most prominent icon in Connecticut history, a tree in which e
their royal charter when agents of King James II desired to cont   ..... reverse
depicted an eagle of starkly modernistic form, perched, with appropriate legends surrounding. Artist Kreis later used a related eagle motif when he designed the reverse of
the 1936 Bridgeport half dollar. The leaves on the Charter Oak were made much larger
than appropriate for the scale of the image and the size of the tree trunk, artistic license.
Mint records designate the eagle side as the obverse and the Charter Oak as the reverse,
although numismatic opinion has been divided on the matter.

During April and May 1935, the full authorized coinage of 25,000 pieces, plus 18
coins for the Assay Commission, was produced at the Philadelphia Mint. Interest was
strong on the part of Connecticut citizens as well as numismatists. The entire issue
was sold out.

Key to Collecting

Today collectors prize Connecticut Tercentenary half dollars, and they are avidly
desired for inclusion in commemorative sets. Most examples survive in grades in the
high AU and low Mint State levels. Higher-grade coins such as MS-65 are elusive.

Friction and/or marks are often obvious at the ground or baseline of the oak tree on
the obverse and, in particular, on the broad expanse of wing on the reverse. Turn the
coin at several angles to the light to check for hairlines on the wing—if they are there
you will see them (the 1936 Bridgeport half dollar by the same designer is similar in
characteristics of the reverse). Specimens that are otherwise lustrous, frosty, and very
attractive, often have friction on the wing.

(1935) HUDSON SESQUICENTENNIAL HALF DOLLARS

Distribution
10,008

Whitman Coin Guide (WCG™)—1935 Hudson Sesquicentennial 50¢

MS-60	MS-63	MS-64	MS-65	MS-66	MS-67	MS-68
$930	$1,300	$1,600	$4,010	$4,055	$13,684	

CERTIFIED POPULATIONS

MS-60	MS-61	MS-62	MS-63	MS-64	MS-65	MS-66	MS-67	MS-68
23	40	255	937	1,807	1,004	299	29	0

Points of Interest: Few coins were available to the public at the issue price of $1; the
distribution of the issue was widely criticized.

Subject of Commemoration: 150th anniversary of the founding of Hudson, New York.

verse—Half Moon ship captained by Henry Hudson, for whom the Hudson
. the town of Hudson were named. *Reverse*—Neptune seated backward on a
taken from the city seal), with a mermaid blowing a conch shell. Designed by
ester Beach.

Mintage Data: Approved May 2, 1935. *Maximum authorized*—10,000. *Number minted*
(including 8 assay coins)—10,008. *Net distribution*—10,008.

Original Cost and Issuer: $1. Hudson Sesquicentennial Committee through the First
National Bank & Trust Company of Hudson.

An Obscure Event Commemorated

Hudson, New York, a small community located 28 miles south of Albany on the banks
of the Hudson River, was first called Claverack Landing when it was settled by Rensse-
laer family interests as a trading spot—with two storehouses and two wharves—in 1662.
The little town expanded in 1783 and 1784 when former residents of Rhode Island,
Martha's Vineyard, and Nantucket moved there and engaged in commerce, and
renamed the village Hudson. In the following year it was incorporated.

Relatively unknown to the outside world, Hudson, New York, a town of 14,000 residents in the 1930s, took on national importance on the numismatic scene in 1935 when
its 150th anniversary was celebrated. On May 2, 1935, congressional legislation provided for 10,000 commemorative silver half dollars (increased from the original proposal
for 6,000) to be coined.

The Design

Chester Beach, a sculptor who had designed the 1923 Monroe Doctrine and 1935
Lexington-Concord half dollars, and who had prepared models for the 1928 Hawaiian
Sesquicentennial coin, was selected to create the Hudson half dollar. Mayor Frank Wise
polled leaders in the city who agreed that the obverse should display the bust of Henry
Hudson, whereas the seal of the City of Hudson would be ideal as a motif for the
reverse. The seal depicts Neptune seated backward on a whale, accompanied by a mermaid blowing a conch shell.

Beach prepared sketches as directed, as well as an alternate proposal of a design
showing Henry Hudson's flagship, the *Half Moon*, and suggested to the city fathers that
the ship would be preferable to a portrait. This proposal was duly adopted. The result
was a coin which presented a puzzling appearance to many viewers. Nautical scenes
were on both sides—a ship on the obverse and a caricature of Neptune on the reverse.
At the upper left of the ship a fancifully styled *quarter* moon (with a bump on the inside
of the crescent for the nose of the Man in the Moon) apparently was intended to indicate the otherwise unstated name of the ship, *Half Moon*.

Production and Distribution

In June 1935, the Philadelphia Mint produced the full authorization of 10,000 coins plus
eight extra for assay. Toward the end of the next month the pieces were shipped to the
First National Bank and Trust Company of Hudson, for delivery to the Hudson Sesquicentennial Committee. Orders were accepted, beginning the first week of May, by the
Executive Committee of the Sesquicentennial, through John R. Evans at the First
National Bank. The cost was $1 each plus 18 cents for registration and three cents
postage for each two coins. It was intended that sales would commence on June 28,

1935, but only a few days later, on July 2, it was stated that the entire issue h.
out and that no pieces were available. Relatively few collectors had placed orde
time that the "sold out" notice was posted.

Subsequently, Evans informed buyers:

> Reservations for these coins have been accepted since the first part of
> May. The coins were received from the Mint on June 28, and July 2
> the supply was depleted. . . . The demand was so great that our entire
> 10,000 has been exhausted and there are no more available except
> through a few dealers who purchased them.

Two dealers were the main buyers: Guttag Brothers (42 Stone Street, New York
City) and Hubert W. Carcaba (182 Magnolia Avenue, St. Augustine, Fla.). Julius Guttag
of Guttag Brothers was believed to have obtained 7,500 coins for 95¢ each. Guttag's
involvement became an inside joke with his coin dealer competitors, who slyly referred
to Hudson coins as "Guttag half dollars."[11]

Numismatists React

As might be expected, collectors whose orders were returned by the issuing bank were
incensed, and numerous complaints were registered to the ANA, the editor of *The
Numismatist*, the American Numismatic Society, and just about anyone else who would
listen. A deluge of bad publicity overtook the City of Hudson.

Many people suspected foul play, especially since Hudson half dollars were aplenty on
the market and in dealers' stocks at $5 to $7 a short time after the original distribution
ended. Even at those inflated prices, coins were snapped up by eager buyers, and those
speculators who thought to hold back coins soon saw prices reach an even higher level.

Collectors finished last in the Hudson half dollar folly, a harbinger of other things
to come within the next half year, particularly the phony distribution, toward the end of
the year, of the 1935 with "small 1934" Boone half dollars by C. Frank Dunn in Lexington, Kentucky (see preceding listing for the Boone coins, 1934). No set of commemorative half dollars was complete without a Hudson, so collectors gritted their teeth and
paid the going price, resolving to order future issues of other series as early as possible,
so as to avoid disappointment and the possibility of higher prices.

Key to Collecting

Today, the Hudson half dollar is highly desired as one of three rare "type" commemoratives from the Classic Era—the 1928 Hawaiian, this coin, and the 1935 Old Spanish
Trail. Examples are easily available, and "gradeflation" and deep or artificial toning
(making close inspection impossible) have propelled some of them into high certified
grades. True gems, however, are very rare and always have been.

Hudson halves were struck at high speed and with little care to preserve them, with
the result that by the time they were originally distributed the majority of pieces showed
nicks, contact marks, and other evidences of handling. On the ship side, on the center
sail, and on the whale/mermaid side on the figure of Neptune, you will usually see evidence of contact and/or light striking. In addition, the typical specimen will show scattered contact marks overall. Most coins are lustrous and frosty except on the center
devices. Today most known pieces are in the lower Mint State levels, with MS-62 to
MS-64 being typical. Carefully graded MS-65 coins are scarce, and anything higher is
very rare. Take your time when buying one.

ANISH TRAIL HALF DOLLARS

Whitman Coin Guide (WCG™)—1935 Old Spanish Trail 50¢

MS-60	MS-63	MS-64	MS-65	MS-66	MS-67	MS-68
$1,400	$1,700	$1,860	$2,145	$2,415	$3,432	

CERTIFIED POPULATIONS

MS-60	MS-61	MS-62	MS-63	MS-64	MS-65	MS-66	MS-67	MS-68
21	12	81	383	1,345	1,828	854	145	5

Points of Interest: This was a private venture of numismatist L.W. Hoffecker.

Subject of Commemoration: 400th (more or less) anniversary of explorer Alvar Núñez Cabeza de Vaca's travels on the Old Spanish Trail.

Designs: *Obverse*—Steer skull. *Reverse*—Map of the Southeastern states and a yucca tree. Designed by L.W. Hoffecker; models were prepared by Edmund J. Senn.

Mintage Data: Authorized June 5, 1935. *Maximum authorized*—10,000. *Number minted*—10,008.

Original Cost and Issuer: $2. L.W. Hoffecker trading as the El Paso Museum Coin Committee.

A Cozy Arrangement

The 1935 Old Spanish Trail half dollar represents another instance of an issue primarily designed for the exploitation of coin collectors. L.W. Hoffecker, who was to keep his fences mended by investigating later abuses of commemorative half dollars on behalf of the ANA and serving as president of the ANA from 1939 through 1941, was the originator of this promotion. Throughout the 1930s Hoffecker was extremely successful in diverting attention away from himself, so that criticisms directed toward the Hudson half dollar, the Boone pieces, and others did not fall on his shoulders as well. Hoffecker earned his living in the mortgage and loan business and as a rare coin dealer (trading as Watkins Coin Company, Box 553, El Paso, through the early 1950s).

In 1929 Hoffecker had set himself up as chairman of the Gadsden Purchase Commission in El Paso, essentially a one-man organization, and had sought to have a commemorative half dollar issue of 10,000 coins to be sold for $1.50 each. Despite approval of the bill in Congress, President Herbert Hoover vetoed the Gadsden Purchase proposal. Undaunted, Hoffecker tried again, this time with the Old Spanish Trail half dollar in 1935. The second time around, Hoffecker visited Washington several times, became friends with congressmen, and even had a five-minute visit with President Franklin D. Roosevelt ("that saved us").[12]

The El Paso Museum Committee was the lofty-sounding name used by Hoffecker to distribute the coins, although the Museum never benefited from what seems to have been a one-man operation, except to receive two coins!

Design and Distribution

The half dollars were to represent the 400th anniversary of a trail used by early explorer Alvar Núñez Cabeza de Vaca, "Cabeza de Vaca" meaning in Spanish, "head of a cow." There was no reason to have celebrated the anniversary of the year 1535, since the explorer's stay in what later became the United States extended from 1528 to 1536. A representation of a steer, facing the viewer, was adopted as the obverse motif for the coin, a punning reference to the name of the explorer. The reverse of the Old Spanish Trail half dollar showed a yucca tree in full bloom, superimposed on a map showing the early trail extending from the coast of Florida to El Paso, with the city name EL PASO at the end of the route. Hoffecker himself designed the piece, and plaster models were prepared in mid-July 1935 by Edmund J. Senn, an unemployed El Paso sculptor.

In September 1935, 10,008 pieces were struck, and all but the extra eight assay coins were subsequently sent to El Paso. Hoffecker offered these at $2 each. Most seem to have been sold to those who ordered them, after which he announced that they were sold out. But this was a lie—he had kept many coins for himself.

The outstanding financial and public relations success scored by the distribution of the Old Spanish Trail half dollars inspired Hoffecker to become involved further, and the next year saw him working in El Paso in an arrangement whereby he was the official outlet for half dollars made to commemorate an event in distant Elgin, Illinois.

Key to Collecting

Unlike the other two "types" with just 10,000 strikes, the Old Spanish Trail halves were handled with care at the Mint and during shipping, yet most show scattered contact marks. Check the highest relief parts of the cow's head for friction. Most grade from MS-65 upward. The fields are usually somewhat satiny and gray, not deeply lustrous and frosty.

(1935–1936) CALIFORNIA-PACIFIC EXPOSITION HALF DOLLARS

Distribution

1935-S: 70,132
1936-D: 30,092

Whitman Coin Guide (WCG™)—1935-S California-Pacific Int'l Exposition 50¢

MS-60	MS-63	MS-64	MS-65	MS-66	MS-67	MS-68
$130	$155	$175	$200	$265	$1,350	$9,350

CERTIFIED POPULATIONS

MS-60	MS-61	MS-62	MS-63	MS-64	MS-65	MS-66	MS-67	MS-68
22	15	149	847	3,421	7,670	1,790	153	7

1936-D California-Pacific International Exposition 50¢

MS-60	MS-63	MS-64	MS-65	MS-66	MS-67	MS-68
$150	$165	$190	$200	$300	$2,295	

CERTIFIED POPULATIONS

MS-60	MS-61	MS-62	MS-63	MS-64	MS-65	MS-66	MS-67	MS-68
10	5	34	366	2,356	5,250	1,012	94	1

Points of Interest: The 180,000 melted 1935-S coins were recoined into 1936-D San Diego half dollars, and 150,000 of these were melted!

Subject of Commemoration: The California-Pacific International Exposition held in San Diego.

Designs: *Obverse*—Minerva seated (from California State Seal). *Reverse*—Parts of two buildings, the Chapel of St. Francis and the California Tower, at the California-Pacific International Exposition. Designed by Robert Aitken.

Mintage and Melting Data: 1935-S: Authorized May 3, 1935. *Maximum authorized*— 250,000. *Number minted* (including 132 assay coins)—250,132. *Number melted*— 180,000. *Net distribution*—70,132. **1936-D:** Authorized May 6, 1936 (special authorization for recoinage of melted 1935-S half dollars). *Maximum authorized*— 180,000. *Number minted* (including 92 assay coins)—180,092. *Number melted*—150,000. *Net distribution*—30,092.

Original Cost and Issuer: 1935-S: $1 (increased to $3 in 1937; dropped to $2 in 1938). **1936-D:** $1.50 (increased to $3 in 1937; reduced to $1 in 1938). California-Pacific International Exposition Company.

Exposition Coins

The California-Pacific International Exposition held in San Diego saw the issuance of commemorative pieces popularly known today as San Diego half dollars. $20 million was spent to stage the event in Balboa Park in that city, but fewer than four million people eventually attended. Located in California about 10 miles from the Mexican border, San Diego, home of a large naval base, was and is a popular tourist attraction, shipping port, and commercial area. The exposition sought to popularize the advantages of the seaport city. A brochure advised visitors to the exposition that "living costs are low in San Diego. More than 200 hotels. Rates range from $1 per day."

Legislation approved May 3, 1935, provided for the coinage of not more than a quarter million silver half dollars for sale in connection with "the fulfillment of ideals and purposes" of the exposition, one such purpose being profit. To stimulate interest on the part of collectors, coinage was to be accomplished at two different mints (interestingly enough, not including Philadelphia).

Robert Aitken, who had been associated with certain earlier commemorative series (most notably the Panama-Pacific $50 gold coins), prepared the designs for the San Diego half dollar, which were translated into dies by the Medallic Art Company in New York. The obverse depicted elements of the California State Seal. The reverse showed parts of two exposition buildings.

Minting, Melting, and Distribution

The total coinage came about in an interesting way. The original authorization provided for not more than 250,000 pieces without any specific date given, except it was noted that the exposition would be held in 1935 and 1936. During August 1935 the San Francisco Mint produced the entire authorization of 250,132 pieces (the odd 132 being for assay), which were sent to the exposition and offered for sale for $1 each. The large production figure was not attractive to collectors, especially in view of only 10,000 having been made for the highly sought-after Hudson issue of recent notoriety, and interest was not strong—despite an extensive campaign involving news releases and advertising.

The exposition petitioned Congress to pass additional legislation, which was accomplished on May 6, 1936, providing:

> The director of the Mint is authorized to receive from the California-Pacific International Exposition Company, or its duly authorized agents, not to exceed 180,000 silver 50-cent pieces heretofore coined under authority of an Act of Congress approved May 3, 1935, and recoin the same [the unsold 1935-S pieces] under the same terms and conditions as contained in said Act: Provided that the coins herein authorized shall be of the same design, shall bear the date 1936 irrespective of the year in which they were minted or issued, and shall be coined at one of the mints of the United States.

This curious recoinage proposal was implemented, and Denver was selected as the site for coinage of 180,092 pieces dated 1936. Earlier the exposition petitioned Congress to authorize the production of 1936 coins at all three mints, but the request was denied.

Offered at $1.50 each, the sales of 1936-D San Diego half dollars were even less satisfactory than seen for 1935-S, and eventually a huge quantity amounting to 150,000 pieces went back to the Treasury for melting, leaving a net distribution of just one-sixth of the original coinage, which coins, it must be remembered, in turn were made from silver taken from unsold coins of the 1935-S issue. All of this activity certainly kept Mint employees busy, but whether it was productive for anyone else is a matter for debate.

The 1935-S San Diego half dollars were placed on sale at the exposition grounds on August 12, 1935, and were offered for $1 each plus shipping charges for those who ordered by mail. Emil Klicka, treasurer of the exposition, tried his best to sell the pieces, but the high published mintages were his undoing. A number of pieces were retained by the exposition, apart from those returned for melting, and were subsequently offered in 1937 at $3 each—as if raising the price would make them seem "rare" and do something for the sales effort.

Years later in the 1980s, a hoard of nearly 10,000 1935-S and close to 6,000 1936-D halves was dispersed. Many were sent to PCGS and mostly graded MS-64 and 65.

Key to Collecting

Both the 1935-S and 1936-D issues were coined with deeply frosty and lustrous surfaces, giving them a very attractive appearance. The design made them susceptible to bag-marks and other evidences of handling, particularly on the figure of Minerva on the obverse, and most survivors, even in higher Mint State levels, show evidence of same. Check the bosom and knees of Minerva on the obverse and the high points of the building on the reverse for friction and/or handling marks. Minerva, in particular, usually displays some graininess or contact marks, even on coins given high numerical grades. Most coins are deeply lustrous and frosty. On the 1935 San Francisco coins the "S" mintmark is usually flat, and on the Denver coins the California Tower is often lightly struck at the top. The eye appeal is usually excellent.

(1935–1939) Arkansas Centennial Half Dollars

Distribution

1935: 3,012; 1935-D: 5,505;
　　　　1935-S: 5,506
1936: 9,660; 1936-D: 9,660;
　　　　1936-S: 9,662
1937: 5,505; 1937-D: 5,505;
　　　　1937-S: 5,506
1938: 3,156; 1938-D: 3,155;
　　　　1938-S: 3,156
1939: 2,104; 1939-D: 2,104; 1939-S: 2,105

Whitman Coin Guide (WCG™)—1935 Arkansas Centennial 50¢

MS-60	MS-63	MS-64	MS-65	MS-66	MS-67	MS-68
$150	$175	$200	$270	$580	$3,385	

CERTIFIED POPULATIONS

MS-60	MS-61	MS-62	MS-63	MS-64	MS-65	MS-66	MS-67	MS-68
10	10	86	453	989	778	184	13	1

1935-D Arkansas Centennial 50¢

MS-60	MS-63	MS-64	MS-65	MS-66	MS-67	MS-68
$135	$155	$170	$265	$735	$3,025	

CERTIFIED POPULATIONS

MS-60	MS-61	MS-62	MS-63	MS-64	MS-65	MS-66	MS-67	MS-68
5	3	30	235	667	671	270	56	1

1935-S Arkansas Centennial 50¢

MS-60	MS-63	MS-64	MS-65	MS-66	MS-67	MS-68
$135	$155	$170	$265	$745	$3,025	

CERTIFIED POPULATIONS

MS-60	MS-61	MS-62	MS-63	MS-64	MS-65	MS-66	MS-67	MS-68
7	5	48	237	708	667	242	27	0

1936 Arkansas Centennial 50¢

MS-60	MS-63	MS-64	MS-65	MS-66	MS-67	MS-68
$130	$155	$165	$260	$781	$3,935	

CERTIFIED POPULATIONS

MS-60	MS-61	MS-62	MS-63	MS-64	MS-65	MS-66	MS-67	MS-68
7	10	83	397	854	473	123	12	0

1936-D Arkansas Centennial 50¢

MS-60	MS-63	MS-64	MS-65	MS-66	MS-67	MS-68
$130	$155	$165	$250	$732	$2,945	

CERTIFIED POPULATIONS

MS-60	MS-61	MS-62	MS-63	MS-64	MS-65	MS-66	MS-67	MS-68
10	8	52	372	872	629	221	26	2

1936-S Arkansas Centennial 50¢

MS-60	MS-63	MS-64	MS-65	MS-66	MS-67	MS-68
$130	$155	$165	$255	$745	$3,935	

CERTIFIED POPULATIONS

MS-60	MS-61	MS-62	MS-63	MS-64	MS-65	MS-66	MS-67	MS-68
16	9	75	343	831	604	161	11	0

1937 Arkansas Centennial 50¢

MS-60	MS-63	MS-64	MS-65	MS-66	MS-67	MS-68
$140	$165	$176	$350	$7,750	$5,585	

CERTIFIED POPULATIONS

MS-60	MS-61	MS-62	MS-63	MS-64	MS-65	MS-66	MS-67	MS-68
5	9	65	311	703	399	125	6	0

1937-D Arkansas Centennial 50¢

MS-60	MS-63	MS-64	MS-65	MS-66	MS-67	MS-68
$140	$165	$176	$320	$1,144	$3,660	$30,800

CERTIFIED POPULATIONS

MS-60	MS-61	MS-62	MS-63	MS-64	MS-65	MS-66	MS-67	MS-68
6	12	49	276	665	577	180	18	0

1937-S Arkansas Centennial 50¢

MS-60	MS-63	MS-64	MS-65	MS-66	MS-67	MS-68
$140	$165	$176	$380	$1,370	$5,585	

CERTIFIED POPULATIONS

MS-60	MS-61	MS-62	MS-63	MS-64	MS-65	MS-66	MS-67	MS-68
8	12	83	314	676	344	74	5	1

1938 Arkansas Centennial 50¢

MS-60	MS-63	MS-64	MS-65	MS-66	MS-67	MS-68
$200	$210	$220	$560	$1,331	$5,035	

CERTIFIED POPULATIONS

MS-60	MS-61	MS-62	MS-63	MS-64	MS-65	MS-66	MS-67	MS-68
6	6	45	241	473	313	91	7	0
PF-60	PF-61	PF-62	PF-63	PF-64	PF-65	PF-66	PF-67	PF-68
0	0	0	1	0	0	0	0	0

1938-D Arkansas Centennial 50¢

MS-60	MS-63	MS-64	MS-65	MS-66	MS-67	MS-68
$200	$205	$220	$540	$1,276	$4,704	

CERTIFIED POPULATIONS

MS-60	MS-61	MS-62	MS-63	MS-64	MS-65	MS-66	MS-67	MS-68
3	11	56	189	459	344	134	21	0
PF-60	PF-61	PF-62	PF-63	PF-64	PF-65	PF-66	PF-67	PF-68
0	0	0	0	1	0	0	0	0

1938-S Arkansas Centennial 50¢

MS-60	MS-63	MS-64	MS-65	MS-66	MS-67	MS-68
$200	$205	$220	$610	$1,606	$2,915	

CERTIFIED POPULATIONS

MS-60	MS-61	MS-62	MS-63	MS-64	MS-65	MS-66	MS-67	MS-68
8	4	56	245	458	284	70	3	0
PF-60	PF-61	PF-62	PF-63	PF-64	PF-65	PF-66	PF-67	PF-68
0	0	0	0	1	0	0	0	0

1939 Arkansas Centennial 50¢

MS-60	MS-63	MS-64	MS-65	MS-66	MS-67	MS-68
$350	$375	$400	$895	$2,525	$12,460	

CERTIFIED POPULATIONS

MS-60	MS-61	MS-62	MS-63	MS-64	MS-65	MS-66	MS-67	MS-68
4	6	55	211	417	241	45	2	0

1939-D Arkansas Centennial 50¢

MS-60	MS-63	MS-64	MS-65	MS-66	MS-67	MS-68
$350	$375	$400	$860	$2,230	$6,960	$33,000

CERTIFIED POPULATIONS

MS-60	MS-61	MS-62	MS-63	MS-64	MS-65	MS-66	MS-67	MS-68
5	4	36	204	401	277	86	10	1

1939-S Arkansas Centennial 50¢

MS-60	MS-63	MS-64	MS-65	MS-66	MS-67	MS-68
$350	$355	$390	$835	$2,046	$6,960	

CERTIFIED POPULATIONS

MS-60	MS-61	MS-62	MS-63	MS-64	MS-65	MS-66	MS-67	MS-68
3	5	71	180	372	231	111	6	0

Points of Interest: The set celebrated the 1836–1936 Arkansas Centennial a year early.

Subject of Commemoration: Centennial of the admission of Arkansas into the Union.

Designs: *Obverse:* Portraits of Miss Liberty and Indian. *Reverse:* Arkansas State Seal. Designed by Edward Everett Burr; models were prepared by Emily Bates of Arkansas.

Mintage and Melting Data: Authorized May 14, 1934. *Maximum authorized*—500,000 (maximum total for all issues 1935 onward). **1935-P-D-S:** *Number minted* (including 5, 5, and 6 assay coins)—13,012, 5,505, 5,506. *Net distribution*—13,012, 5,505, 5,506. **1935-P-D-S:** *Number minted* (including 10, 10, and 12 assay coins)—10,010, 10,010, 10,012. *Number melted*—350, 350, 350. *Net distribution*—9,660, 9,660, 9,662. **1937-P-D-S:** *Number minted* (including 5, 5, and 6 assay coins)—5,505, 5,505, 5,506. *Net distribution*—5,505, 5,505, 5,506. **1938-P-D-S:** *Number minted* (including 6, 5, and 6 assay coins)—6,006, 6,005, 6,006. *Number melted*—2,850, 2,850, 2,850. *Net distribution*—3,156, 3,155, 3,156. **1939-P-D-S:** *Number minted* (including 4, 4, and 5 assay coins)—2,104, 2,104, 2,105. *Net distribution*—2,104, 2,104, 2,105.

Original Cost and Issuers: 1935: $1 per coin; however, few Denver and San Francisco coins were sold at this price as B. Max Mehl bought nearly the entire mintage and soon raised the "issue price" to $2.75 each. **1936:** $1 per coin; then on February 1, 1936, $1.50 per coin; then $4.50 per set of three; then $6.75 per set of three; price for unsold sets was raised to $10 on March 1, 1940. **1937:** $8.75 per set of three. **1938:** $8.75 postpaid per set of three; $10 after July 1, 1938; $12 on and after March 1, 1940. **1939:** $10 per set of three. Issuers: **1935, 1936, 1938, 1939:** Arkansas Centennial Commission throughout. **1935:** B. Max Mehl bought quantities and retailed them at higher prices. **1937:** Stack's.

Another Controversial Series Is Created

The district comprising Arkansas was explored by Hernando de Soto in 1541, followed, more than a century later, by the French Jesuit Father Marquette in 1673. In 1686 the French formed a settlement known as Arkansas (or Arkansaw, as it was often spelled in the early days). In 1720 the area was granted to John Law, known to history as the promulgator of the South Seas Bubble speculation. In 1762, Spain gained control of the district, it went back to France in 1780, and in 1803 it was sold with the Louisiana Purchase to the U.S. government. For a time (1812–1819) Arkansas was part of the territory of Missouri. Finally, on June 15, 1836, Arkansas was admitted to the Union as the 25th state.

Since the State of Arkansas joined the Union in 1836, most people who contemplated the matter in a reasonable light believed that the logical time to celebrate the centennial would be 100 years later or in 1936. Such thinkers, however, did not reckon with the profit motive, so when it came to the subject of selling coins, Arkansas started its birthday party early—in 1935—and kept it going until 1939. As was the case with the Boone issues, the prolonging of the Arkansas coins and the creation of multiple varieties from different mints was done simply to create rarities for collectors. What were perceived as erratic and inequitable methods of distribution of the Arkansas issues were the cause for numerous complaints which precipitated in the congressional shutdown of commemorative coinage in 1939.

Obverse or Reverse?

The coins had their inception with a group known as the Arkansas Honorary Centennial Celebration Commission (later shortened to Arkansas Centennial Commission). On May 14, 1934, a congressional resolution was approved authorizing the production of 500,000 silver half dollars to be issued only to said commission or its authorized agent, "and at such times as they shall be requested by such commission or any such agent, and upon payment to the United States of the face value of such coins."

Edward Everett Burr, a Chicago artist, designed the Arkansas half dollar. The models were created by Miss Emily Bates, who at one time was an Arkansas resident. In keeping with practice at the time, the hub dies were prepared by the Medallic Art Company of New York. During the design process various ideas were considered. The one finally implemented showed conjoined portraits, facing left, of an Indian, intended to be a native Arkansas resident of 1836, and a young girl, representative of an Arkansas citizen of 1936.

The reverse depicted an eagle with outstretched wings, standing on the sun (from which prominent rays emanated), with a parallelogram in the background, partly visible, with stars in the border and enclosing additional stars and the word ARKANSAS, adapted from the state flag. There was some confusion as to which was the obverse side and which was the reverse, for the dates 1836 and 1936 appeared on the portrait side, denoting the centennial span, whereas the eagle side displayed the actual date of issue of the coin. Original correspondence concerning the design, preserved in the National Archives, however, indicates clearly that the portrait side was intended as the obverse.

Market Plans and Problems

The Arkansas Centennial Commission wanted to market coins as soon as possible. Plans were made for the production of coinage at the earliest possible date. In May 1935 10,008 pieces were struck in Philadelphia and, apart from the eight pieces reserved for assay, the coins were shipped to Arkansas, where they were sold during the next several months. In November of the same year, 5,505 pieces were struck in Denver and 5,506 in San Francisco. An additional group of 3,000 Philadelphia Mint coins was ordered. The original offering price was $1 per coin. It developed that many 1935 Philadelphia Mint coins were sold at that price, but that only a few Denver and San Francisco coins were—for B. Max Mehl purchased nearly all of the branch mint coins in a bulk transaction and soon raised the "issue price" to $2.75 each.

Early in January 1936, by which time the commemorative craze had been fanned from a spark into a flame by the unavailability and subsequent skyrocketing value of the low-mintage 1935 with "small 1934" Boone issues, Mehl felt that the market could stand a higher price for the Arkansas issues, so he offered his supply of 1935 coins at the advanced price of $2 for the Philadelphia pieces and $2.75 each for the branch mints. A "special offer" enabled a buyer to acquire a pair of branch mint pieces for $5.

Notwithstanding all of the enthusiasm he expressed in his advertising, which ceaselessly proclaimed them as wonderful investments, apparently Mehl was less than satisfied with the deal, for he did not seek to handle as an original distributor the next Arkansas coins, those dated 1936. During 1936, the actual centennial year, the Arkansas Centennial Commission handled the bulk of sales. A.W. Parke, secretary of the Commission, first offered each of the three Philadelphia, Denver, and San Francisco coins for $1 apiece. On February 1, 1936, he raised the price to $1.50 per coin, and again later to $4.50, offered only as a set of three. Still later Parke decided that unsold sets should be sold for $6.75, which was equal to $2.25 per coin. Sales were sluggish, particularly after the crash in the commemorative market which occurred in late summer, and thousands of unsold pieces were wholesaled to dealers (including B. Max Mehl) at little, if anything, over face value.

By end of the year 1936 it was decided to go the dealer route once again for distribution of subsequently dated coins. The franchise was given to Stack's, a firm which had opened the year before in New York City under the ownership of Joseph, Morton, and Shirley Stack. It fell to Joseph Stack to be in charge of the advertising and distribution of the Arkansas sets. Black leatherette cases were made up for the 1937 offering. Of the 5,500 1937 sets struck, Stack's announced the intention to reserve 500 for distribution to citizens of Arkansas, and the balance of 5,000 was to be offered to the numismatic fraternity, a reflection, undoubtedly accurate, of the fact that at the time commemoratives were made more to turn a profit from collectors than they were to be part of a valid celebration. Besides, by 1937, the anniversary of the Arkansas Centennial was over. Stack's offered the 1937-dated sets for $8.75 each. (Stack's had a related distribution in early 1937 of a "special issue" of 1936-dated Arkansas 50¢ pieces bearing on one side the portrait of Sen. Joseph Robinson of Arkansas and on the other the standard eagle motif as used on Arkansas half dollars since 1935. These are described separately in the present text under the 1936 heading for Robinson-Arkansas half dollars.)

Joseph B. Stack sent the following comment in a letter to dealer Walter P. Nichols dated April 24, 1937:

> Believe me, when I reach the age of eighty, I never want to look at another commemorative. Until then, if there is money to be made in it, I'll play with them. Otherwise, I will extend the glory to our fellow numismatists. Believe it or not, we start sending out the new headaches [1937 Arkansas sets] during the coming week.

In 1938 the Arkansas Centennial Commission once again offered sets directly to collectors. The mintage quantity was raised to 6,000 coins from each of the three mints, and the price remained the same. On July 1, 1938, the official issue price was raised to $10 per set. Sales of 1938 Arkansas sets proved disappointing, and just 3,150 sets eventually found buyers. In the November 1939 issue of *The Numismatist*, A.W. Parke stated in a full-page advertisement that 1,850 sets of the 1938 Arkansas coins had gone back to the Mint. Parke offered the remaining 1938-dated sets for $8.75 each, stating there would be "no advance in price . . . for the present. . . . If there are still coins on hand December 1, the surplus will be sent back to the Mint, and museum specimens made of the few remaining. Should this be done there will be a material price increase in the handful left." Later, an additional 1,000 1938 sets were sent to the Mint for melting. In 1938 Parke also offered unsold 1936 sets at $6.75 per set. He noted that his next advertisement would announce a price advance if there were any coins left to sell.

Projections for coin sales were much less optimistic for the following year, and in 1939 just 2,100 Arkansas sets were offered for $10 each, representing a new high initial price. At the new high issue price of $10 per set, apparently sales were brisk, for the low mintage was attractive to those few collectors and speculators who remained in the market. Parke announced that the issue had sold out quickly. They hadn't. On March 1, 1940, he announced that unsold 1936 sets would be raised in price to $10 and unsold 1938 sets to $12. Further (who was he kidding?): "Through a lucky trade I have acquired 10 sets of 1939s which I hold at $20 per set. They won't last long, for so far as I know, they are the only ones on the market."

Key to Collecting

Arkansas half dollars have never been popular with collectors, translating into the advantage that low-mintage coins are very inexpensive for the specialist who must have one of each variety.

The Arkansas sets were produced with a satinlike, almost "greasy" finish, which many collectors and others found to be unattractive. In addition, the prominence of the girl's portrait on the center of the obverse made that part of the coin prone to receiving bagmarks, scuffs, and other evidences of handling with the result that relatively few pieces present a pleasing appearance. The reverse area where the ribbon crosses the eagle's breast is often very weak. Before "gradeflation," the leading certification services labeled very few coins as MS-65. Later, the interpretations loosened, and today MS-65 coins are common.

The satiny, "greasy" surface is such that even freshly minted coins appeared as if they had been dipped or cleaned repeatedly. Today most specimens grade from about MS-60 through, say, MS-63, but are often certified higher. This is particularly true of 1935 and 1936 coins. Some examples are lightly struck on the eagle just behind its head. Issues of 1937–1939 are usually more satisfactory but still are not deeply lustrous. Grading Arkansas half dollars is a black art, so to speak, and often the experts will disagree by a point or two or three.

(1936) ALBANY (NEW YORK) CHARTER ANNIVERSARY HALF DOLLARS

Distribution
17,671

Whitman Coin Guide (WCG™)—1936 Albany (NY) Charter Anniversary 50¢

MS-60	MS-63	MS-64	MS-65	MS-66	MS-67	MS-68
$335	$400	$425	$605	$726	$2,118	$19,250

CERTIFIED POPULATIONS

MS-60	MS-61	MS-62	MS-63	MS-64	MS-65	MS-66	MS-67	MS-68
15	29	154	734	2,293	2,297	1,096	174	7

Points of Interest: Modeled from a live beaver kept in the artist's studio.

Subject of Commemoration: The 250th anniversary of the granting of a charter to the city of Albany, New York, an event of strictly local significance.

Designs: *Obverse*—A beaver chewing a maple branch. The beaver is on Albany's city seal and the maple is New York's official tree. *Reverse*—Depicts the city's first mayor, Peter Schuyler, and his secretary, Robert Livingston, accepting the charter in 1686 from Governor Thomas Dongan of New York. Designed by Gertrude K. Lathrop.

Mintage and Melting Data: Authorized on June 16, 1936. *Maximum authorized—25,000. Number minted* (including 13 assay coins)—25,013. *Number melted—7,342. Net distribution—17,671.*

Original Cost and Issuer: $1. Albany Dongan Charter Coin Committee.

Conception and Design

In 1936 Albany, the capital of New York State since 1797, sought to commemorate the 250th anniversary of its city charter, granted in 1686 by New York Governor Thomas Dongan, by issuing a half dollar. On June 16, 1936, a bill was passed providing for not more than 25,000 silver half dollars to be produced (of a single design and struck at a single mint), an increase from the small quantity of 10,000 coins originally requested. Thus was created another U.S. legal tender coin to commemorate an anniversary of strictly local significance. Even in Albany itself, few citizens were even slightly interested in this obscure anniversary.

The Albany Dongan Charter Committee selected Miss Gertrude Lathrop to design the pieces. Lathrop, born in Albany on December 24, 1896, had achieved recognition as a sculptress. Her sketches and models depicted, on the obverse, a beaver (a common mammal in the area) facing to the viewer's right, gnawing on a branch of maple. While preparing the motifs, the sculptor kept a live beaver in her studio (through the courtesy of the state Conservation Department). The reverse depicted a group of three standing men in colonial costume, representing Governor Thomas Dongan bidding goodbye to Peter Schuyler and Robert Livingston. An eagle flies above them.

Minting and Distribution

In October 1936, the full authorized coinage of 25,000 pieces, plus 13 extra examples for the Assay Commission, was effected at the Philadelphia Mint. The Committee offered coins for sale at $2 each. At first these were referred to as Albany Dongan half dollars, because of the Committee's name, but later they became known simply as Albany halves. By this point in autumn 1936, interest in commemoratives had dwindled sharply, and despite a lot of advertising puffery and hyperbole on the part of the issuing committee, thousands of pieces remained unsold.

The committee continued offering Albany half dollars for six more years. At one time Abe Kosoff was given the opportunity to purchase the entire remaining stock for just $50 above face value for the lot, but he declined since he did not envision a resale possibility! In 1943 some 7,342 unsold, unwanted coins were sent to the Philadelphia Mint and melted. Quantities still remained on hand, however. Les Zeller advised the author that circa 1954, it became known that the State Bank of Albany had between 1,600 and 2,400 undistributed pieces in its vaults, and was willing to sell them for the issue price of $2 each. Jacob Cheris, Charles French, Dr. Kenneth Sartoris, and other local dealers and collectors quickly purchased the entire supply.

Key to Collecting

The design of the Albany half dollar has always been considered pleasing by numismatists, and the issue has always ranked high on the popularity list of coins from the era. This issue was fairly carefully handled, and most examples are relatively free of marks in the fields. Most specimens are lustrous and frosty, although the frost has satinlike aspects. Albany half dollars are readily available on the market, with typical grades being from MS-63 to MS-65.

The hip of the beaver on the obverse is the first and most obvious area for friction and contact marks, and nearly all coins show at least some minor evidence of contact at this point. On the reverse scattered marks are often seen, especially on the sleeve of the figure on the left.

(1936) BATTLE OF GETTYSBURG ANNIVERSARY HALF DOLLARS

Distribution
26,928

Whitman Coin Guide (WCG™)—1936 Battle of Gettysburg Anniversary 50¢

MS-60	MS-63	MS-64	MS-65	MS-66	MS-67	MS-68
$475	$515	$560	$790	$1,065	$2,871	$52,800

CERTIFIED POPULATIONS

MS-60	MS-61	MS-62	MS-63	MS-64	MS-65	MS-66	MS-67	MS-68
38	32	226	960	2,827	2,348	736	120	4

Points of Interest: Dated 1936 and struck in 1937 for an anniversary to be commemorated in 1938.

Subject of Commemoration: 75th anniversary in 1938 of the Battle of Gettysburg.

Designs: *Obverse*—Portraits of Union and Confederate soldiers. *Reverse*—Union and Confederate shields. Designed by Frank Vittor.

Mintage and Melting Data: Authorized June 16, 1936. *Maximum authorized*—50,000. *Number minted* (including 28 assay coins)—50,028. *Number melted*—23,100. *Net distribution*—26,928.

Original Cost and Issuer: $1.65. The Pennsylvania State Commission, Hotel Gettysburg, Gettysburg. Price later raised to $2.65 and offered by the American Legion, Department of Pennsylvania.

Another Confusing Anniversary

To observe the 75th anniversary of one of the most famous Civil War conflicts, the 1863 Battle of Gettysburg, Congress on June 16, 1936, provided for the coinage of not more than 50,000 silver half dollars of a single design and struck at a single mint. The 75th anniversary was to be held in 1938, but once again the promoters sniffed an immediate profit and simply could not wait. The Commission originally requested 20,000 coins from Philadelphia, 15,000 from Denver, and 15,000 from San Francisco to make up the quantity—an idea that was rejected. The coins were dated 1936, a year completely irrelevant to the situation.

The Pennsylvania State Commission, located at the Hotel Gettysburg in Gettysburg, hired Frank Vittor, a Philadelphia artist, to prepare designs. On the obverse he depicted two busts, one of a Confederate and the other of a Union soldier. The inscription, BLUE AND GRAY REUNION, referred to an event scheduled for July 1 through 3, 1938. The reverse showed two shields divided by a fasces—one representing the Union and the other the Confederacy—with the date 1936 below. The dates 1863–1938 were to the left and right at the border.

In June 1937, 50,028 coins were struck at the Philadelphia Mint. Thus we have a situation similar to that of the Delaware half dollar: a coin dated 1936 struck in 1937 for an event scheduled to take place in 1938, still another shameful example of commemorative half dollar exploitation. Paul L. Roy, executive secretary of the Pennsylvania State Commission, held out the hope that he would have Denver and San Francisco coins until the very end, when he reluctantly told those who had ordered sets of three different coins that he would send them three examples all from the same mint (Philadelphia). Refunds were offered to anyone not wanting that quantity. Single coins were priced at $1.65.

By May 15, 1937, Paul L. Roy had mailed a postcard containing a blatant lie:

> Because of the large oversubscription and the tremendous demand, which we will not be able to fill, we will appreciate your limiting your order to your actual needs in order that all who desire may secure one of the new half dollars.

There must have been some quintessential aspect of being a distributor of commemoratives, that prompted otherwise supposedly respectable people to be dishonest!

The reunion between the Blue and the Gray eventually took place as scheduled in 1938, and among those in attendance was President Franklin Delano Roosevelt, who dedicated the Eternal Light Peace Memorial. Commemorative half dollars were among the souvenirs on sale there.

In August 1938, *The Numismatist* reported that Paul L. Roy had announced that the unsold balance of the Gettysburg coins had been turned over to the American Legion, Department of Pennsylvania, for further distribution. The American Legion raised the price from $1.65 each to $2.65 in the hope that this would make the coins appear to be rare and a good investment. 23,100 remained unsold and were subsequently melted.

Key to Collecting

The 1936 Gettysburg half dollars, properly called Battle of Gettysburg half dollars, are popular with collectors today. Examples are fairly plentiful on the market. Most specimens grade from about MS-63 to MS-65 and are deeply frosty and lustrous. Most coins show scattered contact marks, which are most evident on the cheeks of the soldiers on the obverse and, on the reverse, on the two shields (particularly at the top of the Union shield on the left side of the coin).

(1936) BRIDGEPORT (CONNECTICUT) CENTENNIAL HALF DOLLARS

Distribution
25,015

Whitman Coin Guide (WCG™)—1936 Bridgeport (CT) Centennial 50¢

MS-60	MS-63	MS-64	MS-65	MS-66	MS-67	MS-68
$175	$200	$220	$330	$616	$2,712	

CERTIFIED POPULATIONS

MS-60	MS-61	MS-62	MS-63	MS-64	MS-65	MS-66	MS-67	MS-68
27	17	179	803	2,695	2,402	841	61	1

Points of Interest: The obverse depicts P.T. Barnum, America's best-known showman. The eagle on the reverse is similar to that used by the same artist on the 1935 Connecticut Tercentenary half dollar.

Subject of Commemoration: The 100th anniversary of the incorporation of the city of Bridgeport.

Designs: *Obverse*—Head of P.T. Barnum, Bridgeport's best-known citizen. *Reverse*—An eagle in the Art Deco style. Designed by Henry Kreis.

Mintage and Melting Data: Authorized May 15, 1936. *Minimum authorized*—25,000 (unlimited maximum). *Number minted* (including 15 assay coins)—25,015. *Net distribution*—25,015.

Original Cost and Issuer: $2. Bridgeport Centennial, Inc. through the First National Bank and Trust Co. and other banks.

Bridgeport Celebrates Its Centennial

Although Bridgeport, Connecticut was founded in 1639 and was an important center during the 17th and 18th centuries, the city was not incorporated until 1836. In 1936 the city fathers decided to celebrate the 100th anniversary of this event. A committee styling itself as Bridgeport Centennial, Incorporated aided with the preparation of congressional legislation, approved on May 15, 1936, which specified that no fewer than 25,000 silver half dollars of a single design be struck at a single mint. The bill further provided that "the coins herein authorized shall bear the date 1936, irrespective of the year in which they are minted or issued," placing no expiration time on minting nor limit to the quantities that could be ordered. Accordingly, a strict reading of the legislation suggests that Bridgeport had the authority to order as many additional half dollars as it wanted, and could have produced an unlimited number of 1936-dated coins until kingdom come!

P.T. Barnum

Henry G. Kreis, the sculptor who designed the 1935 Connecticut Tercentenary half dollar, and who in 1936 prepared the model for the Robinson side of the Robinson-Arkansas half dollar, created the designs for the Bridgeport half dollar.

The obverse motif depicted P.T. Barnum, Bridgeport's most famous citizen, whereas the reverse showed a modernistic eagle quite similar in concept to that used on the 1935 Connecticut Tercentenary piece. The Medallic Art Company of New York City finalized the models, and the striking of 25,015 coins was accomplished in September 1936 at the Philadelphia Mint.

P.T. Barnum excited America and Europe with many attractions including the Fee-jee Mermaid, Joice Heth (an aged lady who claimed to have cared for George Washington in his infancy), Jumbo (the huge elephant whose name survives today as an adjective denoting large size), General Tom Thumb, the pageant of Lalla Rookh, and others. Jenny Lind, the "Swedish Nightingale," a relatively unknown singer brought to America by Barnum and launched on this side of the Atlantic with an unprecedented publicity campaign, became famous overnight. Barnum's American Museum in New York City was that metropolis's main tourist attraction in the 1850s and early 1860s.

Barnum's career had many setbacks—as referenced in the title of his life story, *Struggles and Triumphs*. He co-signed a note for the Jerome Clock Company, an enterprise that became defunct, leaving him with a large obligation, although he had reaped no benefits. As a matter of principle Barnum eventually repaid every cent—a tribute to his integrity.

Distribution of the Coins

Bridgeport Centennial half dollars were shipped from the Philadelphia Mint to Bridgeport and sold through the First National Bank and Trust Company and other financial institutions in that city. The offering price was set at $2 each, with a limit of five coins per customer. Distribution began about September 1, missing many local celebrations which ran from June 4 through October 3. Sales proceeded at a satisfactory pace, however, and probably about 20,000 coins found ready buyers.

It was announced in *The Numismatist*, in February 1938, that the unsold Bridgeport half dollars had been acquired by the Community Chest and Council, Inc. of Bridgeport, which was going to offer them for sale. A quantity estimated to be on the order of several thousand pieces remained unsold, and was eventually wholesaled for a small premium above face value through dealers.

Key to Collecting

Bridgeport half dollars are readily available on the market. Most are in Mint State levels from MS-62 to MS-64, and cleaned or lightly polished pieces are often seen. Pristine MS-65 pieces are readily available. Friction and/or marks are often obvious on the cheek of P.T. Barnum on the obverse and, in particular, on the broad expanse of eagle wing on the reverse. Turn the coin at several angles to the light to check for hairlines on the wing—if they are there you will see them. Some specimens are from dies with lightly polished fields and have a prooflike or partially prooflike appearance in those areas.

(1936) CINCINNATI MUSICAL CENTER HALF DOLLARS

Distribution
1936: 5,005
1936-D: 5,005
1936-S: 5,006

Whitman Coin Guide (WCG™)—1936 Cincinnati Music Center 50¢

MS-60	MS-63	MS-64	MS-65	MS-66	MS-67	MS-68
$330	$375	$550	$840	$1,452	$9,581	

CERTIFIED POPULATIONS

MS-60	MS-61	MS-62	MS-63	MS-64	MS-65	MS-66	MS-67	MS-68
10	3	78	322	923	396	130	6	0

1936-D Cincinnati Music Center 50¢

MS-60	MS-63	MS-64	MS-65	MS-66	MS-67	MS-68
$330	$375	$550	$790	$1,287	$4,906	$33,000

CERTIFIED POPULATIONS

MS-60	MS-61	MS-62	MS-63	MS-64	MS-65	MS-66	MS-67	MS-68
7	5	46	247	934	986	467	52	2

1936-S Cincinnati Music Center 50¢

MS-60	MS-63	MS-64	MS-65	MS-66	MS-67	MS-68
$330	$375	$550	$840	$1,690	$15,081	

CERTIFIED POPULATIONS

MS-60	MS-61	MS-62	MS-63	MS-64	MS-65	MS-66	MS-67	MS-68
10	5	86	397	1,094	381	61	2	0

Points of Interest: This issue was a personal project for the profit of numismatist Thomas G. Melish, complete with phony announcements and statements. The 50th anniversary commemorated had no basis in historical fact.

Subject of Commemoration: These coins were supposedly struck to commemorate the 50th anniversary in 1936 of Cincinnati as a center of music.

Designs: *Obverse*—Head of Stephen Foster. *Reverse*—Female holding a lyre, personifying music. Designed by Constance Ortmayer.

Mintage and Melting Data: Authorized March 31, 1936. *Maximum authorized*—15,000. **1936-P-D-S:** *Number minted* (including 5, 5, and 6 assay coins)—5,005, 5,005, 5,006. *Net distribution*—5,005, 5,005, 5,006.

Original Cost and Issuer: $7.75 per set of three (actually $7.50 plus 25¢ for the display container with cellophane slide front). Cincinnati Musical Center Commemorative Coin Association, Ohio (Thomas G. Melish).

Of, By, and For Thomas G. Melish

The 1936 Cincinnati half dollars are closely related to L.W. Hoffecker's Old Spanish Trail coins, in that they also were conceived expressly for the purpose of earning money by sales to collectors. The Cincinnati coins were an issue of, by, and for Thomas G. Melish, an entrepreneur and enthusiastic numismatist of his era. Both Melish and Hoffecker were prominent members of the ANA, good customers of leading dealers, and held themselves out as paragons of honesty. In reality, both were hypocrites.

Melish devised a scheme where a group styling itself as the Cincinnati Musical Center Commemorative Coin Association sought to commemorate, as the congressional authorization of March 31, 1936, stated, "the 50th anniversary of Cincinnati, Ohio as a center of music, and its contribution to the art of music for the past 50 years." To increase the potential for profit the requested issue was for just 15,000 coins to be struck at three mints, creating an encitingly low mintage of just 5,000 coins per variety. Even more profit was envisioned by Melish when he originally proposed a bill which provided for "not more than 15,000 (10,000 Philadelphia Mint, 3,000 San Francisco Mint, and 2,000 Denver Mint)," thus creating 1936-D coins which would have been rarities.

There was a small problem: nothing musical worth commemorating occurred in Cincinnati 50 years earlier in 1886. That didn't make any difference. To be sure, a group known as the Liederkranz Society was formed that year and was composed of German immigrants and others who staged songfests, but few would consider that this obscure occasion was worthy of a nationally distributed coin.

Charles Moore, chairman of the Commission of Fine Arts, endeavored to investigate the situation, obviously smelling a rat, and was unable to find *anyone* in musical circles in Cincinnati who knew the first thing about the proposed half dollar! Accordingly, designs submitted by Miss Constance Ortmayer, showing on the obverse the bust of Stephen Foster and on the reverse a goddess holding a lyre, were found to be ludicrous.

Minting and Distribution

In July 1936 the full authorized issue of 15,000 coins was struck in quantities divided approximately equally among the Philadelphia, Denver, and San Francisco mints: 5,005, 5,005, and 5,006, respectively, the odd pieces being reserved for the Assay Commission. Seeking as much profit as possible at the beginning, Melish and his associates set an issue price of $7.75 per set of three coins, the highest figure of any set up to that time. Each set was mounted in a black leatherette Wynne brand holder, faced with a celluloid slide.

The first 200 sets bore a notarized statement, pasted on the reverse of the holder, attesting that it was from the initial group. In correspondence with a collector, Melish noted:

> These numbered sets were sent to the secretary of the Treasury, the treasurer of the United States, and various senators and representatives. . . . The various mints operated the presses very slowly until the first 1200 coins were struck. The coins were caught in gloved hands and were then put in cellophane envelopes and enclosed in manila envelopes numbered from 1 to 200.

Advertising and publicity solicited orders at the $7.75 issue price, but most who submitted orders found that they were not early enough—indeed they couldn't have been early enough—for the entire issue was "sold out" virtually the moment that news of it appeared (even before it was officially put on sale), according to distributor Melish. Obviously, he had paid attention to, and learned from, what C. Frank Dunn had done with the infamous 1935 "small 1934" Boone sets.

Only a small number of sets were sold at the $7.75 price. Most who ordered had their remittances returned with a notice the coins were sold out. Immediately sets jumped in price on the market to $40, then to $50. As it so happened, at these higher levels many coins became available, most of which are said to have been cautiously parceled out by Melish and other insiders, who had held back at least 2,000 sets. For many years thereafter, the story of the Cincinnati sets was given as an example of the wrong way to do things.

Up to this point, typical congressional laws provided that the authorized coinage of commemoratives be executed "at the *mints* of the United States," giving permission for more than one location. After the Cincinnati issue, the practice was stopped, and subsequent authorizations stated "a mint."

Key to Collecting

Despite the questionable design and origin of the Cincinnati half dollars, the motifs were pleasing to many and today are considered to be among the more attractive in the series. Because nearly all sets went into the hands of collectors and investors, most still exist today in varying degrees of Uncirculated preservation, primarily MS-63 to 65 (per today's somewhat loose interpretation of the ANA grading standards). True gem Mint State specimens are rare. Most coins were carelessly handled at the mints. Nearly all show scattered contact marks, most particularly on the higher areas of Stephen Foster's portrait on the obverse and on the bosom and skirt of the Goddess of Music on the reverse. Cincinnati coins have somewhat satiny or "greasy" surfaces, instead of fields with deep luster and frost. Denver Mint coins are found, on the average, in slightly higher grades than their Philadelphia and San Francisco Mint counterparts.

(1936) CLEVELAND CENTENNIAL HALF DOLLARS

Distribution
50,030

Whitman Coin Guide (WCG™)—1936 Cleveland Centennial 50¢

MS-60	MS-63	MS-64	MS-65	MS-66	MS-67	MS-68
$146	$155	$180	$250	$594	$2,724	$22,000

CERTIFIED POPULATIONS

MS-60	MS-61	MS-62	MS-63	MS-64	MS-65	MS-66	MS-67	MS-68
56	70	397	1,689	4,164	3,626	979	76	4

Points of Interest: Distributed by Thomas G. Melish, who attempted to make low-mintage rarities, but who was unsuccessful.

Subject of Commemoration: The centennial celebration of Cleveland, Ohio, on the occasion of the Great Lakes Exposition held there in 1936.

Designs: *Obverse*—Head of Moses Cleaveland. *Reverse*—Map of the Great Lakes region with a compass point at the city of Cleveland. Designed by Brenda Putnam.

Mintage and Melting Data: Authorized May 5, 1936. *Minimum authorized*—25,000, *Maximum authorized*—50,000. *Number minted* (including 30 assay coins)—50,030. *Net distribution*—50,030.

Original Cost and Issuer: 1 coin @$1.65; 2 @$1.60; 3 @$1.58; 5 @$1.56; 10 @$1.55; 20 @$1.54; 50 @$1.53; 100 @$1.52. Cleveland Centennial Commemorative Coin Association (Thomas G. Melish, Cleveland).

Another Melish Enterprise

The Cleveland Centennial and Great Lakes Exposition took place in Cleveland from June 27 to October 4, 1936, at a 150-acre site on the shore of Lake Erie. Artistic, industrial, and other accomplishments of the Ohio city were showcased, as were public amusements and other attractions, all in connection with the 100th anniversary of Cleveland's incorporation. Costing about $25 million, the exposition attracted approximately four million visitors.

Moses Cleaveland, founder of the city, was born in Connecticut in 1754 and studied law at Yale College. In 1796 he was named a brigadier general in the U.S. army. In the same year he came to Ohio with 50 emigrants from Schenectady, New York, to settle and engage in farming—selecting a site, where the Cuyahoga River empties into Lake Erie, which had served as a trading post.

At the time, the Western Reserve, as that area of Ohio was called, was a magnet for New Englanders, who left the difficult farming conditions of the rocky eastern soil to cultivate the richer soil bordering Lake Erie. Reuben Harmon Jr., the Vermont coiner, was among many to make the journey (although not with Moses Cleaveland).

In 1940, historian Stuart Mosher wrote, "Though the place was originally called Cleaveland in his honor, the spelling was to undergo a minor change. When the first newspaper, the *Cleveland Advertiser*, was established, the headline was found to be too long for the form and the editor cut out the letter 'a,' a revision that was readily accepted by the public." Cleveland was incorporated as a city in 1836. One hundred years later in 1936, Cleveland was a leading shipping and manufacturing center and was well known for its interest in the arts.

The act authorizing commemorative half dollars for the anniversary occasion was approved on May 5, 1936, and provided for the coinage of not less than 25,000, but not more than 50,000, silver half dollars of a single design to be coined at a single mint. Numismatic entrepreneur Thomas G. Melish was behind the venture, and served as treasurer of the Cleveland Centennial Commemorative Coin Association—in *Cincinnati*—which announced its intention to offer the coins to the general public and others for $1.50 each. Lee Hewitt, editor, commented in the *Numismatic Scrapbook*, May 1936: "It seems strange that Mr. Melish, living in Cincinnati, should be the distributor of the Cleveland issue."

The wily Melish had asked his friends in Congress to authorize for him *several* different commemorative half dollars and also to permit additional Cleveland half dollars to be issued with the small date 1937 in addition to the regular date 1936—but these dreams of additional profits did not come true.

Design, Minting, and Distribution

Brenda Putnam, a sculptress of renown, was named as designer of the Cleveland half dollar. A bust of Moses Cleaveland, facing left, dominates the obverse. The reverse shows an outline map of the Great Lakes region with a compass (drawing instrument) describing the area, with the axis on a large star representing the location of Cleveland. Other cities on the Great Lakes are indicated by smaller stars, notably (left to right as they appear on the coin) Duluth, Milwaukee, Chicago, Toledo, Detroit, Buffalo, Toronto, and Rochester. This device was the official insignia of the Great Lakes Exposition.

Melish ordered the first 25,000 coins in July 1936, in which month the requisite quantity (plus 15 extra for assay) was produced at Philadelphia. Sales took place at the exposition in Cleveland, and through Thomas G. Melish's office in far-away Cincinnati, the latter serving as the depot for mail orders.

In order to promote sales, a form letter was sent to collectors which stated, in part:

> We have already been approached by a speculator who wished to buy the entire issue. We advised him that we were not interested.... When these coins are released to the banks in Ohio we anticipate that the entire issue will be sold out within one to three days. All orders will be filled in the rotation received. If you get left on this issue it will be your own fault, not ours.

Sensing an additional demand, the Cleveland Centennial Commemorative Coin Association ordered an additional 25,000 pieces, which were struck in February 1937 but dated 1936, since the congressional enabling act required the entire issue to bear the 1936 date. There was no difference in appearance between 1937-produced coins (technically restrikes) and those minted in the year stated in the design.

Melish stated that the sale was "a landslide." In truth, thousands remained unsold. Many of these went to dealers Abe Kosoff and Sol Kaplan, both close friends of the distributor. In an effort to stimulate interest in Cleveland half dollars and to increase the value of those already in his possession, Sol Kaplan ran numerous advertisements seeking to buy additional pieces.

Key to Collecting

Today 1936 Cleveland half dollars represent the most plentiful commemorative issue surviving from the year 1936, a 12-month span that saw more new designs issued than any other time in American history. Nearly all coins are in Uncirculated grade, typically from MS-63 to MS-65. Scattered marks are usually most evident on Moses Cleaveland's hair and cheek on the obverse, and on the land (non-lake) areas of the map on the reverse. This issue was not handled with care at the Mint. Most Cleveland half dollars are very lustrous and frosty.

(1936) COLUMBIA (SOUTH CAROLINA) SESQUICENTENNIAL HALF DOLLARS

Distribution
1936: 9,007
1936-D: 8,009
1936-S: 8,007

Whitman Coin Guide (WCG™)—1936 Columbia (SC) Sesquicentennial 50¢

MS-60	MS-63	MS-64	MS-65	MS-66	MS-67	MS-68
$280	$320	$330	$410	$550	$1,062	$11,000

CERTIFIED POPULATIONS

MS-60	MS-61	MS-62	MS-63	MS-64	MS-65	MS-66	MS-67	MS-68
9	4	35	202	838	1,290	797	110	2

1936-D Columbia (SC) Sesquicentennial 50¢

MS-60	MS-63	MS-64	MS-65	MS-66	MS-67	MS-68
$270	$300	$325	$405	$495	$900	$7,425

CERTIFIED POPULATIONS

MS-60	MS-61	MS-62	MS-63	MS-64	MS-65	MS-66	MS-67	MS-68
9	6	29	181	625	994	1,085	329	41

1936-S Columbia (SC) Sesquicentennial 50¢

MS-60	MS-63	MS-64	MS-65	MS-66	MS-67	MS-68
$285	$320	$335	$420	$590	$1,008	$13,750

CERTIFIED POPULATIONS

MS-60	MS-61	MS-62	MS-63	MS-64	MS-65	MS-66	MS-67	MS-68
10	4	31	221	693	1,097	504	174	10

Points of Interest: This coin was designed by a sculptor at a local college.

Subject of Commemoration: The 150th anniversary of the designation of Columbia as the capital of the State of South Carolina

Designs: *Obverse*—Justice with sword and scales; at the left is the Capitol of 1786, and on the right, the Capitol of 1936. *Reverse*—Palmetto tree (the state emblem). Designed by A. Wolfe Davidson.

Mintage and Melting Data: Authorized March 18, 1936. *Maximum authorized*—25,000. **1936-P-D-S:** *Number minted and distribution*—9,007, 8,009, 8,007.

Original Cost and Issuer: $6.45 per set of three (single coins $2.15 each). Columbia Sesqui-Centennial Commission.

Another Set of Three Half Dollars

The city of Columbia, South Carolina was established as the capital of the state in 1786, although the General Assembly did not meet in its new Capitol building there until 1790. Earlier the capital was Charleston. To celebrate the 150th anniversary of the 1786 resolution to change the capital city, Columbia proposed to sell a set of commemorative half dollars containing one coin from each of the Philadelphia, Denver, and San Francisco mints. Subsequently, the Act of March 18, 1936 was passed by Congress, allowing 25,000 half dollars to be coined at the various mints—shortly before this practice was prohibited.

The Columbia Sesqui-Centennial (*sic*) Commission named A. Wolfe Davidson, a 32-year-old sculptor at Clemson College, to design the work, a choice that was viewed with disdain by the Commission of Fine Arts: "The models lack artistic merit and are unsatisfactory for translation into a memorial coin." Regardless, a promotional brochure noted:

> The sculptor whose selection has been approved by the Treasury Department and the Fine Arts Commission is A. Wolfe Davidson, of Clemson College, S.C. Mr. Davidson is an outstanding sculptor of the state and is, at present, engaged in sculptoring [*sic*] the bust of Thomas Clemson, the founder of the State Agricultural & Mechanical College.

The obverse depicted the goddess of Justice standing between the Capitol buildings of 1786 on the left and 1936 on the right. The reverse represented a palmetto tree (the state emblem) surrounded by stars. The half dollar was attractive in its simplicity, and few numismatists felt moved to be critical.

In Columbia, there were sesquicentennial festivities from March 22 to 29, 1936, but the coins had not been minted yet (indeed, the congressional enabling act had just passed a few days earlier). The production of the coins was completed by the end of September and consisted of 9,007 pieces produced at Philadelphia, 8,009 at Denver, and 8,007 at San Francisco. Orders were taken at $2.15 per single coin or $6.45 for a set of three. By October 19, 1936, orders received by the issuing commission were said to have been for 15,000 coins more than were minted—despite a lackluster market for commemoratives. Apparently, most of the 15,000 extra coins ordered represented quantities desired by dealers.

The Columbia sets were distributed to buyers from December 8 through 19. Most if not all single orders placed for sets were filled. In an advertising circular, the Columbia Sesqui-Centennial Commission stated, "Residents of the City of Columbia will be given the privilege of making their purchases during the first 24 hours after the coins are placed on sale. Mail orders will then be filled. It is the desire of the Commission that the coin be sold to private collectors rather than dealers." There were never any unsold remainders.

Key to Collecting
The supply of Columbia Sesquicentennial half dollars was widely distributed at the time of issue, and examples are readily obtainable today. Most are MS-63 to MS-65. Treated with care at the mints, most coins show lustrous surfaces with very few handling marks. Nearly all, however, show friction on the bosom of Justice and, to a lesser extent, on the high areas of the palmetto tree foliage on the reverse.

(1936) DELAWARE TERCENTENARY HALF DOLLARS
Distribution
20,993

Whitman Coin Guide (WCG™)—1936 Delaware Tercentenary 50¢

MS-60	MS-63	MS-64	MS-65	MS-66	MS-67	MS-68
$335	$380	$405	$480	$745	$2,035	

CERTIFIED POPULATIONS

MS-60	MS-61	MS-62	MS-63	MS-64	MS-65	MS-66	MS-67	MS-68
25	18	175	737	2,184	2,150	931	120	4

Points of Interest: Dated 1936 and struck in 1937, this issue commemorated a 1938 event. Some numismatists consider the ship side to be the obverse.

Subject of Commemoration: The 300th anniversary of the landing of the Swedes in Delaware.

Designs: *Obverse*—Old Swedes Church. *Reverse*—The ship *Kalmar Nyckel*. Designed by Carl L. Schmitz.

Mintage and Melting Data: Authorized May 15, 1936. *Minimum authorized*—25,000 (unlimited maximum). *Number minted* (including 15 assay coins)—25,015. *Number melted*—4,022. *Net distribution*—20,993.

Original Cost and Issuer: $1.75. Delaware Swedish Tercentenary Commission through the Equitable Trust Company of Wilmington.

An Array of Dates
In March 1638, Swedish colonists, who had departed Göteborg aboard the *Kalmar Nyckel* and the *Fogel Grip* in 1637, arrived in Delaware Bay and anchored at Port Christina, the site of present-day Wilmington, Delaware. They soon established a fur-trading outpost. Later, the region fell under the control of first the Dutch, then the British, and in 1682, William Penn. In 1776, Delaware became one of the 13 original states, and in 1787, it became the first state to ratify the Constitution.

It was desired to celebrate the 300th anniversary of the landing of the Swedes in 1938, but proponents of an appropriate commemorative half dollar for the event couldn't wait that long. Legislation approved on May 15, 1936, provided for no fewer than 25,000 silver half dollars to be struck at a single mint and of a single design. Authorized and dated 1936, the half dollars were actually struck in 1937—for an anniversary scheduled to take place in 1938—another reflection of the abuse of the commemorative half dollar coining privilege.

Design and Distribution

The Delaware Swedish Tercentenary Commission staged a design competition, with a $500 prize, which was won by Carl L. Schmitz, a French-born sculptor who had studied at the Beaux Arts Institute of Design in New York. His entry was judged by Chief Engraver John R. Sinnock and noted sculptor Dr. Robert Tait MacKenzie.

A descriptive leaflet noted:

> On the obverse [*sic*] of the commemorative half dollar appears the *Kalmar Nyckel*, the ship in which the Swedish colonists arrived in this country. This design is made from a model made in Sweden, a copy of the authentic model of the ship now in the Swedish Naval Museum. The reverse shows the Old Swedes Church at Wilmington, dedicated in 1699 and still standing near "The Rocks" in the city of Wilmington and in use. It is said to be the oldest Protestant church building in the United States still used for worship.

The issuing commission designated the ship side of the Delaware Tercentenary half dollar as the obverse; Mint records designated the church side as the obverse. Today collectors agree with the Mint records.

In March 1937, 25,017 Delaware half dollars were struck at the Philadelphia Mint. The Delaware Swedish Tercentenary Commission offered the coins for $1.75 each through the Equitable Trust Company of Wilmington, Delaware. All but 4,022 were sold. The undistributed coins were returned to the Mint to be melted. As was the case with several other 1936 issues, these coins were plentiful in numismatic circles for the next decade or two.

Key to Collecting

Today the 1936 Delaware Tercentenary half dollar is popular with numismatists. Most examples seen are graded MS-64 and MS-65, attributed, it seems, without respect to the usually extensive original planchet nicks and marks. On the church side, marks will often be seen on the roof of the structure, with occasional marks in other areas as well. On the reverse, the center sail on the ship usually shows contact marks, and graininess and nicks from the original planchet. Most Delaware halves are very lustrous and frosty.

(1936) Elgin (Illinois) Centennial Half Dollars

Distribution
20,015

Whitman Coin Guide (WCG™)—1936 Elgin (IL) Centennial 50¢

MS-60	MS-63	MS-64	MS-65	MS-66	MS-67	MS-68
$265	$290	$305	$355	$550	$1,122	$15,950

CERTIFIED POPULATIONS

MS-60	MS-61	MS-62	MS-63	MS-64	MS-65	MS-66	MS-67	MS-68
10	8	82	620	2,507	3,081	1,455	202	8

Points of Interest: Authorized in 1936 for an anniversary that had already taken place in 1935. Some profit from the sale of this issue went toward the work on a statue in Elgin, which was not completed and erected in its designated place until 2001.

Subject of Commemoration: 100th anniversary of the 1835 founding of the city of Elgin, Illinois, and to provide funds for the erection of the *Pioneer Memorial* statuary group.

Designs: *Obverse*—Head of a pioneer (detail from the statue on the reverse). *Reverse*—*Pioneer Memorial* statuary group. Designed by Trygve Rovelstad.

Mintage and Melting Data: Authorized June 16, 1936. *Maximum authorized*—25,000. *Number minted (including 15 assay coins)*—25,015. *Number melted*—5,000. *Net distribution*—20,015.

Original Cost and Issuer: $1.50. Elgin Centennial Monumental Committee, El Paso, Texas (L.W. Hoffecker in charge); banks in and near Elgin, including the First National Bank of Elgin, the Elgin National Bank, and the Union National Bank.

Hoffecker Scores Another Coup

The fact that commemorative half dollars pertaining to Elgin, Illinois, were distributed by L.W. Hoffecker, a rare coin dealer located in distant El Paso, Texas, immediately arouses suspicion. Unlike the Old Spanish Trail coins distributed by Hoffecker, the main recipient of the profit was to be a legitimate civic project: to erect a statue. Hoffecker was in the right place at the right time, and acting as distributor, he turned a profit, somewhat modest in this instance, on the sale of each coin.

The Elgin Centennial half dollar wasn't Hoffecker's idea. It started out when Trygve A. Rovelstad, a sculptor who lived in Elgin, sought financing for a monumental statue, the *Pioneer Memorial*, to be erected in an Elgin park, but was unable to raise the necessary funds. He learned of recent issues of commemorative half dollars, and decided that he himself could design such a coin to provide the money needed. On May 27, 1935, a bill was introduced into the House of Representatives, which provided

> That, in commemoration of the one hundredth anniversary of the founding of the city of Elgin, Illinois and the erection of the heroic *Pioneer Memorial*, there shall be coined by the director of the Mint (not more than) ten thousand silver 50-cent pieces . . . of a special appropriate design containing a replica of the *Pioneers*. . . . Such coins herein authorized shall be issued at par and only upon request of the chairman of the coinage committee, Elgin Centennial Monumental Committee. Such coins may be disposed of at par or at a premium by said committee, and all proceeds shall be used in furtherance of the erecting of the *Pioneer Memorial*.

The above news appeared in *The Numismatist* in July 1935. Among those reading the notice was L.W. Hoffecker, who addressed an inquiry on July 11, 1935, to the Elgin Centennial Monumental Committee, stating that he had just finished "getting a bill passed for the Old Spanish Trail coin and we are now working on the plaque from which to make the dies."

Although Trygve A. Rovelstad had the best of intentions, his bill was getting nowhere in Congress. Hoffecker provided many useful tips. On September 26, 1935, he wrote a lengthy letter to Rovelstad to explain that it took expertise, such as he possessed, to shepherd a commemorative bill through Congress. Hoffecker noted that for his own issue of the Old Spanish Trail half dollar, a personal visit was held with President Franklin D. Roosevelt—an arrangement "that saved us"—implying that he could do the same for the Elgin bill.

So confident was Hoffecker that he could work effectively with Rovelstad, that he told the sculptor how to proceed; although at this time the legislation was still in committee in Congress. In the same letter, Hoffecker instructed Rovelstad on the steps necessary after the bill passed and how sculptors would attempt to manipulate him to introduce their own ideas to the design. He went on to say how much he enjoyed distributing the 1935 Old Spanish Trial coins, asking if Rovelstad's committee would "entertain an offer to handle the entire issue?" and giving a rough guideline of how he'd handle the sale.

In a letter dated October 12, 1935, to Rovelstad, Hoffecker cautioned: "It would not be good for either of us if the word got out that you had disposed of the entire issue to me." The effort was successful. Hoffecker was appointed as distributor. The arrangement was to be for all 10,000 to be shipped to him in El Paso, Texas, where he would take care of everything. Contrary to his expectations, Congress did not pass the bill for 10,000 coins, nor would it agree to have them made at different mints. The effort dragged on into 1936. Eventually, Hoffecker had to settle for 25,000 coins from a single mint, which was becoming the standard practice for the more newly authorized 1936 coins.

The Design

Trygve A. Rovelstad, whose talents were superb, had designed the *Pioneer Memorial* group of statuary, intended to be cast in bronze and to measure 12 feet high. He made a model of the group and also a medal depicting it. Rovelstad prepared designs for the Elgin Centennial half dollar using the *Pioneer Memorial* as a motif, as specified in the legislation.

On the obverse was depicted the head of a man facing to the left (the head of the leftmost figure in the *Pioneer Memorial*) with the lettering PIONEER widely spaced above, and the dates 1673–1936 below. The 1936 date referred to the year the coins were issued. The reverse design showed the entire *Pioneer Memorial*, a group of frontier people (four adults and a baby) who might have settled the area in 1835.

The entire situation was rather mixed up, because the 1673 date, representing the year fathers Joliet and Marquette explored the area, does not seem to have anything to do with anything else on the coin. The 1936 date had nothing to do with the centennial of the city, which, as noted, was celebrated in 1935. The coins were offered by Hoffecker for $1.50 each. The coins were not ready to be shipped until the autumn, by which time the commemorative bubble had burst. Hoffecker and some others bought quantities of unsold remainders, after which 5,000 were shipped back to the Philadelphia Mint and melted.

Although profits were to have gone toward completion of the statue, the concrete base for which was laid in 1934, funds were insufficient, and the project languished for six decades, despite great efforts by Rovelstad and his wife Gloria. Rovelstad died in 1990. Finally, in 2001 the *Pioneer Memorial* was erected in a town park, amidst much celebration.

Key to Collecting

Elgin half dollars seem to have been handled with particular care at the time of minting, with the result that the pieces have fewer bagmarks than many others of the same era.

Marks, when seen, are apt to be on the cheek of the pioneer on the obverse, or on the statue figures on the reverse. Sometimes the heads of the statue figures are lightly struck and show graininess from the surface of the original planchet. The surfaces of many 1936 Elgin half dollars have a mattelike appearance (seemingly a combination of a lustrous circulation strike and a Matte Proof) quite different from other commemorative issues of the year. Others are fairly frosty. On many coins a bright spot is seen on the reverse below the A of AMERICA, the result of an inadvertent polishing on a small area of the die. Chief Engraver Sinnock made a few Matte Proofs at the Mint by pickling coins in acid, perhaps as many as 10. Typical coins grade in the MS-64 to 66 range and are fairly plentiful today.

(1936) LONG ISLAND TERCENTENARY HALF DOLLARS

Distribution
81,826

Whitman Coin Guide (WCG™)—1936 Long Island Tercentenary 50¢

MS-60	MS-63	MS-64	MS-65	MS-66	MS-67	MS-68
$100	$125	$140	$440	$1,220	$6,600	

CERTIFIED POPULATIONS

MS-60	MS-61	MS-62	MS-63	MS-64	MS-65	MS-66	MS-67	MS-68
136	139	565	1,796	3,667	1,962	572	66	0

Points of Interest: This large-mintage issue was distributed on a quota basis to various Long Island counties.

Subject of Commemoration: 300th anniversary of the settling of Long Island, New York.

Designs: *Obverse*—Portraits of a Dutch settler and an Algonquin Indian. *Reverse*—A sailing ship. Designed by Howard Kenneth Weinman.

Mintage and Melting Data: Authorized April 13, 1936. *Maximum authorized*—100,000. *Number minted* (including 53 assay coins)—100,053. *Number melted*—18,227. *Net distribution*—81,826.

Original Cost and Issuer: $1. Long Island Tercentenary Committee, through various banks and other outlets.

Long Island Memorialized

In the year 1636, the first white settlement on Long Island at Jamaica Bay was established, an event memorialized 300 years later with a celebration. The Long Island Tercentenary Committee helped formulate a congressional resolution that was signed into law on April 13, 1936, and which provided for up to 100,000 silver half dollars of a "single design" to be coined at "a mint"—thus prohibiting a multiplicity of exploitative variations. Congress was becoming wise!

Well in advance of the passage of the bill, the Long Island Tercentenary Committee approached Howard Kenneth Weinman, son of famous sculptor Adolph A. Weinman (who designed the 1916 "Mercury" dime and Liberty Walking half dollar), to prepare sketches for the proposed commemorative half dollar. Weinman created a motif depicting, on the obverse, the conjoined heads of a Dutch settler and a male Algonquin Indian. The reverse design was a representation of a Dutch sailing ship of the period, quite similar to the *Half Moon* pictured on the reverse of the 1935 Hudson half dollar. Although the Commission of Fine Arts approved the model, some minor changes were made. Weinman had the proper surname—complaints that probably would have been voiced concerning the work of just about any other artist, were notably absent in correspondence involving Weinman's work on this Long Island coin.

Coinage of the entire authorized issue of 100,000 pieces, plus 53 additional coins for assay, took place in Philadelphia in August 1936, too late to be sold during the May 1936 Long Island Tercentenary celebrations. The coins were shipped to Long Island, where they were distributed through banks for $1 each.

Distribution was widespread, and enough were coined that anyone who desired an example could buy one. No profiteering took place, and no criticisms were voiced concerning the method of distribution. Although collectors undoubtedly accounted for the sale of tens of thousands of pieces, citizens of Long Island were enthusiastic buyers as well. More than 80,000 were marketed, a creditable piece of work by any standard.

Key to Collecting

Today, Long Island half dollars are among the most plentiful survivors from issues of the 1930s. As is the case with most other issues of the era, pieces were minted and handled carelessly, and at the time of distribution most showed nicks, bagmarks, and other evidences of contact, particularly on the ship's sails on the reverse. Numerous pieces that show friction are undoubtedly from the tens of thousands of coins originally distributed to the general public. Such coins usually grade from AU-50 to MS-60. Check for friction and/or evidences of handling on the cheek and hair of the Dutch settler on the obverse and, in particular, on the largest sail on the ship on the reverse. Most coins have a satiny or slightly "greasy" luster and are not deeply frosty; this is the way they were struck. Long Island half dollars grading MS-64 to 66 are readily obtainable.

(1936) LYNCHBURG (VIRGINIA) SESQUICENTENNIAL HALF DOLLARS

Distribution
20,013

Whitman Coin Guide (WCG™)—1936 Lynchburg (VA) Sesquicentennial 50¢

MS-60	MS-63	MS-64	MS-65	MS-66	MS-67	MS-68
$265	$300	$310	$380	$715	$2,162	

CERTIFIED POPULATIONS

MS-60	MS-61	MS-62	MS-63	MS-64	MS-65	MS-66	MS-67	MS-68
16	21	123	692	1,842	2,050	865	127	5

Points of Interest: Depicted on the obverse is Carter Glass, who was living at the time.

Subject of Commemoration: The 150th anniversary of Lynchburg, Virginia's charter.

Designs: *Obverse*—Portrait of Carter Glass. *Reverse*—Standing figure of Miss Liberty. Designed by Charles Keck.

Mintage and Melting Data: Authorized May 28, 1936. *Maximum authorized*—20,000. *Number minted* (including 13 assay coins)—20,013. *Net distribution*—20,013.

Original Cost and Issuer: $1. Lynchburg Sesqui-Centennial Association.

A Local Event Commemorated

In 1936, Lynchburg, Virginia celebrated the sesquicentennial of its 1786 city charter, an event hardly of statewide importance, let alone national significance. Be that as it may, the congressional Act of May 28, 1936, authorized the production of a quantity of Lynchburg Sesquicentennial coins not to exceed 20,000 silver half dollars to be coined of a single design at a single mint.

Lynchburg was proud of her living citizens in 1936, and a brochure noted that they included such personalities as Senator Carter Glass, Lady Nancy Astor, Mrs. Charles Dana Gibson (wife of the artist), Douglas S. Freeman, Samuel Untermyer, Robert L. Owen, Col. Edwin Halsey, S.S. Van Dyne (*nom de plume of* William Huntington Wright, mystery writer), and the Warner brothers (of motion picture fame).

On the recommendation of president Charles Moore of the Commission of Fine Arts, Charles Keck was chosen to create the motifs. (Earlier Keck had designed the 1915-S Panama-Pacific gold dollar and the 1927 Vermont half dollar.)

Although it was considered appropriate that John Lynch, after whom the city was named, be featured on the obverse, no likeness of Lynch existed. After due consideration, the Association selected Senator Carter Glass, a citizen of Lynchburg at the time, for the honor. Glass raised a token protest over the use of his image, but it was approved anyway. Born in Lynchburg on January 4, 1858, Glass entered the newspaper business and then politics, becoming a state senator in 1899. From 1903 to 1918 he was a U.S. congressman. In the latter year he resigned to accept an appointment as secretary of the Treasury under President Woodrow Wilson, a position he filled until 1920. Later in his life, until his death in 1946, Glass was a Virginia state senator.

The reverse of the Lynchburg Sesquicentennial half dollar showed the goddess Liberty standing with Monument Terrace (with its Confederate Monument) and the old Lynchburg Courthouse in the background.

In September 1936, the Philadelphia Mint struck the authorized 20,000 coins plus an extra 13 for the Assay Commission. Offered at $1 each (considered to be a reasonable price for such a restricted issue) the Lynchburg half dollars found a ready market following their release on September 21, and were distributed widely, mostly on an individual basis. Lynchburg celebrated its anniversary from October 12 through 16 with parades, pageants, exhibits, and other attractions. Local residents bought many half dollars at the event. Before long, the entire supply was gone.

Key to Collecting

Most Lynchburg half dollars are in higher grades, with MS-65 and 66 being easy to find. Some show graininess (from striking) on the high areas of the obverse portrait and on the bosom and skirt of the figure on the reverse, or show evidences of handling or contact in the same areas. Surfaces are often somewhat satiny, instead of deeply lustrous and frosty. Often the reverse field is semi-prooflike. This issue must have been handled with particular care at the Mint.

(1936) NORFOLK (VIRGINIA) BICENTENNIAL HALF DOLLARS

Distribution
16,936

Whitman Coin Guide (WCG™)—1936 Norfolk (VA) Bicentennial 50¢

MS-60	MS-63	MS-64	MS-65	MS-66	MS-67	MS-68
$575	$605	$665	$680	$705	$781	$2,530

CERTIFIED POPULATIONS

MS-60	MS-61	MS-62	MS-63	MS-64	MS-65	MS-66	MS-67	MS-68
15	7	47	229	822	1,616	3,299	1,339	193

Points of Interest: This coin bears five dates as part of the design, none of which is the date of mintage (1937).

Subject of Commemoration: 300th anniversary of the land grant for Norfolk, Virginia and the 200th anniversary of the establishment of Norfolk as a borough.

Designs: *Obverse*—Norfolk City Seal. *Reverse*—Royal mace. Designed by William Marks Simpson and his wife Marjorie Emory Simpson.

Mintage and Melting Data: Authorized June 28, 1937. *Maximum authorized—25,000. Number minted* (including 13 assay coins)—25,013. *Number melted*—8,077. *Net distribution*—16,936.

Original Cost and Issuer: $1.50 locally ($1.65 by mail for the first coin, $1.55 each for additional specimens). Norfolk Advertising Board, Norfolk Association of Commerce.

Another Obscure Anniversary

Among the most obscure events ever memorialized on a commemorative coin was the conversion of Norfolk, Virginia, founded as a village in 1682, to the borough form of government in 1736. In 1936, the city fathers thought that the 200th anniversary of the town's borough status should be brought to national attention by issuing commemorative half dollars. The year 1936 was also the 300th anniversary of the 1636 land grant on which Norfolk was founded. On June 28, 1937, a bill was passed to authorize the production of a quantity not to exceed 25,000 silver Norfolk Bicentennial half dollars, to be struck of a single design and at a single mint—never mind that the anniversary to be celebrated had already passed.

William Marks Simpson, a Baltimore sculptor, and his wife Marjorie Emery Simpson were named to prepare the designs. (Mr. Simpson created the 1937 Roanoke and Antietam issues as well.)

The obverse of the 1936-dated Norfolk Bicentennial half dollar stands as the most cluttered commemorative design ever produced. It contains inscriptions in three concentric circles, enclosing a three-masted ship at the center. Below that are a plow and three sheaves of wheat, taken from the seal of the city. The reverse has enough lettering for two coins, at the center of which is the Royal Mace of Norfolk.

The Norfolk Advertising Board, Inc. offered the coins for $1.50 each to local buyers, $1.65 by mail. The commemorative market had slumped by the time these coins were available, and sales were difficult. On July 5, 1938, the issuer sent a circular letter to numismatists, noting that 5,000 unsold pieces had been returned to the Philadelphia Mint, resulting in a net issue of just 20,000. The letter urged collectors to send in their orders.

If at first you don't succeed, then try again. Notice was sent to collectors again on September 13, 1938, pointing out the financial advantages of having extra coins on hand once the issue was sold out.

In the meantime several thousand coins were sold to dealers, and bulk quantities remained in numismatic circles for years afterward.

Key to Collecting

Norfolk Bicentennial half dollars are fairly plentiful today. Most seen are in high Mint State levels. The cluttered nature of the design had a positive effect: all of the lettering served to protect the fields and devices from nicks and marks, with the result that MS-65 and 66 coins are plentiful. Check the sails of the ship and the high points of the mace for friction.

(1936) RHODE ISLAND (PROVIDENCE) TERCENTENARY HALF DOLLARS

Distribution
1936: 20,013
1936-D: 15,010
1936-S: 15,011

Whitman Coin Guide (WCG™)—1936 Rhode Island (Providence) Tercentenary 50¢

MS-60	MS-63	MS-64	MS-65	MS-66	MS-67	MS-68
$115	$145	$165	$275	$550	$2,065	

CERTIFIED POPULATIONS

MS-60	MS-61	MS-62	MS-63	MS-64	MS-65	MS-66	MS-67	MS-68
26	10	76	526	1,779	1,936	691	38	1

1936-D Rhode Island (Providence) Tercentenary 50¢

MS-60	MS-63	MS-64	MS-65	MS-66	MS-67	MS-68
$180	$205	$210	$480	$1,395	$1,624	

CERTIFIED POPULATIONS

MS-60	MS-61	MS-62	MS-63	MS-64	MS-65	MS-66	MS-67	MS-68
13	11	90	437	1,381	1,472	617	69	0

1936-S Rhode Island (Providence) Tercentenary 50¢

MS-60	MS-63	MS-64	MS-65	MS-66	MS-67	MS-68
$110	$145	$165	$275	$517	$2,558	

CERTIFIED POPULATIONS

MS-60	MS-61	MS-62	MS-63	MS-64	MS-65	MS-66	MS-67	MS-68
16	10	98	490	1,277	1,159	360	25	0

Points of Interest: Otherwise upstanding citizens issued phony news releases to promote the sale of these coins.

Subject of Commemoration: 300th anniversary of the founding of Providence, Rhode Island.

Designs: *Obverse*—Roger Williams and Indian. *Reverse*—Elements from Rhode Island State Seal. Designed by Arthur Graham Carey and John Howard Benson.

Mintage and Melting Data: Authorized May 2, 1935. *Maximum authorized*—50,000. **1936-P-D-S:** *Number minted and distribution*—20,013, 15,010, 15,011. Assay coins: 13, 10, 11.

Original Cost and Issuer: $1. Rhode Island and Providence Plantations Tercentenary Committee, Inc.

A Set of Three Coins

The 300th anniversary of the landing of Roger Williams in Rhode Island on June 24, 1636, and the subsequent establishment of the Providence Plantations furnished the occasion for issuing 1936-dated commemorative half dollars. Curiously, no reference to the city of Providence appeared on the coins. Roger Williams, depicted on the coins, was born in England and came to America in 1631. In Massachusetts he quarreled with religious and colony leaders and had the audacity to suggest that settlers should compensate the native Indians for land taken. Williams was commanded to leave, and an effort was made to send him back to England. He escaped with four companions and in early 1636 settled on the shore of Narragansett Bay and established a settlement named Providence—in gratitude for God's help when he was in distress. He negotiated with the Indians and, true to his principles, purchased the land for the new colony. The community grew under a government which permitted freedom of religious expression and the separation of church and state. In 1644, several towns in the area were combined under a charter incorporating the Providence Plantations.

Providence Tercentenary half dollars, commonly called Rhode Island Tercentenary half dollars, were authorized by Congress in an act approved on May 2, 1935, as part of the bill that also provided for Hudson commemoratives. The issue of Providence coins was set at 50,000 silver half dollars. Eventually the coins were produced at three mints.

John Howard Benson, an instructor at the Rhode Island School of Design, and his friend, silversmith Arthur Graham Carey, created the motifs. The obverse depicted Roger Williams kneeling in a canoe, his right hand raised in greeting and his left hand holding a Bible, while an Indian standing on a rock extends his hands (ostensibly in greeting, or perhaps in the gesture known as "good," in sign language). In the distance is the "sun of religious liberty" with resplendent rays. The scene represented Roger Williams arriving in his canoe at Slate Rock. The reverse illustrated an anchor with HOPE above and other lettering below and surrounding.

The entire design is in rather shallow relief, but distinctly defined. This style was inspired by shallow carvings on gravestones in Concord, Massachusetts and elsewhere. After appropriate reduction of the models and preparation of master dies by the Medallic Art Company, 20,013 pieces were struck at the Philadelphia Mint in January 1936, followed in February by 15,010 in Denver, and 15,011 in San Francisco.

A publicity blitz ensued, and news releases, advertisements, and other messages called nationwide attention to the distribution, which was set to take place on March 5, 1936. The Rhode Island Hospital National Bank was the focal point of the activity and distributed allotments to 30 banking outlets. In addition, nearly 7,000 coins were assigned to Horace M. Grant, who owned Grant's Hobby Shop in Providence. Phony announcements stated that the entire issue was sold out in six hours. It soon developed that some insiders, including Grant, still had coins available—but for higher prices.

Key to Collecting

Rhode Island half dollars are readily available singly and in sets, with typical grades being MS-63 to MS-65, with contact marks on the canoe on the obverse and the shield on the reverse. Higher level coins such as MS-66 and 67 are not hard to find, but are elusive in comparison to the lesser condition pieces. The 1936 (in particular) and 1936-S are sometimes found with prooflike surfaces.

Check the prow of the canoe (especially) and the high points of the figures for handling marks. On the reverse the anchor and surrounding areas should be checked, but these are not as crucial as the obverse characteristics. Most specimens have a combination satiny–frosty surface. Many are light gray in color.

(1936) ROBINSON-ARKANSAS HALF DOLLARS

Distribution
25,265

Whitman Coin Guide (WCG™)—1936 Robinson-Arkansas 50¢

MS-60	MS-63	MS-64	MS-65	MS-66	MS-67	MS-68
$160	$185	$200	$455	$924	$2,772	$20,350

CERTIFIED POPULATIONS

MS-60	MS-61	MS-62	MS-63	MS-64	MS-65	MS-66	MS-67	MS-68
23	68	253	1,165	2,607	1,574	517	78	1

Points of Interest: Sen. Joseph Robinson, depicted on the coin, was living at the time the coins were issued; although they were dated 1936, the coins were minted in 1937.

Subject of Commemoration: Centennial of the admission of Arkansas into the Union; Sen. Joseph T. Robinson.

Designs: *Obverse*—Portrait of Joseph T. Robinson. *Reverse*—Arkansas State Seal. Designed by Edward Everett Burr.

Mintage and Melting Data: Authorized June 26, 1936. *Maximum authorized*—50,000 (minimum 25,000). *Number minted* (including 15 assay coins)—25,265. *Net distribution*—25,265.

Original Cost and Issuer: $1.85. Stack's, New York City.

Congress Bends the Rules

Arkansas commemorative half dollars, first issued in 1935 and bearing a design with Miss Liberty and an Indian on the obverse and an eagle on the reverse, were not popular with collectors, and many complaints were made concerning them (see earlier listing of the 1935–1939 Arkansas series). Adding ammunition to the naysayers was a special issue created in 1936, featuring a new design, although the creation of a new design for an existing series was contrary to prevailing government policy.

The origin of the new design came about in 1936, when the Texas Centennial Commission pushed a bill (S. 3721, January 16, 1936), which ultimately proved unsuccessful, to create five new reverse designs for their half dollar. The Arkansas Centennial Commission, sniffing a similar profit possibility, thought it a good idea to request *three* new Arkansas reverses as an amendment to the Texas bill. The Act of June 26, 1936, eventually resulted and authorized the issuance of 50,000 Arkansas coins of *one* new design, in addition to those of the regular centennial style.

A.W. Parke, who was the spokesman for the Arkansas Centennial Commission and the prime moving force of the group, originally stated that the supplementary design would illustrate one side of an old coin (the exact coin was not specified, nor was it stated whether the obverse or reverse would be used) of a type which early explorer Hernando de Soto was said to have presented to an Indian woman during his exploration of the territory that would later become Arkansas. Other considerations intervened, and it was decided to use the portrait of a well-known living politician.

The Design

Featured on the obverse of the coin was the image of Joseph T. Robinson, Democratic senator from Arkansas, a living individual who was well known at the time. Robinson had served in the House of Representatives from 1903 to 1913 and was elected governor of Arkansas in the latter year, resigning soon thereafter in order to serve in the U.S. Senate, where he remained until his death on July 14, 1937.

Enid Bell, a New Jersey artist, designed the obverse of the new coin. Henry G. Kreis, earlier the creator of the 1935 Connecticut and 1936 Bridgeport half dollar motifs, made the finished model from her sketch. The motif was approved by the Commission of Fine Arts on December 23, 1936, too late for coinage and distribution to occur in the year in which the proposed coins were to be dated.

The reverse of the Robinson-Arkansas half dollars incorporated that used on Arkansas Centennial half dollars from 1935 onward. Following the wording of the legislation, an official announcement was made that the Robinson side was really the reverse, whereas the Arkansas side, which contained the date, was the obverse (even though it was the *reverse* of the regular Arkansas coins). This nomenclature was followed by a number of people at the time. Today, most designate the Robinson portrait side as the obverse.

Distribution

In January 1937, 25,265 specimens of the 1936-dated Robinson-Arkansas half dollars were struck at the Philadelphia Mint and sent to Stack's, which by that time had been named as the official distributor for 1937 Arkansas P-D-S sets. The New York City firm offered Robinson coins at $1.85 each. On the back of its subscription application for the coins, the following notice appeared: "From all outward appearances, this issue will be oversubscribed and sold the day the coins will be released."

Unfortunately, sales plodded along at an unsatisfactory rate, for the issue was criticized by many in the numismatic fraternity. In any event, by early 1937 commemorative half dollars of all types were out of favor with many collectors and nearly all speculators.

In *The Numismatist* in February 1939, Stack's placed an advertisement offering for sale to the highest bidder 500 Robinson-Arkansas half dollars (and also 500 sets of

1935 Texas commemorative half dollars). Bids were to be received on or before February 15, 1939. This represented only a small portion of the unsold Robinson-Arkansas pieces.

Finally, the remaining Robinson coins, said to have amounted to 8,000 pieces, were wholesaled to Abe Kosoff, who maintained a coin business in the same city. Other large lots may have been sold to still other dealers (or perhaps Kosoff redistributed them), but in any event, there were large quantities of unsold Robinson-Arkansas half dollars in dealers' hands as late as the 1950s. An original mint bag of 1,000 coins was reported to exist in Arkansas in 1991.

Key to Collecting

Most known Robinson-Arkansas (or, if you prefer, Arkansas-Robinson half dollars) are in Mint State, for nearly all (perhaps all?) were originally sold to collectors and dealers. Examples are plentiful today. Typical grades are MS-62 to MS-64. The portrait of Sen. Robinson is apt to display friction and contact marks, for the coins were not handled with care at the time of production. Some examples are lightly struck on the eagle just behind the head.

(1936) SAN FRANCISCO–OAKLAND BAY BRIDGE HALF DOLLARS

Distribution
71,424

Whitman Coin Guide (WCG™)—1936 San Francisco–Oakland Bay Bridge 50¢

MS-60	MS-63	MS-64	MS-65	MS-66	MS-67	MS-68
$185	$235	$245	$365	$666	$1,705	$14,850

CERTIFIED POPULATIONS

MS-60	MS-61	MS-62	MS-63	MS-64	MS-65	MS-66	MS-67	MS-68
60	54	342	1,016	2,581	2,603	1,151	169	16

Points of Interest: In addition to other methods of distribution, these coins could be bought by driving up to booths at the bridge entrances.

Subject of Commemoration: The opening of the San Francisco–Oakland Bay Bridge linking the two California cities.

Designs: *Obverse*—Grizzly Bear. *Reverse*—San Francisco–Oakland Bay Bridge and part of San Francisco. Designed by Jacques Schnier.

Mintage and Melting Data: Authorized June 26, 1936. *Maximum authorized*—200,000. *Number minted* (including 55 assay coins)—100,055. *Number melted*—28,631. *Net distribution*—71,424.

Original Cost and Issuer: $1.50. Coin Committee of the San Francisco–Oakland Bay Bridge Celebration.

A Bridge Opening Commemorated

The San Francisco–Oakland Bay Bridge was opened to the public in November 1936, furnishing the occasion for a commemorative half dollar and its distribution. The coin had been approved months earlier on June 26, in a congressional bill authorizing a quantity not to exceed 200,000 half dollars, to be made of a single design and struck at a single mint. Almost immediately the issuing commission announced its intention to have fewer made: "The present plans of this Committee include issuance of 100,000 one-half dollars."

Work on the bridge began on July 9, 1933. Spanning four and a half miles over water and connecting in the middle of the bay with Yerba Buena Island, upon completion the bridge was eight and one-half miles long. It linked San Francisco and Oakland, rendering obsolete the ferry that had been used since 1851. Some 200,000 tons of steel, 70,815 miles of cable, and one million cubic yards of concrete were used in its construction, which cost $77 million. It has always been a point of interest to Bay area tourists that maintenance painting of the bridge is continuous.

This bridge was often confused with the better-known Golden Gate Bridge crossing the entrance of San Francisco Bay, the construction of which was also begun in 1933. The original bill (H.R. 12397) authorized "the coinage of 50-cent pieces in commemoration of the completion of the bridges in the San Francisco Bay Area." The bill (S. 4464) finally approved on June 26, 1936, mentioned only the San Francisco–Oakland Bay Bridge.

Jacques Schnier, a young Romanian sculptor who made his home in San Francisco and whose works were well known in California, prepared the designs for the coin. The obverse depicted a grizzly bear and the reverse showed the Ferry Building and the San Francisco end of the bridge in question, with a view toward Yerba Buena Island and Oakland. The entire coin was executed in a modernistic style. The reverse was extremely detailed and had no completely smooth or "field" surface. Models were reduced to die form by the Medallic Art Company of New York, which prepared the master dies for other issues of the era as well.

In November 1936, 100,055 San Francisco–Oakland Bay Bridge half dollars were struck at the San Francisco Mint. The coins were offered for sale for $1.50 each by the San Francisco Clearing House Association (a group which had distributed 1925-S California Diamond Jubilee half dollars 11 years earlier). The actual celebration for the bridge completion was scheduled to be held November 12 to 14, at which time "all the colorful charm of San Francisco will be spread for our visitors" (per an official brochure).

Numerous coins were sold at booths near the entrances to the bridge, making it the first time that a commemorative coin was originally distributed on a drive-up basis. Coins were sold by mail by the San Francisco–Oakland Bay Bridge Celebration. Many coins remained unsold, and in 1937, 28,631 examples were melted.

Key to Collecting

Today, 1936 Bay Bridge half dollars, as they are usually called, are readily available. Most examples are in the range of MS-62 to 64, typically with contact marks on the grizzly bear motif. In general, scattered marks are seen on the bear on the obverse. The reverse design, being complex with many protective devices, is apt to appear mark-free, unless viewed at an angle under a strong light. From a technical or numerical viewpoint the reverse grade of a typical specimen is apt to be a point or two higher than the obverse grade. The fields of this coin often have a "greasy" appearance, rather than being deeply lustrous and frosty.

(1936) WISCONSIN TERRITORIAL CENTENNIAL HALF DOLLARS

Distribution
25,015

Whitman Coin Guide (WCG™)—1936 Wisconsin Territorial Centennial 50¢

MS-60	MS-63	MS-64	MS-65	MS-66	MS-67	MS-68
$255	$280	$320	$415	$550	$930	$9,680

CERTIFIED POPULATIONS

MS-60	MS-61	MS-62	MS-63	MS-64	MS-65	MS-66	MS-67	MS-68
12	12	94	445	1,854	3,223	2,268	499	30

Points of Interest: According to provisions of the congressional enabling acts of the Wisconsin, Bridgeport, and Delaware half dollars, coinage was to be a minimum of 25,000, but there was no stated maximum, and an unlimited quantity could have been made at the time. This coin, like a few other commemoratives, also bears a *day* date, 4th of July Anno Domini 1836. Remainder coins were still being sold by the state in the 1950s.

Subject of Commemoration: 100th anniversary of the establishment of the territorial government in Wisconsin.

Designs: *Obverse*—Badger. *Reverse*—An arm, pickaxe, and ore mound. Designed by David Parsons. Benjamin Hawkins made changes to conform with technical requirements.

Mintage and Melting Data: Authorized May 15, 1936. *Minimum authorized*—25,000 (unlimited maximum). *Number minted* (including 15 assay coins)—25,015. *Net distribution*—25,015.

Original Cost and Issuer: $1.50 plus 7¢ postage for the first coin, 2¢ postage for each additional coin (later sold for $1.25 each in lots of 10 coins; still later sold for $3 per coin). Wisconsin Centennial Coin Committee (also known as the Coinage Committee of the Wisconsin Centennial Commission). Unsold remainders were distributed by the State Historical Society into the 1950s.

Another Obscure Anniversary

The year 1936 marked the 100th anniversary of the establishment of the territorial government in Wisconsin, and it was deemed appropriate to observe the occasion with a commemorative half dollar issue. Wisconsin did not join the Union until 12 years after 1836, so the centennial is not of statehood but is, as noted, of the establishment of the territorial government—a rather obscure event to observe with a nationally distributed commemorative coin bearing the date 1936.

On May 15, 1936, a congressional bill was approved that provided for no fewer than 25,000 coins to be struck of a single design and at a single mint, in connection with the event commemorated. It is worth noting that on May 15, 1936, Congress also approved half dollars pertaining to Bridgeport, Connecticut and to Delaware, and that, although a minimum amount of 25,000 was specified, there was no upper limit. Presumably, the issuing commissions could have ordered any higher number desired.

The Coinage Committee of the Wisconsin Centennial Celebration selected David Goode Parsons, an art student at the University of Wisconsin, to prepare the designs. The Committee stated that the territorial seal should be used on one side and a badger on the other. The Mint found Parsons's models to be poorly executed and rejected them, after which the Committee suggested that the Treasury Department name a suitable artist. The Commission of Fine Arts recommended New York sculptor Benjamin Hawkins, who took up the work and vastly revised it, so that the finished product bore little resemblance to what Parsons originally created.

The obverse shows a stout badger facing to the viewer's left, standing on a small log, with three vertical arrows and a stiff olive branch behind, representing hostilities with native Indians and eventual peace. In its final form, the reverse depicted the simple design used on the Wisconsin Territorial seal, consisting of a forearm holding a pickaxe above a small mound of earth and rock clumps, said to represent lead ore. Below appears the inscription 4TH DAY OF JULY / ANNO DOMINI / 1836, referring to the date when the first territorial governor, Henry Dodge, took office.

The coins were struck in July 1936 to the extent of 25,015 pieces. Sales by mail were made to collectors and dealers. Many others found buyers at the Wisconsin Centennial celebration in Madison, held from June 27 to July 5, 1936. Large quantities remained unsold, and a decade later pieces could be ordered in groups of 10 for $1.25 each from the State Historical Society. By January 2, 1952, the Society had raised its price to $3 per coin (plus postage of 7¢ for the first coin and 1¢ for each additional piece).

Key to Collecting

Today examples are readily available, with most being in MS-62 to 64, although higher grades are not rare. The flank of the badger is an obvious spot to check for friction, which is nearly always present if you look closely enough. The miner's hand is another checkpoint. Most Wisconsin halves are very lustrous and frosty, except for the higher areas of the design (which often have a slightly polished appearance).

(1936) YORK COUNTY (MAINE) TERCENTENARY HALF DOLLARS

Distribution
25,015

Whitman Coin Guide (WCG™)—1936 York County (ME) Tercentenary 50¢

MS-60	MS-63	MS-64	MS-65	MS-66	MS-67	MS-68
$220	$300	$350	$425	$450	$670	$4,125

CERTIFIED POPULATIONS

MS-60	MS-61	MS-62	MS-63	MS-64	MS-65	MS-66	MS-67	MS-68
28	14	98	492	1,594	2,691	2,232	748	47

Points of Interest: Quantities of unsold coins were on hand as late as the 1950s.

Subject of Commemoration: The 300th anniversary of the founding of York County, Maine.

Designs: *Obverse*—Brown's Garrison. *Reverse*—York County Seal. Designed by Walter H. Rich.

Mintage Data: *Maximum authorized*—30,000. *Number minted* (including 15 assay coins)—25,015.

Original Cost and Issuer: $1.50 ($1.65 postpaid to out-of-state buyers). York County Tercentenary Commemorative Coin Commission, York National Bank, Saco, Maine.

Yet Another Obscure Celebration

The world will little remember the 300th anniversary of the founding of York County, Maine, but it furnished the occasion for the issuance of a half dollar authorized by Congress on June 26, 1936. By this time the illogical seems to have become the logical, at least so far as votes by Congress went. The legislation provided that not more than 30,000 pieces were to be struck at a single mint and of a single design.

The Committee for the Commemoration of the Founding of York County, in charge of arrangements, tapped Portland artist Walter H. Rich to create the designs. These were translated into models (apparently made of brass rather than the usual plaster or clay) by the G.S. Pacetti Company of Boston, from which the Medallic Art Company made dies.

The obverse design depicted a stockade representing Brown's Garrison (the original settlement in York County; later the site of the York National Bank in Saco) with a rising sun in the background and a horse and rider in the foreground. The motif was taken from a sketch printed in *The Proprietors of Saco*, a 1931 work by Frank C. Deering. The reverse illustrated the seal of York County, consisting of a cross within a shield, with a pine tree at the upper left.

Distribution was handled through the committee, which variously styled itself in printed literature as the York County Commemorative Coin Commission, the York County Tercentenary Commemorative Coin Commission, and, as stated on the enabling legislation, the Committee for the Commemoration of the Founding of York County.

Walter P. Nichols, an ardent numismatist and later a member of the ANA Board of Governors (elected for two years in 1939), personally supervised all aspects of the release of the pieces and was careful to do everything in a proper manner. His actions became a model for other groups who intended to issue half dollars, and he corresponded with many of them to share his experiences and give advice. Much of this is recounted in the present author's compilation, *An Inside View of the Coin Hobby in the 1930s: The Walter P. Nichols File.*

At the outset 10,000 pieces were reserved for residents of Maine, and 15,000 were earmarked for sale out of state. At the original issue price of $1.50, apparently more than half went to Mainers. Those ordering from out of state paid $1.65 per coin and accounted for thousands more. After the initial burst of enthusiasm, about 6,000 remained unsold and continued to be distributed through the 1950s, well after Nichols's death (on August 8, 1941). Historian Arlie Slabaugh related that the Association sold pieces in the 1950s for $15.50 per group of 10, and at that price, the remainders were quickly liquidated.

When the present writer's firm auctioned coins from the Nichols estate in 1984, a few York County half dollars were included, so technically it can be said that complete distribution was not concluded until that late date.

Key to Collecting

This issue was well handled at the Mint and in distribution, and most examples are in higher grades and are relatively free of marks. Obverse points to check for friction include the horse and rider and the stockade. On the reverse, the top of the shield is a key point. Some coins have been brushed and have a myriad of fine hairlines; these can be detected by examining the coin at various angles to the light. MS-64 and 65 coins are readily found in the marketplace.

(1937) Battle of Antietam Anniversary Half Dollars

Distribution
18,028

Whitman Coin Guide (WCG™)—1937 Battle of Antietam Anniversary

MS-60	MS-63	MS-64	MS-65	MS-66	MS-67	MS-68
$735	$820	$905	$1,030	$1,400	$1,980	$12,650

CERTIFIED POPULATIONS

MS-60	MS-61	MS-62	MS-63	MS-64	MS-65	MS-66	MS-67	MS-68
35	16	91	471	1,556	2,191	1,532	330	29

Points of Interest: With the 1925 Stone Mountain and 1936 Gettysburg issues, this was one of three commemorative half dollars specifically relating to the Civil War; this coin also bears a *day* date of September 17, 1862.

Subject of Commemoration: The 75th anniversary of the famous Civil War battle to thwart Lee's invasion of Maryland.

Designs: *Obverse*—Generals Robert E. Lee and George B. McClellan. *Reverse*—Burnside Bridge. Designed by William Marks Simpson.

Mintage and Melting Data: Authorized June 24, 1937. *Maximum authorized*—50,000. *Number minted* (including 28 assay coins)—50,028. *Number melted*—32,000. *Net distribution*—18,028.

Original Cost and Issuer: $1.65. Washington County Historical Society, Hagerstown, Maryland.

The Only Strictly 1937 Commemorative

The 1937 Antietam half dollar has the distinction of being the only commemorative half dollar first authorized in 1937 and actually produced and sold during the same year. Moreover, it recalled an anniversary that actually took place in 1937. As such it was a paragon of commemorative virtue! It did not lack for fallen idols as companions, including several 1936-dated half dollars struck in 1937, not to forget lingering exploitative issues of Boone, Oregon Trail, Texas, and Arkansas.

Observation of the 75th anniversary of the Battle of Antietam furnished the occasion for a commemorative half dollar authorized by an act Congress approved on June 24, 1937. The enabling legislation specified that no more than 50,000 silver half dollars of a single design be produced at a single mint, to be delivered on request to the Washington County Historical Society of Hagerstown, Maryland.

The original offering circular gave details of the conflict commemorated. The issue was often referred to in brochures as the Lee-McClellan half dollar which, presumably, was more personal than the Battle of Antietam half dollar.

Design and Distribution

William Marks Simpson, the Baltimore sculptor who had designed the 1937 Roanoke and 1936 Norfolk half dollars, was named to prepare the models, which were in due course translated to die form by the Medallic Art Company of New York. The finished design featured on the obverse the busts of generals George B. McClellan and Robert E. Lee, and on the reverse the Burnside Bridge at Antietam, site of the most casualty-ridden skirmish of the Civil War.

Some 50,028 coins were struck at the Philadelphia Mint in August 1937 and shipped to the Washington County Historical Society, which sold them for $1.75 each. The first specimen struck was presented to President Franklin Delano Roosevelt on August 12, 1937.

Despite the avowed interest of the commission in preventing speculators from acquiring the issue, no limit was placed on the quantity that could be ordered. The point was moot, in any event, for by the summer of 1937, few speculators were even the slightest bit interested in commemorative half dollars.

The promoters tried their best to sell the pieces through intense advertising in numismatic periodicals, and most pieces likely were distributed in this manner, at $1.65 each.

By any account, the Antietam half dollar effort was a failure, for of the 50,000 coins produced for general sale, 32,000 were eventually returned to the Treasury Department for melting. There was no negative publicity associated with the distribution of Antietam half dollars, for by that point the subject had been largely exhausted in the numismatic press and elsewhere.

Key to Collecting

Antietam half dollars were handled with care. Friction, when it does occur, is often seen on the high parts of General Lee's portrait on the obverse and, on the reverse, on the bridge and trees. More often seen are scattered small marks, particularly on the upper part of the obverse. Most examples are very lustrous and frosty. MS-65 and finer coins are plentiful in the marketplace.

(1937) ROANOKE ISLAND (NORTH CAROLINA) ANNIVERSARY HALF DOLLARS

Distribution
29,030

Whitman Coin Guide (WCG™)—1937 Roanoke Island (NC) Anniversary 50¢

MS-60	MS-63	MS-64	MS-65	MS-66	MS-67	MS-68
$300	$320	$345	$375	$460	$965	$5,500

CERTIFIED POPULATIONS

MS-60	MS-61	MS-62	MS-63	MS-64	MS-65	MS-66	MS-67	MS-68
12	11	105	513	2,365	3,306	1,764	421	33

Points of Interest: No upper limit was placed on this coinage, and at the time an unlimited quantity could have been struck (as was also the case with 1936-dated Bridgeport, Delaware, and Wisconsin issues).

Subject of Commemoration: The 350th anniversary of the establishment of a colony sponsored by Sir Walter Raleigh (Ralegh) on Roanoke Island, North Carolina.

Designs: *Obverse*—Portrait of Sir Walter Raleigh. *Reverse*—Ellinor Dare and her baby, Virginia. Designed by William Marks Simpson.

Mintage and Melting Data: *Minimum authorized*—25,000 (unlimited maximum). *Number minted* (including 30 assay coins)—50,030. *Number melted*—21,000. *Net distribution*—29,030.

Original Cost and Issuer: $1.65. Roanoke Colony Memorial Association of Manteo.

The Lost Colony Commemorated

On June 24, 1936, an act of Congress was approved that authorized the coinage of no fewer than 25,000 silver half dollars "in commemoration of the three hundred and fiftieth anniversary of Sir Walter Raleigh's colony on Roanoke Island, North Carolina, known in history as the Lost Colony, and the birth of Virginia Dare, the first child of English parentage to be born on the American continent." The occasion was strictly a local celebration to be held at Old Fort Raleigh in August 1937.

Raleigh (1552?–1618; preferred original spelling: Ralegh), was a favorite in the court of Queen Elizabeth and, according to legend, spread his cloak on a puddle to prevent Her Majesty from being splashed by a passing coach. An accomplished writer, explorer, and soldier, Raleigh was given a patent to explore districts of America. In 1584 he sent two ships to the New World to find a place suitable for settlement. In 1585, seven additional ships, with 107 colonists aboard, were dispatched. (Raleigh himself never visited America.) Despite Raleigh's efforts, no permanent colony was made until 1587, when his new company, the City of Raleigh in Virginia, (which gave the would-be settlers stock in the enterprise) formed a colony on Roanoke Island. On August 18, 1587, a child, Virginia, was born to Ananias Dare and Ellinor (also referred to as Eleanor or Elinor) White Dare. In 1590, John White, representing Raleigh in the governing of the colony, visited Roanoke Island, but his granddaughter Virginia Dare and the settlers were nowhere to be seen, although the word CROATAN, the name of a nearby island, was found carved on a tree. The fate of the settlers has never been determined. It has been conjectured that they may have been killed, or, perhaps more likely, absorbed into the community of nearby Indians—who had been friendly to the colonists.

The Roanoke Colony Memorial Association enlisted Baltimore artist William Marks Simpson to prepare the designs. On the obverse is a portrait of Raleigh, said to have been modeled after movie actor Errol Flynn. The reverse shows the standing figure of Ellinor Dare holding her child, Virginia. Many inscriptions surround.

In January 1937, 25,015 Roanoke half dollars were struck at the Philadelphia Mint, followed by 25,015 more in June. The Roanoke Colony Memorial Association of Manteo (located in Manteo, North Carolina) offered them at $1.65 each. Sales proved to be difficult because the commemorative market was in a slump. Only 29,000 found buyers, some of these not until several years later. Fully 21,000 coins went back to the Philadelphia Mint to be melted.

Key to Collecting

Handled with care at the Mint, most coins are in high grades today, with MS-65 pieces being plentiful. On the obverse, check Raleigh's cheek and hat for marks, and on the reverse, check the higher areas of the standing figure. Partially prooflike pieces are sometimes seen (and offered as "presentation pieces" or "prooflike presentation pieces"). Most coins are lustrous and frosty.

(1938) NEW ROCHELLE (NEW YORK) 250TH ANNIVERSARY HALF DOLLARS

Distribution
15,266

Whitman Coin Guide (WCG™)—1938 New Rochelle (NY) 250th Anniversary 50¢

MS-60	MS-63	MS-64	MS-65	MS-66	MS-67	MS-68
$435	$470	$500	$615	$900	$1,716	$19,250

CERTIFIED POPULATIONS

MS-60	MS-61	MS-62	MS-63	MS-64	MS-65	MS-66	MS-67	MS-68
11	4	68	375	1,742	2,269	1,181	202	16
PF-60	PF-61	PF-62	PF-63	PF-64	PF-65	PF-66	PF-67	PF-68
0	1	0	0	0	0	3	1	0

Points of Interest: These coins were struck in 1937, a year before the date appearing on them. The coins were conceived by the Westchester County Coin Club.

Subject of Commemoration: The 250th anniversary of the founding of New Rochelle, New York.

Designs: *Obverse*—John Pell and a fatted calf, from New Rochelle history. *Reverse*—Fleur-de-lis. Designed by Gertrude K. Lathrop.

Mintage and Melting Data: Authorized May 5, 1936. *Maximum authorized*—25,000. *Number minted* (including 15 assay coins)—25,015. *Number melted*—9,749. *Net distribution*—15,266.

Original Cost and Issuer: $2. New Rochelle Commemorative Coin Committee through the First National Bank of New Rochelle, New Rochelle, New York.

Issued by a Coin Club

The 1938 New Rochelle half dollar, commemorating a strictly local event of no national importance, is especially amusing. Although it is dated 1938 and no mention of any other contemporary date appears, the issue was struck in 1937. Here we have a coin authorized in 1936, struck in 1937, and carrying the date 1938—certainly a perplexing situation! Actually, by this time, illogical situations have become the rule, not the exception.

The Westchester County Coin Club of New Rochelle, headed by numismatist Pitt M. Skipton, planned the issue, which was carefully executed so that no sensibilities would be offended. New Rochelle resident Julius Guttag, who earlier was very active as a partner in the Guttag Brothers firm of numismatists and securities dealers (and who scooped up all of those Hudson half dollars in 1935), served as chairman of the sales committee. Guttag was remembered in later years as the founder, in the 1920s, of National Coin Week, sponsored by the ANA.

The enabling congressional legislation, passed on May 5, 1936, stated that "in commemoration of the 250th anniversary of the founding of the settlement of the city of New Rochelle, New York, there shall be coined at a mint of the United States . . . not to exceed 25,000 silver 50-cent pieces." The bill further provided that the authorized coins should bear the date 1938, irrespective of when they were minted. This provision, like others of its era, would seem to authorize restriking as well as *prestriking* the coins. Apparently, the striking of coins in the year in which the pieces were dated was no longer of concern to the government. Indeed, the rule had been violated so many times that it hardly was a rule anymore.

Design and Distribution

Gertrude K. Lathrop, who had created the design for the Albany, New York half dollar, was selected to create the motifs for the New Rochelle issue—after the Commission of Fine Arts had criticized sketches made earlier by one Lorillard Wise, who was characterized as being inexperienced in designing coins or medals. Lathrop created an obverse design depicting a fatted calf, facing to the right, with a rope around its neck. John Pell, early owner of the land upon which the city of New Rochelle is situated, was shown pulling on the rope, in acknowledgment of an early deed provision under which Pell sold his land in an agreement that provided a fat calf would be tendered in payment on June 24 every year thereafter (if demanded). The reverse depicted an iris (the French fleur-de-lis) taken from the seal of the city and its French namesake, La Rochelle. On the coin, the fields were unusually flat and open, providing a surface that sharply highlighted the motifs and lettering. The Commission of Fine Arts approved Lathrop's work in February 1937.

In April 1937 the Philadelphia Mint struck 25,015 1938-dated New Rochelle commemorative half dollars, which were turned over to the First National Bank of New Rochelle—for the government felt that issuing such pieces through the Westchester County Coin Club would set an unfavorable precedent (although it is hard to see how this could have been worse than selling 1935 Old Spanish Trail and 1936 Elgin coins to coin dealer L.W. Hoffecker, or shipping the entire production of 1936 Cincinnati halves to one clever numismatist, Thomas G. Melish).

In addition to pieces sold locally through banks and elsewhere for $2 each, the New Rochelle Commemorative Coin Committee filled mail orders from an office at 20 Summit Avenue. Advertisements offered one coin for $2.18, two coins for $4.21, and five coins for $10.27—the odd amounts being reimbursement for postage and insurance.

The New Rochelle half dollars sold fairly well, considering the depressed market of the era. While citizens of that city undoubtedly purchased numerous examples, the main market consisted of collectors and dealers. When all was said and done, 9,749 remainder coins were melted. Just prior to this some members of the Westchester Coin Club purchased hundreds of unsold coins for face value.

Key to Collecting

New Rochelle half dollars received better-than-average care and handling during the minting and distribution process. Some examples show very light handling marks, but most are relatively problem-free. Some show areas of graininess or light striking on the high spots of the calf on the obverse, and on the highest area of the iris on the reverse. Today the typical coin is apt to be in Mint State, usually MS-64 or higher. The majority of pieces have lustrous, frosty surfaces, but occasionally an example with prooflike surfaces is encountered (these are sometimes offered as "presentation pieces").

(1946) IOWA CENTENNIAL HALF DOLLARS

Distribution
100,057

Whitman Coin Guide (WCG™)—1946 Iowa Centennial 50¢

MS-60	MS-63	MS-64	MS-65	MS-66	MS-67	MS-68
$120	$145	$150	$264	$305	$480	$2,420

CERTIFIED POPULATIONS

MS-60	MS-61	MS-62	MS-63	MS-64	MS-65	MS-66	MS-67	MS-68
24	13	128	655	2,396	4,547	3,952	1,081	87

Points of Interest: The distribution figure includes 500 set aside for later distribution in 1996 (which was done satisfactorily that year) and a further 500 for distribution in 2046. Technically, the distribution of Iowa half dollars has not yet been completed.

Subject of Commemoration: Centennial of the admission of Iowa into the Union.

Designs: *Obverse*—The Old Stone Capitol at Iowa City. *Reverse*—An eagle adapted from the Iowa State Seal. Designed by Adam Pietz.

Mintage Data: Authorized August 7, 1946. *Maximum authorized*—100,000. *Number minted* (including 57 assay coins)—100,057.

Original Cost and Issuer: $2.50 to in-state buyers, $3 out of state. Iowa Centennial Committee, Des Moines, Iowa.

A New Commemorative Issue

President Franklin Delano Roosevelt had been succeeded in the White House by Harry S. Truman when the first new commemorative design since the 1938 New Rochelle became a reality. Collectively, numismatists shouted "Hooray!" when legislation was approved on August 7, 1946. By this time, the deceptions and hucksterism of the 1930s were largely forgotten, and prices of early commemoratives, which had touched bottom in the market in 1941, had recovered nicely. It was time for some more.

The subject observed was the 1846–1946 centennial of Iowa statehood. In 1838 Iowa became a territory of the United States, and on December 28, 1846, it was admitted to the Union. The capital was Burlington until 1839, when Iowa City received that distinction, which it retained until Des Moines was chosen in 1857.

The design of the Iowa Centennial half dollar was handled through the office of Mint Director Nellie Tayloe Ross, who gave the project to Adam Pietz, a medalist who had served on the staff of the Engraving Department. He had resigned in early 1946 to resume private practice.

In November, 100,057 coins were struck. All but the 57 Assay Commission coins were shipped to Iowa the same month, and put on sale. By this time the coin market was exceedingly strong, and the pieces found a ready sale at $2.50 each to residents of Iowa and $3 to buyers located elsewhere, with 5,000 examples reserved for out-of-state purchasers. The available pieces were sold out by March 1947, by which time the price had been raised to $3 to all comers. At least 90,000 were sold within the state, and, remarkably, per

Committee records, "practically 85,000 of these were sold under a plan of distribution and sale which restricted one coin to a customer."

Key to Collecting

In the years since 1946, Iowa half dollars have been popular and plentiful on the market. Most known specimens are in varying degrees of Mint State, with MS-63 and 64 being typical—although with "gradeflation," many pieces graded at these levels 20 years ago are now in MS-65 and 66 holders.

The nature of the design, without open field areas, is such that a slight amount of friction and contact is usually not noticeable. Points to check are the clouds above the Capitol, as well as the high points of the building on the obverse, and the head and neck of the eagle on the reverse. Most examples are lustrous and frosty.

(1946–1951) BOOKER T. WASHINGTON MEMORIAL HALF DOLLARS

Distribution
1946: 1,000,546; 1946-D: 200,113;
          1946-S: 500,279
1947: 100,017; 1947-D: 100,017;
          1947-S: 100,017
1948: 20,005; 1948-D: 20,005;
          1948-S: 20,005
1949: 12,004; 1949-D: 12,004;
          1949-S: 12,004
1950: 12,004; 1950-D: 12,004;
          1950-S: 512,091
1951: 510,082; 1951-D: 12,004;
          1951-S: 12,004

Whitman Coin Guide (WCG™)—1946 Booker T. Washington Memorial 50¢

MS-60	MS-63	MS-64	MS-65	MS-66	MS-67	MS-68
$20	$25	$30	$55	$172	$2,035	$11,000

CERTIFIED POPULATIONS

MS-60	MS-61	MS-62	MS-63	MS-64	MS-65	MS-66	MS-67	MS-68
13	7	36	309	1,712	1,973	646	68	4

1946-D Booker T. Washington Memorial 50¢

MS-60	MS-63	MS-64	MS-65	MS-66	MS-67	MS-68
$25	$30	$35	$70	$210	$2,052	

CERTIFIED POPULATIONS

MS-60	MS-61	MS-62	MS-63	MS-64	MS-65	MS-66	MS-67	MS-68
4	4	16	159	978	1,149	384	50	2

1946-S Booker T. Washington Memorial 50¢

MS-60	MS-63	MS-64	MS-65	MS-66	MS-67	MS-68
$20	$26	$28	$60	$176	$1,474	

CERTIFIED POPULATIONS

MS-60	MS-61	MS-62	MS-63	MS-64	MS-65	MS-66	MS-67	MS-68
3	1	29	218	1,455	1,938	594	95	4

1947 Booker T. Washington Memorial 50¢

MS-60	MS-63	MS-64	MS-65	MS-66	MS-67	MS-68
$35	$50	$56	$85	$792	$1,034	

CERTIFIED POPULATIONS

MS-60	MS-61	MS-62	MS-63	MS-64	MS-65	MS-66	MS-67	MS-68
3	1	1	35	496	763	144	6	0

1947-D Booker T. Washington Memorial 50¢

MS-60	MS-63	MS-64	MS-65	MS-66	MS-67	MS-68
$35	$50	$60	$96	$850	$965	

CERTIFIED POPULATIONS

MS-60	MS-61	MS-62	MS-63	MS-64	MS-65	MS-66	MS-67	MS-68
0	0	3	42	352	553	142	1	0

1947-S Booker T. Washington Memorial 50¢

MS-60	MS-63	MS-64	MS-65	MS-66	MS-67	MS-68
$35	$50	$56	$85	$495	$4,198	

CERTIFIED POPULATIONS

MS-60	MS-61	MS-62	MS-63	MS-64	MS-65	MS-66	MS-67	MS-68
4	0	6	44	361	806	327	17	0

1948 Booker T. Washington Memorial 50¢

MS-60	MS-63	MS-64	MS-65	MS-66	MS-67	MS-68
$50	$90	$75	$90	$440	$964	

CERTIFIED POPULATIONS

MS-60	MS-61	MS-62	MS-63	MS-64	MS-65	MS-66	MS-67	MS-68
1	0	0	12	424	918	223	6	0

1948-D Booker T. Washington Memorial 50¢

MS-60	MS-63	MS-64	MS-65	MS-66	MS-67	MS-68
$50	$66	$75	$85	$370	$3,784	

CERTIFIED POPULATIONS

MS-60	MS-61	MS-62	MS-63	MS-64	MS-65	MS-66	MS-67	MS-68
0	0	2	27	443	846	323	17	0

1948-S Booker T. Washington Memorial 50¢

MS-60	MS-63	MS-64	MS-65	MS-66	MS-67	MS-68
$50	$66	$77	$80	$370	$4,059	

CERTIFIED POPULATIONS

MS-60	MS-61	MS-62	MS-63	MS-64	MS-65	MS-66	MS-67	MS-68
1	1	6	31	353	960	418	31	1

1949 Booker T. Washington Memorial 50¢

MS-60	MS-63	MS-64	MS-65	MS-66	MS-67	MS-68
$80	$85	$95	$121	$270	$5,984	

CERTIFIED POPULATIONS

MS-60	MS-61	MS-62	MS-63	MS-64	MS-65	MS-66	MS-67	MS-68
1	0	0	36	436	866	316	12	0

1949-D Booker T. Washington Memorial 50¢

MS-60	MS-63	MS-64	MS-65	MS-66	MS-67	MS-68
$77	$80	$85	$105	$194	$704	$3,850

CERTIFIED POPULATIONS

MS-60	MS-61	MS-62	MS-63	MS-64	MS-65	MS-66	MS-67	MS-68
1	0	4	44	465	836	308	20	0

1949-S Booker T. Washington Memorial 50¢

MS-60	MS-63	MS-64	MS-65	MS-66	MS-67	MS-68
$80	$85	$95	$121	$240	$2,409	

CERTIFIED POPULATIONS

MS-60	MS-61	MS-62	MS-63	MS-64	MS-65	MS-66	MS-67	MS-68
1	0	2	25	288	938	508	33	0

1950 Booker T. Washington Memorial 50¢

MS-60	MS-63	MS-64	MS-65	MS-66	MS-67	MS-68
$70	$75	$85	$100	$345	$7,359	

CERTIFIED POPULATIONS

MS-60	MS-61	MS-62	MS-63	MS-64	MS-65	MS-66	MS-67	MS-68
0	0	2	21	313	648	215	8	0

1950-D Booker T. Washington Memorial 50¢

MS-60	MS-63	MS-64	MS-65	MS-66	MS-67	MS-68
$65	$75	$80	$100	$360	$7,359	

CERTIFIED POPULATIONS

MS-60	MS-61	MS-62	MS-63	MS-64	MS-65	MS-66	MS-67	MS-68
0	0	0	27	370	651	196	5	0

1950-S Booker T. Washington Memorial 50¢

MS-60	MS-63	MS-64	MS-65	MS-66	MS-67	MS-68
$25	$30	$35	$70	$190	$3,509	

CERTIFIED POPULATIONS

MS-60	MS-61	MS-62	MS-63	MS-64	MS-65	MS-66	MS-67	MS-68
4	2	13	59	530	1,244	598	50	0

1951 Booker T. Washington Memorial 50¢

MS-60	MS-63	MS-64	MS-65	MS-66	MS-67	MS-68
$25	$30	$35	$60	$352	$4,884	

CERTIFIED POPULATIONS

MS-60	MS-61	MS-62	MS-63	MS-64	MS-65	MS-66	MS-67	MS-68
1	0	7	115	994	982	175	9	1

1951-D Booker T. Washington Memorial 50¢

MS-60	MS-63	MS-64	MS-65	MS-66	MS-67	MS-68
$55	$66	$75	$85	$380	$3,650	

CERTIFIED POPULATIONS

MS-60	MS-61	MS-62	MS-63	MS-64	MS-65	MS-66	MS-67	MS-68
1	0	3	29	304	679	293	21	0

1951-S Booker T. Washington Memorial 50¢

MS-60	MS-63	MS-64	MS-65	MS-66	MS-67	MS-68
$55	$66	$75	$85	$315	$2,134	

CERTIFIED POPULATIONS

MS-60	MS-61	MS-62	MS-63	MS-64	MS-65	MS-66	MS-67	MS-68
0	1	1	14	174	738	500	53	0

Points of Interest: The Booker T. Washington sets, with their multiplicity of varieties, were a rerun of the abusive issues of the 1930s.

Subject of Commemoration: The life and accomplishments of educator Booker T. Washington.

Designs: *Obverse*—Portrait of Booker T. Washington. *Reverse*—The Hall of Fame and a slave cabin, with extensive lettering. Designed by Isaac Scott Hathaway.

Mintage Data: Signed into law by President Harry S Truman on August 7, 1946. *Maximum authorized*—5,000,000, with dates not specified. **1946-P-D-S:** *Number minted* (including 546, 113, and 279 assay coins)—1,000,546, 200,113, 500,279. *Net distribution*—700,546 (estimated), 50,000 (estimated), 500,279 (estimated). **1947-P-D-S:** *Number minted* (including 17 assay coins each mint)—100,017, 100,017, 100,017. *Net distribution*—6,000 (estimated), 6,000 (estimated), 6,000 (estimated). **1948-P-D-S:** *Number minted* (including 5 assay coins each mint): 20,005, 20,005, 20,005. *Net distribution*—8,005, 8,005, 8,005. **1949-P-D-S:** *Number minted* (including 4 assay coins each mint)—12,004, 12,004, 12,004. *Net distribution*—6,004, 6,004, 6,004. **1950-P-D-S:** *Number minted* (including 4, 4, and 91 assay coins)—12,004, 12,004, 512,091. *Net distribution*—6,004, 6,004, 62,091 (estimated). **1951-P-D-S:** *Number minted* (including 82, 4, and 4 assay coins)—510,082, 12,004, 12,004. *Net distribution*—210,082 (estimated), 7,004, 7,004.

Original Cost and Issuer: 1946: Booker T. Washington Birthplace Memorial Commission, Inc. Rocky Mount, Virginia (Dr. S.J. Phillips in charge), Stack's, Bebee Stamp & Coin Company (a.k.a. Bebee's). **Later issues:** Costs and distributors varied; see text.

The 1930s Scenario Redux

The commemorative bandwagon began to roll again in 1946. While the Iowa issue received little or no criticism due to the obvious purpose of its issue, and the fact that the coins were distributed by the state, the same cannot be said for the other new issue of 1946—a special series of commemorative half dollars sold through the Booker T. Washington Birthplace Memorial Commission.

Marketed under the direction of commission member Dr. S.J. Phillips, these half dollars were ostensibly produced to honor one of America's best known black educators. Phillips, according to an account, was "the public relations representative of 500,000 colored Elks and 4.5 million colored Baptists who will participate in the sale of these commemoratives." Further, from the same account:

> Mr. Phillips and Booker T. Washington's only surviving child, Mrs. Portia Washington Pittman, visited the office of the chairman of the Coinage, Weights and Measures Committee . . . and outlined a plan. They are anxious that every Negro boy shall have one of these commemorative coins in his possession, as an inspiration to emulate the ideals and teachings of Booker T. Washington, who through a life of constructive efforts on behalf of his people rose from a boyhood of slavery to the Hall of Fame. . . . In view of the above mentioned objectives the chairman . . . feels this bill has unusually meritorious objectives and, furthermore, from the standpoint of the Treasury, rather than increasing the amount of money in circulation it would actually withdraw five millions of dollars from circulation, while the Treasury would be making a profit of one and one-quarter million dollars.

Congressional legislation was approved on August 7, 1946, concurrent with the bill authorizing Iowa half dollars. The act provided that Booker T. Washington commemorative coins could be produced by plural mints of the United States for a period not to exceed five years after passage, up to the quantity of 5 million pieces—sowing the seeds for precisely the same sort of abuse that characterized the long-lived Arkansas, Boone, Oregon Trail, and Texas issues of a decade earlier. The target was, obviously, the coin collecting fraternity—now considered to be ripe for further exploitation. An even broader market was envisioned for the sale of single pieces to the general public, although it stretches credulity to think that non-numismatists would want to acquire them by dates and mintmarks.

A Sudden Change of Designs

To be featured on the coin was Booker T. Washington, who was born into slavery circa 1858 in Franklin County, Virginia. As a young adult after the Civil War, he received a formal education (unlike the majority of his black brethren). By 1879 Washington was an instructor at the Hampton Industrial Institute in Virginia, which he had attended earlier. In 1881 he headed a facility for the education of blacks in Alabama—the Tuskegee Institute—which in time achieved nationwide fame. Later in his life he received honorary degrees from Dartmouth and Harvard and wrote an autobiography, *Up From Slavery*. His death occurred in Tuskegee on November 14, 1915. By that time he was widely recognized as America's foremost black educator.

Charles Keck, who had produced the models for the 1915-S Panama-Pacific gold dollar, the 1927 Vermont half dollar, and the 1936 Lynchburg half dollar, was asked to design the Booker T. Washington issue, following motifs suggested by Dr. S.J. Phillips. Keck's models of the new design were accepted both by Phillips and the Mint. Around this time, black artist Isaac Scott Hathaway entered the scene and offered to prepare, at no charge, his own models for the half dollar, employing for the obverse a motif said to have been taken from the only life mask of Booker T. Washington in existence (made years earlier by Hathaway). The Commission of Fine Arts considered both the Keck and Hathaway portraits of Booker T. Washington for the obverse, and recommended Hathaway's depiction—much to the anger of Keck.

The reverse design was adapted by Hathaway from a sketch provided by an unnamed member of the Commission of Fine Arts, and depicted the Hall of Fame at New York University, where a bust of Booker T. Washington was enshrined. At the bottom of the coin a rustic log cabin appeared, with the inscription FROM SLAVE CABIN TO HALL OF FAME separating it from the Hall of Fame above.

Distribution

In December 1946, the Philadelphia Mint struck 1,000,000 Booker T. Washington half dollars for distribution, plus 546 for assay, whereas in the same month 200,000 (plus 113 for assay) were made at Denver and 500,000 (plus 279 for assay) at San Francisco—a quantity that could furnish 200,000 P-D-S sets plus hundreds of thousands of extra Philadelphia Mint coins. Dr. Phillips envisioned that the 15 million black Americans would snap up the entire issue within three months. Some were sold this way—but not many. The Commission quickly found there was no practical way to publicize the coins and get orders to the general public, without incurring expenses greater than the revenue from the coins sold.

An advertisement in *The Numismatist*, January 1947, invited collectors to order 1946 sets directly from the Booker T. Washington Birthplace Memorial for $1 each for Philadelphia and San Francisco coins and $1.50 for Denver coins, plus 10¢ postage per coin. The coin market was as hot as a firecracker, and thousands were sold in this manner. Apparently, unsold quantities were soon dumped into circulation—possibly by the Commission (which does not seem to have been well financed)—because they began popping up in pocket change. Perplexed as to what to do next, the Commission called upon Stack's, the New York City dealers established in 1935 and experienced in the sale of such coins as distributor of the 1936 Robinson-Arkansas and other issues. In *The Numismatist* in January 1947, the firm proclaimed, "Important Notice! We have been appointed authorized agents of the Booker T. Washington Commemorative Half Dollar."

By that time, collector dissatisfaction with the quality of the 1946 coins was becoming widespread. A typical experience was related by F.H. Hisken, a Seattle collector whose comments appeared in the February 1947 issue of *The Numismatist*:

> We recently received ten sets of the new Booker T. Washington commemorative half dollars, and after examining them, promptly returned them to the Commission. Every single one of them was bruised and nicked, and, in particular, damages appeared on the right jaw which is slightly in relief. I can see no reason for sending out commemorative coins in such condition. There is enough premium being charged to justify special handling of these coins, at least on the pieces which are being sold to collectors.

In 1947 the Commission acted with caution and ordered just 100,000 each of the coins from three mints. Stack's and the Commission each solicited orders for $6 per set. Stack's had agreed to sell 1,000 sets per year, which was easily done and soon exceeded. But numismatic demand did not come close to the number minted. Eventually, all but about 6,000 sets were melted. The Commission kept scanty records, and much information about what happened has had to be pieced together from interviews, stray documents, and other sources. Mint reports are incomplete.[13]

In 1948, the Commission enlisted the Bebee Stamp & Coin Company, because Stack's indicated no further interest in the coins—the quality of which was alienating customers. In a letter to the author dated December 17, 1990, Aubrey Bebee recalled that S.J. Phillips was appointed president of the Booker T. Washington Memorial at Rocky Mount, Virginia, and how surprised and disappointed he was that the 1946 and 1947 issues weren't selling. After discussions at the Treasury Department, Phillips contacted Bebee's about handling distribution of the coins. Bebee's agreed to pay $3 to the memorial commission and $1.50 to the Federal Reserve for each set, starting with 1948. Due to slow demand and despite higher authorized numbers, only 8,000 sets were issued in 1948, and 6,000 per year for 1949 through 1951.

The husband and wife team of Aubrey and Adeline Bebee moved to Omaha, Nebraska, in 1952 and soon changed their trade name to Bebee's, Inc. Sales of the half dollars remained slow, and Bebee's stocked thousands of unsold coins. Mintages of sets remained low, and quantities continued to be melted. In 1950 the Commission ordered, from the San Francisco Mint, 500,000 extra coins for a promotion involving schools and hospitals, plus more than 500,000 from the Philadelphia Mint in 1951. Sales fizzled, and most were melted. No records were kept as to the number distributed. Many of these coins were placed into circulation.

In October 1951, Bebee advised that "thousands of sets of 1948, 1949, 1950, and 1951 Booker T. Washington Memorial half dollars have been returned to the mints to be melted," and that now the price for 1951 sets was $10.

Key to Collecting
Of all commemorative half dollar issues produced up to this point, the Booker T. Washington half dollars were made with the least amount of care during the coining process at the mints. At the time of release, nearly all specimens were poorly defined on the obverse

design and were laden with abrasions and bagmarks. Many have graininess and marks, from the original planchet surface that did not strike up fully, on Washington's cheek. Most examples seen in the numismatic market today are *really* MS-60 to MS-63, but "gradeflation" has propelled many to the MS-65 level—a grade hardly ever seen in the late 1980s when the certification services were stricter. Many other coins have natural or artificial toning which masks the true grades and facilitates gem certification. Prooflike coins are sometimes seen. These are not at all mirrorlike, but are still different from the normal mint frost. Issues include 1947-S (in particular), 1948-S, 1949, and 1951-S.

That said, the Booker T. Washington half dollars are exceedingly cheap in relation to their low mintages. For best value, seek out pieces certified MS-63 or 64, and cherrypick for quality. Some of these will be every bit as nice as other coins labeled MS-65 or 66.

(1951–1954) Carver/Washington Half Dollars

Distribution
1951: 110,018; 1951-D: 10,004;
        1951-S: 10,004
1952: 2,006,292; 1952-D: 8,006;
        1952-S: 8,006
1953: 8,003; 1953-D: 8,003;
        1953-S: 108,020
1954: 12,006; 1954-D: 12,006;
        1954-S: 122,024

Whitman Coin Guide (WCG™)—1951 Carver/Washington

MS-60	MS-63	MS-64	MS-65	MS-66	MS-67	MS-68
$40	$50	$60	$305	$1,700	$4,430	

CERTIFIED POPULATIONS

MS-60	MS-61	MS-62	MS-63	MS-64	MS-65	MS-66	MS-67	MS-68
5	3	30	172	711	291	36	1	0

1951-D Carver/Washington

MS-60	MS-63	MS-64	MS-65	MS-66	MS-67	MS-68
$50	$55	$60	$155	$1,080	$4,430	

CERTIFIED POPULATIONS

MS-60	MS-61	MS-62	MS-63	MS-64	MS-65	MS-66	MS-67	MS-68
2	0	5	101	604	531	55	1	0

1951-S Carver/Washington 50¢

MS-60	MS-63	MS-64	MS-65	MS-66	MS-67	MS-68
$50	$55	$60	$135	$965	$4,430	

CERTIFIED POPULATIONS

MS-60	MS-61	MS-62	MS-63	MS-64	MS-65	MS-66	MS-67	MS-68
0	0	1	29	447	998	205	7	0

1952 Carver/Washington 50¢

MS-60	MS-63	MS-64	MS-65	MS-66	MS-67	MS-68
$25	$30	$45	$60	$472	$10,470	

CERTIFIED POPULATIONS

MS-60	MS-61	MS-62	MS-63	MS-64	MS-65	MS-66	MS-67	MS-68
18	18	66	470	2,652	1,931	298	12	0

1952-D Carver/Washington 50¢

MS-60	MS-63	MS-64	MS-65	MS-66	MS-67	MS-68
$50	$55	$70	$205	$1,150	$4,430	

CERTIFIED POPULATIONS

MS-60	MS-61	MS-62	MS-63	MS-64	MS-65	MS-66	MS-67	MS-68
1	0	6	88	589	393	26	0	0

1952-S Carver/Washington 50¢

MS-60	MS-63	MS-64	MS-65	MS-66	MS-67	MS-68
$50	$55	$65	$140	$616	$9,100	

CERTIFIED POPULATIONS

MS-60	MS-61	MS-62	MS-63	MS-64	MS-65	MS-66	MS-67	MS-68
1	0	3	29	517	701	132	3	0

1953 Carver/Washington 50¢

MS-60	MS-63	MS-64	MS-65	MS-66	MS-67	MS-68
$50	$60	$70	$240	$1,150	$4,430	

CERTIFIED POPULATIONS

MS-60	MS-61	MS-62	MS-63	MS-64	MS-65	MS-66	MS-67	MS-68
1	0	8	122	562	380	30	0	0

1953-D Carver/Washington

MS-60	MS-63	MS-64	MS-65	MS-66	MS-67	MS-68
$50	$60	$70	$225	$1,405	$4,430	

CERTIFIED POPULATIONS

MS-60	MS-61	MS-62	MS-63	MS-64	MS-65	MS-66	MS-67	MS-68
0	0	4	91	607	291	24	0	0

1953-S Carver/Washington

MS-60	MS-63	MS-64	MS-65	MS-66	MS-67	MS-68
$40	$45	$50	$90	$635	$7,720	

CERTIFIED POPULATIONS

MS-60	MS-61	MS-62	MS-63	MS-64	MS-65	MS-66	MS-67	MS-68
2	0	4	106	915	1,046	121	8	0

1954 Carver/Washington 50¢

MS-60	MS-63	MS-64	MS-65	MS-66	MS-67	MS-68
$50	$55	$65	$145	$930	$4,430	

CERTIFIED POPULATIONS

MS-60	MS-61	MS-62	MS-63	MS-64	MS-65	MS-66	MS-67	MS-68
1	0	2	107	820	502	67	0	0

1954-D Carver/Washington 50¢

MS-60	MS-63	MS-64	MS-65	MS-66	MS-67	MS-68
$50	$55	$65	$180	$2,250	$4,430	

CERTIFIED POPULATIONS

MS-60	MS-61	MS-62	MS-63	MS-64	MS-65	MS-66	MS-67	MS-68
2	1	7	137	759	361	13	0	0

1954-S Carver/Washington 50¢

MS-60	MS-63	MS-64	MS-65	MS-66	MS-67	MS-68
$30	$33	$50	$70	$781	$10,470	

CERTIFIED POPULATIONS

MS-60	MS-61	MS-62	MS-63	MS-64	MS-65	MS-66	MS-67	MS-68
1	0	18	194	990	791	96	4	0

Points of Interest: On the map of the U.S.A. on the reverse Delaware was omitted.

Subject of Commemoration: The lives and accomplishments of George Washington Carver and Booker T. Washington.

Designs: *Obverse*—Portraits of George Washington Carver and Booker T. Washington. *Reverse*—Map of the United States (Delaware omitted). Designed by Isaac Scott Hathaway.

Mintage Data: Signed into law by President Harry S Truman on September 21, 1951. *Maximum authorized*—3,415,631 (total for all issues 1951 onward; consisting of 1,581,631 undistributed Booker T. Washington coins which could be converted into Carver/Washington coins, plus the unused 1,834,000 earlier authorization for Booker T. Washington coins). The following include author's estimates: **1951-P-D-S:** *Number minted* (including 18, 4, and 4 assay coins)—110,018, 10,004, 10,004. *Net distribution*—20,018 (estimated), 10,004 (estimated), 10,004 (estimated). **1952-P-D-S:** *Number minted* (including 292, 6, and 6 assay coins)—2,006,292, 8,006, 8,006. *Net distribution*—1,106,292 (estimated), 8,006 (estimated), 8,006 (estimated). **1953-P-D-S:** *Number minted* (including 3, 3, and 20 assay coins)—8,003, 8,003, 108,020. *Net distribution*—8,003 (estimated), 8,003 (estimated), 88,020 (estimated). **1954-P-D-S:** *Number minted* (including 6, 6, and 24 assay coins)—12,006, 12,006, 122,024. *Net distribution*—12,006 (estimated), 12,006 (estimated), 42,024 (estimated).

Original Cost and Issuer: 1951-P-D-S: $10 per set. **1952-P-D-S:** $10 per set; many Philadelphia coins were sold at or near face value through banks. **1953-P-D-S:** $10 per set; some 1953-S coins were distributed at or near face value (Bebee's prices $9 until January 15, 1952, $10 after that date). **1954-P-D-S:** Official sale price: $10 per set; some 1954-S coins were paid out at face value (Bebee's prices for sets $9 until January 20, 1954, $12 after that date). Issued mainly by the Carver-Washington Coin Commission acting for the Booker T. Washington Birthplace Memorial Foundation (Booker Washington Birthplace, Virginia) and the George Washington Carver National Monument Foundation (Diamond, Missouri). Also, for some issues, these dealers: Stack's, Bebee Stamp & Coin Company, Sol Kaplan, and R. Green.

If At First You Don't Succeed

Dr. S.J. Phillips of the Booker T. Washington Birthplace Memorial Association endeavored to continue the distribution of commemorative half dollars. Although vast quantities of unsold Booker T. Washington pieces remained on hand by the summer of 1951, he was able to persuade Congress to pass a new bill providing for the melting of all unsold pieces in the hands of the Commission plus those retained by the Treasury and not called for by the Commission, with the resultant metal to be recoined into pieces of an entirely new design featuring black leaders Dr. George Washington Carver and Booker T. Washington.

The profits from the new coins were to go to "oppose the spread of Communism among Negroes in the interest of the national defense." These were the days of McCarthyism, and many citizens felt that Communist agents were lurking on every street corner. There was little objection to the proposal, for few questioned that blacks (and others) should be kept away from the Communist influence.

In addition to the metal available from melting down earlier-dated Booker T. Washington half dollars, an unused authorization remained for earlier pieces that had not been struck, and this could be applied to the new Carver/Washington issues as well, giving a maximum authorization of 3,415,631 pieces. Anyone who studied the situation in 1951 would have realized that this was far beyond the probable potential market. Phillips relocated, at least on paper, and now headed the Carver-Washington Coin Commission, headquartered at Booker Washington Birthplace, Virginia, which, according to the Carver-Washington letterhead, was "acting for [the] George Washington Carver National Monument Foundation [and the] Booker T. Washington Birthplace Memorial Commission."

Isaac Scott Hathaway, who created the Booker T. Washington half dollar motif, was tapped to prepare the designs of the new Carver/Washington issue. After discussion with the Commission of Fine Arts, the motifs were altered. Models were sent to the Mint. Chief Engraver Gilroy Roberts found the relief too high, and said the coins would not strike up properly. He lowered the relief, after which hubs, master dies, and working dies were made. The result was a coin design which historian Donald Taxay in *U.S. Mint and Coinage* (1966) designated as "particularly ugly."

Cornelius Vermeule in *Numismatic Art in America* (1971) noted of the reverse—"A map labeled U.S.A. marks a low point in pictorial imagination, and it is rather sad that the splendid series of commemorative coins, so much an ornament to the arts of the United States, should reach its conclusion in 1954 with a reverse so impoverished of ideas and devoid of artistry."

Distribution commenced through the Carver-Washington Coin Commission. Dealer response was lukewarm at best, based on the poor reception of the earlier Booker T. Washington coins, but Stack's, Bebee Stamp & Coin Co., Sol Kaplan, and R. Green contributed to the sales efforts. Most collectors ignored them. In March 1953 a letter published in *The Numismatist* from R.B. Minard, a California collector, included this:

> Collectors in general are fast reaching the point whenever the B.T.W. coins are mentioned of placing the tongue in cheek. The original purpose of the coin is being defeated, and Washington along with Carver is being castigated through these continual issues. It would seem that like Old Man River, they must keep rolling along. For goodness sake let's not become maudlin over these two great men, and call a halt somewhere. . . . Let's not allow this respect to be debased by a yearly issuance of a particular coin that is fast becoming silly and idiotic. . . . Let each collector individually and the ANA get behind this movement and rectify a situation that smells.

Certain expanded mintages for 1952 (Philadelphia), 1953-S, and 1954-S were intended for wide distribution (including through banks) but the effort was a failure, and many pieces were dumped at or close to face value. In the meantime the collectors' market absorbed several thousand or more P-D-S sets, but most sets remained unsold. Eventually 1,091,198 Carver/Washington coins were returned for melting. The charitable activities to which the profits of the Booker T. Washington and Carver/Washington halves were to have been directed benefited very little. Few records were kept of distribution, and today for some varieties it is not known how many were spent or melted. By 1955 the Chase National Bank in New York City (antecedent to today's J.P. Morgan Chase Bank) had thousands on hand and was willing to dispose of them at face value, but there were few takers.

The series simply faded away in 1954. The Treasury Department was so distressed with the complaints received about these coins and their poor reception (not that the Treasury created the designs or distributed them), that for years afterward when the subject of new commemorative coins came up in forums or in Congress, the Department recited a litany of abuses and effectively ended any further discussion.

Key to Collecting

Carver/Washington half dollars have never been popular with collectors. Nearly all coins were handled casually at the mints and also during the distribution process. Most were not fully struck up, with the result that under magnification many tiny nicks and marks can be seen on the higher parts, from marks on the original planchet that were not obliterated during the striking process. In the 1980s and early 1990s, very few were certified as MS-65 or better by the leading services. Then, "gradeflation" took place, and MS-65 and higher coins are common. The coins themselves have not changed.

On the plus side of the equation, these coins are very inexpensive in relation to their low mintages for certain varieties. Nowhere else in American numismatics are low-mintage Uncirculated legal tender coins available as cheaply as for the 1946–1951 Booker T. Washington and 1951–1954 Carver/Washington half dollars.

No commemoratives were made from 1955 through 1981. In 1982, they were again made. By this time, silver coins were no longer used in circulation. New commemoratives were made either in clad metal, as for half dollars, or in silver and gold. Those in precious metals were sold at prices far above the face values marked on the coins. The coins remained legal tender, but no one would want to spend them.

Henceforth, commemoratives were issued by the Bureau of the Mint, later called the U.S. Mint. It was customary to include a surcharge or fee as part of the purchase cost, which usually went to the group or other entity that persuaded Congress to authorize the coins. Accordingly, many issues have reeked of politics, resulting in coins commemorating obscure subjects of little or no national, historical, or numismatic significance. Others have commemorated persons, places, things, and events of great importance.

(1982) George Washington
250th Anniversary Half Dollars

Distribution
1982-D: 2,210,458 Uncirculated
1982-S: 4,894,044 Proof

Whitman Coin Guide (WCG™)—1982-D George Washington 250th Anniv 50¢

MS-65	MS-66	MS-67	MS-68	MS-69	MS-70
$10	$20	$30	$61	$590	

CERTIFIED POPULATIONS

MS-65	MS-66	MS-67	MS-68	MS-69	MS-70
89	289	618	1,160	172	0

1982-S George Washington 250th Anniversary 50¢ Proof

PF-65	PF-66	PF-67	PF-68	PF-69	PF-70
$7.65	$11	$12	$13	$25	$275

CERTIFIED POPULATIONS

PF-65	PF-66	PF-67	PF-68	PF-69	PF-70
26	69	174	554	11,328	110

Points of Interest: This was the first new commemorative issue since 1954. These were still available from the Bureau of the Mint as late as December 31, 1985.

Subject of Commemoration: The 250th anniversary of the birth of George Washington.

Designs: *Obverse*—George Washington on horseback. *Reverse*—Mount Vernon. Designed by Chief Engraver Elizabeth Jones. Some modeling of the reverse by Matthew Peloso.

Mintage Data: Authorized by Public Law 97-014, signed by President Ronald Reagan on December 23, 1981. *Maximum authorized*—10,000,000. *Number minted*—1982-D 478,716, 1982-S 868,326. *Net distribution*—1982-D 2,689,204 Uncirculated, 1982-S 5,762,370 Proof.

Original Cost and Issuer: Issued by the U.S. Mint.

Launching a New Era

The observation in 1982 of the 250th anniversary of George Washington's birth provided the opportunity for the Treasury Department to produce a new commemorative coin, to begin a new era of special issues. By this time, there had been vast changes in the relationship between the Treasury Department and collectors. Mrs. Donna Pope, director of the Mint, was well on the way to forging a closer bond, than had ever existed before, between the Mint and the numismatic fraternity. (She eventually accomplished this in spades; her administration is remembered as one of the finest ever.)

On December 23, 1981, legislation provided for the production of not more than 10 million silver Washington half dollars of .900 fine silver, an alloy which had not been used for regular coinage since 1964. It was specified that profits from the issue were to be applied to the national debt. Coins were to be dated 1982 and produced until December 1983 (which was, in effect, an authorization of restrikes).

The Washington commemorative had its inception in the summer of 1980 when David John, a 31-year-old numismatist from Georgia, came to Washington to do post-graduate work at Georgetown University. He became a legislative assistant to Rep. Doug Barnard Jr., of Augusta, Georgia, a Democrat and member of the Banking, Finance, and Urban Affairs Committee. "I was looking at a new edition of the 'Red Book,'" John later recalled, "and the pages of the bicentennial coinage made me think of commemoratives. Then I ran across the story of the Washington quarter in another book, and a flash of mental addition gave me 1982, the 250th anniversary of Washington's birth, for an ideal new commemorative."

David John prepared a proposal which was approved by Rep. Barnard, who had it converted into legislative terms as H.R. 2524. The assistance Rep. Frank Annunzio (who was to become very important in other commemorative legislation of the decade) and others was enlisted. John soon learned that Annunzio had been working on a similar Washington commemorative proposal for a silver dollar. "We wanted to get a flow of commemorative coins started," Annunzio said, "but not a deluge of them like some small-time dictator who puts out a coin on every pretext he can find, every time you turn around. Just then Doug Barnard came up with his bill, and we were happy to go along. The only problems were technical."

The Treasury Department, which had been against commemorative proposals for many years—ever since the Carver/Washington issues—warmly endorsed this one. In congressional testimony, U.S. Treasurer Angela M. (Bay) Buchanan ended the suspense and delighted numismatic listeners with the words, "At the outset, let me inform you that the Treasury Department supports this proposal. . . ."

In the Words of the Artist

Chief Engraver Elizabeth Jones, who had ascended to the post in 1981 following the retirement of Frank Gasparro, was selected to prepare the design, which was done with the assistance of staff engraver Matthew Peloso, who worked on the reverse. In a letter to the author, Ms. Jones recalled her artistic process. After notification that she would design the George Washington coin, her first reaction was to have him on a horse. Her research brought her to the museum in the historic Second Bank of the United States building in Philadelphia. There she was stunned by a large oval painting by Rembrandt Peale. It was the perfect image of Washington on horseback and the basis for much of the obverse of the coin. However, Ms. Jones had access to a private collection that included a volume of portraits of Washington drawn only from life. She used this as her main inspiration for the actual portrait of Washington.

For the reverse, Ms. Jones researched Washington's birthplace, as the legislation stipulated its inclusion. When she submitted drawings of the reconstructed house, Treasury Department officials requested that she use Mount Vernon, since it was so connected with Washington in the public's mind and was more beautiful. Later the Commission of Fine Arts requested changes to the building. For the eagle, the CFA asked that the 1792 half dollar design chosen by Ms. Jones be changed to the eagle from the reverse of the 1804 silver dollar. Ms. Jones has never seen the logic in this. She felt "it would have been more significant if a coin design of his lifetime were to have been used."

Into the Marketplace

Some further revisions were made, after which the new commemorative became a reality to be produced at two mints: the Proofs at San Francisco and the Uncirculated (with frosty surfaces) coins at Denver. Dies, however, were produced at the Philadelphia Mint. The 1982 Washington half dollars were offered at different prices over time. The initial advertising campaign broke in magazines in July 1982. Orders for 1982 Washington commemorative half dollars were accepted beginning on July 7. Issue prices were set at $8.50 for the Uncirculated 1982-D coins and $10.50 for the Proof 1982-S coins. Later, the Treasury raised the official issue prices to $10 and $12 each in order to protect earlier purchasers and to stimulate demand. Orders could be placed directly with the Bureau of the Mint, or coins could be purchased through local banks and other agencies, which acquired them in bulk (defined as 100 or more coins), at a discount.

Quantity production of Uncirculated strikes (the term *circulation strikes* is not necessarily appropriate, for the coins were not intended for circulation) began in Denver in October 1982. The first modern commemorative first-strike ceremony had taken place there on July 1, when Donna Pope pushed a button to stamp the first coin—one of just five 1982-D Washington half dollars struck by five of the nearly 75 guests. The affair was held in a cramped room in the lower-level production area of the Denver Mint. (Later in the same day, another first-strike ceremony for Proofs took place in San Francisco.) By year's end, 695,698 pieces had been made at the Denver facility. In 1983 and 1984, some 1,514,804 pieces were restruck at Denver from 1982 dies.

At the San Francisco Mint, 3,307,645 Proofs were struck and released through the end of the year 1982. In 1983, an additional 1,586,399 were released, restruck from 1982 dies. Additional 1982-S pieces were restruck, on demand, through 1983 until an official end was made to production at both mints in the end of December 1983.

Unsold pieces remained in inventory through December 31, 1985, when the official sales program was terminated. Subsequently, unsold pieces were melted. The sale of

more than seven million coins was a resounding success—
the attractiveness of the design, and the Mint administra
netted more than $36 million profit, a sum deposited to th
reduce the national debt.

Key to Collecting

Today, Uncirculated 1982-D and Proof 1982-S Washin
the market and are readily available in as-issued conditi
regarded as part of the modern commemorative series.

(1983–1984) Los Angeles Olympic Games Commemoratives

Distribution

1983-D silver dollar
    discus thrower:
      174,014 Uncirculated

1983-P silver dollar
    discus thrower:
      294,543 Uncirculated

1983-S silver dollar
    discus thrower:
      174,014 Uncirculated
      and 1,577,025 Proof

1984-P silver dollar
    Olympic coliseum:
      217,954 Uncirculated

1984-D silver dollar
    Olympic coliseum:
      116,675 Uncirculated

1984-S silver dollar
    Olympic coliseum:
      116,675 Uncirculated
      and 1,801,210 Proof

1984-P Olympic gold $10: 33,309 Proof

1984-D Olympic gold $10: 34,533 Proof

1984-S Olympic gold $10: 48,551 Proof

1984-W Olympic gold $10:
      381,085 Uncirculated
      and 75,886 Proof

Whitman Coin Guide (WCG™)—1983-P Olympic Discus Thrower $1

MS-65	MS-66	MS-67	MS-68	MS-69	MS-70
$16	$18	$22	$24	$35	$7,500

CERTIFIED POPULATIONS

MS-65	MS-66	MS-67	MS-68	MS-69	MS-70
2	5	27	148	1,291	15

Discus Thrower $1

	MS-66	MS-67	MS-68	MS-69	MS-70
	$20	$22	$28	$38	$2,550

POPULATIONS

	MS-66	MS-67	MS-68	MS-69	MS-70
	14	50	115	852	3

3-S Olympic Discus Thrower $1

MS-65	MS-66	MS-67	MS-68	MS-69	MS-70
$16	$20	$22	$28	$40	$5,000
PF-65	PF-66	PF-67	PF-68	PF-69	PF-70
$14	$15	$17	$22	$33	

CERTIFIED POPULATIONS

MS-65	MS-66	MS-67	MS-68	MS-69	MS-70
1	2	49	132	427	2
PF-65	PF-66	PF-67	PF-68	PF-69	PF-70
16	29	108	278	1,747	4

1984-P Olympic Coliseum $1

MS-65	MS-66	MS-67	MS-68	MS-69	MS-70
$16	$22	$25	$30	$36	$2,475

CERTIFIED POPULATIONS

MS-65	MS-66	MS-67	MS-68	MS-69	MS-70
15	52	135	404	1,264	24

1984-D Olympic Coliseum $1

MS-65	MS-66	MS-67	MS-68	MS-69	MS-70
$18	$20	$22	$28	$39	

CERTIFIED POPULATIONS

MS-65	MS-66	MS-67	MS-68	MS-69	MS-70
0	17	1755	199	936	4

1984-S Olympic Coliseum $1

MS-65	MS-66	MS-67	MS-68	MS-69	MS-70
$18	$20	$25	$28	$40	
MS-65	MS-66	MS-67	MS-68	MS-69	MS-70
$14	$15	$16	$17	$33	$1,250

CERTIFIED POPULATIONS

MS-65	MS-66	MS-67	MS-68	MS-69	MS-70
2	9	76	211	890	5
PF-65	PF-66	PF-67	PF-68	PF-69	PF-70
10	45	101	281	2,079	45

1984-P Olympic Gold $10 Proof

PF-65	PF-66	PF-67	PF-68	PF-69	PF-70
$370	$375	$380	$390	$420	$7,500

CERTIFIED POPULATIONS

PF-65	PF-66	PF-67	PF-68	PF-69	PF-70
6	31	83	212	2,564	230

1984-D Olympic Gold $10 Proof

PF-65	PF-66	PF-67	PF-68	PF-69	PF-70
$370	$375	$380	$390	$420	$5,500

CERTIFIED POPULATIONS

PF-65	PF-66	PF-67	PF-68	PF-69	PF-70
7	15	50	124	1,449	9

1984-S Olympic Gold $10 Proof

PF-65	PF-66	PF-67	PF-68	PF-69	PF-70
$370	$375	$380	$390	$420	$4,000

CERTIFIED POPULATIONS

PF-65	PF-66	PF-67	PF-68	PF-69	PF-70
5	12	44	107	1,231	141

1984-W Olympic Gold $10

MS-65	MS-66	MS-67	MS-68	MS-69	MS-70
$400	$410	$420	$440	$450	$2,250
PF-65	PF-66	PF-67	PF-68	PF-69	PF-70
$320	$375	$380	$390	$420	$4,500

CERTIFIED POPULATIONS

MS-65	MS-66	MS-67	MS-68	MS-69	MS-70
12	23	81	202	3,586	20
PF-65	PF-66	PF-67	PF-68	PF-69	PF-70
6	23	56	67	17	0

Points of Interest: The 1983 Olympic dollar was the first commemorative silver dollar since the 1900 Lafayette issue. The 1984 dollar, with headless torsos on the obverse, created more controversy than any commemorative design up to this time. The $10 gold coin was the first commemorative of this denomination, and the first of its denomination struck since 1933. This was also the first commemorative to be struck at four different mints.

Subject of Commemoration: 1984 Los Angeles Summer Olympic Games.

Designs: 1983 Discus Thrower silver dollar: *Obverse*—Representation of the traditional Greek discus thrower inspired by the ancient work of the sculptor Myron. *Reverse*—the Head and upper body of an American eagle. Designed by Chief Engraver Elizabeth Jones. **1984 Olympic Coliseum silver dollar:** *Obverse*—Robert Graham's headless torso sculptures at the entrance of the Los Angeles Memorial Coliseum. *Reverse*—Perched eagle looking back over its left wing. Designed by Robert Graham. **1984 Olympic Runners $10 gold:** *Obverse*—Two runners holding aloft the Olympic torch. Designed by John Mercanti from a concept by James Peed. *Reverse*—Adaptation of the Great Seal of the United States. Designed by John Mercanti.

Mintage Data: 1983 Discus Thrower: Authorized by Public Law 97-220 signed by President Ronald Reagan on July 22, 1982. *Maximum authorized*—50,000,000 totally for 1983 and 1984. *Actual distribution*—1983-P Discus Thrower Silver Dollar 294,543 Uncirculated; 1983-D 174,014 Uncirculated; 1983-S 174,014 Uncirculated and 1,577,025 Proof. **1984 Olympic Coliseum silver dollar:** Authorized by Public Law 97-220, signed by President Ronald Reagan on July 22, 1982. *Maximum authorized*—50,000,000 totally for 1983 and 1984. *Actual distribution*—1984-P 217,954 Uncirculated; 1984-D 116,675 Uncirculated; 1984-S 116,675 Uncirculated and 1,801,210 Proof. **1984 Olympic Runners $10 gold:** Authorized by Public Law 97-220 signed by President Ronald Reagan on July 22, 1982. *Maximum authorized*—2,000,000. *Actual distribution*—1984-P 33,309 Proof; 1984-D: 34,533 Proof; 1984-S 48,551 Proof; 1984-W 75,886 Uncirculated and 381,085 Proof.

Original Cost and Issuer: 1983 silver dollars: Uncirculated, $28; Proof $24.95 in advance (later $29, still later $32). **1984 silver dollars:** $28; Proof $32 (later, $35). Sales closed January 18, 1985. **1984 gold $10:** Uncirculated, $339, Proof $353. Part of the

$10 surcharge per $1 and $35 per $10 went to the U.S. Olympic Committee and the Los Angeles Olympic Organizing Committee. More than a dozen purchase options and combinations were also offered. Issued by the U.S. Mint.

Politics Rears Its Head

The 1984 Summer Olympic Games, scheduled to be held in Los Angeles, furnished the opportunity to issue several varieties of silver and gold coins for fund-raising purposes, including the first commemorative silver dollar since the 1900 Lafayette issue.

The issue became a political football when Lazard Frères, the international banking firm, sought to combine its interests with the Occidental Petroleum Corporation (whose chairman, Armand Hammer, was well connected in political circles). The conglomerate persuaded certain legislators, including Senator Alan Cranston of California, to back a bill for 29 different coins to be sold through Occidental Petroleum (which, presumably, would set up a numismatic department).

The stage was being prepared for private profit—reminiscent of the commemorative distribution abuses and cronyism of the 1930s. On May 10, 1981, Cranston's bill called for a 29-piece set consisting of four different $100 gold pieces, four different $50 gold pieces, 16 different $10 silver pieces, and five different copper-nickel dollars. The silver and gold pieces were to be made in both Uncirculated and Proof finishes, whereas the copper-nickel pieces were to be made in Uncirculated finish only, yielding a total combination possibility of 53 different coin varieties. This made anything that the Oregon Trail or Boone Bicentennial coin people did in the 1930s seem tame by comparison.

The numismatic community reacted in horror! The numismatic press took up the cause, as did collectors and dealers. ANA President Adna Wilde went to Washington to testify before Congress, as did the present author and numerous others, including spokespeople from the numismatic press. The Treasury Department was forced to remain silent, as were Mint officials, many of whom privately recoiled at the brazen attempt to take over the distribution of commemorative coinage.

Burnett Anderson observed the Olympic coin debate on Capitol Hill and filed a report with *Coins Magazine* on May 28, 1982, describing the climax of the yearlong battle. The scheme was rejected by a vote of 302 to 84. Most collectors and dealers marked the vote as a victory, since most opposed the large number of designs and the high markups under private distribution. The vote's outcome was unexpected and "was widely reported as a new version of the biblical David and Goliath." Representing David was Representative Frank Annunzio (D-Illinois), chairman of the House Subcommittee on Consumer Affairs and Coinage. Representing Goliath were powerful corporations, highly placed members of the Reagan administration, and Olympic committees.

After a number of suggestions and modifications were considered, the office of Representative Frank Annunzio drafted a bill for three coins, which eventually served as the basis for the Act of July 22, 1982 (Public Law 97-220), which authorized 50 million silver $1 pieces and 2 million gold $10 pieces. It was specified that each $1 piece would include a surcharge of $10 or more and each $10 piece a surcharge of $50 or more. Thus was launched a practice that numismatists soon found to be undesirable—because in effect, it made them pay for various projects beyond the cost of coins themselves. In time, this would develop into a huge boondoggle, because politically connected interests successfully lobbied the passing of many irrelevant commemorative bills—the scenario of the 1990s.

In the instance of the Olympic commemoratives, half the surcharge wa for the U.S. Olympic Committee and the other half for the Los Angeles Olyr nizing Committee. Distribution was through the Treasury Department.

Three Coin Designs

Chief Engraver Elizabeth Jones designed the 1983 Olympic silver dollar, which feature on the obverse several conjoined outlines, in three layers, of a discus thrower as if in stroboscopic motion. The reverse, which showed the head and shoulders of an eagle, was designed by Elizabeth Jones and modeled by Mint engraver John Mercanti.

Robert Graham, who created the bronze sculptures placed at the gateway to the Los Angeles Coliseum, designed the 1984 Olympic silver dollar coin (made of the same fineness as the 1983 issues). His obverse depicted two headless figures on a lintel supported by two columns, with an Olympic flame between the figures and an outline of the Coliseum below. The reverse illustrated a perched eagle with its head turned over its left shoulder—an attractive and quite bold representation of the national bird—with an olive branch but lacking the customary arrows (for war or defense). The obverse of the 1984 Olympic silver dollar received criticism from viewers, and the Fine Arts Commission stated the design was without question a "loser," but the coin became a reality at the insistence of the Los Angeles Olympic Organizing Committee.

The $10 gold coin was the first commemorative to be struck in this metal since the 1926 Sesquicentennial $2.50 gold pieces. The obverse design was modeled at the Philadelphia Mint by staff engraver John Mercanti after a sketch by James M. (Jim) Peed of the Bureau of the Mint's Washington office. Depicted were male and female runners ("Dick and Jane," according to the facetious remarks of some observers, including Rep. Frank Annunzio) holding a torch. Both JM and JP initials appear at the lower left. This unusual double signature resulted from a conversation between Mint Director Donna Pope and the present writer, when she sought historical precedents for this (of which there are many).

Sales of the Olympics coins continued until January 25, 1985. Coins were offered singly and also as part of various sets and packaging options. When figures were tallied, it was announced that fewer than 5 million coins had been sold from the authorization of 52,000,000. Although the 1984 dollar created controversy, perhaps because of this it was the best selling single coin in the program, with 116,675 Uncirculated and 1,801,210 Proof coins reaching buyers. The Bureau of the Mint, as it was then known, acquitted itself well in the eyes of the collecting fraternity. The shortfall in sales was seen as the result of greed on the part of the Olympics people—not at all as a plan of either the Mint or the Treasury Department. The dramatic hearings and debates in Congress served as a landmark, and no doubt forever ended the idea of having a "pet" entity in the private sector take control of a commemorative program. The sins and abuses of the past, dating back nearly 100 years, would have no modern equivalents.

Key to Collecting

The silver dollars in both Uncirculated and Proof format cost less today than they did at the time of issue. The vast quantities issued (never mind that 52 million were not sold) made them common. Today, the aftermarket is supported by collectors, not by Olympic sports enthusiasts. Current values represent true collector demand. The $10 gold coins are necessarily expensive due to their gold content, but are still quite reasonable, on average at about the original issue price. Nearly all surviving coins are in superb gem preservation.

OF LIBERTY
OMMEMORATIVES

ted

,027 Proof
oo-P silver dollar:
   723,635 Uncirculated
1986-S silver dollar:
   6,414,638 Proof
1986-W $5 gold:
   95,248 Uncirculated
   and 404,013 Proof

Whitman Coin Guide (WCG™)—1986-D Statue of Liberty 50¢

MS-65	MS-66	MS-67	MS-68	MS-69	MS-70
$8	$15	$16	$17	$20	$3,250

CERTIFIED POPULATIONS

MS-65	MS-66	MS-67	MS-68	MS-69	MS-70
7	17	63	186	2,328	24

1986-S Statue of Liberty 50¢ Proof

PF-65	PF-66	PF-67	PF-68	PF-69	PF-70
$6.75	$11	$12	$15	$22	$725

CERTIFIED POPULATIONS

PF-65	PF-66	PF-67	PF-68	PF-69	PF-70
8	21	94	75	9,202	255

1986-P Statue of Liberty $1

MS-65	MS-66	MS-67	MS-68	MS-69	MS-70
$16	$18	$22	$28	$32	$2,250

CERTIFIED POPULATIONS

MS-65	MS-66	MS-67	MS-68	MS-69	MS-70
1	5	37	240	3,336	118

1986-S Statue of Liberty $1 Proof

PF-65	PF-66	PF-67	PF-68	PF-69	PF-70
$14	$15	$16	$17	$33	$900

CERTIFIED POPULATIONS

PF-65	PF-66	PF-67	PF-68	PF-69	PF-70
24	52	162	528	8,811	270

1986-W Statue of Liberty Gold $5

MS-65	MS-66	MS-67	MS-68	MS-69	MS-70
$210	$215	$220	$225	$230	$575
PF-65	PF-66	PF-67	PF-68	PF-69	PF-70
$190	$195	$200	$210	$230	$1,750

CERTIFIED POPULATIONS

MS-65	MS-66	MS-67	MS-68	MS-69	MS-70
0	2	10	89	2,453	736
PF-65	PF-66	PF-67	PF-68	PF-69	PF-70
0	4	51	293	6,261	668

Points of Interest: The clad half dollar was the first commemorative in clad format. The $5 was the only commemorative coin of the decade to sell its entire authorized quantity.

Subject of Commemoration: The 100th anniversary of the dedication of the Statue of Liberty in New York City harbor in 1886.

Designs: Clad half dollar: *Obverse*—Ship of immigrants steaming into New York harbor, with the Statue of Liberty greeting them in the foreground and the New York skyline in the distance. Designed by Edgar Z. Steever IV. *Reverse*—Scene of an immigrant family with their belongings on the threshold of America. Designed by Sherl Winter. **Silver dollar:** *Obverse*—Statue of Liberty in the foreground, with the Ellis Island immigration center behind her. *Reverse*—Liberty's torch, along with the words GIVE ME YOUR TIRED, YOUR POOR, YOUR HUDDLED MASSES YEARNING TO BREATHE FREE. Both sides designed by John Mercanti. Matthew Peloso assisted with the reverse. **$5 gold:** *Obverse*—Face and crown of the Statue of Liberty. *Reverse*—American eagle in flight. Designed by Elizabeth Jones (some work on the model of the reverse was done by Philip Fowler).

Mintage Data: Clad half dollar: Authorized by the Act of July 9, 1985. *Maximum authorized*—25,000,000. *Number minted*—1986-D 928,008 Uncirculated; 1986-S 6,925,827 Proof. **Silver dollar:** Authorized by the Act of July 9, 1985. *Maximum authorized*—10,000,000. *Number minted*—1986-P 723,635 Uncirculated; 1986-S 6,414,638 Proof. **$5 gold:** Authorized by the Act of July 9, 1985. *Maximum authorized*—500,000. *Number minted*—1986-W 95,248 Uncirculated and 404,013 Proof.

Original Cost and Issuer: Clad half dollar: 1986-D Uncirculated, $5 pre-order, later $6; 1986-S Proof, $6.50 pre-order, afterward $7.50. **Silver dollar:** 1986-P Uncirculated, $20.50 pre-issue, later $22; 1986-S Proof, $22.50, later $24. **Gold $5:** Uncirculated, $160 to pre orders, afterward $165; Proof, $170, later $175. Various sets and packaging options were also offered. Issued by the U.S. Mint.

Liberty Enlightening the World

The 100th anniversary of the dedication of the Statue of Liberty in New York City harbor in 1886 furnished the occasion for the issuance of commemorative coins in 1986. The statue, officially known as *Liberty Enlightening the World*, was the work of French sculptor Frédéric Auguste Bartholdi and had been presented to the United States by the government of France. Since that time, it has been America's most visible symbol of freedom.

Conceived by Bartholdi in 1865, the statue was planned to be ready for the 1776–1876 centennial anniversary of the United States. By that time, however, only a small part of the work had been completed, and Bartholdi had to be content with exhibiting just the hand and torch of Miss Liberty at the 1876 Centennial Exhibition in Philadelphia. This element of the statue proved to be such an attraction that it stayed in America drawing visitors until its return to France four years later. In 1884, the statue was completed in Paris, after which it was dismantled and shipped to the United States in 214 numbered crates. Erection work commenced on Bedloe's Island in New York harbor and was completed by October 28, 1886, when the Statue of Liberty was dedicated by President Grover Cleveland. In 1924 it was designated as a national monument.

By the early 1980s the statue was in serious need of restoration. Beginning in 1982, plans were made to do the necessary work as well as to restore the vacant buildings on nearby Ellis Island—which had been used to process the immigration of millions of Europeans and others who sailed past Lady Liberty. Some of them may have known the concluding words to Emma Lazarus's poem, *The New Colossus*:

> Give me your tired, your poor; Your huddled masses yearning to breathe free; The wretched refuse of your teeming shore; Send these, the homeless, tempest-tost to me; I lift my lamp beside the golden door!

A Set of Three Denominations

Representative Frank Annunzio sponsored a bill which, after emendation, became law on July 9, 1985, authorizing the production of commemorative coins to assist in fundraising for restoration of the Statue of Liberty and the structures on Ellis Island. In 1982 President Ronald Reagan appointed Lee A. Iacocca, chairman of the board of the Chrysler Corporation, to head the project. At the time Iacocca was heralded in the public and financial press as the savior of the third-largest U.S. auto maker, a firm that had fallen on hard times, and which survived only because of a financial bailout by Congress. Under Iacocca's leadership Chrysler prospered, the loan was eventually repaid, and Iacocca became a folk hero. The project galvanized public attention, and all numismatic eyes faced forward as well.

David L. Ganz, numismatic attorney and writer, signed on as an adviser and proposed that a clad half dollar be added to the suite of proposed coins, since such a coin would be affordable to just about everyone. This was approved, setting a trend that eventually included other commemorative half dollars into the 21st century. The silver dollar and a $5 gold coin (the first such American commemorative) completed the offering. Maximum authorizations were 25,000,000 half dollars, 10,000,000 dollars, and 500,000 $5 pieces.

Within the Mint, discussions were held concerning the designs. Chief Engraver Elizabeth Jones recalled the event, in a letter:

> The Statue of Liberty coins were an in-house competition. Numerous designs were submitted by the entire staff, but only I submitted drawings, about 10, for the gold. My staff . . . told me . . . that I, as chief engraver, should do the gold. I was truly appreciative of their gesture, so that is why only I entered drawings for the $5 gold. Philip Fowler did part of the beginning work on the model for the reverse.

The final choices of submitted art were made by Secretary of the Treasury James A. Baker III.

For the half dollar, designs by Edgar Z. Steever IV and Sherl Joseph Winter were chosen. Steever created the obverse, and Winter produced the reverse. The obverse, according to a Treasury Department news release, "focuses on the growing New York skyline of about 1913, with the Statue's uplifting gesture welcoming an in-bound liner. The scene is set against the sun rising in the east to convey the start of a different life in the New World."

The 1986 Statue of Liberty silver dollars, also known as Ellis Island silver dollars, were designed by John Mercanti, engraver at the Philadelphia Mint. The obverse depicted the Statue of Liberty in the foreground, with the main building at Ellis Island in the distance to the left. Mint publicity described the design as follows: "The Statue of Liberty silver dollar was created from the artist's feeling of majesty derived from the frontal view of the Statue." The reverse illustrated a hand holding a torch, taken from the Statue of Liberty, and an excerpt in four lines from Emma Lazarus's poem, *The New Colossus*.

The obverse of the gold $5 coin, by Elizabeth Jones, featured a close view of the face and crown of the Statue of Liberty, while the reverse illustrated an American eagle in flight, seemingly about to land. This created a sensation in the numismatic community, was widely discussed, and received Krause Publications' Coin of the Year Award. The entire authorization of a half million coins was spoken for—the only complete sweep sellout of any commemorative coin of the 1980s.

Public contributions to the restoration project exceeded expectations even before the commemoratives became a reality. The coin sales program extended from November 1, 1985, through December 31, 1986. Distribution of the Statue of Liberty coins was through direct mail, nationwide merchandising firms, and more than 4,500 banks in coordination with sales efforts for the related silver commemorative issues. As was the case with other commemoratives of the era, many pieces were struck in advance of the date appearing on the coins. By this time little attention was paid to often-quoted and often-violated Mint policy that coins should be struck only in the year appearing on the dies.

Funds raised by coin sales were the icing on the cake. "It was the most successful commemorative coin program in the history of the Mint. More than 15 million gold, silver, and half dollar Liberty coins were sold," a Treasury Department news release observed, forgetting to mention that this was less than half of expectations (not by the Treasury, but by Congress). More than $83 million was raised in coin surcharges for the Statue of Liberty–Ellis Island Foundation, a record.

Key to Collecting

So many 1986 Statue of Liberty commemoratives were issued that the aftermarket affords the possibility of purchasing the coins in and around the original offering price, with the dollar being slightly below the cost at the time of issue. Nearly all coins are superb gems.

(1987) CONSTITUTION BICENTENNIAL COMMEMORATIVES

Distribution
1987-P silver dollar:
    723,635 Uncirculated
1987-S silver dollar:
    2,747,116 Proof
1987-W gold $5:
    212,445 Uncirculated
    and 651,659 Proof

Whitman Coin Guide (WCG™)—1987 Constitution Bicentennial $1

MS-65	MS-66	MS-67	MS-68	MS-69	MS-70
$16	$19	$22	$30	$35	$335

CERTIFIED POPULATIONS

MS-65	MS-66	MS-67	MS-68	MS-69	MS-70
0	4	9	116	3,460	245

1987-S Constitution Bicentennial $1 Proof

PF-65	PF-66	PF-67	PF-68	PF-69	PF-70
$14	$15	$17	$20	$30	$750

CERTIFIED POPULATIONS

PF-65	PF-66	PF-67	PF-68	PF-69	PF-70
11	38	154	550	3,889	112

1987-W Constitution Bicentennial Gold $5

MS-65	MS-66	MS-67	MS-68	MS-69	MS-70
$210	$215	$220	$225	$230	$390
PF-65	PF-66	PF-67	PF-68	PF-69	PF-70
$190	$195	$200	$210	$230	$1,000

CERTIFIED POPULATIONS

MS-65	MS-66	MS-67	MS-68	MS-69	MS-70
2	0	10	89	3,263	1,320
PF-65	PF-66	PF-67	PF-68	PF-69	PF-70
1	6	39	374	7,051	1,395

Points of Interest: A quill pen was featured on three of the four sides of the two coins.

Subject of Commemoration: The 200th anniversary of the U.S. Constitution.

Designs: Silver dollar: *Obverse*—Quill pen, a sheaf of parchment, and the words WE THE PEOPLE. *Reverse*—Cross-section of Americans from various periods representing contrasting lifestyles. Designed by Patricia Lewis Verani. **$5 gold:** *Obverse*—Stylized eagle holding a massive quill pen. *Reverse*—Large quill pen. Designed by Marcel Jovine.

Mintage Data: Authorized by Public Law 99-582, signed by President Ronald Reagan on October 29, 1986. *Maximum authorized*—Silver dollar 1,000,000; $5 gold 1,000,000. *Number minted*—1987-P dollar: 723,635 Uncirculated; 1987-S 2,747,116 Proof; $5 Gold 1987-W 214,225 Uncirculated and 651,659 Proof.

Original Cost and Issuer: Silver dollar: $22.50 pre-issue price, $26 afterward. **$5 gold:** Uncirculated $195 pre-issue, afterward $215; Proof $200 pre-issue, afterward $225. Surcharges of $7 for the dollars and $35 for the $5 pieces went to reducing the national debt. Various sets and packaging options were also offered. Issued by the U.S. Mint.

The Constitution Commemorated

In connection with the 200th anniversary of the U.S. Constitution, observed in 1987, Congress authorized the production of 10 million commemorative silver dollars and one million gold half eagles. Following a competition involving 11 outside and six Mint artists and sculptors, each of whom received $1,000 for submitting four sketches, an announcement was made on March 31, 1987, that the designs had been chosen by Secretary of the Treasury James A. Baker III in consultation with an assistant, John Rogers. Chief Engraver Elizabeth Jones did not submit sketches, since the short time frame did not allow her to create designs she considered appropriate.

The designs were critiqued by the Commission of Fine Arts, which suggested some changes. The design selected for the dollar was disliked, and members recommended that other sketches be revisited for a more attractive motif. This was not done. In the marketplace, the motifs were criticized by many. Mint Director Donna Pope commented that many thought the Mint had gone "feather crazy," with a quill pen featured on three of the four coin sides.

The coins were available for sale through June 20, 1988. The coin market was very strong at the time, with interest focused on gold and silver coins. Although the sales did not come close to the optimistic expectations of the legislation, about four million coins were sold, a strong showing.

Key to Collecting
On the aftermarket, the value fell below the issue prices. Today, these coins remain inexpensive. Nearly all are superb gems.

(1988) SEOUL (SOUTH KOREA) OLYMPIC GAMES COMMEMORATIVES

Distribution
1988-D silver dollar:
      191,368 Uncirculated
1988-S silver dollar:
      1,359,366 Proof
1988-W gold $5:
      62,913 Uncirculated
      and 281,465 Proof

Whitman Coin Guide (WCG™)—1988-D Seoul Olympics $1

MS-65	MS-66	MS-67	MS-68	MS-69	MS-70
$16	$19	$22	$30	$35	$4,000

CERTIFIED POPULATIONS

MS-65	MS-66	MS-67	MS-68	MS-69	MS-70
2	1	28	160	1,399	21

1988-S Seoul Olympics $1 Proof

PF-65	PF-66	PF-67	PF-68	PF-69	PF-70
$14	$15	$17	$20	$33	$2,000

CERTIFIED POPULATIONS

PF-65	PF-66	PF-67	PF-68	PF-69	PF-70
5	23	100	306	1,695	6

1988-W Seoul Olympics Gold $5

MS-65	MS-66	MS-67	MS-68	MS-69	MS-70
$210	$215	$220	$225	$230	$925
PF-65	PF-66	PF-67	PF-68	PF-69	PF-70
$190	$195	$200	$210	$230	$2,350

CERTIFIED POPULATIONS

MS-65	MS-66	MS-67	MS-68	MS-69	MS-70
0	1	9	65	1,463	348
PF-65	PF-66	PF-67	PF-68	PF-69	PF-70
1	5	36	278	3,566	837

Points of Interest: Elizabeth Jones's $5 obverse design is considered by many to be the high point of commemorative art of the late 20th century.

Subject of Commemoration: U.S. participation in the Seoul Olympiad.

Designs: Silver dollar: *Obverse*—One hand holds a Olympic torch as another hand holds another torch to ignite it. Designed by Patricia Lewis Verani. *Reverse*—Olympic rings surrounded by a wreath. Designed by Sherl Joseph Winter. **$5 gold:** *Obverse*—Nike, goddess of Victory, wearing a crown of olive leaves. Designed by Elizabeth Jones. *Reverse*—Stylized Olympic flame. Designed by Marcel Jovine.

Mintage Data: Authorized by Public Law 100-141, signed by President Ronald Reagan on October 28, 1987. *Maximum authorized*—10,000,000 silver dollars; 1,000,000 gold $5. *Number minted*—1988-D silver dollar 191,638 Uncirculated; 1,359,366 Proof; 1988-W Olympiad Gold $5: 62,913 Uncirculated, 281,456 Proof.

Original Cost and Issuer: Silver dollars: Uncirculated, $22 pre-issue price through May 15, 1988, $27 afterward. **$5 gold:** Uncirculated, $200 pre-issue, $225 afterward; Proof, $205 pre-issue, afterward $235. Various packaging and set options were also offered. Surcharges of $7 and $35 per coin went to the U.S. Olympic Committee. Issued by the U.S. Mint.

Another Olympic Issue

The holding of the 1988 Summer Olympic Games in Seoul, Republic of South Korea, furnished the opportunity for the issuance of commemorative silver dollars and $5 gold coins. Designs were solicited from 10 private sculptors and seven on the Mint staff, each submitter receiving $1,000 for the effort. The Commission of Fine Arts made selections from 60 outside and 24 Mint designs submitted—the first time the Commission had been invited to participate in the initial review. Each entry was marked with a code letter and number to conceal the identity of the artist.

The commemorative dollar featured two Olympic torches on the obverse (not a choice of the Commission of Fine Arts) and the Olympic rings on the reverse, with appropriate lettering. It was a non-event in terms of acclaim in numismatic circles. In contrast, the $5 coin was praised to the skies.

For the half eagle, Chief Engraver Elizabeth Jones created a portrait of Nike, the ancient goddess of Victory. The reverse was by Marcel Jovine, a Closter, New Jersey artist. Numismatic columnist Ed Reiter commentedthat the classic obverse and modern reverse never should have been mated. "Aesthetically, the marriage is a bad one, " he wrote.

Coin World editor Beth Deisher paid tribute by calling Jones's head of Nike "one of the most beautiful of all U.S. coin designs."

There was trouble in paradise—or at least a glitch—when GreyCom, the advertising agency hired to promote sales of the 1988 Olympic coins, wanted to rush into print to encourage business; and in the absence of having an actual photograph of the 1988-W $5 gold coin (for it wasn't ready yet), the agency used a computerized representation of the Jones motif embossed on various sales literature. Chief Engraver Jones was justifiably miffed. *Coin World* described GreyCom's unfortunate depiction as "ugly" and not even good enough for a counterfeit!

The 1988 *Annual Report of the Director of the Mint* described the sales effort for the 1988 Olympic commemorative coins. These coins were marketed through direct mail, telemarketing, international marketing, bulk, consignment and over-the-counter sales. Major retailers and more than 900 financial institutions sold U.S. Olympic coins to their customers, making U.S. Olympic coins available to the American public in all 50 states at more than 8,500 locations.

Some observers suggested that, because the event was not held in the United States, it was not an appropriate subject for American coinage. In any event, despite strong sales efforts, the program did not capture nationwide attention. When results were totaled, about 2.5 million coins had been sold from an authorization of 11 million.

Key to Collecting
Both coins are inexpensive, indeed cheaper than the original issue prices. Once again, the numismatic market, representing actual buyers and sellers, is not extensive enough to maintain the price of hundreds of thousands of coins purchased by the public, then sold when their novelty passed. Nearly all coins are superb gems.

(1989) CONGRESS BICENTENNIAL COMMEMORATIVES

Distribution

1989-D clad half dollar:
    163,753 Uncirculated
1989-S clad half dollar:
    767,897 Proof
1989-D silver dollar:
    135,203 Uncirculated
1989-S silver dollar:
    762,198 Proof
1989-W gold $5:
    46,899 Uncirculated
    and 164,690 Proof

Whitman Coin Guide (WCG™)—1989-D Congress Bicentennial 50¢

MS-65	MS-66	MS-67	MS-68	MS-69	MS-70
$12	$16	$18	$19	$25	

CERTIFIED POPULATIONS

MS-65	MS-66	MS-67	MS-68	MS-69	MS-70
11	27	26	124	1,357	1

1989-S Congress Bicentennial 50¢ Proof

PF-65	PF-66	PF-67	PF-68	PF-69	PF-70
$9	$11	$12	$15	$24	

CERTIFIED POPULATIONS

PF-65	PF-66	PF-67	PF-68	PF-69	PF-70
5	21	75	254	2,217	28

1989-D Congress Bicentennial $1

MS-65	MS-66	MS-67	MS-68	MS-69	MS-70
$20	$25	$30	$35	$40	$5,650

CERTIFIED POPULATIONS

MS-65	MS-66	MS-67	MS-68	MS-69	MS-70
0	3	25	121	2,108	13

1989-S Congress Bicentennial $1 Proof

PF-65	PF-66	PF-67	PF-68	PF-69	PF-70
$19	$20	$22	$25	$35	$3,000

CERTIFIED POPULATIONS

PF-65	PF-66	PF-67	PF-68	PF-69	PF-70
6	23	68	300	1,711	21

1989-W Congress Bicentennial Gold $5

MS-65	MS-66	MS-67	MS-68	MS-69	MS-70
$185	$200	$210	$220	$230	$365
PF-65	**PF-66**	**PF-67**	**PF-68**	**PF-69**	**PF-70**
$195	$200	$210	$220	$230	$690

CERTIFIED POPULATIONS

MS-65	MS-66	MS-67	MS-68	MS-69	MS-70
0	0	6	46	1,500	441
PF-65	**PF-66**	**PF-67**	**PF-68**	**PF-69**	**PF-70**
2	9	28	166	3,129	680

Points of Interest: To inaugurate the coins, four coining presses weighing seven tons each were brought from the Philadelphia Mint to the east front of the Capitol building, where in a special ceremony on June 14, 1989, the first silver dollars and $5 gold coins were struck (but no half dollars). Later production was accomplished at the Denver, Philadelphia, and West Point mints.

Subject of Commemoration: The 200th anniversary of the operation of Congress under the U.S. Constitution.

Designs: Clad half dollar: *Obverse*—The head of the *Freedom* statue (erected on top of the Capitol dome in 1863) is shown at the center, with inscriptions around, including LIBERTY in oversize letters at the bottom border. The design was by Patricia L. Verani, a Londonderry, New Hampshire sculptor in the private sector. *Reverse*—A distant front view of the Capital is shown, with arcs of stars above and below, with appropriate lettering. William Woodward, a muralist in the private sector, created the design, and the modeling was done by Mint staffer Edgar Z. Steever. **Silver dollar:** *Obverse*—The statue of *Freedom* full length, with a cloud and rays of glory behind. Lettering around the border. Both sides were designed by William Woodward, and models at the Mint were made by Chester Y. Martin. *Reverse*—The mace of the House of Representative the House Chamber when that body is in session. **Gold $5:** *Obverse*—The Capitol is shown, with lettering around. *Reverse*—The eagle in the old Senate depicted, with lettering surrounding. Designed by John Mercanti, whose selection some dissension within the Engraving Department when it was alleged that certain of others had not been reviewed. The *Annual Report of the Director of the Mint*, 19 described the work in glowing terms, with the obverse displaying "a spectacular rendition of the Capitol dome," while the reverse "centers around a dramatic portrait of the majestic eagle atop the canopy overlooking the Old Senate Chamber."

Mintage Data: Authorized by Public Law 100-673, signed by President Ronald Reagan on November 17, 1988. The coins were to be dated 1989 and could be minted through June 30, 1990. *Maximum authorized*—clad half dollars 4,000,000; silver dollars 3,000,000; gold $5 1,000,000. *Number minted*—clad half dollars, 1989-D Uncirculated 163,753, 1989-S Proof 767,897; silver dollars, 1989-D Uncirculated 135,203, 1989-S Proof 762,198; and $5 gold 46,899 Uncirculated and Proof 164,690.

Original Cost and Issuer: Surcharges were included in the price, amounting to $1 for each half dollar, $7 for each dollar, and $35 for each $5, all to go to the Capitol Preservation Fund (although originally it was proposed that 50 percent would go to that fund and the rest to reduction of the national debt). Purchase options were exceptionally extensive and included 12 combinations. Issued by the U.S. Mint.

200 Years of Congress

The 200th anniversary of the operation of Congress under the U.S. Constitution was observed in 1989. The legislative body met in several venues, first in New York City in 1789, then in Philadelphia, then in the new Capitol in Washington in 1800, and later in the present Capitol, which was built after British forces burned the first one in 1814 (during the War of 1812). Then, as now, Congress was a bicameral or two-part institution, with the House of Representatives comprising members based on the population of each state, at a minimum of one person, and the Senate including two people per state, regardless of population. In time, populous states such as New York and California became powerful in the House, while in the Senate each state had the same voting strength. The first Congress in 1789 had 59 representatives and 22 senators from the 11 states that had ratified the Constitution, representing a population of about four million citizens. By the time of the bicentennial in 1989, Congress included 435 representatives and 100 senators from 50 states, in a nation of about 245 million people.

A suite of commemorative coins was authorized to observe the bicentennial: a clad composition half dollar, a silver dollar, and a gold $5. Hopes were high—it was anticipated that every member of Congress would endorse and help sell them. Up to 4 million half dollars, 3 million silver dollars, and 1 million $5 gold coins were authorized.

To diversify the motifs, 11 artists from the private sector were invited to submit designs, as were members of the Engraving Department staff. Amid some dissension and with much commentary from observers on the sidelines, motifs were selected.

According to Mint Director Donna Pope, in an interview with the author, Congress had input on which designs were used. The Senate, having claimed the gold coin as theirs, chose the Capitol dome motif because of the space constraints on the smallest coin. Once Congress made their selections among the designs, the Treasury went along with their choices. Sadly, many members of Congress did not support the program with sales efforts. When final results were tallied, only a small percentage of the authorized coins was struck.

...signs

...of the motifs to be uninteresting as well as repetitive. The ...omas Crawford, which was mounted on the Capitol dome in ...erse of all three coins, albeit in different sizes and elements. ... editor of *COINage* and a well-known personality in the coin ... the Capitol on the obverse of the $5 gold coin was unimag- ...ird on the reverse looked "more like a fricasseed chicken limping ...namber after an especially grueling filibuster."

Robert A. Weinman, past president of the National Sculpture Society, called the designs of the $5 "stodgy and safe," noting that it was "lackluster."

Mico Kaufman, one of the nation's top medalists, commented on how the competitions were run, proclaiming them "a huge waste of time."

Part of the problem, in Kaufman's view, is that selections are made by viewing sketches, not models, and sketches do not necessarily indicate how a finished coin will look. Since the Mint also tries to please the politicians, "you are no longer talking about numismatic art or something you can be proud of; you're talking about politics as usual."

With regard to the Congress Bicentennial designs, Kaufman dismissed them all by saying that "if they were works of art, you'd be hiding them in the cellar."

Cornelius Vermeule imaginatively compared the new Congress Bicentennial coins to eating a fast-food hamburger after starving on a desert island. "You don't kvetch about the quality of [the] food; you're just so glad to see some food. But after your appetite is sated, you want better."

Key to Collecting

Not popular with numismatists in 1989, these coins still languish in the marketplace, with most sales after 1989 recorded at lower-than-issue prices. Exceptions are coins certified in ultra-high grades.

The Uncirculated 1989-D half dollar exists with a misaligned reverse, oriented in the same direction as the obverse, instead of the usual 180 degree separation. These are rare and valuable, but are not widely known. Likely, some remain undiscovered in buyers' hands.

(1990) EISENHOWER CENTENNIAL DOLLARS

Distribution
1990-W: 241,669 Uncirculated
1990-P: 1,144,461 Proof

Whitman Coin Guide (WCG™)—1990-W Eisenhower Centennial $1

MS-65	MS-66	MS-67	MS-68	MS-69	MS-70
$18	$22	$28	$33	$36	$915

CERTIFIED POPULATIONS

MS-65	MS-66	MS-67	MS-68	MS-69	MS-70
7	31	61	134	1,965	94

1990-P Eisenhower Centennial $1 Proof

PF-65	PF-66	PF-67	PF-68	PF-69	PF-70
$18	$20	$22	$25	$36	$800

CERTIFIED POPULATIONS

PF-65	PF-66	PF-67	PF-68	PF-69	PF-70
28	41	74	215	3,886	71

Points of Interest: This is the only U.S. coin to feature two portraits of the same person on the same side. The reverse notes EISENHOWER HOME, not mentioning it was his retirement residence, where he never spent much time.

Subject of Commemoration: The 100th anniversary of the birth of Dwight David Eisenhower, our 34th president.

Designs: *Obverse*—Profile of President Eisenhower facing right, superimposed over his own left-facing profile as a five-star general. Designed by John Mercanti. *Reverse*—Eisenhower retirement home at Gettysburg, a national historic site. Designed by Marcel Jovine, modeled by Chester Y. Martin.

Mintage Data: Authorized by Public Law 100-467 signed by President Ronald Reagan on October 3, 1988. *Maximum authorized*—4,000,000 silver dollars. *Number minted*—241,669 Proof, 1,144,461 Uncirculated.

Original Cost and Issuer: Uncirculated, $23 pre-issue price, afterward $26; Proof, pre-issue $25, afterward $29. Also available as part of a Prestige Proof Set. $7 surcharge went to reduce the public debt. Issued by the U.S. Mint.

A President's Birth Commemorated

The 100th anniversary of the birth of Dwight David Eisenhower furnished the opportunity for the creation of a commemorative silver dollar in 1990, up to four million of them. Eisenhower was best known as Supreme Commander of the Allied Forces in Europe during World War II, and as the person who planned the D-Day invasion of Normandy on June 6, 1944. Later he served as president of Columbia University and still later was elected for two terms as president of the United States (1953 to 1961). During his presidency, Eisenhower held the first summit with Soviet leaders, was the first chief executive to have a televised news conference, balanced the federal budget, and initiated the interstate highway program.

Eisenhower was born on October 14, 1890. On the 1990 centennial date, various celebrations were held around the United States, including at his birthplace in Denison, Texas, his hometown of Abilene, Kansas, his retirement home in Gettysburg, Pennsylvania, and the Kennedy Center in Washington, D.C.

Five outside artists as well as the artists on the Mint Engraving Department staff were invited to submit designs for the coin (but not all did). In August 1989, Secretary of the Treasury Nicholas F. Brady made the final selections, said to have been in consultation with the Commission of Fine Arts and the Eisenhower family. Later, Diane Wolf of the commission said this was not true, and that her group had been shown the sketches after they were chosen. The entire situation, as well as the appearance of the designs, created many complaints within the Mint and also the collecting community.

John Mercanti of the Mint created the obverse motif, which featured a right-facing bust of Eisenhower as an older man, superimposed on a younger, left-facing bust of Eisenhower as a five-star general. New Jersey artist Marcel Jovine produced the reverse, modeled by Mint sculptor-engraver Chester Y. Martin. This showed Eisenhower's retirement home at Gettysburg, Pennsylvania (although no mention of the building's location appears on the coin). Only about a third of the authorized four million coins found buyers.

Key to Collecting
The controversy surrounding these coins now forgotten, Eisenhower dollars are appreciated as an addition to the commemorative series. Examples are plentiful and inexpensive in the marketplace. Nearly all are superb gems.

(1991) KOREAN WAR MEMORIAL DOLLARS

Distribution
1991-D: 213,049 Uncirculated
1991-P: 618,488 Proof

Whitman Coin Guide (WCG™)—1991 Korean War Memorial $1

MS-65	MS-66	MS-67	MS-68	MS-69	MS-70
$25	$30	$35	$40	$45	$500

CERTIFIED POPULATIONS

MS-65	MS-66	MS-67	MS-68	MS-69	MS-70
3	19	44	81	2,313	169

1991-P Korean War Memorial $1 Proof

PF-65	PF-66	PF-67	PF-68	PF-69	PF-70
$20	$22	$24	$27	$40	$3,000

CERTIFIED POPULATIONS

PF-65	PF-66	PF-67	PF-68	PF-69	PF-70
16	34	63	203	1,881	78

Points of Interest: Produced in a great rush, the design displeased many observers. Buyers reacted favorably however, and more than 800,000 were coined. The word "COMMEMORATIVE" is part of the inscriptions.

Subject of Commemoration: The 38th anniversary of the end of the Korean War, a span of years with no special meaning.

Designs: *Obverse*—Featured are two F-86 Sabrejet fighter aircraft flying to the right, a helmeted soldier carrying a backpack climbing a hill, and the inscriptions: THIRTY EIGHT / ANNIVERSARY / COMMEMORATIVE / KOREA / IN GOD / WE TRUST / 1953 / 1991. At the bottom of the coin are five Navy ships above the word LIBERTY. Mint engraver John Mercanti created the model. *Reverse*—Shown is an outline map of North and South Korea, divided. An eagle's head (representing the United States) is depicted to the right. Near the bottom is the symbol of Korea. Inscriptions included E / PLURIBUS / UNUM (in three lines), ONE DOLLAR, and UNITED STATES OF AMERICA. T. James Ferrell of the Mint staff was the engraver.

Mintage Data: Public Law 101-495 of October 31, 1990, provided
not more than 1,000,000 coins, all to be struck in the calendar year
minted—1991-D Uncirculated 213,049; 1991-P Proof 618,488.

Original Cost and Issuer: Proof 1991-P dollars were priced at $28 if ordered
31, 1991, and $31 if ordered later. Uncirculated 1991-D silver dollars were priced
for early orders and $26 if ordered later. A $7 surcharge went to fund the Korean
Veterans Memorial. Issued by the U.S. Mint.

A Curious Anniversary Date

In the annals of commemoratives, one of the more curious entries is the 1991 silver dollar observing the 38th anniversary of the end of the Korean War, struck to honor those
who served there. As to why the 38th—rather than choosing the 50th or some other logical year—the explanation is that during that war, which was never called such at the
time, but was designated as a "conflict," the 38th degree of latitude on the map defined
the division between North and South Korea. On the coin there is no mention of either
a war, conflict, or any other military action. To the uninitiated observer, Korea might
mean anything (except that ships, planes, and a soldier suggest combat).

One million coins were authorized. Originally, a much higher number was
requested, but Mint Director Donna Pope and others cautioned that, based upon past
experience, even a million might be hard to sell—although six out of seven commemorative dollars minted since 1983 achieved or surpassed that mark. The director was right
on target, for slightly more than 800,000 were sold.

As time was of the essence, designs were solicited only from Mint staff. Ideas of
John Mercanti and T. James Ferrell received the nod from Secretary of the Treasury
Nicholas F. Brady, after consultation with the Korean War Veterans Memorial Advi-
sory Board and the American Battle Monuments Commission.

An observer of the Korean coin design in 1991 could not help but wonder how
much more artistic the coin could have been if the designer had been freed from
the necessity of including so many inscriptions—including one which reminded the
viewer that the coin was a "COMMEMORATIVE"—presumably helpful in case
someone thought it was a regular issue silver dollar. There was nothing on either side
to explain the 38th anniversary, although Ferrell's original sketch had the inscription
"38th PARALLEL."

The Commission of Fine Arts, which reviewed the design, criticized it severely. J.
Carter Brown, chairman, suggested, "The lettering styles on the obverse and reverse
should either be the same or compatible with each other." George Hartman commented, "It's a collection of unrelated things in search of a unifying idea."[14]

Mint Director Donna Pope told the author in an interview of the rush involved.
Money was needed fast for the war memorial, and no design competition was held.
The memorial committee was asked what they wanted, and several ideas were given
to the engravers.

The Korean War Veterans Memorial became a reality, but bore no relationship to
the design of the commemorative dollar.

Key to Collecting

As of 2007, gem Uncirculated and Proof coins are available in the marketplace for less
than the original issuing price.

SHMORE GOLDEN
MEMORATIVES

195,199 Uncirculated
1991-S silver dollar:
738,419 Proof
1991-W gold $5:
31,959 Uncirculated
and 111,991 Proof

ms69

Whitman Coin Guide (WCG™)—1991-D Mt Rushmore Golden Anniversary 50¢

MS-65	MS-66	MS-67	MS-68	MS-69	MS-70
$25	$30	$35	$40	$45	$3,250

CERTIFIED POPULATIONS

MS-65	MS-66	MS-67	MS-68	MS-69	MS-70
2	4	13	54	1,431	15

1991-S Mt Rushmore Golden Anniversary 50¢ Proof

PF-65	PF-66	PF-67	PF-68	PF-69	PF-70
$21	$22	$25	$30	$40	$1,150

CERTIFIED POPULATIONS

PF-65	PF-66	PF-67	PF-68	PF-69	PF-70
4	9	29	128	2,596	103

1991-P Mt Rushmore Golden Anniversary $1

MS-65	MS-66	MS-67	MS-68	MS-69	MS-70
$35	$40	$44	$50	$58	$463

CERTIFIED POPULATIONS

MS-65	MS-66	MS-67	MS-68	MS-69	MS-70
3	14	31	42	1,527	315

1991-S Mt Rushmore Golden Anniversary $1 Proof

PF-65	PF-66	PF-67	PF-68	PF-69	PF-70
$31	$32	$35	$37	$50	$1,100

CERTIFIED POPULATIONS

PF-65	PF-66	PF-67	PF-68	PF-69	PF-70
18	40	43	195	2,504	73

1991-W Mt Rushmore Golden Anniversary Gold $5

MS-65	MS-66	MS-67	MS-68	MS-69	MS-70
$320	$330	$340	$350	$375	$550
PF-65	PF-66	PF-67	PF-68	PF-69	PF-70
$225	$235	$245	$255	$275	$750

CERTIFIED POPULATIONS

MS-65	MS-66	MS-67	MS-68	MS-69	MS-70
0	0	1	38	1,062	479
PF-65	PF-66	PF-67	PF-68	PF-69	PF-70
0	4	20	119	2,834	493

Points of Interest: Essentially the same motif was featured on the obverse of each of the three coins. The reverse of the $5 consisted solely of lettering, with no emblems or motifs, the first such instance in the history of U.S. commemorative coins.

Subject of Commemoration: The 50th anniversary of the Mount Rushmore National Memorial.

Designs: Clad half dollar: *Obverse*—View of Mount Rushmore with rays of the sun behind. Designed by Marcel Jovine. *Reverse*—An American bison with the words GOLDEN ANNIVERSARY. Designed by T. James Ferrell of the Mint staff. **Silver dollar:** *Obverse*—View of Mount Rushmore with an olive wreath prominently below. Designed by Marika Somogyi. Model by Chester Y. Martin of the Mint staff. *Reverse*—The Great Seal of the United States, surrounded by a sunburst, above an outline map of the continental part of the United States inscribed SHRINE OF / DEMOCRACY. Designed by Frank Gasparro, former chief engraver of the Mint. **Gold $5:** *Obverse*—An American eagle flying above the monument with LIBERTY and date in the field. Designed by John Mercanti of the Mint staff. *Reverse*—MOUNT RUSHMORE NATIONAL MEMORIAL in script type. Designed by William Lamb, a Rhode Island calligraphic artist. The model was made by William Cousins of the Mint staff.

Mintage Data: Authorized by the Mount Rushmore National Memorial Coin Act (Public Law 101-332, July 16, 1990). *Maximum authorized*—clad half dollar 2,500,000; silver dollar 2,500,000; $5 gold 500,000. *Number minted*—clad half dollar 1991-D: 172,754 Uncirculated; 1991-S: 753,257 Proofs; silver dollar 1991-P: 133,139 Uncirculated; 1991-S: 738,419 Proofs; $5 gold 31,959 Uncirculated and 111,991 Proofs.

Original Cost and Issuer: The price schedule offered discounts if ordered by March 28, 1991: Uncirculated 1991-D half dollar $6 pre-issue discount price, afterward $7. Proof 1991-S half dollar $8.50 pre-issue, afterward $9.50. Uncirculated 1991-P silver dollar: $23 pre-issue, afterward $26. Proof 1991-S silver dollar: $28 pre-issue, afterward $31. Uncirculated 1991-W $5 pre-issue $185; afterward $210. Proof 1991-W $5 pre-issue $195; afterward $225. These prices included surcharges: $35 per half eagle, $7 per silver dollar, and $1 per half dollar. Fifty percent was earmarked for the Mount Rushmore National Memorial Society of Black Hills for the improvement, enlargement, and renovation of the Memorial, with the balance to go to the U.S. Treasury. Other combinations and packaging options were offered. Issued by the U.S. Mint.

Mount Rushmore Commemorated

The Mount Rushmore National Memorial Coin Act (Public Law 101-332, July 16, 1990) provided the authority to produce three types of 1991-dated commemorative coins in observance of the 50th anniversary of the monumental sculpture in stone. Anticipating huge public interest, the legislation provided for up to 2,500,000 each of clad half dollars and silver dollars and 500,000 gold $5 coins to be struck. *Coin World* was pessimistic, and on January 30, 1999, observed: "Of the 15 different commemorative coins struck by the U.S. Mint since 1982, only the 1986 Statue of Liberty gold half eagle struck at West Point sold out."

A design competition was held with 10 artists participating from the private sector, plus Mint staff. Secretary of the Treasury Nicholas F. Brady, in consultation with the Commission of Fine Arts, made the final selections. All featured the Mount Rushmore figures carved in stone by Gutzon Borglum and his staff of about 60 men. Borglum had died in 1941, and is remembered as the creator of the Georgia mountainside sculpture depicted on the 1925 Stone Mountain commemorative half dollar.

The Mount Rushmore sculpture was cut in the rock face of a South Dakota mountain, with images of presidents George Washington, Thomas Jefferson, Theodore Roosevelt, and Abraham Lincoln, side by side, measuring about 60 to 70 feet high.

The work was the brainchild of Doane Robinson, state historian, who in 1923 sought to increase tourism by developing a mountainous site in the Harney National Forest in the Black Hills. Writing to noted Chicago sculptor Lorado Taft on December 28, 1923, Robinson inquired concerning the artist's interest in carving massive figures of "notable Sioux such as Red Cloud, who lived and died in the shadows of those peaks." Taft was in failing health and could not consider the project, which by the spring of 1924 had expanded in Robinson's mind to include figures in stone of Lewis and Clark, Buffalo Bill, and other notables in addition to Sioux.

On August 24, 1924, Robinson contacted Gutzon Borglum at his Stamford, Connecticut studio to ascertain his possible interest, noting that if the sculptor would take on the project, financing of the project could be arranged. Borglum replied by telegram stating that his work on Stone Mountain was proceeding ahead of schedule and, yes, he was interested and could visit the site in September. The artist was enthusiastic about the project. On March 23, 1925, Congress passed a bill approving the project (for it was to be done in a national park) but not providing financing. In the same year the Mt. Harney Memorial Association was formed. The Mt. Harney site was soon abandoned in favor of nearby Mt. Rushmore, which had a suitable stone outcropping on its east side. Work began in 1927. It was Borglum who selected the presidents to be sculpted. Originally, the first figure, Washington, was to be 500 feet high. He also proposed that a huge cavern, the Hall of Records, to measure 350 feet wide, be carved into the mountain. Within it would be a diorama of westward migration, in company with 25 statues of prominent Americans to be selected and carved by Borglum. Architect Frank Lloyd Wright did some preliminary work, but the cavern project was soon abandoned.

Washington was finished in 1930, Jefferson in 1936, Lincoln in 1937, and Roosevelt in 1939. Final details were completed by Borglum's son in 1941. By 1958 the total visitor count numbered 10 million. Since that time, one to two million people have visited each year. (The Memorial was also featured on the 2006 statehood quarter issued by South Dakota.)

Comments from numismatists were generally negative, as expressed in the columns of *Coin World* and *Numismatic News*. The obverse motifs were viewed as redundant by many: one coin would have served the purpose of all three. The reverses were considered to be uninspired. Only a small fraction of the authorized mintage was struck.

Key to Collecting

Examples are easily available today. The coins were carefully struck, with the result that nearly all are superb gems.

(1991) UNITED SERVICE ORGANIZATIONS DOLLARS

Distribution
1991-D: 124,958 Uncirculated
1991-S: 321,275 Proof

Whitman Coin Guide (WCG™)—1991-D USO $1

MS-65	MS-66	MS-67	MS-68	MS-69	MS-70
$20	$25	$30	$35	$45	$425

CERTIFIED POPULATIONS

MS-65	MS-66	MS-67	MS-68	MS-69	MS-70
1	17	39	70	2,205	209

1991-S USO $1 Proof

PF-65	PF-66	PF-67	PF-68	PF-69	PF-70
$20	$22	$24	$27	$40	$4,250

CERTIFIED POPULATIONS

PF-65	PF-66	PF-67	PF-68	PF-69	PF-70
7	26	33	195	1,598	27

Points of Interest: Nowhere on the coin is there a mention of what USO stands for! The correct name is United Service Organizations, but "United Services Organization" also appears in print many times, including in information released by the Treasury Department about this coin.

Subject of Commemoration: The 50th anniversary of United Service Organizations.

Designs: *Obverse*—Consists entirely of lettering, except for a banner upon which appears USO. Inscriptions include IN GOD WE TRUST, 50th *ANNIVERSARY* (in script), USO (on a banner, as noted; with three stars to each side), and LIBERTY 1991. Design by Robert Lamb, a Rhode Island calligraphic artist. Model by William C. Cousins of the Mint staff. *Reverse*—Illustrates an eagle, facing right, with a ribbon inscribed USO in its beak, perched atop a world globe. An arc of 11 stars is in the space below the globe. Inscriptions include UNITED STATES OF AMERICA, FIFTY YEARS / SERVICE (on the left side of the coin), TO SERVICE / PEOPLE (on the right side of the coin), E PLURIBUS UNUM, and ONE DOLLAR. Designed by Mint staff engraver John Mercanti.

Mintage Data: Authorized by Public Law 101-404, October 2, 1990. *Maximum authorized*—1,000,000. *Number minted*—1991-D Uncirculated: 124,958; 1991-S Proof: 321,275.

Original Cost and Issuer: 1991-D Uncirculated dollars were priced at $23 each through July 26, 1991, afterward $26. 1991-P Proofs were priced at $28 for early orders, afterward $31. The price of each coin included a $7 surcharge—50 percent went to the USO, and 50 percent to reduction of the national debt. Issued by the U.S. Mint.

Honoring the USO

In 1991, a commemorative silver dollar was produced to observe the 50th anniversary of the United Service Organizations, a private non-profit group which provides entertainment and other services to members of the U.S. armed forces. Up to one million coins were to be produced in both Uncirculated and Proof finishes, and were intended to be ready by Flag Day on June 14, 1991.

Five artists from the private sector were invited to submit designs, as were members of the Engraving Department staff at the Mint. Members of the Fine Arts Commission, which advised the Treasury Department on this and other designs, but had no final say, generally condemned the motifs, despite approving what seemed to be the best of a poor selection. (The Mount Rushmore coins and the Korean dollar were also criticized.) Commission Chairman John Carter Brown suggested that in the future, more time be taken, and that "high school art classes" could have done better. An effort should be made to interest sculptors and other artists to learn about the coinage medium. "Get them an NEA grant, bring them to Washington." In a letter to Mint Director Donna Pope on January 22, 1991, Brown commented further:

> The design for this coin was considered mediocre at best. Recognizing that the pennant was based directly on the design of the USO flag, it was hoped that there could be at least some refinement in the shape and spacing of the letters. On the reverse, it was unclear whether the motto, beginning 'Fifty Years,' should be read down or across; perhaps shifting the words on the left slightly upward would remove the uncertainty. There is a great multiplicity of lettering styles on this coin; an effort should be made to reduce the number of styles and see that they are compatible.

Secretary of the Treasury Nicholas F. Brady gave his nod, and the coin became a reality. The coin made its debut in a victory parade held on June 8, 1991, saluting troops returning from the Operation Desert Storm action in Kuwait and Iraq several months earlier. A replica of the obverse of the commemorative, measuring 10 feet across, was carried on a float. Unfortunately, neither parade watchers or many other people were inspired to order coins, and less than half the authorized quantity found buyers. Per a General Accounting Office report, the Mint lost $100,000 in their production.

The Mint and the Treasury Department were in a quandary, as revealed in several conversations I had with officials about that time. They really wanted to produce beautiful coins, but did not know how to go about implementing this. Moreover, it was usu-

ally the situation that the sponsors of coins, not the Mint, s
by Congress.

Key to Collecting

Never popular with collectors, the USO dollars were rou
The aftermarket for these and most other artistically co
poor, and as of 2007, the coins are still available for less

194 A GUIDE BOOK

1992-D Columb

| MS-65 |
| $35 |

CERTIFIED PO

| MS-65 |
| 2 |

19

(1992) CHRISTOPHER COLUMBUS QUINCENTENARY COMMEMORATIVES

Distribution

1992-D clad half dollar:
    135,702 Uncirculated
1992-S clad half dollar:
    390,154 Proof
1992-D silver dollar:
    106,949 Uncirculated
1992-P silver dollar:
    385,241 Proof
1992-W gold $5:
    24,329 Uncirculated
    and 79,730 Proof

Whitman Coin Guide (WCG™)—1992-D Columbus Quincentenary 50¢

MS-65	MS-66	MS-67	MS-68	MS-69	MS-70
$14	$15	$16	$20	$28	$550

CERTIFIED POPULATIONS

MS-65	MS-66	MS-67	MS-68	MS-69	MS-70
2	35	53	50	1,261	56

1992-S Columbus Quincentenary 50¢ Proof

PF-65	PF-66	PF-67	PF-68	PF-69	PF-70
$12	$14	$15	$17	$29	$925

CERTIFIED POPULATIONS

PF-65	PF-66	PF-67	PF-68	PF-69	PF-70
7	17	33	164	2,183	142

Quincentenary $1

MS-66	MS-67	MS-68	MS-69	MS-70
$40	$45	$50	$53	$425

POPULATIONS

MS-66	MS-67	MS-68	MS-69	MS-70
4	15	78	1,700	192

2-P Columbus Quincentenary $1 Proof

PF-65	PF-66	PF-67	PF-68	PF-69	PF-70
$39	$40	$45	$50	$65	

CERTIFIED POPULATIONS

PF-65	PF-66	PF-67	PF-68	PF-69	PF-70
10	32	54	208	2,018	18

1992-W Columbus Quincentenary Gold $5

MS-65	MS-66	MS-67	MS-68	MS-69	MS-70
$300	$320	$330	$350	$400	$550
PF-65	**PF-66**	**PF-67**	**PF-68**	**PF-69**	**PF-70**
$250	$260	$270	$280	$305	$1,100

CERTIFIED POPULATIONS

MS-65	MS-66	MS-67	MS-68	MS-69	MS-70
0	0	1	24	907	444
PF-65	**PF-66**	**PF-67**	**PF-68**	**PF-69**	**PF-70**
1	0	8	127	2,012	462

Points of Interest: These commemoratives attracted much less interest than did the Columbus issues for the 400th anniversary in 1892–1893.

Subject of Commemoration: The quincentenary (500th anniversary) of the discovery of the Americas.

Designs: Clad half dollar: *Obverse*—A full-length figure of Columbus walking ashore, with a rowboat and the flagship *Santa Maria* in the background. Mint engraver T. James Farrell designed both sides. *Reverse*—The reverse shows Columbus's three ships—the *Nina, Pinta* and *Santa Maria*. **Silver dollar:** *Obverse*—Columbus standing, holding a flag in his right hand, with something of a cylindrical nature in his left hand, and with a globe on a stand near his left. On the approved sketch, Columbus was depicted holding a telescope, but after it was pointed out that such instrument had not been invented by 1492, it was changed to a scroll on the final coin. Three ships are shown in the distance, in a panel at the top border. Mint engraver John Mercanti created the design. *Reverse*—A split image is shown, depicting exploration in 1492 at the left, with half of a sailing vessel, and in 1992 at the right, with most of a space shuttle shown in a vertical position, with the earth in the distance. Thomas D. Rogers Sr., of the Mint staff created the motif. **Gold $5:** *Obverse*—The artist's conception of Columbus's face is shown gazing to the left toward an outline map of the New World. T. James Ferrell was the designer. *Reverse*—The crest of the Admiral of the Ocean Sea and a chart dated 1492 are depicted, the work of Thomas D. Rogers Sr.

Mintage Data: Authorized by Public Law 102-281, signed by President George H.W. Bush on May 13, 1992. *Maximum authorized*—half dollars 6,000,000; silver dollars 4,000,000; $5 gold 1,000,000. *Number minted*—half dollars 1992-D: 135,702 Uncirculated, 390,154 Proofs; silver dollars 1992-D: 106,949 Uncirculated, 1992-S: 385,241 Proofs; gold dollars 1992-W: 24,329 Uncirculated and 79,730 Proofs.

Original Cost and Issuer: Discounts were available for orders re[ceived] by October 1992, with the regular sales period extending into 1993. [1992] dollar: $8.50 early order price, afterward $9.50. 1992-P dollar: $27, a[fter] Proof 1992-W $5 gold: $190, afterward $225. Various combination offers, [along] with regular Proof sets, were available. Surcharges of $1 per half dollar, $7 per [dollar,] and $35 per half eagle benefited the Christopher Columbus Quincentenary Coins a[nd] Fellowship Foundation. Issued by the U.S. Mint.

The 500th Anniversary of Columbus' Landing

The 500th anniversary of Christopher Columbus's first trip to the new world was observed in 1992 by a suite of commemoratives—once again, a clad half dollar, silver dollar, and $5 gold coin. Surcharges were levied to benefit the newly established Christopher Columbus Quincentenary Coins and Fellowship Foundation. The numismatic tradition fit in nicely with the World's Columbian Exposition coins of a century earlier—the half dollars issued in 1892 and 1893.

The 20th century Columbus commemoratives arose from a bill introduced in Congress by Representative Frank Annunzio, Democrat from Illinois, who had been prominent in coinage legislation for quite some time. His encouragement of earlier commemoratives had landed him the ANA Award of Merit in 1985.

When Representative Annunzio presented H3253 to the House, he recounted how Columbus's voyage and discovery changed 15th-century maps and the course of history. The legislation would authorize the minting of gold, silver, and coppernickel coins in 1991 and 1992 to commemorate the discovery of the New World by Columbus. Profits from their sale would fund the Christopher Columbus Fellowship Foundation Columbus Scholar program, a program that supports new discovery in any field of endeavor for the benefit of mankind.

No action followed. Representative Annunzio reintroduced the legislation in 1991. Controversy ensued. *Coin World* editor Beth Deisher suggested that a portion of the surcharges, say half, be used to benefit coin collecting (such as to endow the National Numismatic Collection at the Smithsonian), since numismatists were likely to be the main buyers. In another commentary, Deisher opined that the 1992 anniversary of the founding of the Mint in 1792 might be a more worthy event to honor. Others, including Deputy Director of the Mint Eugene Essner, questioned the need for the proposed foundation. Some naysayers reminded readers that Columbus was a latecomer to America whose accomplishments were, in any event, a prelude to genocide and exploitation.

Despite such objections, the Columbus coins became a reality. The Fine Arts Commission resented having to consult with the new foundation regarding the designs. Some motifs proposed were found to be incorrect or controversial. Native Americans were shown fully clothed, whereas Columbus in his journal had described them as naked. Moreover, having the word "Liberty" next to these about-to-be-enslaved people seemed to be inappropriate. The solution was to remove the Indians completely.

The sales period began in August 1992 and extended to June 1993. Although the designs echoed the same theme, the depictions were diverse. Sales were abysmal in relation to the 11 million authorized, and only slightly more than a million were sold.

Key to Collecting

Examples in the marketplace remain reasonably priced, although at a premium over the offering cost—quite unlike certain other commemoratives of the era. Nearly all are superb gems.

GAMES COMMEMORATIVES

TIVES, 1892 TO DATE 195

...ited

1992...
504,50...
1992-W gold $5:
27,732 Uncirculated
and 77,313 Proof

received or postmarked
Proof 1992-S half
afterward $31.
including
dollar,
nd

MS 68

Whitman Coin Guide (WCG™)—1992-P XXV Olympic Games 50¢

MS-65	MS-66	MS-67	MS-68	MS-69	MS-70
$10	$11	$14	$17	$26	$375

CERTIFIED POPULATIONS

MS-65	MS-66	MS-67	MS-68	MS-69	MS-70
0	3	11	46	1,121	166

1992-S XXV Olympic Games 50¢ Proof

PF-65	PF-66	PF-67	PF-68	PF-69	PF-70
$25	$28	$30	$35	$50	$2,250

CERTIFIED POPULATIONS

PF-65	PF-66	PF-67	PF-68	PF-69	PF-70
0	2	9	66	2,094	17

1992-D XXV Olympic Games $1

MS-65	MS-66	MS-67	MS-68	MS-69	MS-70
$28				$40	

CERTIFIED POPULATIONS

MS-65	MS-66	MS-67	MS-68	MS-69	MS-70
3	26	56	198	2,528	66

1992-S XXV Olympic Games $1 Proof

PF-65	PF-66	PF-67	PF-68	PF-69	PF-70
$26	$25	$30	$35	$48	$2,250

CERTIFIED POPULATIONS

PF-65	PF-66	PF-67	PF-68	PF-69	PF-70
6	6	53	187	1,496	20

1992-W XXV Olympic Games Gold $5

MS-65	MS-66	MS-67	MS-68	MS-69	MS-70
$300	$310	$320	$330	$340	$400
PF-65	PF-66	PF-67	PF-68	PF-69	PF-70
$200	$215	$220	$225	$280	$875

CERTIFIED POPULATIONS

MS-65	MS-66	MS-67	MS-68	MS-69	MS-70
0	0	1	8	1,008	494
PF-65	PF-66	PF-67	PF-68	PF-69	PF-70
1	2	8	40	1,896	519

Points of Interest: The silver dollar got all of the attention, seemingly depicting base-ball star Nolan Ryan and copied from a popular trading card, although the facial features were slightly different. The Denver Mint half dollar had a lettered edge, the first on any U.S. commemorative.

Subject of Commemoration: The games of the XXV Olympic Summer and Winter Games held in Europe.

Designs: Clad half dollar: *Obverse*—A pony-tailed female gymnast doing the stretch against a background of stars and stripes, a motif by Mint artist William Cousins. *Reverse*—The Olympic torch and an olive branch, with CITIUS / ALTIUS / FORTIUS nearby in three lines, Latin for "faster, higher, stronger." Mandatory inscriptions are on both sides. Steven M. Bieda, a Wisconsin artist, was the designer. **Silver dollar:** *Obverse*—A pitcher is shown about to throw a ball to a batter. The image fit closely that of Fleer's card showing popular player Nolan Ryan, of the Texas Rangers, although the designer, John R. Deecken, denied there was any connection when queried on the subject by the Treasury Department. A Fleer spokesman said, "Copying is the sincerest form of flattery." The Denver Mint Uncirculated dollars have XXV OLYMPIAD incuse four times around the edge, alternately inverted, on a reeded background. These are the first lettered-edge U.S. coins since the 1933 $20 double eagle. *Reverse*—A shield, intertwined Olympic rings, and olive branches make up the main design, created by Marcel Jovine. **Gold $5:** *Obverse*—A sprinter running forward with a vertical U.S. flag in the background, a design by James Sharpe, modeled at the Mint by T. James Ferrell. *Reverse*—A heraldic eagle with five Olympic rings and USA above, a design by James Peed.

Mintage Data: Authorized by the 1992 Olympic Commemorative Coin Act, Public Law 101-406, signed by President George H.W. Bush on October 3, 1990. *Maximum authorized*—half dollars 6,000,000; silver dollars 4,000,000; $5 gold 500,000. *Number minted*—half dollars 1992-P: 161,607 Uncirculated; 1992-S: 519,645 Proofs. Silver dollars 1992-D: 187,552 Uncirculated; 1992-S: 504,505 Proofs. $5 gold: 1992-W: 27,732 Uncirculated and 77,313 Proofs.

Original Cost and Issuer: Uncirculated 1992-P half dollar $6 pre-issue price, afterward $7.50. Proof 1992-P half dollar $8.50, afterward $9.50. Uncirculated 1992-D dollar $24, afterward $29. Proof 1992-S dollar $28, afterward $32. Uncirculated 1992-W $5 gold $185, afterward $215. Proof 1992-W $5 gold $195, afterward $230. Surcharges of $1 per half dollar, $7 per dollar, and $35 per half eagle benefited the U.S. Olympic Committee. Issued by the U.S. Mint.

Commemorating the XXV Olympiad

In 1992 the XXV Winter Olympic Games were held in Albertville and Savoie, France, while the Summer Games took place in Barcelona, Spain. Although the events did not take place in the United States, the rationale for a commemorative coin issue was, in part, to raise money to train American athletes. The same line of reasoning had been used for the coins made in connection with the 1988 Olympic Games held in Seoul, Korea.

Expectations were high—almost, but not quite, as optimistic as for the Columbus Quincentenary coins of the same year. A maximum of six million clad half dollars, four million silver dollars, and 500,000 gold $5 coins were authorized.

Although the designs were varied and depicted three different sports, interest by purchasers was lukewarm at best, and only about 1.5 million coins were sold in all.

Key to Collecting
Examples are easily available today for prices representing a modest advance on the cost at the time of issue. Nearly all are gems.

(1992) WHITE HOUSE 200TH ANNIVERSARY DOLLARS

Distribution
1992-D: 123,803 Uncirculated
1992-W: 375,849 Proof

Whitman Coin Guide (WCG™)—1992 White House 200th Anniversary $1

MS-65	MS-66	MS-67	MS-68	MS-69	MS-70
$36	$40	$44	$50	$55	$400

CERTIFIED POPULATIONS

MS-65	MS-66	MS-67	MS-68	MS-69	MS-70
4	17	42	107	1,831	205

1992-W White House 200th Anniversary $1 Proof

PF-65	PF-66	PF-67	PF-68	PF-69	PF-70
$25	$28	$30	$35	$55	$800

CERTIFIED POPULATIONS

PF-65	PF-66	PF-67	PF-68	PF-69	PF-70
12	31	45	159	1,793	36

Points of Interest: This coin is one of few depicting Washington buildings that sold out its full authorized limit.

Subject of Commemoration: 200th anniversary of the laying of the cornerstone of the White House.

Designs: *Obverse*—The north portico of the White House is sh㿰
without shrubbery or background. Foliage, two trees, and a fountain
nal sketch, but were removed at the suggestion of the Fine Arts Co
designer was Edgar Z. Steever IV of the Mint staff. *Reverse*—James Hoban
the first White House, in a half-length portrait with the original entra
Chester Y. Martin of the Mint staff was the designer.

Mintage Data: Authorized by Public Law 102-281, signed by President George H
Bush on May 13, 1992. *Maximum authorized*—500,000. *Number minted*—1992-D silv
dollar 123,803 Uncirculated, 1992-W 375,849 Proof.

Original Cost and Issuer: 1992-D Uncirculated dollars were offered for $23 and $28
for the Proof. Both were sold out. A surcharge of $10 per coin was for the preservation
of the public rooms in the White House. Issued by the U.S. Mint.

The White House Commemorated

The 1992 bicentennial of the laying of the cornerstone of the White House on October
13, 1792, served to catalyze legislation for another commemorative dollar. In that year,
other observances included the publishing of books about the White House, lectures on
its history, and the burial of a time capsule, at the southwest corner, by President
George H.W. Bush and his wife Barbara.

James Hoban, an Irish immigrant, was the original White House architect and also
supervised its construction. In 1800, it was first occupied. In 1814, marauding British
soldiers set it afire, reducing the interior to ashes. Hoban supervised its rebuilding, completed in 1817, forming the essence of the structure that exists today—although many
changes have been made over the years.

The authorization of the commemorative limited production to no more than
500,000, an amount perhaps more realistic than for the typical commemorative dollar
of the preceding decade. Mint artists began work on sketches. The original obverse
design, by Edgar Z. Steever IV, showed the White House as it appeared in actuality,
with landscaping around. This was viewed as being "too busy" by the Fine Arts Commission, and a bare structure was the result.

The reverse sketch, by John Mercanti, showed a view of the building, with a nearby
plaque inscribed "MAY NONE BUT HONEST AND WISE MEN EVER RULE
UNDER THIS ROOF," a statement made by John Adams. John Carter Brown, chairman of the Commission, found that the plaque resembled a T-shirt or a TV antenna
and, in a separate comment, that "MEN" in the inscription excluded the possibility of a
woman president. The design was scrapped, and replaced by a different motif, by
Chester Y. Martin, showing James Hoban, architect of the structure.

The authorized mintage was just right, and the issue was sold out on August 13,
1992—within the pre-issue price period.

Key to Collecting

The White House dollar has remained popular ever since its issuance. Examples are
readily available today and are nearly always found in superb gem preservation, as issued.

...HTS COMMEMORATIVES

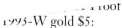

...wn in a plan view, ...were in the origi-...mission. The ...architect of ...nce door. ...W. ...er

...Proof

1993-W gold $5:
     23,266 Uncirculated
     and 78,651 Proof

MS69

Whitman Coin Guide (WCG™)—1993-W Bill of Rights 50¢

MS-65	MS-66	MS-67	MS-68	MS-69	MS-70
$25	$27	$30	$35	$40	$340

CERTIFIED POPULATIONS

MS-65	MS-66	MS-67	MS-68	MS-69	MS-70
1	6	23	94	1,333	113

1993-S Bill of Rights 50¢ Proof

PF-65	PF-66	PF-67	PF-68	PF-69	PF-70
$16	$17	$18	$20	$35	$2,150

CERTIFIED POPULATIONS

PF-65	PF-66	PF-67	PF-68	PF-69	PF-70
3	5	42	218	1,939	18

1993-D Bill of Rights $1

MS-65	MS-66	MS-67	MS-68	MS-69	MS-70
$26	$28	$35	$40	$45	$550

CERTIFIED POPULATIONS

MS-65	MS-66	MS-67	MS-68	MS-69	MS-70
2	18	51	97	1,618	131

1993-S Bill of Rights $1 Proof

PF-65	PF-66	PF-67	PF-68	PF-69	PF-70
$19	$20	$25	$30	$36	$1,700

CERTIFIED POPULATIONS

PF-65	PF-66	PF-67	PF-68	PF-69	PF-70
8	27	52	195	1,869	25

1993-W Bill of Rights Gold $5

MS-65	MS-66	MS-67	MS-68	MS-69	MS-70
$350	$370	$390	$410	$425	$450
PF-65	PF-66	PF-67	PF-68	PF-69	PF-70
$250	$270	$300	$325	$350	$1,400

CERTIFIED POPULATIONS

MS-65	MS-66	MS-67	MS-68	MS-69	MS-70
0	1	1	20	992	928
PF-65	PF-66	PF-67	PF-68	PF-69	PF-70
0	2	10	124	2,392	329

Points of Interest: The 1992 date of issue has no particular meaning regarding an anniversary of the man or text commemorated.

Subject of Commemoration: The 1789 Bill of Rights proposed by James Madison.

Designs: Clad half dollar: *Obverse*—James Madison seated at a desk, penning the Bill of Rights. Montpelier, Madison's Virginia home, is shown in plan view in the distance. Designed by T. James Ferrell of the Mint staff. *Reverse*—A hand holds a flaming torch, with inscriptions to each side. Designed by Dean McMullen. **Silver dollar:** *Obverse*—Portrait of James Madison facing right and slightly forward. Designed by William Krawczewicz, employed with the Bureau of Engraving and Printing. *Reverse*—Montpelier shown in plan view. Designed by Dean McMullen. **$5 gold:** *Obverse*—Portrait of Madison, waist up, reading the Bill of Rights. Designed by Scott R. Blazek. *Reverse*—Quotation by Madison with an eagle above and small torch and laurel branch at the border below. Designed by Joseph D. Peña.

Mintage Data: Authorized by Public Law 101-281, part of the White House Commemorative Coin Act, on May 13, 1992. *Maximum authorized*—1,000,000 half dollars; 900,000 silver dollars; 300,000 gold $5. *Number minted*—1993-W clad half dollar 193,346 Uncirculated; 1993-S clad half dollar 586,315 Proof; 1993-D silver dollar 98,383 Uncirculated; 1993-S silver dollar: 534,001 Proof; 1993-W gold $5: 23,266 Uncirculated and 78,651 Proof.

Original Cost and Issuer: Uncirculated 1993-W half dollar $9.75 pre-issue price, afterward $11.50. Proof 1993-S half dollar $12.50, afterward $13.50. Uncirculated 1993-D dollar $22, afterward $27. Proof 1993-S dollar $25, afterward $29 Uncirculated 1993-W $5 gold $175, afterward $205. Proof 1993-W $5 gold $185, afterward $220. $10 surcharge per coin paid to the James Madison Memorial Scholarship Trust Fund. Issued by the U.S. Mint.

The Bill of Rights Commemorated

The White House Commemorative Coin Act of May 13, 1992, also included a provision for a series of Bill of Rights coins, a set of three, including the clad half dollar, silver dollar, and $5 gold. These honored President James Madison and the Bill of Rights, added to the Constitution in 1789, and intended to give basic rights and freedoms to all (in practice, women and blacks were excluded from many privileges). The coin project came out of the blue, so to speak. The 1992 date was not any particular anniversary relating to either the Bill of Rights or to Madison. The coins were made possible by political clout wielded by the Madison Foundation, which sought to cash in on the current fad for issuing series of coins with surcharges going to various privileged entities.

On June 1, 1992, U.S. Treasurer Catalina Vasquez Villalpando announced a nationwide competition seeking designs for the James Madison / Bill of Rights Commemorative

Coin Program, with all entries to be received by August 31. Secretary of the Treasury Nicholas F. Brady selected his favorite motifs from 815 submissions, which were then sent to the Commission of Fine Arts for review. Many changes were suggested, including simplifying the appearance of Madison's residence, Montpelier. This structure, in the hills of Virginia, was the seat of the Madison family for many years.

The coins were among the better sellers of the era, although numbers were far below expectations. The ANA arranged to have 9,656 of the half dollars marked on the edge with a serial number and initials of the ANA and the Madison Foundation, a promotion that was noted in numismatic newspapers at the time and is mentioned today in the *Guide Book of United States Coins.*

Key to Collecting
Following the pattern of other commemoratives of the early 1990s, these coins are readily available on the market, typically in superb gem preservation.

(1993) 50TH ANNIVERSARY OF WORLD WAR II COMMEMORATIVES

Distribution
1993-P clad half dollar:
    197,072 Uncirculated
    and 317,396 Proof
1993-D silver dollar:
    107,240 Uncirculated
1993-W silver dollar:
    342,041 Proof
1993-W gold $5:
    26,342 Uncirculated
    and 67,026 Proof

Whitman Coin Guide (WCG™)—1993 50th Anniversary of WWII 50¢

MS-65	MS-66	MS-67	MS-68	MS-69	MS-70
$30	$35	$40	$45	$55	$675
PF-65	PF-66	PF-67	PF-68	PF-69	PF-70
$30	$35	$40	$45	$50	$2,500

CERTIFIED POPULATIONS

MS-65	MS-66	MS-67	MS-68	MS-69	MS-70
0	1	6	55	1,198	64
PF-65	PF-66	PF-67	PF-68	PF-69	PF-70
3	3	17	125	1,700	18

1993-D 50th Anniversary of WWII $1

MS-65	MS-66	MS-67	MS-68	MS-69	MS-70
$30	$35	$40	$50	$55	$600

CERTIFIED POPULATIONS

MS-65	MS-66	MS-67	MS-68	MS-69	MS-70
4	5	24	34	1,768	460

1993-W 50th Anniversary of WWII $1 Proof

PF-65	PF-66	PF-67	PF-68	PF-69	PF-70
$40	$45	$50	$55	$65	$1,650

CERTIFIED POPULATIONS

PF-65	PF-66	PF-67	PF-68	PF-69	PF-70
8	16	29	141	2,018	41

1993-W 50th Anniversary of WWII Gold $5

MS-65	MS-66	MS-67	MS-68	MS-69	MS-70
$400	$425	$450	$475	$500	$850

PF-65	PF-66	PF-67	PF-68	PF-69	PF-70
$335	$350	$375	$400	$450	$5,250

CERTIFIED POPULATIONS

MS-65	MS-66	MS-67	MS-68	MS-69	MS-70
0	0	4	17	957	335

PF-65	PF-66	PF-67	PF-68	PF-69	PF-70
0	0	9	101	1,757	175

Points of Interest: The World War II Monument erected in Washington, in part financed by the proceeds of coin sales, included a statement by President Franklin D. Roosevelt: "Yesterday, December 7, 1941, a date which will live in infamy, the United States of America was suddenly and deliberately attacked. With confidence in our armed forces, with the unbounding determination of our people, we will gain the inevitable triumph." In actuality, the words "so help us God" concluded the statement, but, apparently, modern "political correctness" prompted the omission on the monument. The monument to be built in France and dedicated on D-Day was never constructed, despite several million dollars provided from coin sales. An investigation of fraud was launched by the Justice Department, but no charges were brought and no money was recovered.

Subject of Commemoration: The 50th anniversary of the involvement of the United States in World War II, 1941 to 1945.

Designs: Clad half dollar: *Obverse*—The heads of a soldier, sailor and airman are shown superimposed on a V (for victory), with a B-17 bomber flying overhead. George Klauba was the designer. *Reverse*—An American Marine is shown as he participates in the takeover of a Japanese-held island in the South Pacific. A carrier-based fighter plane flies overhead. Bill J. Leftwich was the designer. **Silver dollar:** *Obverse*—An American soldier is shown as he runs ashore on the beach in Normandy during the D-Day invasion on June 6, 1944, launched from England to liberate France. Mint engraver Thomas D. Rogers Sr. designed both sides. *Reverse*—The reverse illustrates the shoulder patch used on a uniform of Dwight D. Eisenhower's Supreme Headquarters Allied Expeditionary Force, with a quotation from Eisenhower. **$5 gold:** *Obverse*—An American soldier holds his rifle and raises his arm to indicate victory. Charles J. Madsen created the motif. *Reverse*—A large V (for victory) is at the center, with three dots and a dash over it, the Morse code for that letter. Branches are to each side. Edward Southworth Fisher was the designer.

Mintage Data: Authorized by Public Law 102-414, signed by President William J. Clinton on October 14, 1992. *Maximum authorized*—clad half dollar 2,000,000; silver dollar 1,000,000; $5 gold 300,000. *Number minted*—half dollar 1993-P: 197,072 Uncirculated and 317,396 Proof; silver dollar 1993-D: 107,240 Uncirculated, 1993-W: 342,041 Proof; $5 gold 1993-W: 26,342 Uncirculated and 67,026 Proof.

Original Cost and Issuer: 1993-P half dollars, Uncirculated: $8 pre-issue price, $9 afterward; Proof: $9 pre-issue, $10 afterward. 1993-D silver dollar, Uncirculated: $23 pre-issue,$28 afterward. 1993-W silver dollar, Proof: $27 pre-issue, $31 afterward. 1993-W $5 gold: Uncirculated, $170 pre-issue, $200 afterward; Proof: $215 pre-issue, $245 afterward. Combination offers were also made. Surcharges of $2, $8, and $35 for the three coins were paid to the American Battle Monuments Commission to aid in the construction of the World War II Monument in the nation's capital, and to the Battle of Normandy Foundation to assist in the erection of a monument in France. Issued by the U.S. Mint.

A War to Remember

In 1992, American involvement in World War II was still fresh in the memories of many men and women who had fought on land, sea, or in the air, or who had done their duty on the home front. The war began in the 1930s with the Japanese occupation of China and the 1939 German invasion of Poland and Czechoslovakia. By the early 1940s, the so-called Axis powers consisted of Germany (under Hitler and the Nazis), Japan, and Italy. Fighting them on several fronts were England, Russia, and other countries, plus resistance movements within occupied lands. The United States acted as the "arsenal of democracy," a popular term, and provided munitions to England in particular. Many Americans volunteered to enter combat overseas, joining the armed forces of other countries.

Following the surprise invasion by the Japanese of the Pearl Harbor Navy Base in Hawaii on December 7, 1941, America declared war. The conflict lasted until August 1945, when atomic bombs dropped on the Japanese cities of Hiroshima and Nagasaki brought the long conflict to an end.

Public Law 102-414 of 1992 provided for the usual suite of coins—a clad half dollar, silver dollar, and $5 gold piece—to be issued in commemoration of the 1941–1945 war. Approval of the designs by the American Legion, Veterans of Foreign Wars of the United States, American Veterans of World War, Korea and Vietnam (AMVETS), and the Disabled American Veterans, was mandated. It was further specified that the dollar use the Battle of Normandy as a theme, and the $5 reflect the Allied victory in the war.

Authorized mintages were two million half dollars, one million silver dollars, and 300,000 gold half eagles. New, higher surcharges of $2 were tacked on the price of the half dollar and $8 on the dollar, while $35 on the gold coin was as before. Although they were authorized in 1992, the coins were struck and sold in 1993.

A design competition was launched, and the works of five artists were selected, only one of them, Thomas D. Rogers Jr., being from the Mint staff.

Despite the importance of the war commemorated, the coins met with a lukewarm response by purchasers. Those who sought a single example of a given denomination opted for a Proof, this being the historic pattern. When sales were tallied, they fell far short of expectations. By this time commemoratives were becoming routine, with many complaints about their frequency and high cost. No longer was a new coin a novelty.

Key to Collecting
Examples are easily enough found in the marketplace today and are nearly always of superb gem quality.

(1993) THOMAS JEFFERSON DOLLARS

Distribution
1993-P: 266,927 Uncirculated
1993-S: 332,891 Proof

Whitman Coin Guide (WCG™)—1993-P Thomas Jefferson $1

MS-65	MS-66	MS-67	MS-68	MS-69	MS-70
$27	$28	$35	$44	$58	$350

CERTIFIED POPULATIONS

MS-65	MS-66	MS-67	MS-68	MS-69	MS-70
7	42	86	231	2,585	427

1993-S Thomas Jefferson $1 Proof

PF-65	PF-66	PF-67	PF-68	PF-69	PF-70
$30	$35	$40	$45	$50	$3,250

CERTIFIED POPULATIONS

PF-65	PF-66	PF-67	PF-68	PF-69	PF-70
4	12	72	178	1,602	15

Points of Interest: On the reverse, Monticello is shown with shrubbery. The same building on the 1938 Jefferson nickel had shrubbery in the original design, but this feature was eliminated by the Treasury Department.

Subject of Commemoration: The 250th anniversary of Jefferson's birth.

Designs: *Obverse*—Head of Thomas Jefferson, with the neck especially prominent. Both sides designed by T. James Ferrell. *Reverse*—Monticello, Jefferson's home.

Mintage Data: Authorized under Public Law 103-186, signed by President William J. Clinton on December 14, 1993. *Maximum authorized*—600,000. *Number minted*—1993-P silver dollar 266,927 Uncirculated; 1993-S silver dollar 332,891 Proof.

Original Cost and Issuer: 1993-P silver dollar, Uncirculated, $27 pre-issue, $32 afterward. 1993-S silver dollar, Proof, $31 pre-issue, $35 afterward. Surcharge of $10 per coin paid to the Jefferson Endowment Fund. Issued by the U.S. Mint.

Honoring Thomas Jefferson
The 250th anniversary in 1993 of the birth of Thomas Jefferson in 1743 furnished the occasion for a commemorative silver dollar. T. James Ferrell of the Mint staff created both obverse and reverse designs, including a portrait based on an 1805 painting by Gilbert Stuart. Although the coins are dated 1743–1993, they were not made until 1994. Sometimes the coin is described as 1993 (1994) in numismatic listings.

Stung by continuing poor sales of commemorative coins, the maximum for the Jefferson dollar was set at 600,000. This figure proved to be realistic, and the issue was a sellout, a rare occurrence. Among the options was a package containing an Uncirculated dollar, a $2 bill, and a *1994* Jefferson nickel with special finish, of which 167,703 were sold (in 1997, a related arrangement with a special nickel was made with the Botanic Garden dollar).

Key to Collecting

Although the Jefferson dollar was a sellout in its time, examples are easily found in the numismatic marketplace and are nearly always of superb gem quality. Most in demand, from the enthusiasm of five-cent piece collectors, are the special sets with the Jefferson nickel.

(1994) U.S. Capitol Bicentennial Dollars

Distribution
1994-D: 68,332 Uncirculated
1994-S: 279,579 Proof

Whitman Coin Guide (WCG™)—1994-D U.S. Capitol Bicentennial $1

MS-65	MS-66	MS-67	MS-68	MS-69	MS-70
$25	$26	$28	$33	$40	$390

CERTIFIED POPULATIONS

MS-65	MS-66	MS-67	MS-68	MS-69	MS-70
1	4	40	39	1,674	459

1994-S U.S. Capitol Bicentennial $1 Proof

PF-65	PF-66	PF-67	PF-68	PF-69	PF-70
$28	$30	$32	$35	$45	$3,250

CERTIFIED POPULATIONS

PF-65	PF-66	PF-67	PF-68	PF-69	PF-70
3	9	41	194	1,495	29

Points of Interest: American flags are not often seen on commemoratives; this coin shows five.

Subject of Commemoration: The 200th anniversary of the beginning of the U.S. Capitol building in Washington.

Designs: *Obverse*—Dome of the Capitol with stars surrounding the *Freedom* statue. Designed by William C. Cousins of the Mint staff. *Reverse*—Shield with four American flags, branches, and surmounted by an eagle, a motif based on the center area of a stained glass window near the House and Senate grand staircases (produced by J. & G. Gibson, of Philadelphia, in 1859 and 1860). Coin design by Mint engraver John Mercanti.

Mintage Data: Authorized by Public Law 103-186, signed by President William J. Clinton on December 14, 1993. *Maximum authorized—*500,000. *Number minted—*1994-D 68,332 Uncirculated, 1994-S 279,579 Proof.

Original Cost and Issuer: 1994-D silver dollar, Uncirculated, $32 pre-issue through October 21, 1994, $37 afterward. 1994-S silver dollar, Proof, $36 pre-issue, $40 afterward. Sales were advertised to end on April 30, 1995, but this was extended to July 15, 1995. The Architectural History Edition included a Proof dollar and a 12-page booklet (priced at $42 pre-issue, $46 afterward). $15 surcharge per coin was paid to the United States Capitol Preservation Commission. A Mint announcement noted that this was to go "for the construction of the Capitol Visitor Center" (itself the subject of a 2001 commemorative dollar). Issued by the U.S. Mint.

Capitol Featured

The 200th anniversary of the U.S. Capitol in Washington, D.C. furnished the occasion for Congress to authorize a coinage of 500,000 commemorative silver dollars. Although the Federal City, as it was called, was laid out in the 1790s, it was not until 1800 that the federal government relocated there from Philadelphia. In honor of the recently deceased first president, the name was changed to Washington City, or, in popular use, Washington. The Capitol building design represented the work of several architects and artists, among them Benjamin Latrobe, Charles Bulfinch, and Constantino Brumidi.

The coin, designed by Mint staff, features the Capitol dome on the obverse, with the statue of *Freedom* (by Thomas Crawford, installed in 1863) at the top encircled by 13 stars. "The image evokes the power and classic grace of the U.S. Capitol," Mint Director Philip N. Diehl noted in a press release.

The reverse illustrates an eagle, shield, and accouterments taken from a stained glass window within the Capitol. Mint sculptor-engraver John Mercanti reflected, "Achieving a faithful representation of the original window took more hours and patience than any other coin in my experience."

Orders were received beginning on July 9, 1994, with the declaration that sales would end on April 30 of the next year. Because the authorization had been used only partially by that time, the sales period was extended to July 15. In an effort to spur sales, federal income tax refund checks mailed out before the July 15, 1995, deadline included promotional material for five different commemorative coin programs. When all was said and done, the program was more than 150,000 short of expectations. It had been anticipated in the 1980s that various congressmen and senators would be enthusiastic promoters of commemoratives depicting buildings in Washington, but this did not prove to be the case. Relatively few ever took notice.

Key to Collecting

Superb gem Mint State and Proof coins are easily available.

(1994) U.S. PRISONER OF WAR MEMORIAL DOLLARS

Distribution
1994-W: 54,893 Uncirculated
1994-P: 224,449 Proof

Whitman Coin Guide (WCG™)—1994-W U.S. POW Memorial $1

MS-65	MS-66	MS-67	MS-68	MS-69	MS-70
$105	$110	$120	$125	$130	$400

CERTIFIED POPULATIONS

MS-65	MS-66	MS-67	MS-68	MS-69	MS-70
0	0	10	63	1,490	520

1994-P U.S. POW Memorial $1 Proof

PF-65	PF-66	PF-67	PF-68	PF-69	PF-70
$48				$65	

CERTIFIED POPULATIONS

PF-65	PF-66	PF-67	PF-68	PF-69	PF-70
4	13	51	245	1,515	12

Points of Interest: Proceeds from coin sales were earmarked to construct the museum.

Subject of Commemoration: The Prisoner of War Memorial Museum to be built in Andersonville, Georgia. The museum opened on April 9, 1998.

Designs: *Obverse*—Eagle with a chain on one leg flies through a circle of barbed wire, representing flight to freedom. Designed by Tom Nielsen, a decorated former prisoner of war employed by the Bureau of Veterans Affairs. Model made by Mint engraver Alfred F. Maletsky. *Reverse*—Plan view, with landscaping, of the proposed National Prisoner of War Museum. Designed by Mint engraver Edgar Z. Steever.

Mintage Data: Authorized by Public Law 103-186, signed by President William J. Clinton on December 14, 1993. *Maximum authorized*—500,000. *Number minted*—1994-W Uncirculated 54,893, 1994-P Proof 224,449.

Original Cost and Issuer: 1994-W silver dollar, Uncirculated, $27 pre-issue through September 9, 1994, $32 afterward. 1994-P silver dollar, Proof, $31 pre-issue, $35 afterward. Sales were advertised to end on April 30, 1995, but this was extended to July 15, 1995. A surcharge of $10 per coin went to the construction of the museum. Issued by the U.S. Mint.

Museum Proposed

The proposed National Prisoner of War Museum set the stage for the issuance of a silver dollar observing the tribulations of prisoners held by foreign military powers. Andersonville, Georgia, site of a notorious Confederate prison housing Union soldiers, was to be the site. A Mint announcement noted:

> [The aim is] to communicate the prisoner of war (POW) experience regardless of when, where, why, or how the individual was captured or imprisoned. For the first time hundreds of POW artifacts and documents will be used to help visitors understand the horrors, stress, and suffering of those denied their freedom during periods of war. The museum will provide a long awaited tribute to American POWs from the American Revolution to the recent Somalian peace-keeping efforts.

A mintage of 500,000 was authorized. The Mint began taking orders on July 29, 1994, with special discounts in effect through September 9. At the Florida United Numismatists convention in Orlando in January 1995, several former prisoners of war were on hand to meet and greet numismatists and to promote the coins. The order deadline was April 30,

1995, extended to July 15, 1995, in an effort to stimulate sales. This was part of a suite of programs including the Vietnam Veterans Memorial and Women in Military Service Memorial silver dollars, all with similar ordering information and deadlines. Interest was not widespread, and fewer than 300,000 were sold, mostly in Proof format.

Key to Collecting
The 1994-W dollar is in special demand due to its relatively low mintage. Both varieties are seen with frequency in the marketplace and are nearly always superb gems.

(1994) WOMEN IN MILITARY SERVICE MEMORIAL DOLLARS

Distribution
1994-W: 69,860 Uncirculated
1994-P: 249,278 Proof

Whitman Coin Guide (WCG™)—1994-W Women in Military Memorial $1

MS-65	MS-66	MS-67	MS-68	MS-69	MS-70
$45	$50	$55	$60	$65	$325

CERTIFIED POPULATIONS

MS-65	MS-66	MS-67	MS-68	MS-69	MS-70
0	2	10	78	2,733	679

1994-P Women in Military Memorial $1 Proof

PF-65	PF-66	PF-67	PF-68	PF-69	PF-70
$40	$42	$45	$50	$60	

CERTIFIED POPULATIONS

PF-65	PF-66	PF-67	PF-68	PF-69	PF-70
8	24	39	204	1,583	16

Points of Interest: Proceeds from coin sales were earmarked to construct the memorial complex.

Subject of Commemoration: Women in military service and the erection of a monument honoring them.

Designs: *Obverse*—Servicewomen from the Army, Marine Corps, Navy, Air Force, and Coast Guard, with the names of these branches around the border. Designed by T. James Ferrell of the Mint staff. *Reverse*—A diagonal view of the front of the proposed the Women In Military Service for America Memorial. T. James Ferrell of the Mint staff was the designer.

Mintage Data: Authorized by Public Law 103-186, signed by President William J. Clinton on December 14, 1993. *Maximum authorized*—500,000. *Number minted*—1994-W 69,860 Uncirculated; 1994-P 249,278 Proof.

Original Cost and Issuer: 1994-W silver dollar, Uncirculated, $27 pre-issue through September 9, 1994, $32 afterward. 1994-P silver dollar, Proof, $31 pre-issue, $35 afterward. Sales were advertised to end on April 30, 1995, but this was extended to July 15, 1995. Issued by the U.S. Mint.

Women in Military Service Memorial

By 1994, approximately 1,800,000 women had served with American armed services. Among the earliest, Margaret Corbin is remembered for joining her husband in the Battle of Fort Washington in the Revolutionary War. On July 6, 1779, the Continental Congress awarded her the first national pension for a woman wounded in battle. Records indicate that about 6,000 women served in the Civil War, 1,500 in the Spanish-American War, 34,000 in World War I, 400,000 in World War II, 22,000 in the Korean conflict, and 7,500 in Vietnam. Many distinguished themselves in combat. In 1994, memories were fresh of their service in the Gulf War, in which 37,213 women participated.

To honor women in the military and help fund the Women In Military Service For America Memorial at the ceremonial entrance to Arlington National Cemetery (which became a reality and opened in October 1997 on a 4.2 acre site), Public Law 103-186 provided for the issuance of 500,000 commemorative silver dollars. Buyer interest was lukewarm—about on a par with other commemorative dollars of this time—and far below the authorized maximum. At the Bureau of the Mint (as it was called at the time), commemoratives often caused losses due to the expense of production and marketing. While the recipients of the despised (by collectors) surcharges collected large sums, the basic work was done by the Mint, entailing much effort.

Key to Collecting

Following the situation for other commemoratives of the era, these are easily enough found on the market and are usually in superb gem grades.

(1994) VIETNAM VETERANS MEMORIAL DOLLARS

Distribution
1994-W: 52,290 Uncirculated
1994-P: 332,891 Proof

Whitman Coin Guide (WCG™)—1994-W Vietnam Veterans Memorial $1

MS-65	MS-66	MS-67	MS-68	MS-69	MS-70
$95	$100	$110	$120	$130	$475

CERTIFIED POPULATIONS

MS-65	MS-66	MS-67	MS-68	MS-69	MS-70
0	0	69	91	1,579	317

1994-P Vietnam Veterans Memorial $1 Proof

PF-65	PF-66	PF-67	PF-68	PF-69	PF-70
$61	$70	$75	$80	$85	$1,700

CERTIFIED POPULATIONS

PF-65	PF-66	PF-67	PF-68	PF-69	PF-70
2	8	45	245	1,688	8

Points of Interest: Issued as a fund-raiser to tap the wallets of collectors. Otherwise the 10th anniversary attracted hardly any notice.

Subject of Commemoration: 10th anniversary of the dedication of the Vietnam Veterans Memorial Wall in Washington, D.C.

Designs: *Obverse*—A hand touching the Wall. In the distance to the right is the Washington Monument. Designed by John Mercanti of the Mint staff. *Reverse*—Three military medals and ribbons surrounded with lettering. Designed by Thomas D. Rogers, Sr. of the Mint staff.

Mintage Data: Authorized by Public Law 103-186, signed by President William J. Clinton on December 14, 1993. *Maximum authorized*—500,000. *Number minted*—1994-W 52,290 Uncirculated; 1994-P 332,891 Proof.

Original Cost and Issuer: 1994-W, Uncirculated, $27 pre-issue through September 9, 1994, $32 afterward. 1994-P, Proof, $31 pre-issue, $35 afterward. Sales were advertised to end on April 30, 1995, but this was extended to July 15, 1995. Issued by the U.S. Mint.

A Popular Memorial

In Washington, D.C., the Vietnam Veterans Memorial, often called the Memorial Wall, has been one of the city's prime attractions since it was dedicated in 1984. Although the significance of the Wall is beyond question, whether numismatists should be tapped to buy coins to celebrate its 10th anniversary was a matter of serious question in 1994. Striking a coin to observe anything a decade after it happened or was built seemed to be a stretch of greed.

The surcharge of $10 included in the purchase price of each coin was to go to the construction of a visitors' center near the Memorial for approximately two million or more annual visitors. The center was said to be of special use for young people, who could "learn the lessons of the Vietnam War and develop a better understanding of character, service, sacrifice, and patriotism," according to a news release.

Sales were above average for a commemorative dollar of the era, but still amounted to fewer than 400,000 coins, significantly below the authorization. The spate of new coins promoted by the Mint had caused many collectors to have buyer exhaustion, as reflected by many editorials and letters in the numismatic media. To keep a collection complete, commemoratives for the World Cup, Prisoner of War Museum, Women in Military Service, U.S. Capitol Bicentennial, and the 1993 (but sold in 1994) Jefferson coins had to be purchased—with no end in sight, because other commemorative coin bills were being proposed constantly in Congress. Excitement was a rare element in any commemorative release of the period.

Key to Collecting

Gem specimens are easily available. The aftermarket price for this dollar is stronger than for most others of the early 1990s.

(1994) WORLD CUP TOURNAMENT COMMEMORATIVES

Distribution

1994-D clad half dollar:
168,208 Uncirculated

1994-P clad half dollar:
609,354 Proof

1994-D silver dollar:
81,524 Uncirculated

1994-S silver dollar:
577,090 Proof

1994-W gold $5:
22,447 Uncirculated
and 89,614 Proof

Whitman Coin Guide (WCG™)—1994-D World Cup 50¢

MS-65	MS-66	MS-67	MS-68	MS-69	MS-70
$12	$14	$15	$19	$28	$1,925

CERTIFIED POPULATIONS

MS-65	MS-66	MS-67	MS-68	MS-69	MS-70
2	12	22	83	1,215	38

1994-P World Cup 50¢ Proof

PF-65	PF-66	PF-67	PF-68	PF-69	PF-70
$10	$11	$13	$15	$26	

CERTIFIED POPULATIONS

PF-65	PF-66	PF-67	PF-68	PF-69	PF-70
4	3	29	112	2,250	4

1994-D World Cup $1

MS-65	MS-66	MS-67	MS-68	MS-69	MS-70
$30	$35	$40	$45	$50	$2,850

CERTIFIED POPULATIONS

MS-65	MS-66	MS-67	MS-68	MS-69	MS-70
0	5	15	57	1,351	51

1994-S World Cup $1 Proof

PF-65	PF-66	PF-67	PF-68	PF-69	PF-70
$30	$32	$35	$50	$65	$1,450

CERTIFIED POPULATIONS

PF-65	PF-66	PF-67	PF-68	PF-69	PF-70
5	2	23	115	2,132	57

1994-W World Cup Gold $5

MS-65	MS-66	MS-67	MS-68	MS-69	MS-70
$360	$380	$400	$425	$450	$3,750
PF-65	PF-66	PF-67	PF-68	PF-69	PF-70
$265	$275	$285	$300	$325	$7,500

CERTIFIED POPULATIONS

MS-65	MS-66	MS-67	MS-68	MS-69	MS-70
1	0	6	38	853	198
PF-65	PF-66	PF-67	PF-68	PF-69	PF-70
0	2	13	68	1,666	249

Points of Interest: In terms of mintage goals, this program was one of the greatest failures in the history of American commemorative coinage.

Subject of Commemoration: The culmination of soccer games among 141 nations, in which the United States was chosen to host the XV FIFA World Cup playoff.

Designs: Clad half dollar: *Obverse*—A soccer player in action, on the run with a ball near his feet. The designer was Richard T. LaRoche. *Reverse*—The World Cup USA logo at the center, flanked by branches, as adapted by Dean McMullen. This motif was used on all three coins in the series. **Silver dollar:** *Obverse*—Two competing soccer players converge on a soccer ball in play. Designed by Dean McMullen (modeled by Mint engraver T. James Farrell), who also did the reverses of the three coins. *Reverse*—Motif as described for the half dollar. **Gold $5:** *Obverse*—The World Cup trophy. Designed by William J. Krawczewicz. *Reverse*—Motif as described for the half dollar.

Mintage Data: *Maximum authorized*—clad half dollar 5,000,000; silver dollar 5,000,000; $5 gold 750,000. *Number minted*—clad half dollar, 1994-D 168,208 Uncirculated; 1994-P 609,354 Proof. Silver dollar 1994-D 81,524 Uncirculated; 1994-S: 577,090 Proof. Gold $5 1994-W: 22,447 Uncirculated and 89,614 Proof.

Original Cost and Issuer: Uncirculated 1994-D half dollar $8.75 pre-issue price, afterward $9.50. Proof 1994-P half dollar $9.75, afterward $10.50. Uncirculated 1994-D dollar $23, afterward $28. Proof 1994-S dollar $27, afterward $31. Uncirculated 1994-W $5 gold $170, afterward $200. Proof 1994-W $5 gold $185, afterward $220. Surcharges went to the World Cup Organizing Committee. Issued by the U.S. Mint.

Soccer in America

One of the mysteries of American life that puzzles foreigners is the absence of widespread interest in soccer. Elsewhere in the world, it is the most popular sport, handily outranking baseball and football on a global basis. The National Soccer Hall of Fame in Oneonta, New York, is not known to many. Despite this, the United States was chosen to host the XV FIFA World Cup playoff series (that would cap contests involving the incredible number of 141 different competing countries, resulting in 94 qualifiers). To the surprise of many, attendance at the 52 matches was excellent. The Rose Bowl in Pasadena, California, was the site of the finals, when Brazil won 2-1 over Bulgaria.

Congress mandated a huge program of commemorative coins involving 5 million each of a clad half dollar and silver dollar and 750,000 $5 gold coins. When the dust settled, of the 10,750,000 coins authorized, sales dribbled in for a total of less than 1.5 million, a failure by any evaluation, despite 25 percent of the sales being to foreign buyers. *Coin World* opined that the "designs didn't help matters," and that the many recent commemoratives had caused buyer fatigue. The U.S. Mint stated it lost $3.5 million in the effort, noting that there simply were too many commemorative programs in progress, each with excessive mintage expectations.[15] The only winner in the World Cup scenario seemed to be the recipient of the detested surcharge.

Collectors blamed the Mint for creating coins that few people wanted, and with designs that many viewed as unattractive. The complaints should have gone to Congress instead. Faced with so many coins to produce, often with very short deadlines, the Mint simply had no time to call for designs to be submitted from leading artists and to evaluate them. Just about everything was rush-rush-rush.

Key to Collecting
Never popular to begin with, the World Cup coins are reasonably priced as a result. Nearly all are superb gems.

(1995) CENTENNIAL OLYMPIC GAMES COMMEMORATIVES

Distribution
1995 Various: See data below.
1996 Various: See data below.

Whitman Coin Guide (WCG™)—1995-S Olympic Basketball 50¢

MS-65	MS-66	MS-67	MS-68	MS-69	MS-70
$25	$28	$30	$35	$40	$325
PF-65	PF-66	PF-67	PF-68	PF-69	PF-70
$19	$20	$22	$25	$35	$3,000

CERTIFIED POPULATIONS

MS-65	MS-66	MS-67	MS-68	MS-69	MS-70
1	0	9	64	1,879	336
PF-65	PF-66	PF-67	PF-68	PF-69	PF-70
0	5	18	76	1,725	166

1995-S Olympic Baseball 50¢

MS-65	MS-66	MS-67	MS-68	MS-69	MS-70
$25	$28	$30	$35	$40	$365
PF-65	PF-66	PF-67	PF-68	PF-69	PF-70
$20	$22	$25	$27	$35	$2,750

CERTIFIED POPULATIONS

MS-65	MS-66	MS-67	MS-68	MS-69	MS-70
0	0	7	74	1,966	182
PF-65	PF-66	PF-67	PF-68	PF-69	PF-70
1	1	8	58	1,269	81

1996-S Olympic Swimming 50¢

MS-65	MS-66	MS-67	MS-68	MS-69	MS-70
$180	$185	$190	$195	$200	$2,800
PF-65	PF-66	PF-67	PF-68	PF-69	PF-70
$36	$38	$40	$45	$55	$2,250

CERTIFIED POPULATIONS

MS-65	MS-66	MS-67	MS-68	MS-69	MS-70
2	5	11	42	698	56
PF-65	PF-66	PF-67	PF-68	PF-69	PF-70
0	4	10	75	1,043	26

1996-S Olympic Soccer 50¢

MS-65	MS-66	MS-67	MS-68	MS-69	MS-70
$125	$130	$135	$140	$150	$650
PF-65	PF-66	PF-67	PF-68	PF-69	PF-70
$105	$110	$115	$120	$130	$2,000

CERTIFIED POPULATIONS

MS-65	MS-66	MS-67	MS-68	MS-69	MS-70
0	1	8	36	670	114
PF-65	PF-66	PF-67	PF-68	PF-69	PF-70
0	2	11	67	1,109	25

1995-D Olympic Gymnastics $1

MS-65	MS-66	MS-67	MS-68	MS-69	MS-70
$85	$88	$90	$95	$100	$375

CERTIFIED POPULATIONS

MS-65	MS-66	MS-67	MS-68	MS-69	MS-70
0	3	8	71	1,511	243

1995-P Olympic Gymnastics $1 Proof

PF-65	PF-66	PF-67	PF-68	PF-69	PF-70
$58	$60	$62	$65	$75	$5,000

CERTIFIED POPULATIONS

PF-65	PF-66	PF-67	PF-68	PF-69	PF-70
3	14	22	122	1,662	26

1995-D Paralympics $1

MS-65	MS-66	MS-67	MS-68	MS-69	MS-70
$105	$110	$115	$120	$125	$500

CERTIFIED POPULATIONS

MS-65	MS-66	MS-67	MS-68	MS-69	MS-70
0	0	4	47	1,211	274

1995-P Paralympics $1 Proof

PF-65	PF-66	PF-67	PF-68	PF-69	PF-70
$65	$68	$70	$75	$80	$1,300

CERTIFIED POPULATIONS

PF-65	PF-66	PF-67	PF-68	PF-69	PF-70
1	2	17	130	1,488	30

1995-D Olympic Track & Field $1

MS-65	MS-66	MS-67	MS-68	MS-69	MS-70
$110	$115	$120	$125	$135	$850

CERTIFIED POPULATIONS

MS-65	MS-66	MS-67	MS-68	MS-69	MS-70
0	1	4	30	679	135

1995-P Olympic Track & Field $1 Proof

PF-65	PF-66	PF-67	PF-68	PF-69	PF-70
$52	$55	$60	$65	$70	

CERTIFIED POPULATIONS

PF-65	PF-66	PF-67	PF-68	PF-69	PF-70
2	6	14	101	1,581	41

1995-D Olympic Cycling $1

MS-65	MS-66	MS-67	MS-68	MS-69	MS-70
$165	$170	$175	$180	$190	$950

CERTIFIED POPULATIONS

MS-65	MS-66	MS-67	MS-68	MS-69	MS-70
0	2	5	48	729	162

1995-P Olympic Cycling $1 Proof

PF-65	PF-66	PF-67	PF-68	PF-69	PF-70
$47	$50	$55	$60	$70	$2,600

CERTIFIED POPULATIONS

PF-65	PF-66	PF-67	PF-68	PF-69	PF-70
0	6	18	126	1,124	19

1996-D Olympic Tennis $1

MS-65	MS-66	MS-67	MS-68	MS-69	MS-70
$360	$365	$375	$380	$390	$800

CERTIFIED POPULATIONS

MS-65	MS-66	MS-67	MS-68	MS-69	MS-70
0	0	9	39	671	75

1996-P Olympic Tennis $1 Proof

PF-65	PF-66	PF-67	PF-68	PF-69	PF-70
$90	$95	$100	$105	$120	

CERTIFIED POPULATIONS

PF-65	PF-66	PF-67	PF-68	PF-69	PF-70
1	5	20	84	518	0

1996-D Olympic Paralympics $1

MS-65	MS-66	MS-67	MS-68	MS-69	MS-70
$420	$430	$440	$450	$460	$1,425

CERTIFIED POPULATIONS

MS-65	MS-66	MS-67	MS-68	MS-69	MS-70
0	1	4	35	746	212

1996-P Olympic Paralympics $1 Proof

PF-65	PF-66	PF-67	PF-68	PF-69	PF-70
$90	$95	$100	$105	$120	

CERTIFIED POPULATIONS

PF-65	PF-66	PF-67	PF-68	PF-69	PF-70
1	7	15	122	1,257	0

1996-D Olympic Rowing $1

MS-65	MS-66	MS-67	MS-68	MS-69	MS-70
$380	$385	$390	$395	$405	$1,375

CERTIFIED POPULATIONS

MS-65	MS-66	MS-67	MS-68	MS-69	MS-70
0	0	3	19	538	62

1996-P Olympic Rowing $1 Proof

PF-65	PF-66	PF-67	PF-68	PF-69	PF-70
$75	$78	$80	$85	$95	

CERTIFIED POPULATIONS

PF-65	PF-66	PF-67	PF-68	PF-69	PF-70
2	8	15	95	1,086	0

1996-D Olympic High Jump $1

MS-65	MS-66	MS-67	MS-68	MS-69	MS-70
$430	$435	$440	$450	$470	$2,900

CERTIFIED POPULATIONS

MS-65	MS-66	MS-67	MS-68	MS-69	MS-70
0	1	2	29	587	62

1996-P Olympic High Jump $1 Proof

PF-65	PF-66	PF-67	PF-68	PF-69	PF-70
$60	$62	$65	$70	$85	

CERTIFIED POPULATIONS

PF-65	PF-66	PF-67	PF-68	PF-69	PF-70
0	7	21	97	1,056	0

1995-W Olympic Torch Runner Gold $5

MS-65	MS-66	MS-67	MS-68	MS-69	MS-70
$740	$740	$755	$760	$780	$1,525
PF-65	PF-66	PF-67	PF-68	PF-69	PF-70
$380	$385	$390	$395	$420	$3,000

CERTIFIED POPULATIONS

MS-65	MS-66	MS-67	MS-68	MS-69	MS-70
2	0	8	21	533	339
PF-65	PF-66	PF-67	PF-68	PF-69	PF-70
0	0	3	9	14	0

1995-W Olympic Stadium Gold $5

MS-65	MS-66	MS-67	MS-68	MS-69	MS-70
$1,095	$1,125	$1,175	$1,200	$1,250	$2,150
PF-65	PF-66	PF-67	PF-68	PF-69	PF-70
$475	$485	$490	$510	$525	$2,000

CERTIFIED POPULATIONS

MS-65	MS-66	MS-67	MS-68	MS-69	MS-70
0	0	3	17	712	268
PF-65	PF-66	PF-67	PF-68	PF-69	PF-70
0	0	2	4	8	0

1996-W Olympic Flag Bearer Gold $5

MS-65	MS-66	MS-67	MS-68	MS-69	MS-70
$1,120	$1,150	$1,175	$1,225	$1,275	$1,600
PF-65	PF-66	PF-67	PF-68	PF-69	PF-70
$615	$640	$665	$685	$715	$6,250

CERTIFIED POPULATIONS

MS-65	MS-66	MS-67	MS-68	MS-69	MS-70
0	0	3	19	559	199
PF-65	PF-66	PF-67	PF-68	PF-69	PF-70
0	1	5	34	859	22

1996-W Olympic Flame Gold $5

MS-65	MS-66	MS-67	MS-68	MS-69	MS-70
$1,090	$1,120	$1,140	$1,165	$1,200	$5,000
PF-65	PF-66	PF-67	PF-68	PF-69	PF-70
$640	$650	$660	$675	$725	$7,000

CERTIFIED POPULATIONS

MS-65	MS-66	MS-67	MS-68	MS-69	MS-70
0	0	6	14	638	138
PF-65	PF-66	PF-67	PF-68	PF-69	PF-70
0	0	7	31	1,310	21

Points of Interest: This is the largest of all commemorative programs and also one of the worst performing from a sales viewpoint.

Subject of Commemoration: The Centennial Olympic Games held in Atlanta in 1996.

Designs: 1995-S Basketball clad half dollar: *Obverse*—Men's basketball. Designed by Clint Hansen and modeled by Alfred F. Maletsky. *Reverse*—Symbol of the Atlanta Committee for the Olympic Games superimposed over the Atlantic Ocean as viewed from space. Designed by Mint engraver T. James Ferrell.

1995-S Baseball clad half dollar: *Obverse*—Batter at the plate with catcher and umpire. Designed by Edgar Z. Steever of the Mint staff. *Reverse*—As preceding.

1996-S Swimming clad half dollar: *Obverse*—Male swimmer. Designed by William Krawczewicz. *Reverse*—Symbols of the Olympic games, including flame, torch, rings, Greek column, and 100 (the last to observe the 100th anniversary of the modern Olympic games inaugurated with the 1896 Games in Athens). Designed by Malcolm Farley.

1996-S Soccer clad half dollar: *Obverse*—Women playing soccer. Designed by Clint Hansen. *Reverse*—As preceding.

1995-D and P Gymnastics silver dollar: *Obverse*—Men's gymnastics. Designed by James C. Sharpe. *Reverse*—Clasped hands of two athletes with torch above. Designed by William Krawczewicz and modeled by T. James Ferrell.

1995-D and P Paralympics silver dollar: *Obverse*—Blind runner tethered to a seeing companion in a race. Designed by James C. Sharpe and modeled by Thomas D. Rogers Jr. *Reverse*—As preceding.

1995-D and P Track and Field silver dollar: *Obverse*—Men competing in track and field. Designed by John Mercanti of the Mint staff. *Reverse*—As preceding.

1995-D and P Cycling silver dollar: *Obverse*—Men cycling. Designed by John Mercanti of the Mint staff. *Reverse*—As preceding.

1996-D and P Tennis silver dollar: *Obverse*—Women playing tennis. Designed by James C. Sharpe and modeled by Thomas D. Rogers Jr. *Reverse*—Atlanta Committee for the Olympic Games logo with torch and flame. Designed by Thomas D. Rogers, Sr. of the Mint staff.

1996-D and P Paralympics silver dollar: *Obverse*—Athlete in a wheelchair competing in a track and field competition. Designed by James C. Sharpe. *Reverse*—As preceding.

1996-D and P Rowing silver dollar: *Obverse*—Men rowing. Designed by Bart Forbes. *Reverse*—As preceding.

1996-D and P High Jump silver dollar: *Obverse*—Athlete doing the "Fosbury Flop" maneuver. Designed by Calvin Massey. *Reverse*—As preceding.

1995-W Torch Runner gold $5: *Obverse*—Olympic runner carrying a torch. Both sides designed by Frank Gasparro, former chief engraver at the Mint, and modeled by John Mercanti.

1995-W Stadium gold $5: *Obverse*—Aerial view of the Olympic Stadium from a distance to the side. Designed by Marcel Jovine. *Reverse*—As preceding.

1996-W Flag Bearer gold $5: *Obverse*—Athlete with a flag followed by a crowd. Designed by Patricia L. Verani. *Reverse*—Atlanta Committee for the Olympic Games logo within laurel leaves. Designed by William Krawczewicz.

1996-W Olympic Flame gold $5: *Obverse*—Lighting of the Olympic flame. Designed by Frank Gasparro. *Reverse*—As preceding.

Mintage Data: 1995-S Basketball clad half dollar: *Maximum authorized*—2,000,000. *Number minted*—171,001 Uncirculated; 169,655 Proof.

1995-S Baseball clad half dollar: *Maximum authorized*—2,000,000. *Number minted*—164,605 Uncirculated; 118,087 Proof.

1996-S Swimming clad half dollar: *Maximum authorized*—3,000,000. *Number minted*—49,533 Uncirculated; 114,315 Proof.

1996-S Soccer clad half dollar: *Maximum authorized*—3,000,000. *Number minted*—52,836 Uncirculated;112,412 Proof.

1995-D and P Gymnastics silver dollar: *Maximum authorized*—750,000. *Number minted*—1995-D 42,497 Uncirculated; 1995-P 182,676 Proof.

1995-D and P Paralympics silver dollar: *Maximum authorized*—750,000. *Number minted*—1995-D 28,649 Uncirculated; 1995-P 138,337 Proof.

1995-D and P Track and Field silver dollar: *Maximum authorized*—750,000. *Number minted*—1995-D 24,976 Uncirculated; 1995-P 136,935 Proof.

1995-D and P Cycling silver dollar: *Maximum authorized*—750,000. *Number minted*—1995-D 19,662 Uncirculated; 1995-P 118,795 Proof.

1996-D and P Tennis silver dollar: *Maximum authorized*—1,000,000. *Number minted*—1996-D 15,983 Uncirculated; 1996-P : 92,016 Proof.

1996-D and P Paralympics silver dollar: *Maximum authorized*—1,000,000. *Number minted*—1996-D 14,497 Uncirculated; 1996-P 84,280 Proof.

1996-D and P Rowing silver dollar: *Maximum authorized*—1,000,000. *Number minted*—1996-D 16,258 Uncirculated; 1996-P 151,890 Proof.

1996-D and P High Jump silver dollar: *Maximum authorized*—1,000,000. *Number minted*—1996-D 15,697 Uncirculated; 1996-P 124,502 Proof.

1995-W Torch Runner gold $5: *Maximum authorized*—175,000. *Number minted*—14,645 Uncirculated; 57,442 Proof.

1995-W Stadium gold $5: *Maximum authorized*—175,000. *Number minted*—10,579 Uncirculated; 43,124 Proof.

1996-W Flag Bearer gold $5: *Maximum authorized*—300,000. *Number minted*—9,174 Uncirculated; 32,886 Proof.

1996-W Olympic Flame gold $5: *Maximum authorized*—300,000. *Number minted*—9,210 Uncirculated; 38,555 Proof.

Original Cost and Issuer: Pre-issue prices for sets were at a 7 percent discount, with a six-installment payment plan offered to those interested. Regular price, 32-coin set including Uncirculated and Proof: $2,261; 16-coin set Proof: $1,162; 8-coin set silver only Proof: $237. Over this series' life span, which extended into 1996, eight other set options and a single-coin option were made available. Issued by the U.S. Mint.

1995–1996 Centennial Olympics Coins

The XXVI Olympiad, the Summer Games, were held in Atlanta, Georgia, from July 19 to August 4, 1996. The entire world watched as nations competed, records were set, and medals were won. Invitations were sent to the National Olympic Committees in each of 197 nations, and *all* responded—including nations that formerly composed the Union of Soviet Socialist Republics (USSR).

The Atlanta Olympic Committee knew no bounds in its enthusiasm—some said *greed*—to receive an anticipated $100,000,000 in surcharges from coins sold to collectors. To bolster their argument, the Atlanta group hired McKinsey & Co., a research firm, to make a study—which must have been done in academia, or on the moon, or somewhere outside of the numismatic mainstream. Congress went along with the idea, championed by Representative Douglas Barnard Jr., Democrat from Georgia (important as the key person in the 1982 Washington half dollar program). A far-ranging program of 16 coins dated 1995 and 16 more dated 1996, including Uncirculated and Proof versions of the clad half dollar, silver dollar, and $5 gold coin, was implemented. Not only did the drafters of the legislation add surcharges of unprecedented amounts, but they originally requested that no other commemoratives of any kind except theirs should be issued during the 1995 and 1996 years. Proposed were *silver* half dollars, silver dollars, and $5 gold coins. Congress changed the half dollar to the usual clad format, and denied the exclusivity idea.

What Happened

In summer 1993, invitations were sent to artists. Designs were gathered, and in autumn 1994 illustrations of the final motifs were displayed. The coin program was announced, to commence in January 1995, with many options for purchase. In total, one of every design, in both Uncirculated and Proof formats, cost $2,291. Collectors voted with their pocketbooks, and sales proved dismal in relation to forecasts. Even though sales were extended into calendar year 1997, not a single coin came even close to its projections. One of the worst sellers was the 1997 tennis games silver dollar—and this was supposed to be one of the most popular sports in America. One million were authorized, but only 15,983 Uncirculated and 92,016 Proof coins were sold.

From a numismatic market viewpoint, history repeated itself. Commemoratives that were not popular and that were ignored by buyers at the time, turned into expensive scarcities and rarities on the aftermarket. The Olympic Games themselves were a grand success, with enthusiastic attendance.

Key to Collecting

Although enough 1995 and 1996 Olympics coins are on the aftermarket that finding designs of choice, or forming a set, will be no problem, the undertaking costs far more than the original issue prices. The obverse designs are varied, and in total the collection is an excellent representation of this quadrennial worldwide competition.

(1995) CIVIL WAR BATTLEFIELDS COMMEMORATIVES

Distribution

1995-S clad half dollar:
>119,520 Uncirculated
>and 226,632 Proof

1995-P silver dollar:
>45,866 Uncirculated

1995-S silver dollar:
>437,114 Proofs

1995-W gold $5:
>12,735 Uncirculated
>and 55,246 Proof

Whitman Coin Guide (WCG™)—1995-S Civil War Battlefields 50¢

MS-65	MS-66	MS-67	MS-68	MS-69	MS-70
$50	$55	$60	$65	$75	$690
PF-65	PF-66	PF-67	PF-68	PF-69	PF-70
$40	$42	$45	$50	$60	$2,000

CERTIFIED POPULATIONS

MS-65	MS-66	MS-67	MS-68	MS-69	MS-70
1	0	6	46	945	176
PF-65	PF-66	PF-67	PF-68	PF-69	PF-70
2	9	31	145	1,751	31

1995-P Civil War Battlefields $1

MS-65	MS-66	MS-67	MS-68	MS-69	MS-70
$85	$90	$95	$100	$125	$950

CERTIFIED POPULATIONS

MS-65	MS-66	MS-67	MS-68	MS-69	MS-70
2	2	21	89	1,241	88

1995-S Civil War Battlefields $1 Proof

PF-65	PF-66	PF-67	PF-68	PF-69	PF-70
$80	$85	$90	$95	$115	$2,000

CERTIFIED POPULATIONS

PF-65	PF-66	PF-67	PF-68	PF-69	PF-70
1	12	49	183	1,985	33

1995-W Civil War Battlefields Gold $5

MS-65	MS-66	MS-67	MS-68	MS-69	MS-70
$980	$1,000	$1,050	$1,100	$1,150	$1,875
PF-65	PF-66	PF-67	PF-68	PF-69	PF-70
$550	$575	$600	$625	$675	$4,250

CERTIFIED POPULATIONS

MS-65	MS-66	MS-67	MS-68	MS-69	MS-70
0	0	1	10	674	224
PF-65	PF-66	PF-67	PF-68	PF-69	PF-70
2	3	18	59	1,833	160

Points of Interest: The same person, not a Mint artist, designed the obverses for all three coins.

Subject of Commemoration: Action in battlefields during the Civil War.

Designs: Clad half dollar: *Obverse*—Drummer standing. Designed by Don Troiani, well known artist specializing in Civil War motifs. *Reverse*—Cannon overlooking battlefield with inscription above. Designed by Mint engraver T. James Ferrell. **Silver dollar:** *Obverse*—Soldier offering canteen to a wounded comrade. Designed by Don Troiani. *Reverse*—Gettysburg landscape with a quotation from Joshua Chamberlain, hero in that battle. Designed by John Mercanti of the Mint staff. **$5 gold:** *Obverse*—Bugler on horseback sounding a call. Designed by Don Troiani. *Reverse*—Eagle perched on a shield. Designed by Alfred F. Maletsky of the Mint staff.

Mintage Data: Authorized by Public Law 102-379. *Maximum authorized*—clad half dollar 2,000,000; silver dollar 1,000,000; $5 gold 300,000. *Number minted*—clad half dollar 1995-S 119,520 Uncirculated and 226,632 Proof; silver dollar 1995-P 45,866 Uncirculated; 1995-S 437,114 Proof; $5 gold 12,735 Uncirculated and 55,246 Proof.

Original Cost and Issuer: There were 15 different pre-issue ordering options, from $9.50 for a single uncirculated half dollar, to $455 for a six-coin set with one of each coin in Proof and Uncirculated finishes. Regular prices ranged from $11.75 to $490. Surcharges per single coin: $5 gold, $35; silver dollar, $7; clad half dollar, $2. Proceeds went to the Civil War Trust for the preservation of historically significant battlefields. Issued by the U.S. Mint.

Preserving the Scenes of War

Preserving battlefields associated with the 1861–1865 Civil War formed the topic for a suite of three coins—the usual clad half dollar, silver dollar, and $5 gold coin. Mintages were limited to 2 million, 1 million, and 300,000, respectively. Don Troiani, an artist in the private sector known for his depictions of battle scenes, designed the three obverses, while Mint engravers did the reverses.

Although Civil War history attracts millions of followers and books on the subject are very popular, these coins languished. Total sales amounted to a tiny fraction of expectations. It seems that buyers were sated with all the commemoratives being spewed out by the Mint—not its idea at all, but done on behalf of Congress reacting to greedy constituents.

Key to Collecting
All are readily available in the marketplace today. Most are superb gems.

(1995) Special Olympic Games Dollars

Distribution
1995-W: 89,301 Uncirculated
1995-P: 351,764 Proof

Whitman Coin Guide (WCG™)—1995-W Special Olympics $1

MS-65	MS-66	MS-67	MS-68	MS-69	MS-70
$35	$38	$42	$45	$50	$1,400

CERTIFIED POPULATIONS

MS-65	MS-66	MS-67	MS-68	MS-69	MS-70
0	0	5	39	501	115

1995-P Special Olympics $1 Proof

PF-65	PF-66	PF-67	PF-68	PF-69	PF-70
$27	$28	$30	$32	$45	$3,000

CERTIFIED POPULATIONS

PF-65	PF-66	PF-67	PF-68	PF-69	PF-70
0	2	3	8	4	5

Points of Interest: Created by political favoritism, and historically incorrect in its commemoration. Was the first U.S. coin to portray a living American woman.

Subject of Commemoration: Eunice Shriver, but ostensibly intended for the Special Olympics.

Designs: *Obverse*—Unflattering portrait of Eunice Shriver. From art by Jamie Wyeth designed and modeled by T. James Ferrell of the Mint staff. *Reverse*—Representation of a Special Olympics medal, a rose, and a quotation by Shriver. Designed by Thomas D. Rogers, Sr. of the Mint staff.

Mintage Data: Authorized by Public Law 103-328, signed by President William J. Clinton on September 29, 1994. *Maximum authorized*—800,000. *Number minted*—1995-W 89,301 Uncirculated; 1995-P 351,754 Proof.

Original Cost and Issuer: Pre-issue prices: $31 encapsulated Proof, $29 Uncirculated (ordinary packaging). Regular prices: $35 Proof, $31 Uncirculated. A $10 surcharge on each coin went to the Special Olympics to support the 1995 World Summer Games. Issued by the U.S. Mint.

The Shriver Dollar and Politics

Eunice Kennedy Shriver formed the subject of this commemorative dollar, honoring her as founder of the Special Olympics Games. These quadrennial contests bring together individuals who are mentally retarded or otherwise disabled. They emphasize team play and sportsmanship, rather than athletic prowess. The idea sprang from a movement in the administration of President John F. Kennedy. Eunice was his sister. In 1995 the Games were held in Connecticut, mainly at Yale University Stadium.

This issue has a curious history, and was *almost* the greatest commemorative failure of modern time. Jeff Stark reported in *Coin World* that Phoenix Home Life Mutual Insurance Co. was the corporate benefactor that bought 250,000 coins at the last minute, saving the issue from financial losses. The company remained anonymous until 1998, when it used the coins to give to Special Olympic athletes. The coin was controversial from the start; it depicted the first living female on U.S. coinage, was seen as the result of political nepotism, and was decried as perpetuating historical injustice (many credit Anne [McGlone] Burke with founding the event). Her nephew, Rep. Joseph F. Kennedy II, sponsored the bill and chaired the House committee that oversees coinage.[16]

What a mess! The coin perhaps epitomizes the bad side of commemoratives: a design that was historically inappropriate and incorrect, the result of politics, with motifs rejected by both advisory panels, but approved anyway by the secretary of the Treasury.

Key to Collecting

These coins are plentiful in the marketplace. Most are superb gems.

(1996) National Community Service Dollars

Distribution
1996-S: 23,500 Uncirculated
and 101,543 Proof

Whitman Coin Guide (WCG™)—1996 National Community Service $1

MS-65	MS-66	MS-67	MS-68	MS-69	MS-70
$270	$280	$290	$300	$310	$1,750
PF-65	PF-66	PF-67	PF-68	PF-69	PF-70
$85	$90	$95	$100	$115	$2,250

CERTIFIED POPULATIONS

MS-65	MS-66	MS-67	MS-68	MS-69	MS-70
0	1	4	39	946	141
PF-65	PF-66	PF-67	PF-68	PF-69	PF-70
0	5	18	93	1,189	9

Points of Interest: Faced with an unappealing subject, the Mint resurrected an old medal design by famous sculptor Augustus Saint-Gaudens for the obverse, but not even that saved the day.

Subject of Commemoration: Community service.

Designs: *Obverse*—Standing figure of Liberty, adapted by engraver Thomas D. Rogers, Sr., from a 1905 medal by Augustus Saint-Gaudens. *Reverse*—SERVICE FOR AMERICA in three lines, with a wreath around, and other lettering at the border. Designed by Mint engraver William C. Cousins.

Mintage Data: Authorized by Public Law 103-328, signed by President William J. Clinton on September 29, 1994. *Maximum authorized*—500,000. *Number minted*—1996-S 23,500 Uncirculated and 101,543 Proof.

Original Cost and Issuer: Surcharge of $10 per coin benefited the National Community Service Trust. Issued by the U.S. Mint.

National Community Service Honored

"The more things change, the more they remain the same," it has been said. By 1996 the program of modern commemoratives had sunk into criticism and disfavor that paralleled that of the 1930s, when collectors tired of meaningless events being commemorated on coins often made in multiple varieties to take money from numismatists. By 1996, letters to the editors of *Coin World* and *Numismatic News* endlessly repeated complaints of overly high issue prices, poor designs, and a program that seemed to have run amok. It was a far cry from 1982, when the Mint launched its first modern commemorative, the inexpensive George Washington 250th Anniversary half dollar.

A curious aspect of commemorative coins is that the U.S. Mint had to foot the bill for advertising and promotion. Often handed poor or unappealing concepts, the Mint then received criticism if the programs failed to sell to the expectations of their political promoters. For most modern issues this was a lose-lose proposition for the Mint.

Time had come for reform, and in 1996 Congress decreed that after existing approved programs had run their course, no more than two events could be commemorated on coins each year. There was no stipulation, however, regarding the denominations to be issued within those programs.

In 1996 the National Community Service dollar was the latest in the "Who cares?" category of things commemorated. The sponsor was none other than Representative Joseph D. Kennedy of Massachusetts, of the Eunice Kennedy Shriver dollar connection. To be sure, community service is a fine thing, as are motherhood, the American flag, and apple pie. It was certainly reasonable for collectors to ask, however, why they had to pay the high surcharge of $10 per coin for this new dollar, to go to the National Community Service Trust, which encourages volunteers to work for the public good. Probably not one numismatist in a hundred had ever heard of the group.

To the Mint's credit, staffer Christine Seyfried and others met with numismatists in groups in Denver, Fort Lauderdale, and Baltimore. Not surprisingly, it was learned that they desired commemoratives to honor a significant event in history, and for the designs to be beautiful. The Community Service dollar had neither of these attributes. With sponsors hoping for 500,000 coins to be sold, there was a bit of a problem, it seemed. In an interesting move intended to add a bit of art, the obverse design was taken from a 1905 medal by Augustus Saint-Gaudens made for the Women's Auxiliary of the Massachusetts Civil Service Reform Association.

Marketing commenced on July 12, 1996, in the midst of promotions for the 1995 and 1996 coins for the Atlanta Olympic Games, not to overlook a commemorative dollar for the Smithsonian Institution. To reduce losses from what the Mint was sure would be a losing program, economies were effected in advertising and direct mail. Representative Kennedy was supposed to attract corporate purchasers of bulk quantities, a display at the Premium Incentive Show in New York City was hoped to bring in new buyers, a mailing was made to 5,000 organizations, and the United Way indicated that it would sign up for 250,000 coins.

Corporate sales did not materialize, the trade show brought in few new buyers, and the United Way became embroiled in controversy when it was discovered its national leader was using funds to pay for lavish personal expenses. All of these efforts amounted to just 400 coins sold to new buyers, including just one "bulk" sale of 51 pieces.[17]

Collectors saved the day a bit, but sales were still just about 25 percent of expectations.

Key to Collecting
Uncirculated dollars are scarce by virtue of their low mintage, but demand is scarce as well, with the result that specimens can be purchased easily enough. Both formats are usually seen in superb gem preservation.

(1996) SMITHSONIAN INSTITUTION 150TH ANNIVERSARY COMMEMORATIVES

Distribution
1996-D silver dollar:
      31,320 Uncirculated
1996-P silver dollar:
      129,152 Proof
1996-W $5 gold:
      9,068 Uncirculated
      and 21,772 Proof

Whitman Coin Guide (WCG™)—1996-D Smithsonian 100th Anniversary $1

MS-65	MS-66	MS-67	MS-68	MS-69	MS-70
$165	$170	$175	$180	$195	$550

CERTIFIED POPULATIONS

MS-65	MS-66	MS-67	MS-68	MS-69	MS-70
0	0	2	26	792	231

1996-P Smithsonian 100th Anniversary $1 Proof

PF-65	PF-66	PF-67	PF-68	PF-69	PF-70
$70	$75	$80	$85	$95	$5,250

CERTIFIED POPULATIONS

PF-65	PF-66	PF-67	PF-68	PF-69	PF-70
0	8	19	126	1,234	3

1996-W Smithsonian 100th Anniversary Gold $5

MS-65	MS-66	MS-67	MS-68	MS-69	MS-70
$1,600	$1,625	$1,675	$1,725	$1,800	$4,250

PF-65	PF-66	PF-67	PF-68	PF-69	PF-70
$700	$720	$735	$750	$785	$5,250

CERTIFIED POPULATIONS

MS-65	MS-66	MS-67	MS-68	MS-69	MS-70
0	3	9	19	561	138

PF-65	PF-66	PF-67	PF-68	PF-69	PF-70
0	3	14	46	904	15

Points of Interest: The Smithsonian Institution houses the National Numismatic Collection. Before being moved to the Museum of National History, the collection was housed in the Castle building shown on the coin.

Subject of Commemoration: 150th anniversary of Congress establishing the Smithsonian Institution in Washington, D.C. on August 10, 1846.

Designs: Silver dollar: *Obverse*—The "Castle" building on the Mall in Washington, the original home of the Smithsonian Institution. Branches to each side. Designed by Thomas D. Rogers, Sr. of the Mint staff. *Reverse*—Goddess sitting on top of a world globe. In her left hand she holds a torch, in the right a scroll inscribed ART / HISTORY/ SCIENCE. In the field to the right in several lines is FOR THE INCREASE AND DIFFUSION OF KNOWLEDGE. Designed by Mint staff engraver John Mercanti. **$5 gold:** *Obverse*—Bust of James Smithson facing left. Designed by Mint staff engraver Al Maletsky. *Reverse*—Sunburst with SMITHSONIAN below. Designed by Mint engraver James T. Ferrell.

Mintage Data: Authorized by Public Law 104-96, signed by President William J. Clinton on January 10, 1996. *Maximum authorized*—silver dollars 650,000; $5 gold 100,000. *Number minted*—silver dollars 1996-D 31,320 Uncirculated; 1996-P 129,152 Proof; $5 gold 1996-W 9,068 Uncirculated and 21,772 Proof.

Original Cost and Issuer: 1996-D Uncirculated dollar $30 pre-issue, $32 afterward. 1996-P Proof $33 pre-issue, $37 afterward. 1990-W $5 gold Uncirculated $180 pre-issue, $205 afterward; Proof $195 pre-issue, $225 afterward. The Mint also offered some jewelry items incorporating the commemorative coins. Issued by the U.S. Mint.

Honoring the Smithsonian

Established in 1846, the Smithsonian Institution was funded by the will of James Smithson (1765–1829), an English scientist who had never visited the United States. His remains were brought to America, and in 1904 interred in a special area in the "Castle" building on the Mall in Washington, D.C. His bequest was in the form of more than $500,000 equivalent value in British gold sovereigns. The Smithsonian became America's national museum, supplementing displays at the Patent Office and other locations. The 150th anniversary was celebrated on August 10, 1996, by a special ceremony.

The Smithsonian Institution Sesquicentennial Commemorative Coin Act of 1995, Public Law 104-96, provided for the issuance of up to 650,000 silver dollars and 100,000 gold $5 coins. The issue prices included surcharges of $10 for the dollar and $35 for the half eagle, the proceeds, which eventually totaled $2,683,220, going to the Smithsonian Board of Regents. This time, there was little resistance to this by buyers, since the Smithsonian is home to the National Numismatic Collection of more than a million items. Some years later in 2004, most of the exhibit was dismantled, making way for new displays, the extent of which had not been announced by the press time of this book. In the meantime, in the Castle building a special gallery of rare coin highlights was opened in 2005.

The coins were offered at pre-issue discounts, as usual for commemoratives of the era, as well as in other options, now including a 50,000-set Young Collectors Edition, and some jewelry incorporating the coins.

Although the Smithsonian coins and their designs were appreciated by most numismatists, the market for new commemoratives had run out of steam. The deluge of Olympics and other coins, dozens of new issues, had exhausted the public's enthusiasm, and the bank accounts of most collectors simply could not handle the cost needed to keep current with coins as they came out. Sales proved to be a small fraction of the hoped-for totals.

Key to Collecting

The Smithsonian coins have risen in value considerably since their release. Today examples can be found readily in the marketplace and are nearly always superb gems.

(1997) BOTANIC GARDEN DOLLARS

Distribution
1997-P: 57,272 Uncirculated
and 264,528 Proof

Whitman Coin Guide (WCG™)—1997 Botanic Garden $1

MS-65	MS-66	MS-67	MS-68	MS-69	MS-70
$50	$52	$55	$60	$65	$700
PF-65	**PF-66**	**PF-67**	**PF-68**	**PF-69**	**PF-70**
$45	$47	$50	$55	$75	$1,750

CERTIFIED POPULATIONS

MS-65	MS-66	MS-67	MS-68	MS-69	MS-70
3	8	17	160	1,369	150
PF-65	**PF-66**	**PF-67**	**PF-68**	**PF-69**	**PF-70**
0	6	17	87	1,196	13

Points of Interest: Dated 1820–1995 on one side and 1997 on the other.

Subject of Commemoration: The 165th anniversary of the United States Botanic Garden, or at least inscribed as such.

Designs: *Obverse*—Façade of the United States Botanic Garden in plan view without landscaping. Designed by Edgar Z. Steever of the Mint staff. *Reverse*—A rose at the center with a garland of roses above. The inscription below includes the anniversary dates 1820–1995. Designed by William C. Cousins of the Mint staff. Some listings designate the rose side as the obverse.

Mintage Data: Authorized by Public Law 103-328, signed by President William J. Clinton on September 29, 1994. *Maximum authorized*—500,000. *Number minted*—1997-P 57,272 Uncirculated and 264,528 Proof.

Original Cost and Issuer: Proof $33; Uncirculated $30. A $10 per coin surcharge was designated for the National Fund for the Botanic Garden, after Mint expenses were paid. Issued by the U.S. Mint.

Botanic Garden Commemorative

Not that another commemorative was needed in the tired and glutted market for such coins, but Public Law 103-328 of September 29, 1994, provided for the minting of 500,000 silver dollars to feature the National Botanic Garden in Washington, D.C. It is not sure what was being commemorated, other than trying to make collectors pony up money to support a fairly obscure project. One side of the finished coin bears the dates 1820–1995, perhaps indicating that the 165th anniversary was being celebrated, but the other side is dated 1997, the 167th anniversary. Once again, up was down, black was white, in terms of logic.

Not much was left to the creativity of artists and engravers, for the law specified that the French façade of the U.S. Botanic Garden be shown on the obverse and a rose on the reverse, with the 1820–1995 dates. The marketing efforts of the U.S. Mint were nothing less than heroic, with options including a package with an Uncirculated silver dollar, a $1 paper note, and a Jefferson nickel with a special matte finish.

Again, the minds of prospective buyers were swimming with a confused array of dozens of other commemoratives currently being marketed by the Mint, including 32 for the Atlanta Olympics and stray other coins. As might be expected, sales fizzled, and only a small fraction of the authorization was sold.

Key to Collecting

These coins are readily available on the market today. Nearly all are superb gems. Ironically, the hottest item is the package containing the special-finish Jefferson nickel, the demand coming from collectors of five-cent pieces! Only 25,000 sets were sold. This is déjà vu of the 1993 Jefferson dollar offer.

(1997) NATIONAL LAW ENFORCEMENT OFFICERS MEMORIAL DOLLARS

Distribution
1997-P: 28,575 Uncirculated
and 110,428 Proof

Whitman Coin Guide (WCG™)—1997 National Law Enforcement Memorial $1

MS-65	MS-66	MS-67	MS-68	MS-69	MS-70
$200	$210	$220	$230	$250	$1,000
PF-65	**PF-66**	**PF-67**	**PF-68**	**PF-69**	**PF-70**
$165	$175	$185	$195	$210	$2,750

CERTIFIED POPULATIONS

MS-65	MS-66	MS-67	MS-68	MS-69	MS-70
0	4	4	44	694	115
PF-65	**PF-66**	**PF-67**	**PF-68**	**PF-69**	**PF-70**
0	10	22	87	1,182	13

Points of Interest: Another numismatically meaningless commemorative that registered poor sales.

Subject of Commemoration: National Law Enforcement Officers Memorial on the sixth anniversary of its dedication.

Designs: *Obverse*—United States Park Police officers Robert Chelsey and Kelcy Stefansson making rubbing of a fellow officer's name, from a photograph by Larry Ruggieri. Both sides modeled by Mint engraver Alfred F. Maletsky. *Reverse*—Shield with a rose across it, evocative of the sacrifices made by officers.

Mintage Data: Authorized by Public Law 104-329, signed by President William J. Clinton on October 20, 1996. *Maximum authorized—500,000. Number minted—*1997-P 28,575 Uncirculated, 110,428 Proof.

Original Cost and Issuer: 1997-P Uncirculated, pre-issue $30, afterward $32; Proof $33, afterward $37. A portion of the $10 surcharge on each was earmarked for preservation of the Memorial. Issued by the U.S. Mint.

Monument Commemorated

The National Law Enforcement Officers Memorial at Judiciary Square in Washington, D.C., dedicated on October 15, 1991, was for some reason the subject of yet another commemorative coin in 1997. As to the monument's significance there is no question, for it honors more than 14,000 men and women who gave their lives in the line of duty.

Handed the challenge of finding homes for a half million coins, the Mint gamely set about publicity, suggesting that this was one coin that most collectors would surely want to own:

> The 1997 National Law Enforcement Officers Memorial silver dollar is the final U.S. commemorative coin to be minted this year. Designed and sculpted by Alfred F. Maletsky, this silver dollar is unlike any you've purchased before. Its design beautifully illustrates both the joy of life and the sorrow when a life is taken too soon. These are also the emotions many people experience during visits to the Memorial. It may be hard to believe that so much history and emotion could be captured in a single silver dollar, but once you have added it to your collection, you'll realize that it has indeed been done.

Packaging options included the Signature Set with a Proof dollar, and "a beautiful Memorial cloisonné lapel pin and an official embroidered Memorial patch . . . in an elegant, royal blue presentation case, Insignia Sets are perfect for display, as gifts, or for personal remembrance." Orders were accepted by the Mint beginning on September 22, 1997, with deliveries scheduled to commence on December 15 of the same year. To wring the greatest amount out of the sales program, the coins were available all the way through December 15, 1998.

With many earlier modern commemoratives available on the open market for less than the original price, and with this issue having little or no numismatic or historical interest to most purchasers, sales were dismal. Less than 25 percent of the authorization was sold.

Key to Collecting

Once the distribution figures were published, the missed opportunity was realized. The market price rose to a sharp premium, where it remains today. Nearly all coins approach perfection in quality.

(1997) JACKIE ROBINSON COMMEMORATIVES

Distribution

1997-S silver dollar:
    30,180 Uncirculated
    and 110,002 Proof
1997-W gold $5:
    5,174 Uncirculated
    and 24,072 Proof

Whitman Coin Guide (WCG™)—1997-S Jackie Robinson $1

MS-65	MS-66	MS-67	MS-68	MS-69	MS-70
$110	$115	$120	$130	$145	$2,800
PF-65	PF-66	PF-67	PF-68	PF-69	PF-70
$85	$87	$90	$95	$110	$5,000

CERTIFIED POPULATIONS

MS-65	MS-66	MS-67	MS-68	MS-69	MS-70
0	3	29	121	1,242	61
PF-65	PF-66	PF-67	PF-68	PF-69	PF-70
2	8	41	156	1,081	3

1997-W Jackie Robinson Gold $5

MS-65	MS-66	MS-67	MS-68	MS-69	MS-70
$6,000	$6,100	$6,250	$6,400	$6,600	$8,500
PF-65	PF-66	PF-67	PF-68	PF-69	PF-70
$920	$930	$940	$950	$1,050	$3,750

CERTIFIED POPULATIONS

MS-65	MS-66	MS-67	MS-68	MS-69	MS-70
0	2	7	40	538	74
PF-65	PF-66	PF-67	PF-68	PF-69	PF-70
1	0	9	42	860	38

Points of Interest: The mintage of only 5,174 Uncirculated $5 gold coins is the lowest among modern commemoratives, creating the key to the series.

Subject of Commemoration: 50th anniversary of the first acceptance of a black player in a major league baseball game, Jack ("Jackie") Robinson being the hero.

Designs: Silver dollar: *Obverse*—Robinson in game action stealing home plate, evocative of a 1955 World Series play in a contest between the New York Yankees and the Brooklyn Dodgers. Designed by Mint engraver Alfred F. Maletsky. *Reverse*—50th anniversary logotype of the Jackie Robinson Foundation (a motif worn by all Major League Baseball players in the 1997 season) surrounded with lettering of two baseball accomplishments. Designed by Mint engraver T. James Ferrell. **$5 gold:** *Obverse*—Portrait of Robinson in his later years as a civil rights and political activist. *Reverse*—Detail of the seam on a baseball, Robinson's 1919–1972 life dates, and the inscription "Life of Courage." Designed by James Peed.

Mintage Data: Authorized on October 20, 1996 by Public Law 104-329, part of the United States Commemorative Coin Act of 1996, with a provision tied to Public Law 104-328 (for the Botanic Garden dollar). Coins could be minted for a full year beginning July 1, 1997. *Maximum authorized*—200,000 silver dollars, 100,000 gold $5. *Number minted*—Silver dollars, 1997-S 30,180 Uncirculated and 110,002 Proof; gold $5: 1997-W 5,174 Uncirculated, 24,072 Proof.

Original Cost and Issuer: Silver dollar: 1997-S Uncirculated, pre-issue $30, afterward $32; Proof $33, afterward $37. **$5 gold:** 1997-W Uncirculated, pre-issue through August 15, 1997, $180, afterward $205; Proof pre-issue $195, afterward $225. Surcharges were $10 for the dollar and $35 for the $5, earmarked for the Jackie Robinson Foundation. The surcharges were to go into effect after the Mint's production expenses were covered, and after the first $1,000,000 from silver dollar sales was paid to the *Botanic Garden Foundation*, a curious provision in the combined legislation for this and the Botanic Garden dollar. Issued by the U.S. Mint.

Jackie Robinson Honored

In 1997 two commemorative coins were issued to observe the 50th anniversary of "baseball's proudest moment," as Mint publicity observed, the debut of a black player in Major League Baseball. The watershed event took place at Ebbets Field on April 15, 1947. Earlier, Jackie Robinson had played a year with the Montreal Royals, a Brooklyn Dodgers farm club. Branch Rickey, manager of the Dodgers, selected Robinson for the historical occasion, for he was educated (UCLA graduate and the first there to earn four varsity letters in basketball, football, baseball and track) and a fine athlete, a man who was immune to any real criticism. Prejudice was hardly new to him. As an Army officer at Fort Hood, Texas, during World War II, he faced court martial when he refused to sit at the back of a military bus, "where Negroes belong." He was acquitted, and later was honorably discharged.

Robinson's 1947 debut on the Major League Baseball playing field was controversial, and during the rest of the season he was spat upon, called racial epithets, and suffered other abuses from prejudiced white onlookers. The race barrier had been broken, and there was no turning back. He was later awarded the coveted title of Rookie of the Year.

Congress authorized an issue of up to 200,000 silver dollars and 100,000 $5 gold coins. Anticipating wide interest, the Mint suggested that collectors act on the pre-issue offer as the numbers were limited.

Marketing was innovative, as it had been in recent times, as the U.S. Mint strove heroically to move commemoratives into the hands of buyers. One promotion featured a reproduction of a rare baseball trading card, with the distinction of being the first such card ever issued by the U.S. government.

Mint Director Philip N. Diehl enthused,

> In baseball terms, it's a triple play—a historic coin, a unique collector's card, and the Major League Baseball emblem commemorating the achievements of a great American and an extraordinary athlete.

No matter how important Robinson's legacy was, buyers again voted with their pocketbooks. Sales were wretched. The Jackie Robinson Foundation, which had hoped to receive millions of dollars from the $10 surcharge on the silver dollars and $35 on the gold coins, was distressed. Lobbyists went to work, and the U.S. Senate unanimously passed a bill to extend the sales date of the Robinson coins until December 31, 1998.

This was sent to the House of Representatives, where Michael Castle (Republican from Delaware). chairman of the House Banking Subcommittee on Domestic and International Monetary Policy, and one of the most numismatically aware members Congress has ever had, rejected the bill, noting in part, as reported in *Coin World*:

> I sympathize with the Robinson Foundation receiving less income than expected due to the poor sales of the Jackie Robinson coins. This is due to the fact that overall, too many poorly conceived commemorative coin programs have been imposed on the few collectors who constitute virtually the entire market for these coins. It has nothing to do with the relative merit of the causes that hope to be funded. Therefore, I cannot approve any extension of the sales period that is already mandated by law for the Robinson coins because this would unfairly compete with the sales by other scheduled coins, especially the current Black Patriots Memorial program, which is in even greater trouble and need.

As a curious footnote in this matter, in July 1998 the U.S. Mint reported that 222,933 Jackie Robinson silver dollars had been struck, or 22,933 more than legally authorized. The same document related that 48,500 $5 coins had been produced (from the authorization of 100,000).

The Uncirculated $5 gold coins were ultimately distributed to the extent of only 5,174 pieces, the lowest of any modern commemorative. Most went to the melting pot.

Key to Collecting

Although the Jackie Robinson coins were losers in the sales figures of the U.S. Mint, the small quantities issued made the silver dollars and half eagles winners in the investment sweepstakes, with the $5 coin taking top honors as the key issue among modern commemoratives. Today, each of these can be found without a problem, including the rare and pricey Uncirculated half eagle. Nearly all are in superb gem preservation.

(1997) Franklin D. Roosevelt $5 Gold

Distribution

1997-W: 11,805 Uncirculated and 29,233 Proof

Whitman Coin Guide (WCG™)—1997 Franklin D. Roosevelt Gold $5

MS-65	MS-66	MS-67	MS-68	MS-69	MS-70
$1,190	$1,220	$1,250	$1,280	$1,320	$2,250
PF-65	PF-66	PF-67	PF-68	PF-69	PF-70
$570	$580	$590	$600	$660	$3,500

CERTIFIED POPULATIONS

MS-65	MS-66	MS-67	MS-68	MS-69	MS-70
	0	1	15	615	201
PF-65	PF-66	PF-67	PF-68	PF-69	PF-70
1	1	9	82	1,332	31

Points of Interest: As Roosevelt ended the use of American gold coins in circulation and confiscated many from the public, depicting him on a *gold* coin is one of the most illogical situations in the history of commemoratives.

Subject of Commemoration: Franklin D. Roosevelt, president of the United States 1933–1945.

Designs: *Obverse*—Upper torso and head of Roosevelt facing right, depicting him as either a huge man or else wearing an overly large coat, based on one of the president's favorite photographs, taken when he was reviewing the U.S. Navy fleet in San Francisco Bay. Designed by T. James Ferrell of the Mint staff. *Reverse*—Presidential seal displayed at Roosevelt's 1933 inaugural. Designed by James Peed, and modeled by Thomas D. Rogers Sr.

Mintage Data: Authorized by Public Law 104-329, signed by President William J. Clinton on October 20, 1996. *Maximum authorized*—100,000. *Number minted*—1997-W 29,474 Uncirculated, 11,894 Proof.

Original Cost and Issuer: 1997-W Uncirculated, pre-issue $180, afterward $205; Proof pre-issue $195, afterward $225. Each included a surcharge of $35 for the Franklin Delano Roosevelt Memorial Commission. Issued by the U.S. Mint.

Roosevelt on a *Gold* Coin?

In 1933, newly inaugurated President Franklin D. Roosevelt suspended the mintage and paying out of U.S. gold coins, a foundation of the monetary system since 1795. Soon, he mandated that citizens turn in their gold coins to exchange them for paper money. At the time an ounce of gold was worth $20.67. Soon after Americans surrendered their coins, the Treasury Department raised the value of gold to $35 per ounce, depriving Depression era men and women of untold millions of dollars.

It was thus ironic that Roosevelt, of all people, should have a gold coin commemorating his life! Even more illogical, this was the only coin made, with no silver issues accompanying it. Public Law 104-329 provided for the minting of up to 100,000 gold $5 coins. The year 1997 does not seem to have been a special anniversary date of any kind, as it as 115 years after his birth, 64 years after his inauguration, and 52 years after his death. The reason for issuing this misguided "commemorative" seems to have been a combination of politics and greed. Orders were accepted by the U.S. Mint, beginning on May 15, 1997. Sales were poor, and less than half of the authorized quantity was sold. Because no silver coins were included, this produced the lowest-mintage commemorative event of modern times.

Key to Collecting

Since the mintages for both Uncirculated and Proof formats were low, the prices rose substantially on the aftermarket. Examples are easily available today and are nearly always in superb gem preservation.

(1998) BLACK REVOLUTIONARY WAR PATRIOTS DOLLARS

Distribution
1998-S: 37,210 Uncirculated
and 75,070 Proof

Whitman Coin Guide (WCG™)—1998 Black Revolutionary War Patriots $1

MS-65	MS-66	MS-67	MS-68	MS-69	MS-70
$190	$195	$200	$210	$225	$1,750
PF-65	PF-66	PF-67	PF-68	PF-69	PF-70
$120	$125	$130	$140	$150	$3,500

CERTIFIED POPULATIONS

MS-65	MS-66	MS-67	MS-68	MS-69	MS-70
0	0	4	54	923	158
PF-65	PF-66	PF-67	PF-68	PF-69	PF-70
2	5	32	128	465	6

Points of Interest: Nowhere on the coin is it mentioned that Attucks is black, or that he died as a patriot, or that a Memorial would be erected. Without such information, any owner of the coined would be clueless as to the significance of the motifs on either side.

Subject of Commemoration: Black Revolutionary War patriots and the 275th anniversary of the birth of Crispus Attucks, the first patriot killed in the infamous Boston Massacre in 1770, which was *not* part of the Revolutionary War, although it was among the many incidents that inflamed the passions of Americans.

Designs: *Obverse*—Artist's conception of Crispus Attucks. Designed by Mint engraver John Mercanti. *Reverse*—A black patriot family, a detail from the proposed Black Patriots Memorial. Ed Dwight, the Denver sculptor who designed the Memorial, is credited with the reverse motif on the coin, since it depicts that work.

Mintage Data: Authorized by Public Law 104-329, signed by President William J. Clinton on October 20, 1996. *Maximum authorized*—500,000. *Number minted*—1998-S 37,210 Uncirculated, 75,070 Proof.

Original Cost and Issuer: 1998-S Uncirculated, pre-issue $30, afterward $32; Proof $33, afterward $37. A portion of the $10 surcharge on each was earmarked for the Black Revolutionary War Patriots Foundation. Issued by the U.S. Mint.

The Boston Massacre

Collectors of early American prints treasure each of the several versions of Paul Revere's engraving depicting "The Bloody Massacre Perpetrated in King Street" on March 5, 1770. A line of rifle-wielding British soldiers is shown firing at local citizens, some of whom have collapsed in death. A black man, Crispus Attucks, was the first to fall, a fact well known to those who enjoy American history trivia.

To observe the 275th anniversary of the birth of this particular victim of the unfortunate attack, Congress passed a law providing for 500,000 commemorative silver dollars to be minted and sold, including a portion of the surcharge of $10 per coin to go toward erecting a Black Patriots Memorial in Washington, D.C. No likeness of Attucks survived, so it fell to Mint engraver John Mercanti to create an image of what he may have looked like, to form the obverse motif. The reverse illustrates a small detail from the proposed Memorial, which when finished would be a bronze sculpture, 90 feet long, rising from three to 7.5 feet in height.

Once again, the U.S. Mint tried its best to sell a commemorative that had little chance of success. The dollar did not commemorate a logical anniversary and was viewed as tapping the wallets of collectors in lieu of what should have been a public fund-raising event. Perhaps most important, the market was saturated with huge quantities of earlier modern coins that could be bought for less than the Mint had sold them for.

Various options were offered, including the Black Patriots Coin & Stamp Set with a Proof dollar packaged with four postage stamps featuring abolitionist Frederick Douglas, inventor Benjamin Banneker, soldier Salem Poor, and Underground Railroad conductor Harriet Tubman. Some misinformed publicity suggested that the Boston incident "triggered the Revolutionary War." (If so, the firing of the first shot in the Revolution was a long time coming—five years later, and in a different location.) The Boston Massacre was one of many incidents that inflamed American passions against the British.

The sales program laid an egg. Only 112,280 coins were minted out of 500,000 authorized, one of the poorest showings of the era.

Key to Collecting

Once again these coins became highly desirable when the low mintage figures were published. Examples remain expensive, and deservedly so. Nearly all are superb gems.

(1998) ROBERT F. KENNEDY DOLLARS

Distribution
1998-S: 106,422 Uncirculated
      and 99,020 Proof

Whitman Coin Guide (WCG™)—1998 Robert F. Kennedy $1

MS-65	MS-66	MS-67	MS-68	MS-69	MS-70
$40	$42	$45	$48	$55	$675
PF-65	PF-66	PF-67	PF-68	PF-69	PF-70
$45	$50	$55	$60	$65	$1,900

CERTIFIED POPULATIONS

MS-65	MS-66	MS-67	MS-68	MS-69	MS-70
0	2	17	174	2,343	268
PF-65	PF-66	PF-67	PF-68	PF-69	PF-70
1	2	16	117	1,081	11

Points of Interest: The inscriptions and the only date on the coin, 1998, give the viewer little indication of why Kennedy is being commemorated, save for the word JUSTICE on the reverse.

Subject of Commemoration: 30th anniversary of the death of Robert F. Kennedy, attorney general of the United States appointed by his brother, President John F. Kennedy.

Designs: *Obverse*—Portrait of Robert F. Kennedy. Thomas D. Rogers Sr. designed both sides. *Reverse*—Eagle perched on a shield with JUSTICE above, Senate seal to lower left.

Mintage Data: Authorized by Public Law 103-328, signed by President William J. Clinton on September 29, 1994. *Maximum authorized*—500,000. *Number minted*—1998-S 106,422 Uncirculated, 99,020 Proof.

Original Cost and Issuer: Pre-issue $30, afterward $32; Proof $33, afterward $37. A portion of the $10 surcharge on each was earmarked for the Robert F. Kennedy Memorial. Issued by the U.S. Mint.

Popular American

Robert F. Kennedy, born in 1925 and appointed attorney general by his brother, John F. Kennedy, when he became president in 1981, acquitted himself with distinction in the post, to the surprise of many detractors, some of whom noted that the youthful senator and lawyer had never tried a case in court. Civil rights became a passion, and for this Robert is especially remembered today. On June 8, 1968, he was shot and killed by Sirhan Sirhan, who encountered him in a back passage near the kitchen of the Ambassador Hotel in Los Angeles, where Kennedy was celebrating his win as a presidential candidate in the California primary.

Congress authorized the issuance of a half million commemorative silver dollars dated 1998, the 30th anniversary of Kennedy's death. The Mint, again faced with a tough marketing challenge, offered the coin with praise for the design, the man, and the memorial.

Again the Mint tried hard, and again the market proved resistant. Just slightly more than 40 percent of the 500,000 authorized coins were sold.

Key to Collecting

Upon their publication the mintage figures were viewed as being attractively low from a numismatic viewpoint. Examples are easily found today and are usually superb gems.

(1999) Dolley Madison Dollars

Distribution
1999-P: 89,104 Uncirculated
and 224,403 Proof

Whitman Coin Guide (WCG™)—1999 Dolley Madison $1

MS-65	MS-66	MS-67	MS-68	MS-69	MS-70
$60	$62	$65	$70	$75	$310
PF-65	PF-66	PF-67	PF-68	PF-69	PF-70
$52	$55	$58	$65	$75	$600

CERTIFIED POPULATIONS

MS-65	MS-66	MS-67	MS-68	MS-69	MS-70
1	2	8	61	1,596	544
PF-65	PF-66	PF-67	PF-68	PF-69	PF-70
0	0	17	93	2,090	69

Points of Interest: The design was made by a for-profit firm in the private sector, Tiffany & Co., jewelers, who were permitted to put their trademark on each side, but not the full name of the business, as requested originally. No charge was made for the art. Frustrating to numismatists, even in the 19th century, Tiffany generally did not credit its artists on the many medals it issued. No credit for the artists was given on this coin, although Mint engravers who prepared the models were recognized.

Subject of Commemoration: 150th anniversary of the death of First Lady Dolley Madison.

Designs: *Obverse*—Portrait of Dolley Madison as depicted near the ice house (in the style of classic pergola) on the grounds of the family estate, Montpelier. A bouquet of cape jasmines is to the left. Designed by Tiffany & Co. and modeled by Mint engraver T. James Ferrell. The T&Co. logo is in a flower petal. *Reverse*—Angular view of the front of Montpelier, complete with landscaping. Designed by Tiffany & Co. and modeled by Mint engraver Thomas D. Rogers, Sr. The T&Co. logo is at the base of the trees to the right.

Mintage Data: Authorized by Public Law 104-329, signed by President William J. Clinton on October 20, 1996. *Maximum authorized*—500,000. *Number minted*—1999-P 89,104 Uncirculated and 224,403 Proof.

Original Cost and Issuer: Uncirculated, pre-issue through February 9, 1999, $30, afterward $32; Proof $33, afterward $37. A portion of the $10 surcharge on each was earmarked for the National Trust for Historic Preservation. Issued by the U.S. Mint.

Dolley in the White House

If the myth that Martha Washington was the subject for the 1792 silver half disme is discarded, Dolley Madison, wife of President James Madison, became the first of the first ladies to be depicted on a legal tender U.S. coin. Long spelled as "Dolly" by historians and the public alike, the spelling was later corrected to Dolley. Mrs. Madison served as hostess at the White House for 16 years, during the term of widowed President Thomas Jefferson, and then during her husband's administration. When British troops sacked Washington, D.C., in 1814 and set the White House on fire, she rescued Gilbert Stuart's painting of George Washington by breaking the frame and rolling up the canvas, and carrying it off to safety.

To commemorate the 250th anniversary of her death, Congress provided for the minting of 500,000 commemorative silver dollars, with part of the $10 surcharge to go to the National Trust for Historic Preservation. This was a change from the original proposal to honor President James Madison instead. The Citizens Advisory Committee for Commemorative Coins remonstrated that he had recently (1993) appeared on three different commemorative coins, and he should not be honored again so soon. Not to worry. Dolley Madison came to the forefront and probably sold more coins than her over-commemorated husband could have done on a second go-around. This scenario is not widely known, except to readers of numismatic publications.

In a remarkable departure from tradition, the Dolley Madison designs were created by Tiffany & Company, leading jewelers in the private sector, as specifically recommended by the National Trust for Historical Preservation. Their T&Co. logotype was allowed to be placed on each side—a first in the history of legal tender U.S. coinage. Although this could have been controversial, it was not. The designs, viewed as among the most beautiful in the modern commemorative series, quickly drew the attention of buyers. In the White House on January 11, 1999, successor First Lady Hilary Rodham Clinton conducted a ceremony unveiling the coin, and mentioning Dolley Madison's legacy. She noted that while Mrs. Madison was the first lady first to appear on a coin, Martha Washington had been depicted on Silver Certificates in the 19th century.

Though the entire authorization for the dollars was not used, more than 300,000 coins found buyers—a better showing than many commemorative dollars of the period.

Key to Collecting

The Dolley Madison dollars have been popular with collectors ever since they were first sold. Examples can be obtained with little effort and are usually superb gems.

(1999) GEORGE WASHINGTON DEATH BICENTENNIAL $5 GOLD

Distribution

1999-W: 22,511 Uncirculated and 41,693 Proof

Whitman Coin Guide (WCG™)—1999-W George Washington Death Bicentennial $5

MS-65	MS-66	MS-67	MS-68	MS-69	MS-70
$525	$535	$550	$480	$600	$2,600
PF-65	PF-66	PF-67	PF-68	PF-69	PF-70
$480	$490	$500	$525	$600	$2,000

CERTIFIED POPULATIONS

MS-65	MS-66	MS-67	MS-68	MS-69	MS-70
1	0	0	33	1,196	363
PF-65	PF-66	PF-67	PF-68	PF-69	PF-70
0	2	2	35	1,754	18

Points of Interest: The designs were originally created in the hope they would be used on the 1932 Washington quarter.

Subject of Commemoration: The 200th anniversary of George Washington's death on December 14, 1799.

Designs: Laura Garden Fraser's rejected design for the 1932 quarter dollar was resurrected to create this coin. *Obverse*—the portrait of Washington inspired by the bust modeled in 1785 for French sculptor Jean Antoine Houdon. *Reverse*—a perched eagle with feathers widely separated at left and right.

Mintage Data: Authorized on October 20, 1996 by Public Law 104-329, part of the United States Commemorative Coin Act of 1996. *Maximum authorized*—100,000 pieces (both formats combined). *Number minted*—1999-W gold $5: 22,511 Uncirculated and 41,693 Proof.

Original Cost and Issuer: Uncirculated versions were priced at $180 if ordered by June 25, 1999, and $195 after that. Proof coins were priced at $195 for early orders and $225 after June 25. A two-coin set was priced at $350, increasing to $399. Issued by the U.S. Mint.

Father of Our Country

At his home, Mount Vernon, on the bank of the Potomac River in Virginia, George Washington died on December 14, 1799. His passing was widely mourned. Among the best known mementoes are the silver (mostly) funeral medals sold in 1800 by Jacob Perkins, and featuring the sentiment: HE IS IN GLORY, THE WORLD IN TEARS. By that time, Washington had been depicted on several dozen different varieties of tokens and medals. The earliest to bear his true likeness is the Manly medal distributed in 1790. After his passing, our first president was eulogized as the Father of Our Country. In numismatics he became a favorite subject, and many coins, tokens, medals, and paper money issues were produced, continuing to the familiar Washington quarter and $1 bill of today.

Congress authorized the minting of a $5 commemorative gold coin to observe the 200th anniversary of Washington's death. The legislation included what many called a pork barrel provision—$10 from each coin sale would go to the Mount Vernon Ladies

Association, which cares for Washington's home today. There is no question that the organization is a fine one. The problem is that collectors dislike being forced to donate to this or any other cause when buying coins.

The obverse and reverse motifs were adapted from models created by Laura Gardin Fraser and submitted for consideration during the development of the Washington quarter dollar in 1932. Secretary of the Treasury Andrew W. Mellon rejected her design in favor of one by John Flanagan. Many artists and some numismatists at the time said Fraser's art would have been the better choice. Today, opinion is still divided on the subject.

Although sales fell short of expectations, the coins were well received by numismatists, and the design was highly admired.

Key to Collecting
Readily available in any high grade desired.

(1999) YELLOWSTONE NATIONAL PARK DOLLARS

Distribution
1999-P: 82,563 Uncirculated
and 187,595 Proof

Whitman Coin Guide (WCG™)—1999 Yellowstone National Park $1

MS-65	MS-66	MS-67	MS-68	MS-69	MS-70
$65	$70	$75	$80	$90	$450
PF-65	PF-66	PF-67	PF-68	PF-69	PF-70
$55	$60	$65	$70	$80	$1,500

CERTIFIED POPULATIONS

MS-65	MS-66	MS-67	MS-68	MS-69	MS-70
1	1	9	60	1,487	253
PF-65	PF-66	PF-67	PF-68	PF-69	PF-70
1	8	49	181	1,506	11

Points of Interest: The coin bears the irrelevant date of 1999—the 125th anniversary was actually celebrated in 1997. In any event, the anniversary is not mentioned on the coin, nor are the words "National Park."

Subject of Commemoration: 125th anniversary of the establishment of Yellowstone National Park, an event that was observed 1997.

Designs: *Obverse*—An unidentified geyser (not the famed Old Faithful, for the terrain is different) is shown in action. YELLOWSTONE is above, with other inscriptions to the left center and below, as illustrated. Designed by Edgar Z. Steever IV of the Mint staff. *Reverse*—A bison is shown, facing left. In the background is a mountain range with sun and resplendent rays. William C. Cousins of the Mint staff prepared the design, an adaptation of the seal of the Department of the Interior.

Mintage Data: Authorized on October 20, 1996, by Public Law 104-329, part of the United States Commemorative Coin Act of 1996. The catch-all legislation authorized seven commemoratives to be issued from 1997 to 1999. *Maximum authorized*—500,000 (both formats combined). *Number minted*—82,563 Uncirculated plus 187,595 Proof.

Original Cost and Issuer: Coins were available from July 16, 1999, to July 15, 2000. Proof dollars were available for the pre-issue price of $33 through August 29, 1999, and $37 afterward. Uncirculated dollars were available for $30 pre-issue and $32 afterward. The surcharge of $10 (part of the purchase price of each coin) was earmarked for the Yellowstone National Park and half for the National Park Foundation. Issued by the U.S. Mint.

The First National Park

Yellowstone National Park, the first of many such parks set aside for the public good, was established by Congress on March 1, 1872. Comprising 3,472 square miles, it is located in the northwest corner of Wyoming, with a smaller portion extending into Idaho and Montana. Today it is a magnet for tourists, who enjoy watching Old Faithful and several other geysers, boating on Yellowstone Lake, and appreciating the natural surroundings.

Congress authorized the issuance of 500,000 commemorative silver dollars to observe the 125th anniversary of the park in 1997. Made in Uncirculated and Proof formats, these listed at $33 and $37 each, the price including a $10 surcharge. Richard Giedroyc, in *Coin World*, April 11, 2000, noted that the Yellowstone proceeds would go to park maintenance and improvements, research projects, and archaeological excavations. While he pointed out that virtually all U.S. commemoratives were issued to finance something at collector expense, some of the modern series have been such failures that Congress has passed legislation to compensate the groups who expected to profit from the sale.

In any event, the coins were released two years after the anniversary date. By this time any whispers from the lightly observed occasion had long since faded away. Only slightly more than half of the authorized quantity found buyers.

Key to Collecting

Easily obtainable in the numismatic marketplace, nearly always in high grades. Investors are attracted to coins certified as MS-70 or PF-70, but few can tell the difference between these and coins at the 69 level. Only a tiny fraction of mintage has ever been certified.

(2000) LIBRARY OF CONGRESS BICENTENNIAL ISSUES

Distribution

2000-P silver dollar:
    52,771 Uncirculated
    and 196,900 Proof
2000-W bimetallic $10:
    6,683 Uncirculated
    and 27,167 Proof

Whitman Coin Guide (WCG™)—2000-P Library of Congress Bicentennial $1

MS-65	MS-66	MS-67	MS-68	MS-69	MS-70
$50	$55	$60	$65	$75	$650
PF-65	PF-66	PF-67	PF-68	PF-69	PF-70
$42	$45	$50	$55	$65	$4,350

CERTIFIED POPULATIONS

MS-65	MS-66	MS-67	MS-68	MS-69	MS-70
0	0	0	23	1,285	417
PF-65	PF-66	PF-67	PF-68	PF-69	PF-70
0	6	30	177	1,279	4

2000-W Library of Congress Bicentennial Bimetallic $10

MS-65	MS-66	MS-67	MS-68	MS-69	MS-70
$3,950	$4,000	$4,100	$4,200	$4,400	$5,325
PF-65	PF-66	PF-67	PF-68	PF-69	PF-70
$1,295	$1,325	$1,350	$1,400	$1,500	$5,000

CERTIFIED POPULATIONS

MS-65	MS-66	MS-67	MS-68	MS-69	MS-70
0	0	1	9	893	546
PF-65	PF-66	PF-67	PF-68	PF-69	PF-70
0	0	1	40	1,295	22

Points of Interest: The $10 is the first gold/platinum bimetallic coin struck by the U.S. Mint.

Subject of Commemoration: The bicentennial of the Library of Congress on April 24, 2000.

Designs: Silver dollar: *Obverse*—An open book, with its spine resting on a closed book, with the torch of the Library of Congress dome behind. By Thomas D. Rogers Jr. *Reverse*—The dome part of the Library of Congress. Designed by John Mercanti. **Bimetallic $10:** *Obverse*—The torch of the Library of Congress dome, designed by John Mercanti. *Reverse*—an eagle surrounded by a wreath, designed by Thomas D. Rogers Jr.

Mintage Data: Authorized by Public Law 105-268, signed by President William J. Clinton on October 19, 1996. *Maximum authorized*—500,000 silver dollars, 200,000 bimetallic $10. *Number minted*—silver dollars, 2000-P 52,771 Uncirculated and 196,900 Proof; bimetallic $10, 6,683 Uncirculated and 27,167 Proof.

Original Cost and Issuer: Silver dollar: Proof $28 pre-issue price (through June 6, 2000), $32 afterward; Uncirculated $25 pre-issue price, $27 afterward. **Bimetallic $10:** Proof $395 pre-issue, $425 afterward; Uncirculated $380 pre-issue, $405 afterward. Issued by the U.S. Mint.

The Library of Congress

The Library of Congress, located across the street from the U.S. Capitol in Washington, celebrated its 200th anniversary on April 24, 2000. The institution was founded in 1800, the first year that the government operated in what had earlier been called the Federal City. During the 1790s the seat of government had been Philadelphia. In 1814 the Library was burned by the British, who also destroyed the Capitol and the White House. This was a part of the land campaign in the War of 1812, that ended when Baltimore successfully resisted invasion (memorialized by the *Star Spangled Banner*), and the British sailed home. Soon afterward, Thomas Jefferson sold his personal library of 6,487 books to the government for $23,950, thus forming the nucleus of the new Library of Congress.

Today, the Library is a vast repository that includes 18 million books and more than 100 million other items, including periodicals, films, prints, photographs, and recordings.

The Library of Congress Bicentennial coins were produced to honor the anniversary. Two denominations were made: a dollar in silver and a uniquely configured bimetallic $10 coin with a center of platinum and a border of gold. Mint staff engravers designed the coins with motifs intended to be representative of the Library and its objectives. On April 24, 2000, a special launch ceremony for the coins and related postage stamps was held in the Great Hall of the Thomas Jefferson Building of the Library.

Numismatic response was tepid at best, perhaps because the designs were viewed as having little in the way of artistic beauty.

Key to Collecting

Each of the Library of Congress coins is readily available in the marketplace today, nearly always of the superb gem quality as issued.

(2000) LEIF ERICSON MILLENNIUM DOLLARS

Distribution
2000-P: 28,150 Uncirculated
    and 144,748 Proof

Whitman Coin Guide (WCG™)—2000 Leif Ericson Millinneum $1

MS-65	MS-66	MS-67	MS-68	MS-69	MS-70
$105	$110	$115	$125	$135	$850
PF-65	PF-66	PF-67	PF-68	PF-69	PF-70
$70	$72	$75	$80	$95	$3,000

CERTIFIED POPULATIONS

MS-65	MS-66	MS-67	MS-68	MS-69	MS-70
0	0	1	39	1,366	278
PF-65	PF-66	PF-67	PF-68	PF-69	PF-70
0	3	16	173	1,348	5

Points of Interest: Issued in cooperation with a foreign government, the Republic of Iceland, which also sponsored its own coin, struck at the Philadelphia Mint (but with no mintmark), a silver 1,000 krónur depicting on the obverse Stirling Calder's 1930 sculpture of Ericson, and on the reverse, A stylized eagle, dragon, bull, and giant adapted from the Iceland coat of arms. The coin was designed by Thröstur Magnússon.

Subject of Commemoration: The 1,000th anniversary of the voyage of Viking explorer Leif Ericson to the New World, approximately in the year 1000.

Designs: *Obverse*—Portrait of Leif Ericson, an artist's conception, as no actual image survives—based on the image used on the Iceland 1 krónur coin. The helmeted head of the explorer is shown facing right. Designed by staff engraver John Mercanti. *Reverse*—A Viking long ship with high prow under full sail, FOUNDER OF THE NEW WORLD above, other inscriptions below. Designed by T. James Ferrell of the Mint staff.

Mintage Data: Authorized under Public Law 106-126. *Maximum authorized*—500,000. *Number minted*—28,150 Uncirculated, 144,748 proof.

Original Cost and Issuer: Coins were available from June 21, 2000, to February 28, 2001. Proof dollars were available for the pre-issue price of $33 through August 4, 2000, and $37 afterward. Uncirculated dollars were available for $30 pre-issue and $32 afterward. $10 of the proceeds from each coin was a surcharge given to the Leifur Eiriksson Foundation for funding student exchanges between United States and Iceland. Issued by the U.S. Mint.

Ericson and His Tradition

While popular wisdom often has it that Christopher Columbus "discovered" America in 1492, actually he was a latecomer. Leif Ericson and his crew of Norwegian Viking sailors left home around 1000 A.D. and sailed toward Greenland. They were blown southward, off course to areas along the eastern coast of what is now Canada, where they set up a camp in Newfoundland. They visited a district on the mainland farther to the south designated as Vinland, from the profusion of wild grapes growing there, the land believed to have been today's Cape Cod. Salmon and grain were also in abundance there. Even a brief perusal of modern information about Viking explorations in North America will yield much information and many theories. Possibly, the adventurers also went as far west as the present-day Wisconsin and Minnesota.

To commemorate the millennium of the approximate year of 1000, Congress authorized the minting of commemorative coins in cooperation with the Republic of Iceland. Under a special program the U.S. Mint offered a dollar coin in both Uncirculated and mirror Proof finishes, and an Icelandic silver 1,000 krónur in Proof format. Expectations were high, and a limit of 500,000 was set for the dollars (both formats combined) and 150,000 for the Icelandic coins. Response fell far short, and only a fraction of those figures was coined. In 2000, most Americans were preoccupied with other things, and little notice was paid to this anniversary.

Key to Collecting

These coins are readily available in the marketplace today.

(2001) American Buffalo Commemoratives

Distribution
2001-D: 227,131 Uncirculated
2001-P: 272,869 Proof

Whitman Coin Guide (WCG™)—2001-D American Buffalo $1

MS-65	MS-66	MS-67	MS-68	MS-69	MS-70
$255	$260	$265	$270	$280	$1,070

CERTIFIED POPULATIONS

MS-65	MS-66	MS-67	MS-68	MS-69	MS-70
1	6	57	501	11,580	917

2001-P American Buffalo $1 Proof

PF-65	PF-66	PF-67	PF-68	PF-69	PF-70
$260	$280	$285	$290	$310	$1,400

CERTIFIED POPULATIONS

PF-65	PF-66	PF-67	PF-68	PF-69	PF-70
2	5	60	526	13,083	163

Points of Interest: The design was not original, but was entirely copied from another coin. One of the hottest-selling modern commemorative issues. The Treasury Department capitalized on this popularity by reiterating the design on the American Buffalo $50 gold bullion coins first issued in 2006 (not commemoratives and thus not further discussed here).

Subject of Commemoration: The National Museum of the American Indian, Washington, D.C., which received a portion of the sale proceeds.

Designs: A copy of the 1913 Indian Head / Buffalo nickel, now with modified inscriptions on the reverse. *Obverse*—portrait of a Native American facing right. *Reverse*—a bison standing, facing left. Designed by James Earle Fraser (1913 version), modified by Mint engravers.

Mintage Data: *Maximum authorized*—500,000 under Public Law 106-375, October 27, 2000. *Number minted*—Philadelphia Mint Proofs: 272,869; Denver Mint coins: 227,131.

Original Cost and Issuer: Denver: $30 pre-issue (orders postmarked or received no later than July 25, 2001), regularly $32. Philadelphia Proof: $33 pre-issue, regularly $37. Two-coin set $59.95 pre-issue, $64.95 regularly. 2001-D dollar with replica of a Series 1899 $5 Silver Certificate and two postage stamps, limited to 50,000 sets, $54.95 pre-issue, $59.95 regularly. Issued by the U.S. Mint.

Rebirth of the Buffalo Design

James Earle Fraser's design for the 1913 Indian Head / Buffalo nickel, actually depicting an American *bison*, has long been a numismatic favorite. On September 28, 1999, a ground-breaking ceremony was held for the Smithsonian Institution's National Museum of the American Indian, on the National Mall between the Capitol and the Washington Monument. The secretary of the Treasury authorized a special commemorative dollar to honor the new museum, assuring its popularity by copying the Buffalo nickel design. For many Americans, the buffalo, as nearly everyone calls the animal, is the best-known animal of the plains, in the era when Native Americans populated the territory.

Mint engravers modified James Earle Fraser's design for the 1913 Indian Head / Buffalo nickel, and on the reverse rearranged the lettering, now to include In God We Trust. Coins with Uncirculated or regular finish were made at the Denver Mint, and Proofs were struck at Philadelphia. The term "American Buffalo Commemorative" was used to describe the coins. In late spring 2001, the Mint began accepting advance orders at special discount prices. On May 4, the coin was launched in a ceremony held at the Denver Mint. Examples were made available to buyers on June 11.

On June 21, the Mint announced that all had been sold out. The market price rose immediately, and has stayed at a strong premium ever since.

Key to Collecting

Both varieties of the 2001 American Buffalo were carefully produced to high standards of quality. Nearly all examples today grade at high levels, including MS-70 and PF-70, these ultra-grades commanding a sharp premium for investors. Coins grading 68 or 69 often have little or any real difference in quality and would seem to be the best buys.

(2001) CAPITOL VISITOR CENTER COMMEMORATIVES

Distribution

2001-P half dollar:
    99,157 Uncirculated
    and 77,962 Proof

2001-P dollar:
    35,380 Uncirculated
    and 143,793 Proof

2001-W gold $5:
    6,761 Uncirculated
    and 27,652 Proof

Whitman Coin Guide (WCG™)—2001-P Capitol Visitor Center 50¢

MS-65	MS-66	MS-67	MS-68	MS-69	MS-70
$16	$18	$20	$22	$33	$1,250
PF-65	PF-66	PF-67	PF-68	PF-69	PF-70
$18	$19	$20	$22	$34	

CERTIFIED POPULATIONS

MS-65	MS-66	MS-67	MS-68	MS-69	MS-70
1	1	8	52	2,430	1647
PF-65	PF-66	PF-67	PF-68	PF-69	PF-70
0	0	17	132	1,585	0

2001-P Capitol Visitor Center $1

MS-65	MS-66	MS-67	MS-68	MS-69	MS-70
$40	$42	$44	$50	$55	$1,250
PF-65	PF-66	PF-67	PF-68	PF-69	PF-70
$45	$48	$50	$55	$115	$2,450

CERTIFIED POPULATIONS

MS-65	MS-66	MS-67	MS-68	MS-69	MS-70
0	1	8	79	1,803	370
PF-65	PF-66	PF-67	PF-68	PF-69	PF-70
1	3	21	118	2,136	23

2001-W Capitol Visitor Center Gold $5

MS-65	MS-66	MS-67	MS-68	MS-69	MS-70
$2,200	$2,225	$2,250	$2,275	$2,350	$2,525
PF-65	PF-66	PF-67	PF-68	PF-69	PF-70
$470	$480	$490	$500	$560	$1,250

CERTIFIED POPULATIONS

MS-65	MS-66	MS-67	MS-68	MS-69	MS-70
0	0	2	21	1,657	535
PF-65	PF-66	PF-67	PF-68	PF-69	PF-70
0	2	4	31	1,520	70

Points of Interest: The designs are redundant—one, or at most two, coins could have displayed the same information.

Subject of Commemoration: The proposal to erect a Capitol Visitor Center in Washington, D.C., at the time a concept.

Designs: Clad half dollar: *Obverse*—The north wing of the original Capitol (burned by the British in 1814) is shown superimposed on a plan view of the present building, a concept that will render the viewer clueless, because there is no explanation except the inscription U.S. CAPITOL 1800, which does not explain the larger building. The obligatory IN GOD WE TRUST is above the building. Surrounding is a circle of stars, outside of which is LIBERTY and the date 2001. The designer was Dean McMullen, a retired graphic artist in the private sector, in Portland, Oregon. *Reverse*—Although two well-known sculptor-artists, Alex Shagin and Marcel Jovine, collaborated on this, the result could just as well have been done on a computer graphics program, for in consists only of a mixture of letters, numbers, and five-pointed stars, with no art in the scenic or illustrative sense. Within a circle of 16 stars are inscriptions referring to the first meeting of the Senate and House, plus E PLURIBUS UNUM tossed in. Around the border are the name of our country and the denomination. **Silver dollar:** *Obverse*—The original Capitol is shown with the date 1800, and a much smaller later Capitol with the date 2001—a variation on the same theme as used on the half dollar. Marika Somogyi was the artist. *Reverse*—The reverse, by Mint sculptor-engraver John Mercanti, presents a rather stocky eagle reminiscent of the same artist's reverse for the 1986 silver bullion "Eagle" dollar. In the present incarnation, the national bird wears a ribbon lettered U.S. CAPITOL VISITOR CENTER. **$5 gold:** Both sides are the work of Elizabeth Jones, distinguished former chief engraver at the Mint. Her talents are not tested here. *Obverse*—section of a Corinthian column. *Reverse*—yet another iteration of the 1800 Capitol (interestingly, with slightly different architectural details and proportions than seen on the other coins). Appropriate inscriptions are on both sides.

Mintage Data: Authorized by Public Law 106-126, signed by President William J. Clinton on December 6, 1999. *Maximum authorized*—clad half dollar 750,000; silver dollar 500,000; gold $5 100,000. *Number minted*—clad half dollar: 99,157 Uncirculated and 77,962 Proofs; silver dollar: 35,380 Uncirculated and 143,793 Proofs; gold $5: 6,761 Uncirculated and 27,652 Proofs.

Original Cost and Issuer: Half dollar: Proof, $10.75 pre-issue price through April 20, 2001, $11.50 afterward, Uncirculated pre-issue $7.75, $8.50 afterward. Silver dollar: Proof pre-issue $29, $33 afterward, Uncirculated pre-issue $27, $29 afterward. Gold $5: Proof pre-issue $177, $207 afterward, Uncirculated pre-issue $175, $200 afterward. Coins were available from the Mint from February 29, 2001 to March 1, 2002. Special packaging was available for a slight extra cost. Issued by the U.S. Mint.

The Capitol Visitor Center

In 1991, Congress decided that it would be nice if a Visitor Center be established near the U.S. Capitol building, and if coin collectors would help pay for it with surcharges. Three coins were decided upon: a clad half dollar ($3 surcharge), silver dollar ($10), and $5 gold coin ($35).

It was said that the Capitol Visitor Center would offer free exhibits, films, and would eliminate lengthy waits. As to the waits, presumably many would still want to visit the Capitol itself, for which no plan to eliminate waiting time was presented. It was estimated that about five million people each year sought to take a look at the inside. After the September 11, 2001, terrorist attack on the World Trade Center in New York City and the Pentagon in the District of Columbia, security at the Capitol was heightened—and the concept of the Visitor Center became even more important.

If there was a potential highlight for what proved to be yet another underperforming commemorative issue—with sales far below projections—it was that Elizabeth Jones, former chief engraver at the Mint, was tapped to do the obverse of the $5. The result, however, was hardly a showcase for the remarkable talent she had shown earlier on the 1986 Statue of Liberty $5 and the stunning 1988 Olympiad coin of the same denomination. It simply illustrated the top part of a Corinthian column.

The designs on all three coins were repetitive, each showing the 1800 Capitol building, and two showing the current Capitol (plus Ms. Jones's view of a column on the current Capitol). Such lack of originality did not play well with collectors—it seemed that the lessons of history as evidenced by the poorly reviewed 1991 Mount Rushmore trio had not been assimilated. Buyers stayed away in droves, it might be said, and only a small percentage of the authorized coins found buyers.

Key to Collecting
Today, the Capitol Visitor Center commemoratives are readily available on the market, nearly always in the same gem quality as issued, although the Uncirculated $5 is less often seen than the others. After the distribution figure of only 6,761 was released for that coin, buyers clamored to acquire them, and the price rose sharply. Today, it still sells at one of the greatest premiums of any modern commemorative.

(2002) OLYMPIC WINTER GAMES COMMEMORATIVES

Distribution
2002-D dollar: 40,257
2002-P dollar: 166,864 Proof
2002-W gold $5:
    10,585 Uncirculated
    and 32,877 Proof

Whitman Coin Guide (WCG™)—2002-D Olympic Olympic $1

MS-65	MS-66	MS-67	MS-68	MS-69	MS-70
$40	$42	$45	$50	$55	$425

CERTIFIED POPULATIONS

MS-65	MS-66	MS-67	MS-68	MS-69	MS-70
0	0	1	33	1,935	438

2002-P Olympic Winter Games $1 Proof

PF-65	PF-66	PF-67	PF-68	PF-69	PF-70
$44	$45	$47	$50	$63	$1,450

CERTIFIED POPULATIONS

PF-65	PF-66	PF-67	PF-68	PF-69	PF-70
2	4	15	107	1,805	25

2002-W Olympic Winter Games Gold $5

MS-65	MS-66	MS-67	MS-68	MS-69	MS-70
$600	$620	$640	$660	$700	$950
PF-65	PF-66	PF-67	PF-68	PF-69	PF-70
$520	$540	$565	$580	$640	$1,200

CERTIFIED POPULATIONS

MS-65	MS-66	MS-67	MS-68	MS-69	MS-70
1	0	0	7	1,261	367
PF-65	PF-66	PF-67	PF-68	PF-69	PF-70
0	1	0	14	996	54

Points of Interest: The mintages were remarkably low, considering the worldwide interest in Olympic events. The reverse cityscape included the great Mormon Tabernacle in Salt Lake City. Several design elements are made of geometric shapes and may be puzzling to any observer who does not have a sheet explaining the motifs.

Subject of Commemoration: The 2002 Winter Olympic Games in Salt Lake City, Utah.

Designs: Silver dollar: *Obverse*—A series of angles is supposed to represent a ice crystal, but the disconnected elements bear no resemblance to any crystal seen in nature. Five interlocked Olympic rings and inscriptions complete the picture, including XIX OLYMPIC WINTER GAMES. John Mercanti was the sculptor-engraver. *Reverse*—The skyline of Salt Lake City is shown with exaggerated dimensions, with the rugged Wasatch Mountains in the distance with either a lightning bolt or an Etch-a-Sketch design in the sky overhead. The cityscape included the outline of the Mormon Temple, causing some complaint that a church should not be depicted on a federal coin, but by the time this was noticed, preparation of masters and dies was already underway. In case you missed it on the obverse, the XIX OLYMPIC GAMES is repeated on the reverse. Get it, stupid? Donna Weaver of the Mint staff was the artist. **$5 gold:** *Obverse*—The curious ice crystal dominates, here superimposed over another geometric creation supposed to represent "Rhythm of the Land," but not identified. That's it, except for the date, SALT LAKE, and the mandatory LIBERTY and IN GOD WE TRUST. Donna Weaver claimed credit for the work on both sides. *Reverse*—The outline of the Olympic cauldron is shown, with geometric sails above said to be flames. Lettering completes the picture.

Mintage Data: Authorized by Public Law 106-435, the Salt Lake Olympic Winter Games Commemorative Coin Act, signed by President William J. Clinton on November 6, 2000. Production was accomplished at three mints: Denver and Philadelphia for the $1 and West Point for the $5. *Maximum authorized*—silver dollar 400,000; $5 gold 80,000. *Number minted*—silver dollar 2002-D 40,257; 2002-P 166,864 Proofs; $5 gold 10,585 Uncirculated, 32,877 Proofs.

Original Cost and Issuer: Orders were accepted beginning in October 2001 for delivery in 2002. Pre-issue price for the Proof dollar was $33, raised to $37, while the Proof

$5 was priced at $195 for early birds and $225 for latecomers. Uncirculated dollars were priced at $30 and $32, and the $5 at $180 and $205. A complete set of four coins was available for $440 to early orders, $475 later. Issued by the U.S. Mint.

Coins for the XIX Olympic Winter Games

In February 2002, Salt Lake City, Utah, was the focal point for the XIX Olympic Winter Games, a quadrennial event. Various snow and ice sport competitions were held for entrants from many countries, in an event that spanned 17 days. Alpine events were held in the mountains nearby.

Congress authorized a commemorative silver dollar and $5 gold coin for the games, adding a $10 surcharge to the dollar and $35 to the $5 to help support the 2002 event. The design of the coins attracted little favorable notice outside of advertising publicity, and, once again, sales were dismal—all the more surprising, for Olympic coins often attract international buyers. In the meantime, the U.S. Mint, seeking to add spirit and originality to its coins, was implementing the Artistic Infusion Program, in which outside artists and sculptors could submit designs for coins. (This bore excellent results a few years later with redesigns of the Jefferson nickel.)

Key to Collecting

Although the mintage of the Uncirculated $5 in particular was quite low, there was not much interest in the immediate aftermarket. As might be expected, coins encapsulated as MS-70 and PF-70 sell for strong prices to investors and Registry Set compilers. Most collectors are nicely satisfied with 68 and 69 grades, or the normal issue quality, since the coins are little different in actual appearance.

(2002) WEST POINT (U.S. MILITARY ACADEMY) DOLLARS

Distribution
2002-W: 103,201 Uncirculated
and 288,293 Proof

Whitman Coin Guide (WCG™)—2002-W West Point U.S. Military Academy $1

MS-65	MS-66	MS-67	MS-68	MS-69	MS-70
$30	$32	$34	$36	$45	$240
PF-65	PF-66	PF-67	PF-68	PF-69	PF-70
$28	$30	$32	$34	$45	$500

CERTIFIED POPULATIONS

MS-65	MS-66	MS-67	MS-68	MS-69	MS-70
1	2	12	167	4,297	1,934
PF-65	PF-66	PF-67	PF-68	PF-69	PF-70
3	6	34	227	4,314	231

Points of Interest: Although the Cadet Chapel is shown on the obverse of the dollar, there was no complaint concerning this religious element (unlike squawks about the Mormon church on the 2002 Olympic dollar and IN GOD WE TRUST on all coins). The coins were struck at the West Point Mint, appropriate considering the subject.

Subject of Commemoration: 200th anniversary of the U.S. Military Academy at West Point, NY.

Designs: *Obverse*—A fine depiction of the Academy color guard in a parade, with Washington Hall and the Cadet Chapel in the distance, with minimum intrusion of lettering, projects this to the forefront of commemorative designs of the era. Mint sculptor-engraver T. James Ferrell did the work. *Reverse*—The West Point Bicentennial logotype is shown, an adaptation of the Academy seal, showing at the center an ancient Greek helmet (not a *snail*, as some numismatists suggested) with a sword and shield. John Mercanti created the models from a design handed to him (absolving him from criticism).

Mintage Data: Authorized several years earlier by Public Law 103-328, signed by President William J. Clinton on September 29, 1994. *Maximum authorized*—500,000. *Number minted*—103,201 Uncirculated, 288,293 Proofs.

Original Cost and Issuer: Uncirculated dollars were priced at $30 and Proofs at $32 if ordered by April 29, 2002, after which prices were $32 and $37, respectively. A much-despised surcharge of $10 was included in the price of each, to benefit the Association of Graduates. Issued by the U.S. Mint.

Two Hundred Years of West Point

The U.S. Military Academy at West Point, New York, was authorized by an act signed by President Thomas Jefferson on March 16, 1802. The 200th anniversary in 2002 was a fitting occasion for a commemorative silver dollar, struck, logically enough, at the West Point Mint. Authorization was set at 500,000 coins. Originally, a three-coin program with a clad half dollar, silver dollar, and $5 gold coin had been proposed. Considering the generally lackluster performance of other three-coin sets, concentrating on a single denomination was probably a smart move.

The silver dollars bore a scenic motif on the obverse, with marching cadets, a welcome contrast to overwhelming geometric elements and lettering of some commemoratives of the era. The first strike ceremony was held on March 14, 2002, missing the true bicentennial time by two days. Each Proof received three blows from the modern Gräbener press, which applied a reported 219 tons of pressure.

Collectors, military personnel and veterans, and the general public were enthusiastic, carrying the sales to nearly 80 percent of the authorization, a welcome and remarkable change from the sagging sales of other recent issues. The strong sales raised surcharges of $3,914,940, which were delivered to the recipient organization, according to long-time U.S. Mint spokesperson Michael White.

Key to Collecting

The scenario is familiar: enough coins were struck to satisfy all comers during the period of issue, with the result that there was no unsatisfied demand. The aftermarket contains many coins available for less than the issue price. Coins certified at the MS-70 level appeal to a special group of buyers and command strong premiums.

(2003) FIRST FLIGHT CENTENNIAL COMMEMORATIVES

Distribution

2003-P clad half dollar:
  57,122 Uncirculated and
  109,710 Proof

2003-P dollar:
  53,533 Uncirculated and
  190,240 Proof

2003-W gold $10:
  10,009 Uncirculated and
  21,676 Proof

Whitman Coin Guide (WCG™)—2003-P First Flight Centennial 50¢

MS-65	MS-66	MS-67	MS-68	MS-69	MS-70
$20	$22	$24	$26	$34	$320
PF-65	PF-66	PF-67	PF-68	PF-69	PF-70
$17	$18	$20	$25	$34	$800

CERTIFIED POPULATIONS

MS-65	MS-66	MS-67	MS-68	MS-69	MS-70
0	0	1	13	1,902	865
PF-65	PF-66	PF-67	PF-68	PF-69	PF-70
1	2	11	65	2,034	20

2003-P First Flight Centennial $1

MS-65	MS-66	MS-67	MS-68	MS-69	MS-70
$45	$48	$50	$55	$60	$650
PF-65	PF-66	PF-67	PF-68	PF-69	PF-70
$33	$35	$40	$45	$55	$1,000

CERTIFIED POPULATIONS

MS-65	MS-66	MS-67	MS-68	MS-69	MS-70
1	0	2	46	2,643	902
PF-65	PF-66	PF-67	PF-68	PF-69	PF-70
1	2	22	167	2,785	29

2003-W First Flight Centennial Gold $10

MS-65	MS-66	MS-67	MS-68	MS-69	MS-70
$715	$725	$735	$750	$800	
PF-65	PF-66	PF-67	PF-68	PF-69	PF-70
$565	$575	$595	$615	$665	$4,000

CERTIFIED POPULATIONS

MS-65	MS-66	MS-67	MS-68	MS-69	MS-70
0	0	0	2	854	761
PF-65	PF-66	PF-67	PF-68	PF-69	PF-70
0	0	2	26	889	34

Points of Interest: The trio of coins may have set a record for redundancy and lack of originality, because each had the same central motif: the Wright brothers' plane, which had recently appeared on two statehood quarters as well.

Subject of Commemoration: The 100th anniversary of the Wright brothers' flight on December 17, 1903.

Designs: Clad half dollar: *Obverse*—Wright Monument at Kill Devil Hill on the North Carolina seashore. Designed by John Mercanti. *Reverse*—*Wright Flyer* biplane in flight. Designed by Norman E. Nemeth. **Silver dollar:** *Obverse*—Conjoined portraits of Orville and Wilbur Wright. Designed by Donna Weaver. *Reverse*—Wright brothers' plane in flight. Designed by T. James Ferrell. Designed by Norman E. Nemeth. **$10 gold:** *Obverse*—Portraits of Orville and Wilbur Wright. Designed by Donna Weaver. *Reverse*—Wright Brothers' plane in flight with an eagle overhead. Designed by Norman E. Nemeth.

Mintage Data: Authorized by Public Law 105-124, as an amendment and tag-on to the 50 States Commemorative Coin Program Act (which authorized the statehood quarters), signed by President William J. Clinton on December 1, 1997. *Maximum authorized*—clad half dollars 750,000; silver dollars 500,000; $10 gold 100,000. *Number minted*—clad half dollars 2003-P: 57,122 Uncirculated and 109,710 Proof; silver dollars 2003-P: 53,533 Uncirculated and 190,240 Proof; $10 gold 2003-W: 10,009 Uncirculated and 21,676 Proof.

Original Cost and Issuer: 2003-P clad half dollar, Uncirculated $9.75 pre-issue price through September 26, 2003, $10.75 afterward; Proof $12.50 pre-issue, $13.50 afterward. 2003-P silver dollar, Uncirculated $31 pre-issue price through February 12, 2007, $33 afterward; Proof $33 pre-issue, $37 afterward. 2003-W gold eagle, Uncirculated $340 pre-issue, $365 afterward; Proof $350 pre-issue, $375 afterward. Surcharges of $1 for the half dollar and silver dollar, and $35 for the gold $10 were directed to the First Flight Centennial Foundation, a private nonprofit group founded in 1995. Issued by the U.S. Mint.

100th Anniversary of Powered Flight

On December 17, 1903, Orville and Wilbur Wright successfully flew the biplane they had constructed in their bicycle shop in Dayton, Ohio, the first *manned* powered flight. The *Wright Flyer*, with Orville at the controls, made four flights above the sand at Kill Devil Hill on the outer banks of the North Carolina seacoast. The first covered about 120 feet in 12 seconds, and the longest spanned 852 feet and took slightly less than a minute. Interestingly, the event drew little attention at the time. The Smithsonian Institution, when informed of the accomplishment, repudiated it! This was because the secretary of the Smithsonian, Samuel Pierpont Langley, had achieved powered flight with *unmanned* craft in 1896. This stance was stubbornly maintained for years afterward.

Eventually, the rest of America celebrated the accomplishments of the Wright brothers, who went on to become well known in the production of other aircraft. In the 1920s, when Henry Ford was collecting buildings and artifacts for his Greenfield Village display in Michigan, he scooped up the Dayton bicycle shop and moved it there. In 2001, North Carolina chose the Wright airplane of 1903 as the reverse of its statehood quarter, and in 2002, Ohio did the same thing (but added an astronaut to the scene).

To celebrate the 100th anniversary of powered aircraft flight by Orville and Wilbur Wright in 1903, Congress authorized a set of 2003-dated commemoratives as an amendment to Public Law 105-124 which provided for the statehood quarters program. The lineup included a clad half dollar (750,000 maximum), silver dollar (500,000), and a $10 gold coin (100,000), the last being an infrequent departure from the usual half eagle.

The coins went on sale on August 1, 2003, with special pre-issue discount prices in effect through September 26. The sales period was extended to July 30, 2004. The program was a failure, with fewer than 450,000 coins sold of the 1,350,000 authorized. No doubt, the redundancy of the motifs contributed to this: each had the same reverse motif of the Wright brothers' plane, and the two largest denominations each pictured the Wright brothers. The whole matter produced an unstifled yawn in numismatic circles.

Key to Collecting
In the aftermarket, values fell after sales concluded, with the half dollars going down to nearly half the original issue prices. In time, they recovered. Today, all sell for a premium. Superb gems are easily enough found.

(2004) THOMAS ALVA EDISON DOLLARS

Distribution
2004-P: 68,031 Uncirculated
and 213,409 Proof

Whitman Coin Guide (WCG™)—2004-P Thomas Alva Edison $1

MS-65	MS-66	MS-67	MS-68	MS-69	MS-70
$45	$48	$50	$55	$60	$650
PF-65	PF-66	PF-67	PF-68	PF-69	PF-70
$42	$44	$46	$50	$60	$850

CERTIFIED POPULATIONS

MS-65	MS-66	MS-67	MS-68	MS-69	MS-70
0	1	5	47	2,161	570
PF-65	PF-66	PF-67	PF-68	PF-69	PF-70
2	2	18	107	2,511	44

Points of Interest: Should commemoratives ever be issued for all of Edison's *other* important inventions, dozens of new coins would be in the offing!

Subject of Commemoration: 125th anniversary of the October 21, 1879, demonstration by Thomas Edison of his first successful electric light bulb.

Designs: *Obverse*—Waist-up portrait of Edison holding a light bulb in his right hand. Designed by Donna Weaver. *Reverse*—Light bulb of the 1879 style mounted on a base, with arcs surrounding. Designed by John Mercanti.

Mintage Data. Authorized by Public Law 105-331, signed by President William J. Clinton on December 6, 1999. *Maximum authorized*—500,000. *Number minted*—68,031 Uncirculated and 213,409 Proof.

Original Cost and Issuer: 2004-P, Uncirculated, pre-issue through March 26, 2004, $31, afterward $33; Proof pre-issue $33, afterward $37. Also offered in various packages with added items. The $10 surcharge was to be divided equally among the Port Huron (Mich.) Museum of Arts and History, Edison Birthplace Association, National Park Service, Edison Plaza Museum, Edison Winter Home and Museum, Edison Institute, Edison Memorial Tower, and Hall of Electrical History. Issued by the U.S. Mint.

Honoring the Light Bulb and Its Inventor

On October 21, 1879, Thomas Alva Edison successfully tested an electric light bulb. Using a carbon filament within a glass housing, the bulb remained illuminated for a satisfactory amount of time. This achievement culminated a period in which Edison had tested several hundred different materials and arrangements, without success.

To observe the 125th anniversary of this brilliant occasion, Congress authorized that up to a half million commemorative silver dollars be minted with designs "emblematic of the light bulb and the many inventions made by Thomas A. Edison throughout his prolific life." Earlier, several proposals had been made for commemoratives to be issued in 1997 to observe the 150th anniversary of Edison's February 11, 1847, birth in Milan, Ohio. More than any other American inventor, Edison left behind a long trail of innovations, including the Kinetoscope (first practical movie film projector) and the phonograph, both of which defined entertainment for generations afterward.

Mint engravers Donna Weaver and John Mercanti created the designs, the obverse featuring Thomas Edison and the reverse a light bulb. The dollars went on sale on February 11, 2004 and remained available through December 30, 2004. Sales were satisfactory, but measured, without excitement. To stir up interest, on October 11 the Department of the Interior issued a news release emphasizing the December 31 deadline. More than 200,000 coins remained uncalled for when the order time expired.

Despite sales falling far short of the authorized amount, the Edison dollar was well received by collectors. By this time the yearly profusion of new commemorative issues was history, and complaints about draining buyers' pocketbooks were directed toward Mint products overall—including American "Eagle" silver and gold, and a new series of platinum bullion coins (inaugurated in 1997).

Key to Collecting

Examples are plentiful. Nearly all are superb gems. As was the situation for many other Mint issues of the period, promoters who had coins encased in certified holders marked MS-70 or PF-70 were able to persuade, or at least imply, to investors (but not to seasoned collectors) that coins of such quality were rarities, and obtained strong prices for them. Smart buyers simply purchased examples remaining in Mint holders, of which many were just as nice as the "70" coins.

(2004) LEWIS AND CLARK BICENTENNIAL DOLLARS

Distribution
2004-P: 142,015 Uncirculated
          and 351,989 Proofs

Whitman Coin Guide (WCG™)—2004 Lewis & Clark Bicentennial $1

MS-65	MS-66	MS-67	MS-68	MS-69	MS-70
$40	$42	$45	$50	$60	$625
PF-65	PF-66	PF-67	PF-68	PF-69	PF-70
$35	$37	$40	$42	$55	$625

CERTIFIED POPULATIONS

MS-65	MS-66	MS-67	MS-68	MS-69	MS-70
0	0	0	26	2,923	1047
PF-65	PF-66	PF-67	PF-68	PF-69	PF-70
0	2	7	121	3,984	97

Points of Interest: This was one of the most successful commemorative programs.

Subject of Commemoration: The 200th anniversary of the Lewis and Clark expedition into the Louisiana Territory Purchase.

Designs: *Obverse*—Meriwether Lewis and William Clark standing with a river and foliage in the distance as a separate motif. Lewis holds the barrel end of his rifle in one hand and a journal in the other and is looking at Clark, who is gazing to the distance in the opposite direction. Both sides were designed by Donna Weaver. *Reverse*—Copy of the reverse of the Jefferson Indian peace medal designed by John Reich and presented to Indians on the expedition (the identical motif was also revived for use on one variety of the 2004 Jefferson nickel). Feathers are to the left and right, and 17 stars are above.

Mintage Data: Authorized by Public Law 106-136, signed by President William J. Clinton on December 6, 1999. *Maximum authorized*—500,000. *Number minted*—142,015 Uncirculated, 351,989 Proofs.

Original Cost and Issuer: Uncirculated, pre-issue through June 11, 2004, $33, afterward $35; Proof pre-issue $35, afterward $39. Also offered in various packages with added items. Two-thirds of the $10 surcharge for each coin was earmarked for the National Council of the Lewis and Clark Bicentennial, and one third to the National Park Service for the bicentennial celebration. Issued by the U.S. Mint.

Commemorating (Again) the Louisiana Purchase

The Lewis and Clark expedition of 1804 to 1806, already well recognized on the commemorative gold dollars dated 1903 for the Louisiana Purchase Exposition (St. Louis World's Fair held in 1904) and those of 1904 and 1905 for the Lewis and Clark Exposition (Portland, Oregon, 1905), came to the fore in a new issue. Congress authorized the production of commemorative silver dollars, dated 2004, to observe the bicentennial of the event. Revised Jefferson nickel motifs were made for the same celebration.

America got set for widespread festivities in the Midwest and West in 2004, as towns and cities planned celebrations. Books and pamphlets were published, television programs were produced, and anticipation ran high. The public did not respond as hoped, and some events and festivals drew few visitors. The *Wall Street Journal* reported that the observation was a financial fizzle. Part of the problem may have been media overload. By 2004, attendance at museums and National Parks around the country had diminished from past years, possibly as the Internet, home computers, and other popular gadgets provided stimulation.

Mint artists were invited to submit designs, and those of Donna Weaver were selected from the 14 received. The marketing program included some coins sold with bison rawhide pouches made by Native Americans. The Mint warned that these were not suitable for long-term storage. *Coin World* advised that some made by Wynona and

Errol Medicine of the Standing Rock Sioux, that had been rejected by the Mint due to poor quality, were later sold on eBay, complete with certificates of authenticity. Another package included a replica of the face of the Series of 1901 $10 Legal Tender Note depicting a bison flanked by Lewis and Clark. The packages proved to be very popular, as did the silver dollars themselves—the entire program being a rousing success.

Key to Collecting
Superb gem coins are readily available.

(2005) MARINE CORPS 230TH ANNIVERSARY DOLLARS

Distribution
2005-P: 49,671 Uncirculated
and 548,810 Proof

Whitman Coin Guide (WCG™)—2005 Marine Corps 230th Anniversary $1

MS-65	MS-66	MS-67	MS-68	MS-69	MS-70
$65	$68	$72	$75	$80	$825
PF-65	PF-66	PF-67	PF-68	PF-69	PF-70
$62	$65	$68	$75	$90	$625

CERTIFIED POPULATIONS

MS-65	MS-66	MS-67	MS-68	MS-69	MS-70
0	1	7	61	4,515	4,845
PF-65	PF-66	PF-67	PF-68	PF-69	PF-70
2	11	28	237	8,946	269

Points of Interest: The depiction of the flag raising on Iwo Jima is perhaps the most familiar image from the history of World War II. This was the "poster" sales triumph coin of its era.

Subject of Commemoration: The 60th anniversary of the Battle of Iwo Jima and the 230th anniversary of the Marine Corps.

Designs: *Obverse*—Marines raising the Stars and Stripes over Iwo Jima as shown on the famous photograph by Joe Rosenthal. Modeled by Norman E. Nemeth of the Mint engraving staff. *Reverse*—Eagle, globe, and anchor emblem of the Marine Corps. Modeled by Mint engraver Charles L. Vickers.

Mintage Data: Authorized under Public Law 108-291, signed by President George W. Bush on August 6, 2004. *Maximum authorized*—500,000, later increased to 600,000. *Number minted*—2005-P 49,671 Uncirculated and 548,810 Proof.

Original Cost and Issuer: 2005-P silver dollar, Uncirculated $33 pre-issue price, $35 afterward; Proof $35 pre-issue, $39 afterward. Surcharge of $10 per coin was designated to support construction of the Marine Corps Heritage Center at the base in Quantico, Virginia. Issued by the U.S. Mint.

Recognizing the Marine Corps

To honor the Battle of Iwo Jima and the 230th anniversary of the Marine Corps, Congress authorized an issue of 500,000 commemorative silver dollars to be minted in 2005. A survey taken on behalf of the recipient of the $10 surcharge on each coin, the Marine Heritage Foundation, found demand would be greater than that. The secretary of the Treasury was persuaded to use his legal authority to increase the mintage to 600,000 which he did, to the disapproval of many collectors who had relied on the information first issued concerning the dollars. Ameliorating the situation was the fact that the increase took place before the first orders were accepted on July 20th.

On May 25, 2005, a ceremonial strike ceremony took place, and on July 20 the coin was launched at the Marine Corps base in Quantico, Virginia, with Mint Director Henrietta Holsman Fore officiating. The widespread appreciation of the heritage of the Marine Corps plus the fame of the obverse design taken from Joe Rosenthal's photograph of the flag-raising at Iwo Jima, propelled this coin to remarkable success.

For the first time in recent memory, pandemonium reigned in the coin market, as prices rose, buyers clamored to find all they could, and most dealers were sold out. Within a year, interest turned to other things, and the prices dropped, but not down to the issue levels.

Key to Collecting

Superb gem coins are readily available.

(2005) CHIEF JUSTICE JOHN MARSHALL DOLLARS

Distribution
2005-P: 67,096 Uncirculated
and 196,753 Proof

Whitman Coin Guide (WCG™)—2005 Chief Justice John Marshall $1

MS-65	MS-66	MS-67	MS-68	MS-69	MS-70
$45	$48	$50	$52	$58	$513
PF-65	PF-66	PF-67	PF-68	PF-69	PF-70
$40	$42	$45	$50	$60	$550

CERTIFIED POPULATIONS

MS-65	MS-66	MS-67	MS-68	MS-69	MS-70
0	0	0	15	1,302	833
PF-65	PF-66	PF-67	PF-68	PF-69	PF-70
0	4	11	65	1,863	83

Points of Interest: Sales of this commemorative followed the general trend of others of the era, falling short of the authorized maximum.

Subject of Commemoration: The 250th anniversary of Chief Justice John Marshall's birth.

Designs: *Obverse*—Portrait of Marshall by John Mercanti, adapted from a painting made in March 1808 by Charles-Balthazar-Julien Fevret de Saint-Mèmin, of France. *Reverse*—The old Supreme Court Chamber within the Capitol. Designed by Donna Weaver.

Mintage Data: Authorized by Public Law 108-290, signed by President George W. Bush on August 9, 2004. *Maximum authorized*—400,000. *Number minted*—67,096 Uncirculated and 196,753 Proof.

Original Cost and Issuer: Uncirculated, $33 pre-issue price through June 27, 2005, $35 afterward; Proof, $35 pre-issue, $39 afterward. $10 surcharge per coin went to the Supreme Court Historical Society. Issued by the U.S. Mint.

Honoring a Famous Chief Justice

Chief Justice John Marshall, who served 34 years in that post in the U.S. Supreme Court, was the subject for a commemorative silver dollar in 2005. Sworn in on February 4, 1801, he was the fourth chief justice. His decisions are remembered as fair and just. Many of them helped define the limits of power of the executive and legislative branches in an era in which the provisions of the Constitution were frequently tested.

Observing the 250th anniversary of Marshall's birth (September 24, 1755), the coins were given a feasible limit of 400,000 pieces, to be issued during calendar year 2005. The dollars went on sale on April 25. A special launch ceremony was conducted by Mint Director Henrietta Holsman Fore with Justice Stephen Breyer among those in attendance. The justice reminded listeners that Oliver Wendell Holmes once commented, "If American law were to be represented by a single figure, skeptic and worshipper alike would agree without dispute that the figure could be one alone, and that one would be John Marshall." Chief Justice William Rehnquist was conspicuous by his absence, but had testified before Congress earlier as to Marshall's place in history.

Mint engravers submitted designs, with six depictions of Marshall inspired by a painting by Saint Mèmin, ten from an oil by Rembrandt Peale, and three from a statue by William W. Story. Mint engraver John Mercanti's interpretation of the Saint-Mèmin portrait received the nod. Donna Weaver created the reverse motif depicting the old Supreme Court chamber in the Capitol.

Coins were available at a discount during the pre-issue period, extending to May 25. Later, the discount opportunity was moved forward to June 27. During this time, Uncirculated coins cost $33, and Proofs were priced at $35. Afterward the prices were $35 and $39. A "Chronicles" package was offered with extra items included. In *Numismatic News* on August 2, Peter Lindblad's article, "Ho-Hum Sales for Marshall Coin & Chronicles Set," dryly observed, "As a jurist, John Marshall was a giant, perhaps the most important Chief Justice in the history of the U.S. Supreme Court. Unfortunately, Marshall's influence hasn't been as prevalent in the numismatic realm." In terms of popular interest, the Marshall dollar played second fiddle to the Marine Corps issue, sold out at its 600,000 limit. The Marshall coins totaled about 260,000, or about two-thirds of the authorized 400,000.

Key to Collecting

Superb gem coins are available in the marketplace for little more than the original issue prices.

(2006) BENJAMIN FRANKLIN DOLLARS

Distribution
2006-P "Scientist":
     58,000 Uncirculated
     and 142,000 Proof
2006-P "Founding Father":
     58,000 Uncirculated
     and 142,000 Proof
(above figures are not final)

Whitman Coin Guide (WCG™)—2006 Benjamin Franklin "Scientist" $1

MS-65	MS-66	MS-67	MS-68	MS-69	MS-70
$60	$62	$64	$68	$80	$495
PF-65	PF-66	PF-67	PF-68	PF-69	PF-70
$57	$60	$62	$65	$75	$600

2006 Benjamin Franklin "Founding Father" $1

MS-65	MS-66	MS-67	MS-68	MS-69	MS-70
$60	$62	$65	$70	$75	$450
PF-65	PF-66	PF-67	PF-68	PF-69	PF-70
$55	$57	$60	$65	$75	$375

Points of Interest: Considering Franklin's life and the Continental dollar shown on the reverse of one of the coins, these are among the most numismatically related of all modern commemoratives (but with a nod to the San Francisco Mint commemoratives of the same year).

Subject of Commemoration: The 300th anniversary of Franklin's birth.

Designs: "Scientist": *Obverse*—Franklin standing with a kite on a string, evocative of his experiments with lightning in June 1752. Mint engraver Norman E. Nemeth produced the model. *Reverse*—Franklin's political cartoon, featuring a snake cut apart, titled "Join, or Die," reflecting the sentiment that the colonies should unite during the French and Indian War (and which had nothing to do with perceived offenses by the British, at this early time). This appeared in Franklin's *Pennsylvania Gazette* on May 9, 1754. The reverse was the work of mint engraver Charles Vickers. **"Founding Father":** *Obverse*— Head and shoulders portrait of Franklin facing forward slightly to the viewer's right, with his signature reproduced below. Don Everhart of the Mint staff was the engraver. *Reverse*—Copy of a 1776 Continental dollar within a frame of modern lettering. The mottoes on this coin were suggested by Franklin. Donna Weaver of the Mint staff was the engraver.

Mintage Data: Authorized by Public Law 104-463, the Benjamin Franklin Tercentenary Act, and signed by President George W. Bush on December 21, 2004. *Maximum authorized*—250,000 coins for each design, limiting the total for the program to 500,000 coins. *Number minted*—figures not final.

Original Cost and Issuer: Proof $35 (pre-issue through March 14, 2006, 5 p.m.), $39 after; Uncirculated pre-issue $33, $35 after. A surcharge of $10 per coin was earmarked for the Franklin Institute. Issued by the U.S. Mint.

Franklin Honored

Congress authorized the minting of 500,000 commemorative silver dollars to observe the 2007 tercentenary of Benjamin Franklin's birth. In an unusual move, the legislation specified two different designs, one showing Franklin as a "scientist" and the other as a "Founding Father." The bill took note of his accomplishments, stating he was "the only Founding Father to sign all of our Nation's organizational documents," who printed "official currency for the colonies of Pennsylvania, Delaware, New Jersey and Maryland," and helped design the Great Seal of the United States. He also "designed the first American coin, the 'Continental' penny"—apparently an unstudied reference to what numismatists call the 1776 Continental dollar. Further:

> Franklin made "A penny saved is a penny earned" a household phrase to describe the American virtues of hard work and economical living.
>
> The official United States half dollar from 1948–1963 showed Franklin's portrait, as designed by John Sinnock.
>
> The Franklin Institute Science Museum in Philadelphia houses the first steam printing machine for coinage, used by the United States Mint, which was placed in service in 1836, the 130th anniversary year of Franklin's birth.

Beyond the Franklin half dollar, this founder's portrait was already well known to collectors of early American medals, Civil War and other tokens, and both state-bank and federal paper money.

To honor Franklin's city, "It is the sense of the Congress that the coins minted under this Act should be struck at the U.S. Mint at Philadelphia, Pennsylvania, to the greatest extent possible." And they were. Designs were specified as follows, and were devised by Representative Michael Castle, a representative from Delaware and descendant of Franklin. For a long time Castle had been recognized as one of the most numismatically erudite members of Congress:

> *$1 Coins with younger Franklin image:*
> The obverse shall bear the image of Benjamin Franklin as a young man.
>
> The reverse shall bear an image related to Benjamin Franklin's role as a patriot and a statesman.
>
> *$1 Coins with older Franklin image:*
> The obverse shall bear the image of Benjamin Franklin as an older man.
>
> The reverse shall bear an image related to Benjamin Franklin's role in developing the early coins and currency of the new country.

A ceremonial striking of both coins was held at the Philadelphia Mint on December 19, 2005. Acting U.S. Mint Director David Lebryk officiated. The coins went on sale on January 17, 2006, the 300th anniversary of Franklin's birth.

As the authorization for each of the dollars was for 250,000 coins, and 200,000 of each were sold, the program was a success. Perhaps Congress was nearing an equilibrium in its ability to match output with buyers.

Key to Collecting
Superb gems are easily found in the marketplace.

(2006) SAN FRANCISCO OLD MINT COMMEMORATIVES

Distribution
2006-S silver dollar:
    67,100 Uncirculated
    and 160,870 Proof
2006-S gold $5:
    17,500 Uncirculated
    and 44,174 Proof
(above figures are not final)

Whitman Coin Guide (WCG™)—2006 San Francisco Old Mint $1

MS-65	MS-66	MS-67	MS-68	MS-69	MS-70
$50	$52	$55	$60	$75	$625
PF-65	PF-66	PF-67	PF-68	PF-69	PF-70
$55	$57	$60	$65	$75	$625

2006 San Francisco Old Mint Gold $5

MS-65	MS-66	MS-67	MS-68	MS-69	MS-70
$270	$275	$286	$297	$345	$700
PF-65	PF-66	PF-67	PF-68	PF-69	PF-70
$260	$270	$280	$290	$345	$825

Points of Interest: Designs of old coins, the reverse of the Morgan silver dollar and the Liberty Head $5 gold, were resurrected for use on the commemoratives.

Subject of Commemoration: The 100th anniversary of the 1906 earthquake and fire and to honor the "Granite Lady's" role in San Francisco's recovery from that disaster.

Designs: Silver dollar: *Obverse*—The Second San Francisco Mint as viewed from off the left front corner. Taken from a medal designed by Sherl J. Winter. *Reverse*—Copy of the reverse of a standard Morgan silver dollar of the era 1878–1921, said to have been taken from a 1904-S. Mint artist Joseph Menna made a new model for use on the commemorative. **$5 gold:** *Obverse*—Front view of the portico of the Second San Francisco Mint, with a portion of the building to each side, seemingly redundant to the design of the $1 coin. Designed by Charles L. Vickers, modeled after an 1869 construction drawing by Supervising Architect A.B. Mullet. *Reverse*—Copy of the reverse of the Liberty

Head half eagle with motto IN GOD WE TRUST, as regularly used from 1866 to 1907. A new model was made from a 1906-S coin by Mint artist Don Everhart (an exceptionally talented sculptor who could have done this with one eye closed and one hand behind his back).

Mintage Data: Authorized by Public Law 109-230, the San Francisco Old Mint Commemorative Act, signed by President George W. Bush in June 2006. *Maximum authorized*—silver dollars 500,000; $5 gold 100,000. *Number minted*—figures not final.

Original Cost and Issuer: 2006-S silver dollar, Uncirculated $33 pre-issue price through October 17, 2006, $35 afterward; Proof $35 pre-issue, $39 afterward. 2006-S gold $5, Uncirculated $220 pre-issue, $245 afterward; Proof $230 pre-issue, $255 afterward. Other packaging options were offered, including a combination with the 2006 Benjamin Franklin dollar. Surcharges of $10 and $35 per coin went to the "San Francisco Museum and Historical Society for use for the purposes of rehabilitating the Historic Old Mint in San Francisco as a city museum and an American Coin and Gold Rush Museum." Issued by the U.S. Mint.

"Granite Lady" Recognized

The San Francisco Mint opened for business in March 1854 in a remodeled and slightly expanded building purchased from Curtis, Perry & Ward, operators of Moffat & Company (private coiners of gold and contractors for the United States Assay Office of Gold). From the outset, the facilities were cramped and poorly ventilated, causing many problems. In 1870 the cornerstone was laid for the Second San Francisco Mint, which was dedicated in 1874. Later nicknamed "the Granite Lady," the structure had all of the latest coining equipment and amenities.

During the 1906 earthquake and fire, workers at the Mint used their own well water supply to hose down the roof, saving the structure—the only one to survive in its district. In due course, coinage recommenced, and continued there until 1937, when the Third San Francisco Mint opened on Duboce Street.

Coins made at the several San Francisco Mints have been collectors' favorites for a long time. With much enthusiasm from the numismatic community, Congress passed a law to honor the Second Mint with a pair of commemorative coins dated 2006, the 100th anniversary of its not having been destroyed in the 1906 fire. Accordingly, the honor was for "just showing up," to paraphrase Woody Allen.

Congress found these aspects to be important:

1. The Granite Lady played an important role in the history of the nation.
2. The San Francisco Mint was established pursuant to an Act of Congress of July 3, 1852, to convert miners' gold from the California Gold Rush into coins.
3. The San Francisco Old Mint building was designed by architect A.B. Mullett, who also designed the U.S. Treasury Building and the Old Executive Office Building.
4. The solid construction of the Granite Lady enabled it to survive the 1906 San Francisco earthquake and fire making it the only financial institution that was able to operate immediately after the earthquake as the treasury for disaster relief funds for the city of San Francisco.

5. Coins struck at the San Francisco Old Mint are distinguished by the "S" mint mark.
6. The San Francisco Old Mint is famous for having struck many rare, legendary issues, such as the 1870-S $3 coin, which is valued today at more than $1,000,000, and the 1894-S dime which is comparatively rare.
7. The San Francisco Old Mint Commemorative Coin will be the first commemorative coin to honor a United States mint.

As to the 1870-S $3 coin, today this belongs to the Harry W. Bass Jr. Foundation and is on loan exhibition at the ANA Headquarters in Colorado Springs. There are nine verified 1894-S dimes in numismatic hands, from a coinage said to be just 24 pieces. Number 7 in the above list is a bit embarrassing, for the 200th anniversary of the Philadelphia Mint in 1992 was an occasion begging for a commemorative.

On the Numismatic Front

In 2005, hobby magazines and newspapers enlisted the aid of numismatists to help persuade Congress to pass the needed legislation in the form of H.R. 1953 and S. 1881. Readers rallied, and most, if not all, representatives and senators heard from their coin-collecting constituents. Finally, the program became a reality, with 500,000 silver dollars and 100,000 gold half eagles authorized. Orders were accepted beginning on August 15, 2006, with a pre-issue discount applicable through October 17.

Surcharges of $10 and $35 per coin were to be applied to the San Francisco Mint to improve it as a visitor center and, under the aegis of the ANA, to open an American Coin and Gold Rush Museum. In the meantime, in 2005 and early 2006, just about everybody and his or her brother or sister had an idea as to what the commemorative coins should look like. The tradition of the Gold Rush seemed to be an obvious theme, since this chapter in American history was responsible for the San Francisco Mint being established. Other motifs were advanced.

The finished designs were a disappointment to many. Both obverses showed the same thing—the front of the Mint building, one in an overall view and another with a close-up of the portico. The reverses were not original at all, but were copies of the Morgan silver dollar and the Liberty Head with-motto half eagle reverses—with no specific connection to the San Francisco Mint other than that such coins were once made there, as they were also in Philadelphia, Carson City, Denver, and New Orleans. There was a rush-rush to create designs. Some details of the artistic process were revealed in an article in *Numismatic News*, July 25, under title of "CCAC likes denticles for S.F. Mint":

> A final review of the new designs for the Old San Francisco Mint commemoratives was undertaken July 10 at a meeting of the Citizen Coin Advisory Committee in Washington, D.C. Following "Mint interaction with the recipient organization," Mitch Sanders, CCAC chairman, reported that the renditions of the Old Mint building have been moved from reverse to obverse and the Liberty Heads have disappeared, replaced by classic eagle reverse designs.
>
> The CCAC chose an obverse design for the silver dollar commemorative with denticles as opposed to a virtually identical obverse design without them. The reverse design has denticles, so the obverse should, too, Sanders explained. . . . For the reverse [of the $5], the only design presented was a replica of the 1906 half eagle ($5) reverse.

Secretary of the Treasury Henry M. Paulson Jr., approved the motifs on August 3, just 49 days after President George W. Bush signed the bill.

After the coins were shipped, some packaging proved defective. "Mint halts deliveries of SFOM gold; Plastic capsules popping open, loose $5 coins arriving damaged," proclaimed the headline in an article by Paul Gilkes in *Coin World*, November 11. It was revealed that the Mint had shipped the coins to a private contractor in Memphis, who was processing the orders. Many coins arrived with "nicks or other damage," the same account reported. Eventually, the situation was corrected.

Key to Collecting
Superb gems are easily found in the marketplace.

(2007) JAMESTOWN 400TH ANNIVERSARY COMMEMORATIVES

Distribution
2007-P silver dollar:
Uncirculated and
Proof issues still
being distributed
2007-W gold $5: Uncirculated
and Proof issues still
being distributed

Whitman Coin Guide (WCG™)—2007 Jamestown 400th Anniversary $1

PF-65	PF-66	PF-67	PF-68	PF-69	PF-70
$50	$52	$55	$60	$85	$305

2007 Jamestown 400th Anniversary Gold $5

MS-65	MS-66	MS-67	MS-68	MS-69	MS-70
$262	$264	$275	$286	$335	$700
PF-65	**PF-66**	**PF-67**	**PF-68**	**PF-69**	**PF-70**
$250	$260	$265	$270	$340	$700

Points of Interest: Jamestown was also honored on the 2000 Virginia statehood quarter dollar.

Subject of Commemoration: The 400th anniversary of the settlement of Jamestown, Virginia.

Designs: Silver dollar: *Obverse*—Captain John Smith is shown with an Indian man and woman. Designed by Donna Weaver, recently retired from the Mint engraving staff. *Reverse*—Three sailing ships are shown, déjà vu from the 2000 statehood quarter, but differently arranged. Designed by Susan Gamble, a participant in the recent Artistic Infusion Program at the Mint, created to bring artists in from the private sector to upgrade the quality of coin designs. **$5 gold:** *Obverse*—Captain John Smith is shown with Indian chief Powhatan, who holds a bag of corn. John Mercanti of the Mint staff created the model. *Reverse*—Ruins of the old church at Jamestown. Designed by Susan Gamble.

Mintage Data: Authorized by Public Law 108-289, the Jamestown 400th Anniversary Commemorative Coin Act, signed by President George W. Bush on August 6, 2004. *Maximum authorized*—silver dollars 500,000; gold $5 100,000. *Number minted*—figures not final.

Original Cost and Issuer: 2007-P silver dollar, Uncirculated $33 pre-issue price through February 12, 2007, $35 afterward; Proof $35 pre-issue, $39 afterward. 2006-S gold $5, Uncirculated $220 pre-issue, $245 afterward; Proof $230 pre-issue, $255 afterward. Surcharges of $20 and $35 per coin were intended to fund the public observance of the anniversary. Issued by the U.S. Mint.

Jamestown Settlement Honored

The 400th anniversary of the British settlement of Jamestown, Virginia, was the subject for a pair of commemorative coins issued in 2007. Congress authorized up to 500,000 silver dollars and 100,000 gold half eagles.

Orders were accepted beginning on January 10, 2007. In the first six days the Mint reported sales of 121,286 silver dollars (38,256 Uncirculated and 83,030 Proof) and 32,754 gold $5 (11,472 Uncirculated and 21,282 Proofs), furnishing signs that the program would be strong. By March 18 the totals had climbed to 253,346 dollars and 55,290 gold $5.

(2007) LITTLE ROCK CENTRAL HIGH SCHOOL DESEGREGATION DOLLARS

Distribution
2007-P silver dollar

Whitman Coin Guide (WCG™)—2007 Little Rock Central HS Desegregate $1

MS-65	MS-66	MS-67	MS-68	MS-69	MS-70
$50	$52	$55	$60	$75	$500

Points of Interest: These coins attracted scant media attention and were mostly purchased by numismatists and those on the U.S. Mint mailing list.

Subject of Commemoration: The 50th anniversary of the Little Rock Central High School in Little Rock, Arkansas.

Designs: *Obverse*—The feet of the "Little Rock Nine" students are shown, escorted by a soldier. Designed by Richard Masters, a participant in the Mint's Artistic Infusion Program. *Reverse*—Little Rock Central High School as it appeared in 1957. Designed by Mint staff engraver Don Everhart.

Mintage Data: Authorized by Public Law 109-146, the Little Rock Central High School Desegregation 50th Anniversary Commemorative Coin Act, signed by President George W. Bush on December 22, 2005. *Maximum authorized*—500,000. *Number minted*—figures not final.

Original Cost and Issuer: Uncirculated $33 pre-issue price through June 13, 2007, $35 afterward; Proof $35 pre-issue, $39 afterward. Surcharge of $10 per coin to go to improvements at the Little Rock Central High School National Historic Site. Issued by the U.S. Mint.

Civil Rights Landmark

In September 1957, the Little Rock (Arkansas) Central High School was a segregated facility with no black students allowed. The U.S. Supreme Court in Brown, et al. v. Board of Education of Topeka, et al., 347 U.S. 483 (1954), ruled that this was illegal, but implementation was another matter entirely. Now, the "Little Rock Nine," a group of black students consisting of Ernest Green, Elizabeth Eckford, Melba Pattillo, Jefferson Thomas, Carlotta Walls, Terrence Roberts, Gloria Ray, Thelma Mothershed, and Minnijean Brown, endeavored to enter the portals of the forbidden institution. Under the eye of federal troops, they succeeded.

This action, soon praised by the Rev. Dr. Martin Luther King Jr., and others, brought an effective end to segregation in American schools, although some time was needed for full implementation. In honor of this historic event, Congress voted to authorize up to 500,000 commemorative silver dollars to be issued with the date 2007 and with appropriate designs "emblematic of the desegregation of the Little Rock Central High School and its contribution to civil rights in America." The entire mintage was to take place no later than December 31, 2007. The Mint began accepting orders on May 15.

Coming Attractions

The U.S. Mint has announced forthcoming commemorative coins for the next several years. Included are these:

American Bald Eagle Commemoratives: These will include a 2008 clad half dollar, 2008 silver dollar, and 2008 gold $5.

NASA Commemoratives: These issues are in the discussion stage as this book goes to press. Originally, it was sought to commemorate the 50th anniversaries, in 2008, of the founding of the National Aeronautics and Space Administration (NASA) and the Jet Propulsion Laboratory.

Louis Braille Bicentennial Dollars: Appearing in 2009, these will be silver dollars honoring the 200th anniversary of the birth of the pioneer in a raised-print reading system for the blind.

Lincoln Bicentennial Dollars: These 2009 silver dollars will observe the 200th anniversary of the birth of Abraham Lincoln. (Special designs, intended as part of regular circulating coinage for the Lincoln cent, are also planned for 2009.)

THE SOCIETY FOR UNITED STATES COMMEMORATIVE COINS

The Society for United States Commemorative Coins (SUSCC) is a group of collectors and dealers who share a common interest in the commemorative coins of the United States. SUSCC members collect the coins and related material (e.g., holders, advertising pieces, books, medals, etc.) of the traditional series of commemoratives (1892 to 1954), the modern series (1982 to date) and the circulating series (1976 to date).

SUSCC is dedicated to the compilation and sharing of knowledge about US commemorative coins and to the promotion of the collecting of these fascinating celebrations of American history. To help guide the organization, SUSCC has developed mission and vision statements:

Mission Statement
To help maximize the knowledge and appreciation of United States commemoratives among collectors, dealers and the general public.

Vision Statement
To be the leading source of trusted information and education regarding United States commemoratives, the leading supporter of collectors of the series and the leading advocate of US commemoratives within the hobby.

MEMBERSHIP BENEFITS

All members receive *The Commemorative Trail*, the official journal of SUSCC. Each issue is filled with informative stories about all aspects of commemorative collecting, as well as collecting tips and investing insights that can help maximize the enjoyment of your collection.

SUSCC holds membership meetings at several large regional and national coin shows each year, including the
- American Numismatic Association (ANA) conventions
- Florida United Numismatists (FUN) show
- Baltimore Coin and Currency conventions

Each meeting includes a SUSCC update, an educational program and member door prizes. Each meeting also provides the opportunity to meet fellow commemorative collectors and for the sharing of hobby adventures!

MEMBERSHIP DUES

Annual dues are $20.00 (US) for Adults (18 years of age and older) and $10.00 (US) for Juniors. (Additional postage costs may be incurred for members residing outside of the US; write the SUSCC Secretary for further information.) SUSCC memberships run from January 1st through December 31st.

To join SUSCC, send your name and mailing address (along with a check or money order for your first year's dues) to:

SUSCC
PO Box 2335
Huntington Beach, CA 92647

NOTES

1. Boudinot, of Elizabeth-Town, New Jersey, had served as president of the Continental Congress in 1792. In 1795 he was appointed by President George Washington to be the third director of the Mint. The coins Boudinot "had seen" were undoubtedly patterns of 1792.
2. Certain information about Lewis was presented by John Kleeberg in November 1999 at the Coinage of the Americas Conference (COAC) hosted by the American Numismatic Society.
3. Certain of the minting and other information is similar to that used in early "Official Red Book" titles.
4. Letter dated March 1, 1991.
5. Reported by Anthony Swiatek in 1980.
6. Discovered by Frank DuVall and first published in 1988.
7. *The Numismatist*, January 1903.
8. The identity of the artist was generally unknown to numismatists until Roger W. Burdette located related correspondence in 2002.
9. Per a commentary by Ray Mercer in *The Commemorative Trail*, Spring 1986 issue.
10. *The Encyclopedia of U.S. Silver & Gold Commemorative Coins*, p. 240.
11. Per correspondence from John R. Evans to Walter P. Nichols, undated, circa early July 1935. Also L.W. Hoffecker files. This hitherto unknown information came as a surprise to numismatists when it was published by the present author, including in the 1992 *Commemorative Coins of the United States: A Complete Encyclopedia*. Julius Guttag would later become involved in the distribution of the 1938-dated New Rochelle half dollars.
12. Letter from Hoffecker to Trygve Rovelstad, September 26, 1935.
13. For expanded details and findings see the author's *Commemorative Coins of the United States: A Complete Encyclopedia*, 1992.
14. Paul Gilkes, "Commission Criticizes Coin Designs," *Coin World*, January 30, 1991.
15. Jeff Starck, "1994 World Cup Coins Strong International Sales Don't Kick Up Mintages for Program," *Coin World*, July 11, 2005.
16. "Special Olympics Coin Controversial in Hobby; Shriver First Living Female on U.S. Coin," August 8, 2005.
17. From the Web site of montgomerycoinclub.org.

SELECTED BIBLIOGRAPHY

ANACS Report. Austin, Texas, and Dublin, Ohio: Various issues.

Annual Report of the Director of the Mint. Various years, especially 1891 to date.

Breen, Walter H. *Walter Breen's Encyclopedia of U.S. and Colonial Proof Coins, 1792–1977.* Albertson, New York: FCI Press, 1977; updated, Wolfeboro, N.H.: Bowers and Merena Galleries, 1989.

—*Walter Breen's Complete Encyclopedia of U.S. and Colonial Coins.* New York: Doubleday, Inc., 2008.

Bressett, Kenneth E. (editor). *A Guide Book of United States Coins.* Racine, Wis.: Various modern editions. Earlier editions edited by Richard S. Yeoman.

Bressett, Kenneth E., and Q. David Bowers. *The Official American Numismatic Association Grading Standards for United States Coins.* 6th edition. Atlanta, Georgia: Whitman Publishing, LLC, 2005.

Burdette, Roger W. "Designer of 1920 Maine Centennial Half Dollar Identified." *Coin World*, 2005.

Certified Coin Dealer Newsletter. Torrance, California: Various issues, 2000s to date.

Coin Dealer Newsletter. Torrance, California: Various issues, 1963 to date.

Coin World Almanac. Sidney, Ohio: *Coin World*, 2000.

Coin World. Sidney, Ohio: Amos Press: Various issues, 1960 to date.

Doty, Richard. *America's Money, America's Story.* Iola, Wis.: Krause Publications, 1998.

Numismatic Guaranty Corporation of America Census Report. Sarasota, Fla.: Numismatic Guaranty Corporation of America: Various issues.

Numismatic News. Iola, Wis.: Krause Publications: Various issues, 1952 to date.

Numismatist, The. The American Numismatic Association. Colorado Springs, Colo. (and other addresses): Various issues, 1891 to date.

PCGS Population Report. Newport Beach, Cal. Professional Coin Grading Service: Various issues.

Raymond, Wayte. *Standard Catalogue of United States Coins and Paper Money* (titles vary). Scott Stamp & Coin Co. (and others): New York, 1934 to 1957 editions.

Taxay, Don. *U.S. Mint and Coinage.* New York City, NY: Arco Publishing, 1966.

—*Scott's Comprehensive Catalogue of United States Coinage.* New York: Scott Publications, 1970 (cover date 1971; largely based upon information supplied by Walter H. Breen in a March, 2, 1992, letter to the author). (Revised Edition 1976 updated by Joseph Rose and H. Hazelcorn.)

Treasury Department, U.S. Mint, *et al. Annual Report of the Director of the Mint.* 1891 onward.

Vermeule, Cornelius. *Numismatic Art in America.* Cambridge, Mass.: Belknap Press, Harvard, 1971; 2nd edition, with updating by David T. Alexander, Atlanta, Georgia, Whitman Publishing, LLC, 2007.

INDEX
ALPHABETICAL REFERENCE TO
DATES FOR COMMEMORATIVES

GENERAL INDEX OF COMMEMORATIVES BY PAGE NUMBER